SCHEMES & UNDERTAKINGS

SCHEMES & UNDERTAKINGS

A Study of English Politics
in the Seventeenth Century

Clayton Roberts

OHIO STATE UNIVERSITY PRESS   COLUMBUS

Library of Congress Cataloguing in Publication Data

Roberts, Clayton
  Schemes & undertakings.

  Bibliography: p.
  Includes index.
  1. Great Britain—Politics and government—1603–1714.
I. Title. II. Title: Schemes and undertakings.
DA375. R63   1985   941.06   84-25572
ISBN 0-8142-0377-9

To Cecily, Bob, Cathy, and David

Table of Contents
◦§◦

Preface

~§€~

DURING THE PAST FIFTY YEARS, in reaction to the Whig interpretation of history, historians of English politics have focused upon the story of "influence." They have written of the power of patronage, of "the King's friends," of "management," of pensions, bribes, and place. As the monarch lost his power to govern outside Parliament, he is seen to have won a power to govern through Parliament. By means of a Court party, he could support ministers of his own choice.

Much of this history concerns mid-eighteenth-century politics, but the same point of view has colored the writings of historians of seventeenth- and early eighteenth-century politics. Mena Prestwich has found the earliest beginnings of a system of influence in the reigns of James I and Charles I. Hugh Trevor-Roper has taken Oliver Cromwell to task for overlooking the importance of management. J. R. Jones has written of Clarendon's court dependents, and Andrew Browning has written a magisterial account of the rise of the Court party during the ministry of the Earl of Danby. J. P. Kenyon has examined the "King's friends" in the 1690s, and Patricia Ansell has studied Robert Harley's reliance on patronage in Queen Anne's reign. These are special studies of the rise of a Court party and the use of patronage, but this point of view also pervades the works of David Ogg, Betty Kemp, Geoffrey Holmes, and J. H. Plumb.

This literature has been of great value. The role of the "King's friends" in Parliament, the power that the disposal of place gives to the King, the importance of management in both Houses, the use of place, honors, and pensions to win over men, all this has been explored, illuminated, chronicled, and established. But it is only half the story. At the same time that Clifford and Danby and Sunderland and Harley were building up a Court party in both Houses, a Court party with which to support the crown's greatness and independence, other men, politicians in both Houses, were devising a mechanism by which they could use their popularity in Parliament to wrest office from the King. In the early seventeenth century, this mechanism gained the name of a "parliamentary undertaking." In the reigns of King William and Queen Anne, it was more often called a "scheme of administration." Parliamentary undertakings and schemes of administration have not attracted the attention of historians in the same way that the rise of a Court party has. And yet the parliamentary undertaker who used his power in the House of Commons to wrest office from the King proved ultimately more powerful than the court manager who used place, pension, and title to win over members of the two Houses.

The purpose of this study is to redress the balance by writing the history of parliamentary undertakings from 1603 to 1714. More particularly, its purpose is to establish the existence of such a phenomenon and to stress its importance in the politics of these years.

The first recorded use of the work *undertaker* to describe a politician who undertook to manage Parliament for the King occurred on 12 February 1614. On that day, John Donne, the celebrated dean of Saint Paul's, wrote to a friend, "It is taken ill, though it be but mistaken that certain men (whom they call undertakers) should presume either to understand the House before it sits, or to incline it then. . . . "[1] Within three months the word *undertaker* was on every man's lips—despite Sir Francis Bacon's protest that, though he knew of "undertakers" who would plant Derry or discover the Northwest Passage or dye cloth, he had never heard of any who would dare undertake for the ancient Parliament of England.[2] The last known use of the word to designate one who would undertake to manage Parliament for the King occurs in a letter that Robert Harley wrote to the Duke of Newcastle on 5 December 1707. "I am just come from the two Great men," he wrote (meaning Godolphin and Marlborough). "I believe they are fully sensible of their danger, and that there are [a] number of men, enough to support them, who are ready and willing to do it, if they will but create a confidence in them; I was not willing to be thought an undertaker, and therefore would not name the method which is obvious enough if they please to make use of it."[3]

But though the word *undertaker* disappeared from the political vocabulary of England (to become the sole property of the mortuary trade), the phenomenon did not. Under the name of "schemes of administration," "schemes of government," and just plain "schemes," it continued. Indeed, as early as William's reign the word *undertaking* began to give way to *scheme*. In 1690, upon William's turning to the Church party, John Hampden, a Whig, lamented to Sir Edward Harley, "You say you do not understand the present scheme, I don't know who does, and that which is most melancholy and discouraging is that there seems to be no scheme at all."[4] Twenty-four years later, the expression enjoyed even greater currency. "What can be your new scheme," wrote Jonathan Swift to Lord Bolingbroke's lieutenant, John Arbuthnot, "what are your new provocations? Are you sure of a majority?"[5] During the reigns of William III and Queen Anne, "schemes of administration" might comprehend more than "an undertaking." They might comprehend the naming of men to office in order to secure greater efficiency in administration or greater harmony in the cabinet. But usually concealed within such a scheme was an undertaking to manage Parliament for the monarch.

The following eight chapters are a study of such schemes and undertakings. I have sought in each chapter to tell the story of a single, discrete episode, beginning with Sir Henry Neville's brave, bold undertaking in 1614, and ending with Robert Harley's adroit, devious scheme of 1710. In each instance I have sought to discover the authors of the undertaking, to explore their hopes and fears and purposes, to reveal their illusions and mistakes, to assess their prudence and farsightedness, and to describe the final dénouement of their venture. It is my purpose to study each episode in terms of the politics of that age. How did the political process work? Where did power reside? What unspoken premises guided men's conduct? How were conflicts resolved? How did things get done?

But a second purpose informs this study. I hope not only to illuminate the political process as it worked at a given moment in time but also to show how it changed through time. The world of Robert Harley was not the world of Sir Henry Neville; and though it invites the charge of being a Whig historian to pose the genetic question, I shall do so. I shall in the following chapters seek to offer some explanation of why parliamentary undertaking, a forlorn hope in 1614, became by 1714 an integral part of the political life of Great Britain.

The terms *parliamentary manager*, *court manager*, and *parliamentary undertaker* are central to the argument of this study. For that reason it is essential to define them at the outset. By *parliamentary manager* I mean any politician who manages the King's business in the two Houses of Parliament. It can be regarded as the genus, of which *court manager* and *parliamentary undertaker* are two species. What distinguishes the *court manager* is the fact that he serves the court in the management of Parliament, using place, pension, title, persuasion, and careful management to win men over to policies favored by the King. Clifford, Danby, and the second Earl of Sunderland were archetypal court managers. The *parliamentary undertaker*, on the other hand, uses his popularity in Parliament and his ability to manage Parliament to wrest office from the King. Sir Richard Temple, the Earl of Shaftesbury, and the Junto Whigs were archetypal undertakers. The distinction between the two species lies in the terms upon which they agree to serve the King in the management of Parliament. If they enter office on the court's terms, they are court managers; if they insist on their own terms, they are parliamentary undertakers. The Earl of Shaftesbury understood this distinction well when he wrote to the Earl of Carlisle in 1675 that he did not fear to be accounted "an undertaker," but that he would never accept a place at court unless the present Parliament was dissolved.[6]

Two generous scholars—Professor Henry Snyder, of Louisiana State University, and Professor Henry Horwitz, of the University of Iowa—read the typescript in full and made invaluable comments upon it. I wish to thank them for their kindness and help. They have saved me from many an error of fact and interpretation.

I should also like to thank the Duke of Marlborough for permission to examine the manuscripts at Blenheim Palace, the Duke of Devonshire for permission to use the Finch-Halifax papers at Chatsworth House, and the Marquess of Bath for permission to quote from the Thynne and Coventry Papers at Longleat. Quotations from the Breadalbane Muniments, which are in the Scottish Record Office, appear with the permission of the Keeper of the Records of Scotland. I am indebted to the University of Nottingham Library for allowing me to examine the Portland papers in its possession and to the Trustees of the Portland Estate for permission to quote from them. I am similarly indebted to the Marquess of Downshire and the County Archivist, Berkshire Record Office, for permission to publish extracts from the Trumbull MSS, to Earl Spencer for permission to read and quote from the Halifax MSS at Althorp, to Lady Ravensdale and the Hertfordshire Record Office for allowing me to read and quote from the Panshanger MSS, and to Mr. and Mrs. O. R. Bagot for permission to read and quote from the Levens manuscripts in the Kendal Record Office. The Dr. Williams's Trust kindly granted me permission to read and quote from Roger Morrice's Entring Book in the Dr. Williams's Library, and the Cumbria County Library, at Tullie House, Carlisle, granted me a like permission to read and quote from Bishop Nicholson's Diary in their possession. The brief quotations from the Forster manuscripts are published by courtesy of the Trustees of the Victoria and Albert Museum. Lt-Cdr. Henry Plunkett-Ernle-Erle-Drax kindly granted me permission to publish material from the Erle MSS, now on deposit in Churchill College, Cambridge. Transcripts and translations of Crown copyright records in the Public Record Office appear by permission of the Controller of H.M. Stationery Office, and excerpts from manuscript Add. 7093 in the Cambridge University

Library with the permission of the Syndics of Cambridge University Library. For permission to quote from the Stanhope MSS, I should like to thank the Kent Archives Office and the Trustees of the Chevening Estate, for permission to quote from the Phelips MSS the Somerset Record Office, and for permission to quote from the Finch Collection on deposit in the Leicestershire Record Office, E. R. Hanbury. Finally, I should like to thank the Reigate and Banstead Borough Council and the Surrey Record Office for allowing me to read and to quote from the Somers MSS, Christ Church, Oxford, for permission to read and to quote from the Wake MSS, the New York City Library for permission to quote from Hardwicke MSS XXXIII, the Folger Shakespeare Library for permission to quote from the Newdigate News Letters, the Huntington Library for permission to read and quote from the Stowe and Brydges MSS, and to the Bodleian Library, Oxford, for permission to quote from its Western Manuscripts.

The debt that the historian owes to these archivists, librarians, and owners of manuscripts is much greater than a mere formal acknowledgment can convey. They make the writing of history both possible and agreeable.

Maija Jansson, an editor at the Yale Center for Parliamentary History and editor of the forthcoming *Proceedings in Parliament 1614*, has generously provided me with transcripts of an anonymous parliamentary diary now in the Kenneth Spencer Research Library at the University of Kansas. I am most grateful to her for her kindness.

SCHEMES & UNDERTAKINGS

Chapter I

Sir Henry Neville and the Origins of Parliamentary Undertaking

O N AN AUTUMN DAY IN 1611, John More met his old friend Levinus Munck. More was a servant of Sir Ralph Winwood, the English envoy at the Hague; Munck was secretary to the Earl of Salisbury and knew most of the secrets at court worth knowing. The two men fell to gossiping. "I wonder," said Munck, "from whence should grow so much discourse of Sir Henry Neville to be a Secretary of State or at least a Privy Councillor." More replied that he could hardly believe such discourse, for Neville had not spoken in Parliament for the King and had ranged himself with those patriots thought to be opposed to the courtiers, "which I think he would not have done, if he had aspired to any Court employment." Nevertheless, replied Munck, "he doth seek for some advancement, and that through Sir Thomas Overbury, by the means of Viscount Rochester, who of late hath brought to pass many great and strange matters." "The plot," continued Munck, "was that Sir Henry Neville should undertake to deal with the Lower House, and then (so as my Lord Treasurer would not intermeddle) there was no doubt but that better effects would come of the next Session (which is like to be in February next) than did come of the former."[1]

The former session about which Munck spoke was that held in the autumn of 1610, and its failure furnished the immediate occasion for Sir Henry Neville's undertaking to deal with the Lower House. The autumn session of 1610 had opened on 16 October, with the Commons uneasy at Salisbury's Great Contract. The lord treasurer had proposed that Parliament vote the King an additional revenue of £200,000 a year in return for the abolition of wardship and purveyance. But how, asked members of the House, could they raise such money in the country? And how, added Sir Roger Owen, introducing an idea that would haunt men's minds for a century, could they secure Parliaments hereafter if the King's wants were fully supplied?[2]

Then James dropped a bombshell. If the contract was to go forward, the Commons must add an immediate supply of £500,000 to the £200,000 annual support. The stunned Commons resolved not to proceed with the Great Contract. But disappointment was deep, for the contract comprehended the redress of grievances, and grievances were much on men's minds. Since 1604 Parliament had voted four subsidies and seven fifteenths and still grievances had not been redressed— impositions continued to be levied, purveyances exacted, deprived ministers silenced, pluralities held, proclamations abused, the penal laws unenforced. Robert Cecil, Earl of Salisbury and lord treasurer, stepped in to rescue the session from total failure. He offered eight graces in return for supply. But these graces did not speak to the main grievances weighing upon the nation. Nor was Parliament ready to vote money to a prodigal King, who wasted his treasure on worthless favorites, mostly Scotsmen. "The royal cistern had a leak," cried John Hoskyns.[3] The fifth sessions of James's first Parliament ended in shambles. James fled to Royston, the Commons grew more vehement in speech, and Salisbury struggled on. On 24 November he secured an adjournment, but an adjournment would not content James, who prorogued Parliament on 29 November and dissolved it in January. "No House save the House of Hell," he said, would treat him as the Commons had.[4]

James blamed Salisbury for the failure of the 1610 Parliament, but David Harris Willson is surely nearer the mark when he argues that it was the failure of a system, not the failure of a minister.[5] Salisbury had applied traditional Tudor methods of management, and they had failed. The essence of those methods was leadership by a few able councillors, not the creation of a Court party. There was no packing of a Parliament, only care taken that privy councillors were returned. The Privy Council itself prepared measures for the

Parliament. The senior privy councillor in the Commons nominated the Speaker, upon whose alertness and wisdom so much depended. The councillors, with the Speaker's help, then sought to direct all. They introduced government measures, spoke often and eloquently, whispered advice to the Speaker, moved for committees, proposed conferences, and suggested adjournments. Their interventions were often successful, for they—the Mildmays and Walsinghams of Elizabethan England—were popular and trusted, were one with the House, understood the House. They were, of course, the Queen's servants first, and the Queen was the *primum mobile* by whose motion all the other spheres moved. It was she who sent minatory messages, forbidding the discussion of this bill, hurrying on the passage of that. It was she who threatened to veto, and often did veto, bills that displeased her. It was she who summoned delegations of both Houses to hear scolding speeches or timely, gracious concessions. It all worked by an alchemy that not even its greatest historian, Sir John Neale, pretends to understand.[6]

The political crisis of 1610 forced men to search for solutions to their difficulties. One solution, proposed by the unadventurous and the unimaginative, was to carry on with the Elizabethan system, restore it and make it work. But this was a hopeless solution, for too much water had flowed under the bridge. There were now in the Commons, as John More observed, "patriots that were accounted of a contrary faction to the Courtiers," patriots who could carry the House and who could hold their own with any councillor.[7] And the House, with its claim to free speech, its corporate spirit, its committees, its pride, had gained an independence that hindered its manipulation by the court. At the same time, the privy councillors were in disarray, few in number, wanting in eloquence, and divided from the House by sentiment and policy. But the greatest obstacle to a restoration of the Elizabethan system was the King himself. James was incapable of Elizabeth's bewitching speeches, incapable of attending to the routine duties of parliamentary management, incapable of naming men of stature as councillors and of following their advice. He lacked the magnanimity of spirit that informed

Elizabeth's concessions on purveyances and monopolies. He lacked the tack to leave constitutional issues alone. By her frugality Elizabeth had won the confidence of her subjects; by his prodigality James forfeited that confidence. Elizabeth quarreled with her Parliaments, but beneath those quarrels lay a strange harmony of interest and instinct. Under a Scottish king who exalted the prerogative, listened to favorites, promoted his countrymen, made peace with Spain, and wasted his patrimony, that harmony dissolved away.[8]

There was a second solution: James could abate his expenses, increase his revenue, and "live of his own." Were he to do this, he need not meet Parliament again. England would then enter upon the same path that France was taking, for the French crown sent the Estates General home in 1614, never to meet them again until 1789. Some Englishmen, reported the Venetian ambassador, believed the King would never summon Parliament again.[9] Certainly this was the hope of the Howard faction, led by that master of intrigue the aged, erudite Earl of Northampton. Nor was it an impossible dream. In July of 1610, Salisbury nearly carried it off. When he came to the Treasury in 1608, he found the King's debts to be £597,337 and the annual deficit £78,433. By the spring of 1610, he had reduced the debt to £160,000 and the deficit to £50,000. Had the Great Contract succeeded, about £100,000 would have been added to the King's revenues, raising them from £460,000 a year to £560,000. This sum compares favorably with the average annual revenue during the last five years of Elizabeth's reign, which was £360,519 from ordinary revenues and £125,000 from parliamentary subsidies and fifteenths, a total of £485,519 in all. In short, had the Great Contract taken effect, James's nonparliamentary revenues would have been £75,000 more than Elizabeth's total revenues, parliamentary and nonparliamentary together.[10] No wonder the Commons took fright at the contract and that one bold member suggested that a want of money would serve as a subpoena on the King to give the House better answers hereafter.[11]

Yet it was the King, not the Commons, who first turned against the Great Contract. He probably did so on the advice of Sir Julius Caesar, chancellor of the Exchequer. In August, Sir Julius warned the King that the Great Contract would only increase his revenues by £85,000, a sum that could be gained by a better administration of wards and purveyance, the recovery of assart lands, a more rigorous search for defective titles, and a stricter enforcement of penal laws. Caesar even held out the hope that another £84,000 could be gained from the King's own lands. [12] In essence, Caesar advised the King to rely on projects, and it was this strategy that James pursued for the next four years. As early as 1609, Caesar had drawn up a list of 105 new projects. After 1610 the age of projects began in earnest. The Earl of Northampton joined in the pursuit. In 1612 the council named a committee on projects. They looked at proposals to coin brass farthings, to sell offices, to sell baronetcies, to create a starch monopoly, to lease wastes and commons, to erect alum works, and to prohibit the export of undyed cloth. Some they rejected, some they accepted, but none proved of great profit. "As with projects in chemical businesses," remarked John Chamberlain, it all went up in smoke. By February of 1614, the debt had risen to £680,000, the deficit to £200,000 a year. Matters grew so desperate by 1614 that even Northampton regarded the summoning of a Parliament as the lesser calamity. [13]

Tudor methods had proved unworkable; projects had failed. Were there other solutions? Sir Francis Bacon—philosopher, essayist, lawyer, and politician—believed there were. In late May 1612, a week after the death of the Earl of Salisbury, he wrote a memorial to the King. In subsequent months he wrote others. Bacon's advice contained a remarkable amalgam of naïveté and cynicism. He naïvely imagined that old grievances had died away and that new ones had not arisen, that the King could pretend he was not in want, and that the opposition was broken. All this being true, James should meet Parliament again, resorting to those arts of management that had succeeded in Elizabeth's reign. But the heart of his advice, what was new in it, lay in more cynical recommendations. What should be done, he wondered, to win over or bridle the lawyers, that they might further the King's cause or at least fear to oppose it? And how might the courtiers and the

King's servants be made zealous for the King, and not popular or fearful, as last time? What persons were fit to be brought into the House and what persons to be kept out? How might the boroughs of the Cinque Ports and the duchy be used to bring in well-affected persons, as also those boroughs at the devotion of the King's councillors? And how might men be made to see that it was not safe to form parties in Parliament.[14]

These were Bacon's meditations on the future, but he already had encouraging news about the present. "Yelverton is won," he wrote, "Sandys is fallen off; Crew and Hyde stand to be Serjeants; Brooke is dead; Neville has hopes; Berkeley I think will be respective; Martin has money in his purse; Dudley Digges and Holles are yours." In Bacon's world men were to be won, bought, owned, frightened, bridled, silenced, and seduced; in short, manipulated rather than led. He even believed that hopes of becoming a councillor would make Sir Edward Coke "obsequious." From this cynical view of human nature arose Bacon's strategy for managing Parliament: the King should, through patronage and electoral influence, create a Court party, a party that would then help carry his measures through both Houses.[15]

The use of patronage and electoral influence to create a Court party was no part of parliamentary management during the High Elizabethan period, but neither was it a strategy invented solely by Sir Francis Bacon. Its true origin lay in the 1590s, when the Elizabethan age began to disintegrate. The Earl of Essex, seeking "domestical greatness," sent letters to numerous boroughs promoting the election of his friends. Robert Cecil followed suit in 1597 and 1601, though in 1604, with Essex no longer on the scene, he neglected to do so. He and James soon saw the error of their ways and intervened actively in the 95 by elections that followed, usually with success. Only four boroughs are known to have refused Cecil's nominee. Of the members elected in those 95 elections, one-third were royal officials or persons closely connected with the government. But the strength of the court group was undermined by the independence of its own members. To counteract this the court sought to persuade men privately, outside the House, to support royal measures. Persuasion soon gave way to pressure. James in 1607 berated five lords for opposing his measures in Parliament. Councillors on committees sought, though unsuccessfully, to record the votes of its members. In 1610 James asked Cecil, now Earl of Salisbury, to send him a list of all his servants who had opposed the vote of a fifteenth. The Venetian ambassador observed in 1611 that when a new Parliament is summoned care shall be taken that those hostile to the King shall not be reelected.[16]

Bacon concluded his advice to James with the remark, "Until your Majesty have tuned your instrument [meaning Parliament], you will have no harmony." But he was not the only man aware of the disharmonies in English public life. Sir Henry Neville, remarked John Chamberlain in 1612, takes "great pains to reconcile and set all in tune." But Neville would set all in tune in a way very different from Bacon's. Far from excluding the patriots of 1610 from the next Parliament, he would have the King rely upon them. The exact nature of Neville's proposal, first broached in October 1611, can only be delineated by tracing its history through the year 1612.[17]

The idea of Neville as secretary of state had shocked John More, but by the spring of 1612 it was a commonplace around Whitehall. In early March most men spoke of Sir Thomas Lake and Sir Henry Neville as the two secretaries of state. By April it was thought that Neville was more likely than Lake to succeed Salisbury, who was gravely ill. Salisbury died on 24 May, and rumor at once designated Lake and Neville to be the two secretaries. The intrigues at court for the secretaryship were of a classical nature: the Howards pressed the claims of Lake; Rochester and Overbury favored Neville; the Queen supported Sir Henry Wotton. But some of the canvassing for Neville went beyond the traditional solicitation of patron for client. Parliament men flocked about Neville. They met at Lord Rochester's chambers, where they consulted with the Earl of Southampton and Lord Sheffield. Rumor declared that Southampton and Sheffield would shortly be sworn of the council. On 29 May, Sir Henry Neville's friends told him that the King desired to speak with him and required him to be in readiness. Although he had arranged to wait upon Prince Henry at Richmond that day, he sent his apologies and remained at Whitehall. But no summons came. The next day Neville returned to Whitehall, but the King went hunting. Neville's constant attendance upon the King's pleasure proved fruitless. Too much soliciting by his friends and the flocking of parliament men about him had hurt his cause. James declared in mid-June that he would not have a secretary imposed upon him by Parliament. Southampton retired to Tichfield without his councillorship; Sheffield went off to Yorkshire with nothing more than a grant to prosecute Papists; and men declared Wotton to be the likeliest choice for secretary.[18]

Neville himself returned to Billingbeare, in Berkshire, to the handsome red brick manor house his father had built during Elizabeth's reign. But retirement to the country did not diminish his zeal to serve the King. When James came to Windsor in early July, Neville secured the interview he had vainly sought in June. Two years later Neville told the House of Commons that the King on that occasion had sought him out in order to ask his opinion concerning a Parliament, but the likelier explanation is that Rochester and Overbury had finally persuaded James to meet with Neville.[19] Neville was certainly prepared for the meeting, for he had written a long paper, entitled "An Advice Touching the Holding of a Parliament," which he gave to James on that occasion.[20]

Neville opened his "Advice" by asking whether the King should relieve his wants by Parliament or projects. Those projects adopted since the last Parliament had failed. But admit that projects might succeed in the future, "yet I am clearly of opinion that" no project can be as fit, as honorable, and as necessary as a Parliament. The last Parliament ended in acrimony and discord, report of which spread throughout the realm and into foreign parts. This injured the King, for nothing so emboldens his enemies abroad and discontented persons at home as the belief that prince and people are divided. To erase this belief, the King should summon Parliament, "for there the error grew, and no where else it must be repaired. The harsh conclusion of the former Parliament bred that ill conceit, and the sweet close of another must beget a better." Two notable effects will follow: the relief of the King's wants and the end of the conceit that there is a misunderstanding between King and people.

Neville admitted that there were two objections to his counsels: Parliament might continue adverse and unwilling to relieve His Majesty's wants, and it might play upon his necessities in order to extort unreasonable demands. Both objections, however, were grounded upon the false belief that the last Parliament acted out of evil affection. "Which I do know, and do confidently avow, to be otherwise . . . as one that lived and conversed inwardly with the chief of them that were noted to be most backward, and know their inwardest thoughts in that business. So I dare undertake for the most of them, that his Majesty proceeding in a gracious course towards his people, he shall find those gentlemen exceeding willing to do him service. . . . " True, some things will be expected of him by way of grace. "And without this I dare promise nothing." What things will be expected by Parliament will be hard to determine. "Yet what I have collected out of the desire of sundry of the principal and the most understanding gentlemen, that were of the last Parliament and are like to be of this, I will be bold to deliver in a Memorial hereunto adjoined." These graces will be of small moment to His Majesty but of great value to his subjects. Neville then proposed that Parliament be called at Michaelmas. "And I do not see but in a month or five weeks this point of supplying the King and of his retribution will be easily determined, if it be proposed betimes and followed close afterwards."

There then followed the memorial containing the graces that should be offered by way of retribution for supply.[21] These graces reflected the grievances of a landowning gentry. Thus, persons accused of intruding on royal land should be allowed to keep possession until the King's title was proved. All the King's grants of land not already overthrown in Exchequer should be confirmed. Those possessing licences for alienating land should not be forced to plead those alienations in the Exchequer. And officers of the Exchequer should not charge fees when sheriffs and collectors of subsidies tender their accounts. Neville then rounded off his defense of the landed gentlemen of England by proposing a liberal pardon. The King should pardon all debts to the crown arising before the death of Elizabeth, all unpaid fines for alienations made before March 1603, all reprisals based on grants made before March 1611, and all fines imposed in courts of justice before September 1611.[22]

To these concessions of his own devising, Neville then added the eight graces promised by Salisbury in 1610. They too principally concerned the grievances of landed men. Respite of homage should be abolished; no royal lease should be forfeited for nonpayment of rent; assart and drowned lands should not be called in question; sixty years' possession of land should be sufficient to prescribe against the King; penal laws should be reformed, obsolete laws abolished, the Statute of Wales repealed, and no impositions levied hereafter but by Parliament.[23]

Aside from the promise that no new impositions be levied hereafter but by Parliament, there was nothing in these concessions that spoke to the principal grievances afflicting Englishmen. There was nothing about proclamations, prohibitions, purveyances, or silenced ministers. But neither were these concessions as trivial as their technical language might suggest. Since 1605 a commission to compound for assart lands had wrested £20,000 a year from Englishmen. Exchequer officials were extorting £60, £100, even £170 from sheriffs for passing their accounts. In 1606 an angry Commons summoned the notorious Mr. Typper before it to answer for his energetic search into defective titles to land. During the 1610 sessions, the Commons complained of restraints on alienation, of fines for respite of homage, of proceedings in cases of intrusion, and of searches for concealed wardships and old debts. They had also demanded that an outlaw's just debts be paid before his estate be forfeited to the crown, that sixty years' possession answer against the King, that men not forfeit leases of crown land for nonpayment of rent, and that 34 Henry VIII, which gave the King arbitrary power over Welshmen, be repealed. Puritans and merchants and lawyers might find in these graces little "retribution" for a vote of supply, but the country gentlemen, who made up four-fifths of the House, would find much to be grateful for.[24]

On 5 September, Neville secured a second meeting with James. He spoke for two hours with the King as he hunted. He found those matters "well tasted" that he had proposed at the first meeting. James approved of most of Neville's counsels, though of some he had doubts. Neville thereupon, so he avows, satisfied those doubts. James then told Neville that in a fortnight he would make known his resolution. The fortnight came and went, and there was no resolution. Neville therefore wrote Rochester, asking him to explain to the King that the proposals lately made to him would not injure his prerogative. He accompanied his letter with proposals for administrative reforms, with new concessions, and with a memorial explaining why the course proposed concerning impositions would not prejudice the King's right of imposing. The arguments in this new memorial were tendentious—and appear not to have persuaded James.[25]

Neville's advice and concessions did not make up the whole of his undertaking: in fact, they made up only half of the bargain. The other half was the preferment of himself and his friends to office. The nature of the plot became clear as summer gave way to autumn in 1612. By mid-July men ceased to talk of Wotton as secretary; they now said that Neville and his good friend Sir Ralph Winwood would come in together. A step in that direction was taken when the signet, in Sir Thomas Lake's possession since the death of Salisbury, was delivered to Rochester. Lake was the Howard candidate for secretary; Rochester and Overbury were promoting Neville and Winwood. As Sir Robert Naunton wrote to Winwood on 15 September: "His [Neville's] directions from his friends, you know, continue the same—not to obtrude himself into any petition or pursuit, but to leave it to them wholly, to cull out a time proper for the propounding it with success."[26] By "them" Naunton probably meant Rochester and Overbury, who were with the King at Windsor in early September, busy culling out a proper time. James had appointed a council meeting for 21 September, and they were hopeful that a resolution would be taken then. But Neville had to report to

Winwood that there was much kicking, "both against you and me severally, but more against the coupling of us together."[27]

Some observers of the court scene thought that Rochester intended to keep the signet until he had groomed Overbury for the post of secretary, but Naunton assured Winwood that "we can admit no suspicion of any such underhand meaning in any of the three."[28] The twenty-first of September came, the secret wheels turned, but no resolution followed. Neville was not dismayed. He continued to take great pains to reconcile and set all in tune. "Yet there is exceptions taken to him," wrote Chamberlain in November, "that he cannot be content to come in himself, but he must bring in his man Sir Ralph Winwood, and his champion the Earl of Southampton, and whosoever he thinks good. It may be indeed that the great favourite [Rochester] embracing too much at once will mar all. . . ."[29]

While Rochester worked for him at court, Neville sought to augment his allies in Parliament. In November, Sir Maurice Berkeley, a formidable power in Somersetshire politics, wrote Sir Robert Phelips, son of the Speaker: "I like well of your purpose of treating with Sir Henry Neville and I do assure myself it will be grateful to him to see such as you are so well affected."[30] The undertaking went forward, Rochester the broker at court, Neville the manager in Parliament.

Neville's undertaking was a bold and original scheme. John More found it incredible; Bacon dismissed it as preposterous; James thought it tantamount to Parliament's forcing a secretary upon him. It was a new idea, but like other new ideas, it did not emerge fully armed, like a Pallas Athena from the head of Zeus. It was generated by earlier events and compounded of earlier experiences. Three events in particular led Neville to propose his undertaking. They were a meeting at Salisbury's Hyde Park home in July 1610, a colloquy with James in November, and a consultation with Lake in December.

On 10 July 1610, the Earl of Salisbury, in the Banqueting Hall before both Houses, justified his role in levying impositions. Not content with a public defense, he met privately that night, at his house in Hyde Park, with eight members of the House of Commons, all of them accounted patriots, among them Neville. They met to discuss impositions, but they probably also discussed the Great Contract. What decisions they reached, what bargains they struck are not known, but the very fact that they met privately marked a new era. In Elizabeth's reign men were imprisoned for holding such meetings out of Parliament. The meeting was not well received among the rank and file of the House of Commons; they immediately suspected the eight members of plotting some new design.[31]

In November 1610 Neville acted once more as an intermediary between court and Commons. It was on 16 November, when James summoned 30 members of the Commons to the Council Chamber in order to ask them some direct questions. "Did they," he asked, "think he was in want, as the Treasurer had told them?" Sir Francis Bacon began to answer, though in a style more extravagant than James desired. So the King turned to Neville and commanded him to answer. Neville gave the direct answers that James desired. "Yes, his Majesty was in want." "Then," said James, "tell me whether it belongs to you that are my subjects to relieve me or not." "To this," said Neville, "I must answer with a distinction: where your Majesty's expenses grow by [the needs of] the Commonwealth we are bound to maintain it, otherwise not." Neville then reminded James that they had voted four subsidies and seven fifteenths, yet had had no redress of grievances. James at once demanded to know what those grievances were. "To all their grievances," said Neville, "I am not privy, but to those that are come to my knowledge I will make recital." And so he began to recite them, until he reached the jurisdiction of the Council of Wales, when Sir Herbert Croft interrupted him. "Otherwise," wrote John More, he would have delivered his judgment in all, "in what respect it might be taken."[32]

Then in December 1610, Sir Thomas Lake, acting for Salisbury and the King, consulted with Neville in order to discover who in the House of Commons intended to petition to send all the Scots home.[33]

The germ of Neville's undertaking can be seen in these

three events. Salisbury and Lake had sought him out and the King had singled him out as a man who could speak for the Commons. Though they knew he was one of the opposition— indeed, *because* he was one of the opposition—they had asked his advice. Neville could not have been blind to this fact, and in this perception was born the idea of a parliamentary undertaking. Others, however, had attended both meetings— Sandys, Croft, Berkeley—and had not the ingenuity or boldness or foolhardiness to propose such an undertaking. To understand more fully this episode in Jacobean history, one must understand what manner of man Sir Henry Neville was.

Three qualities—confidence, inventiveness, and ambition—distinguished Neville's character.

The sources of Neville's confidence are not far to seek; they lay in his birth, his wealth, his education, and his experience. Sir Henry was descended from the Nevilles of Abergavenny, a branch of the House of Westmorland. One ancestor had served William the Conqueror as admiral. Another had helped place Henry IV on the throne. His grandfather had been a boon companion of Henry VIII, until he lost his life by joining Exeter's conspiracy. To birth was added wealth when Sir Henry's father, an ally of Warwick and a favorite of Edward VI, secured the Berkshire estates of the bishop of Winchester and, through marriage, acquired the Sussex estates of Sir Thomas Gresham. In 1580 Neville's father was assessed for the subsidy at £100 a year for his Berkshire lands, and was required to pay 20 marks in tax. It was the largest assessment in the county.

Henry received an education befitting the son of a wealthy gentleman and a future deputy lieutenant. He matriculated at Merton College, Oxford, where he initiated a lifelong friendship with his tutor, Henry Savile, later warden of Merton. After a year at Oxford, he traveled abroad, accompanied by Henry Savile. Neville and Savile were frequently joined by Sir Robert Sidney, brother of the author of *Arcadia*. After four years of travel through Germany, Austria, Italy, and France, he returned to England to take up his duties as a gentleman of Berkshire. He served as justice of the peace, sat in five Elizabethan Parliaments, and succeeded his father as master of

Billingbeare in 1593. He was a paradigm of that wealthy, educated gentry class whose growing role in government Sir John Neale has chronicled.[34]

It is doubtful, however, that he would have ever exhibited the audacity he later displayed had he not served as ambassador to France from 1599 to 1601. Possessing wealth, knowing French, stoutly Protestant, and allied by marriage with Cecil, Sir Henry was an obvious choice for ambassador to France. He arrived in Paris on 8 May 1599 and before his departure a year later had held seven audiences with Henry IV, audiences punctuated with bold declarations, quick ripostes, and resolute argument. The debt owed the Queen must be paid, the sale of English cloth at Rouen restored, the shipment of French corn to Spain stopped. Neville's second audience was at Fountainbleau, where Henry IV bid him sit down beside him, talked privately with him for more than an hour, and then showed him about the palace. But neither the majesty of the Most Christian King nor the charm of Henry Bourbon could dissuade Neville from stoutly defending the Queen's interests. He never recovered the debts owed her, but his pertinacity in that cause led to shorter and shorter audiences. The year in Paris also brought Neville into the inner circles of power and gave him a knowledge of men and affairs in Europe. With great skill he anatomized for Cecil Henry IV's council. He presumed to differ from Henry IV himself on the political complexion of the Papal Curia. His own reading of the various courts of Europe reflected a Machiavellian realism wedded to a Protestant idealism. From Paris, Neville went on to Boulogne, where he served as first commissioner at an abortive peace conference with Spain. Upon the collapse of the conference, he returned to London, a wiser, more experienced, more confident man.[35]

While in Paris, Neville displayed not only boldness but inventiveness. Not content merely to defend English policy or to send home foreign intelligence, he sought also to fashion policy. He bombarded Cecil with what he called his "poor opinion." If Her Majesty would banish French wines for a time, the French would treat her more respectfully. The Queen should ask for some payment of the debt in corn, for it could be used in Ireland. The Queen should not, relying upon the amity of France, rush into a peace with Spain that would end the dependence of the States on England. Urging this last point with some warmth, Neville felt constrained to add: "Pardon me I humbly beseech your Honour, that I am entered so far into this argument, for though it belongs rather to my place to advertise, than to interfere or to inforce, yet my zeal to her Majesty's service cannot contain itself within ordinary bounds, and methinks I see somewhat more than I can by a bare advertisement explain."[36]

The flood of advice that poured from Paris revealed an inventive mind. Other events in Neville's life revealed the same. Succeeding to Mayfield manor in Sussex in the late 1580s, he at once entered into the growing iron industry of that county. Through his own native wit and his influence with Lord Burleigh, he seems to have cornered the market in the sale of small ordnance in Sussex.[37] After his ambassador-ship he continued to promote projects. In 1608 he sent Salisbury a proposal for raising £80,000 a year for the King; the scheme was to allow two gentlemen in each parish to pay £5 a year to escape jury duty.[38] In 1613 Neville was active in a plan to establish a trade with Persia through Muscovy, a plan that envisaged placing Prince Charles on the throne of Muscovy.[39] Sir Henry possessed in full measure the optimism, ingenuity, and boldness needed by a Jacobean projector.

He also possessed the ambition characteristic of a Jacobean politician, though his ambition nearly destroyed him in 1601. Neville had not been ambassador in Paris six months before he began to dream of becoming secretary of state. It was an exalted office, but there seemed no reason why Neville should not in time secure it. During Henry VIII's reign, Sir Edward Seymour had observed that three things "raise a man to observation: 1. some peculiar sufficiency, 2. some particular exploit, 3. an especial friend."[40] In his command of French and knowledge of European courts, Neville possessed a peculiar sufficiency. The collection of the debts owed to the Queen would be a particular exploit. And Cecil was an especial friend. But there were obstacles. Neville's sufficiency was marred by a rash judgment, which Cecil had frequently observed. There was little prospect that Neville could wring a single sou from Henry IV. And the prospect arose that Essex might become more powerful at court than Cecil.

In August 1600 Neville returned to England and was at once accosted by Henry Cuffe, an old friend, once professor of Greek at Oxford and now secretary to the Earl of Essex. Cuffe sought in the next six months to enlist Neville among the phalanx of noblemen and gentlemen who rallied behind Essex. In November, Neville met secretly with Essex himself, though it appears they discussed nothing more treasonous than the European scene. Cuffe met often with Neville through the late autumn and early winter, urging him to meet with Sir Charles Danvers and the Earl of Southampton at Drury House. Neville begged off several times, but finally on 2 February 1601 did so. Southampton began by telling Neville that the Earl of Essex had formed a high opinion of him. He then unfolded Essex's plan to gain access to the Queen by overpowering the guard at Whitehall. Neville committed himself to nothing. Several days later he told Cuffe that he would not be an actor in the conspiracy, for he saw that the plot was aimed at Cecil, to whom he was beholden and to whom he was allied. Cuffe replied that all they asked of him was that he be at court when Essex arrived. Neville asked why. Cuffe answered, because Essex "meant to name him to supply some place there." Cuffe later testified that that place was the secretaryship.[41]

Neville found himself in a quandry. Gratitude to Cecil, loyalty to the Queen, and expectations of securing the secretaryship after a second year in Paris dictated that he reveal the plot to Cecil. Yet his own inclinations toward an aggressive Protestant foreign policy had more in common with Essex's policies than Cecil's. There was also a growing estrangement between himself and Cecil. France had just concluded peace with Savoy, removing the only lever England had to wrest concessions from Henry IV. If he returned to Paris and failed to secure the repayment of the debt, he would have little chance of winning high office. Essex held out the hope of high office within a month. Faced with these pressures, Neville took a middle course: he assured Cuffe of his neutrality, remained silent, and went to court that fateful Sunday when Essex and his men rose.[42]

Neville's decision led to disaster, a disaster that was to haunt him for the rest of his life. Essex's revolt failed, and its participants were seized. The Earl himself, a fortnight later, confessed all, including Neville's knowledge of the plot. Cecil immediately sent a warrant for Neville's arrest to Dover, where Neville was about to embark for France. Being guilty only of misprision of treason, Neville escaped with his life, but he spent two years in the Tower and was fined £10,000. As Sir Thomas Hoby observed, when he heard of Sir Henry's misfortune, "his cousin Neville was ambling towards his preferment, and would needs gallop in all the haste, and so stumbled and fell."[43]

James's accession awoke new hopes in Neville. James had always looked upon Essex and his followers as martyrs to his cause. No sooner had he ascended the throne than he released Neville from the Tower and restored him to his titles and fortune. The Venetian ambassador reported that James destined Sir Henry Neville "to great rewards."[44] But the bright dawn soon faded, no advancement came; Cecil remained first minister, controlling patronage, recommending men to office, and denying advancement to Neville. James, told by the Scottish ambassador in Paris that Neville was a Puritan, exhibited a like distrust. James even went so far as to imprison Neville, Southampton, and others in the Tower, having been told that they threatened to kill several of his Scottish favorites, perhaps the King himself. The story proved false, and the men were released; but Neville now knew the true measure of the King's distrust of him.[45] When Cecil in 1605 considered resigning as secretary, Sir Dudley Carleton thought Neville a good replacement. But Cecil clung to office, not only then but in 1608 when he became lord treasurer. Neville would have had to be purblind not to see by 1610 that Cecil's hostility and James's distrust blocked his advancement at court—at least by conventional means.

Denied advancement at court, Neville put his talents to work in Parliament. He had sat in Parliament during Elizabeth's reign, but the nature of his parliamentary service now altered. His earlier parliamentary career had been an introduction to political society and an apprenticeship in government. He regularly supported the policies of the court. Under James he took a more active role and drifted into opposition. He did not, however, become a popular orator or a tribune of the people. He preferred to work through committees, being named in all four sessions of James's first Parliament to the more important committees. He distinguished himself frequently by acting as spokesman for the Commons before the Lords. As committeeman and spokesman, he increasingly allied himself with the opposition. In the session that met in 1605, he found himself working with men of a more radical turn of mind than his own, men who opposed the peace with Spain, who would give no quarter to recusants, who favored free trade, who would not compound for purveyance. He came to admire these country members, and to look with contempt on courtiers.[46]

Neville's consorting with the opposition injured him at court. "This parliament," he wrote Winwood, "has done me no good, where not only speeches and actions, but countenances, and conversations with men disliked, have been observed."[47] In the 1607 session, he broke with the court even more openly, delivering before the Lords a fierce attack upon the proposed union with Scotland, a speech certain to displease James.[48] By 1610 Neville the courtier had traveled far toward becoming Neville the patriot.

Though he traveled far toward the opposition, he remained a courtier. Bacon counted him in 1610 among those with whom the government could work.[49] And herein lay his strength: he was a man of the middle. His experience, his aspirations, his Cecil connection, and his knowledge of men and affairs made him a man of the court. His Berkshire manors, his Protestant prejudices, his commercial ventures, and his political allies made him a man of the country. He was well placed to be a bridge between the two.

He was also peculiarly fitted by temperament to act as that bridge. He was no champion of the common law, as Coke, no passionate orator, as Eliot, no remorseless opponent of court policies, as Pym. Rather he was a fixer, a compromiser, a doer, fertile in expedients, rich in ideas. His wit and ingenuity were as admired by his friends as feared by his enemies. Carleton, a friend, thought him a better lapidary than Bodley; Suffolk, an enemy, warned Northampton against his "trickery wit."[50] His closest friends—Sir Henry Savile, Sir Thomas Bodley, Sir Dudley Carleton, Ralph Winwood, John Chamberlain—were diplomats and scholars, not preachers and lawyers. He quoted Tacitus oftener than the Bible.[51] He saw government not as the triumph of right over wrong but as the daily reconciling of opposed interests among men. He believed that crown and Parliament could cooperate in the good government of the realm. He was, in short, a sensible, pragmatic, tolerant, patriotic Englishman, who believed he had found a way to bring King and Parliament together.

Such was the man who in the autumn of 1612 persisted in his efforts to reconcile and set all in tune. The means to do this were obvious: James should name Neville and Winwood as secretaries, summon Parliament, and entrust its management to them. In return for concessions that would cost him little, they would secure him a vote of supply. The first step in this plot was the nomination of Neville and Winwood as secretaries, and to this purpose Overbury and Rochester exerted all the arts of a courtier. In October they were so near success that Neville secured a license to build a house on Tothill Fields, immediately southwest of the Parliament houses. In December, Neville was nearer the mark than ever; but then, in April of 1613, storm clouds appeared, and by October the whole plan had collapsed. Neville, despairing of preferment, crept off to Billingbeare.[52]

The forces working against the undertaking had proved irresistible. There was in the first place the King's rooted aversion to Neville, an aversion aggravated in January 1613 by Neville's quarrel with Viscount Fenton, one of James's favorites, and exacerbated in May by Neville's alleged support of Sir James Whitelocke's attack upon the legality of the Admiralty commission.[53] Then there was the opposition—continuous, obdurate, and calumnous—of the Howard faction. But the greatest obstacle to his hopes, as Neville came to see, was Sir Thomas Overbury. The very man who was to be the instrument of his advancement proved to be his nemesis. Overbury's neglect of men of place and power, his needless contesting with them, his refusal to serve abroad, his final imprisonment in the Tower, all worked to Neville's disadvantage.[54]

Neville sought to repair the damage by forming an alliance with Southampton and Pembroke, and through them to retain Rochester's support. Viscount Fenton in May 1613 described the alliance thus: "All those that Overbury drew to him and about Rochester are like to make a party [opposed] to the Howards, which I think they would do if they could stir Rochester to it, but he will be wiser. Southampton and Pembroke are joined in that side, and they stand much to have Neville Secretary. They have with them some of the most discontented noblemen of the younger sort, and all the parliament mutineers; yet I think all will not work their end."[55] Fenton prophesied truly. In October, Rochester was drawn into the Howard camp by his marriage to Lady Frances Howard, formerly Lady Essex. Rochester threw over Neville, who now learned the melancholy truth that in Jacobean England power resided in the breast of the favorite.[56]

Neville's undertaking to manage Parliament of the King in return for office might never have caught the eye of the historian had not penury driven James to meet Parliament in 1614. Projects had failed. The revenues of the Court of Wards had not trebled. A like improvement promised in the licences of alienation had turned to smoke. Thus early in February 1614, the council advised the King to summon a new Parliament, to meet on 5 April. The King accepted the council's advice, and writs went out for new elections. Then came reports that the shires were not disposed to return the King's servants. Hearing this, James panicked. He commanded Lake to write to the lords of the council, urging them to use their credit to return "men of good disposition and apt to have due consideration of him and his estate."[57] As a result, letters of recommendation flew through the land, even to the meanest borough. Their number was so great that the world conceived it a packing of Parliament. Sir Thomas Parry, chancellor of the duchy, returned 14 courtiers and servants. "I understand," wrote

Gabaleone, the Piedmontese resident, "that the King has used his offices throughout the country in order to secure the election to Parliament of persons allied to him."[58] So he did, but not upon the advice of Neville. There is no evidence whatever that Neville ever advised the King to attempt to influence the elections to Parliament. Nor were the King's efforts particularly successful. In a House numbering 464 members, 135 courtiers and officials were returned, a number normal for a Jacobean Parliament.[59]

The council also prepared measures for the coming Parliament, including graces to be offered by the King to the Commons. On 12 February the council, probably upon the initiative of the Earl of Suffolk, examined those graces that Salisbury had offered in 1610 and those that Neville had proposed in 1612. In March the council drew up eleven bills to be offered to Parliament, nine of which came from Neville's Memorial. On 9 April the King offered these eleven bills of grace to Parliament. In short, Suffolk and Rochester (now Earl of Somerset) adopted Neville's strategy of offering concessions as a retribution for supply. They did not, however, ask the King to name Neville secretary or give office to his friends or entrust the management of the Commons to him or accept his solution to the problem of impositions. Neville never once met with the council; during these months he remained a spectator to events he could not control.[60]

Yet rumors flew about that the King had entrusted the management of Parliament to the undertakers. John Donne, the eloquent dean of St. Paul's, wrote on 12 February: "It is taken ill, though it be mistaken that certain men (whom they call undertakers) should presume either to understand the House before it sit, or incline it then, and this rumour beforehand . . . must impeach, if it does not defeat, their purpose at last."[61] Five days later Sir John Holles wrote: "They say we shall have a Parliament and the apostates of the last are the proselytes in this and have, as the many headed beast says, contracted for plenty of subsidies."[62] By the middle of March, the many-headed beast had done his work well. "It is bruited abroad," wrote the anonymous author of a memorial in Northampton's papers, "that some few gentlemen that were most opposed to his Majesty in the last Parliament, for particular promotions, will undertake to carry this Parliament for his Majesty's profit and ends, which other men of their like rank and quality do so much condemn and scorn, and take for so great an injury to themselves and the parliament house, as they begin to bandy and to made a faction which is like to break forth to open discontent at their sitting."[63]

"For particular promotions," wrote the anonymous author, they "will undertake to carry this Parliament for his Majesty's profit and ends." But there were no particular promotions. True, Somerset offered Neville a post in the Household in December 1613, but Neville rejected it with scorn.[64] And in late March, the Earl of Suffolk (Northampton's nephew) met with Neville and held out to him the hope of his becoming secretary if he amended his faults in this Parliament. Northampton thereupon accused Suffolk of inclining toward the undertakers. "This troubles me nothing," Suffolk wrote to Somerset, "for if we may do our master the service we wish by our dissembling, I am well contented to play the knave a little with them. . . ."[65]

There was no undertaking in 1614, unless Suffolk's dissembling with Neville and the Council's offering eleven bills of grace be thought an undertaking. Yet there was a spate of rumors of an undertaking. How can one explain the anomaly? Sir Thomas Roe probably hit upon the right explanation when he wrote that the pro-Spanish faction, anxious to see Parliament fail, spread abroad rumors that there was an undertaking.[66] The greatest of the Howards, Northampton, scorned the undertaking as a "pragmatic invention."[67] It was probably his emissaries who traduced as undertakers the chief pillars of the House of Commons and who spread around town, a few days before Parliament met, copies of Neville's memorial. The Earl knew that Neville had proposed an undertaking. What better way to wreck the Parliament than to spread rumors that particular men for particular promotions had engaged to carry the House for the King?

Northampton's emissaries did their work well, for when Parliament met, there was an explosion of anger against the undertakers. There was also an explosion of wrath against the packers, and it is a mistake not to distinguish between the two. James himself distinguished between them when he promptly told Parliament: "For undertakers, I protest, I never was so base [as] to call or rely upon any but your general love, and if any had been so foolish to offer it, yet it had been greater folly in me to have accepted it, and for elections and packing a parliament, I know none of them, nor interceded, and who will doubt of this gives me the lie."[68]

The House of Commons likewise distinguished between the two. On 8 April it ordered the Committee for Privileges to inquire into packing; on 13 April it named a separate committee to draw up a message clearing members of the House from the suspicion of undertaking. The former committee inquired into Sir Thomas Parry's endeavors to compel the voters of Stockbridge to return two courtiers. Bacon, who had advised James to look to his duchy boroughs, sought to stem the tide running against Parry. "Consider the person, a counsellor, representing the King. . . . We live not in Plato his commonwealth, but in times wherein abuses have got the upper hand." But his intervention did no good. The Commons expelled the chief of the packers from the House.[69]

The fate of the undertakers was very different. Sir Richard Weston, later to serve Charles I as lord treasurer, was the first to attack those who sought to take advantage of an interest in the last Parliament to manage the present one. Others rallied behind Weston, declaring that "this contracting sticketh in the House." Sir Herbert Croft, who admitted that he had been saluted by the name of undertaker, favored a message to the King clearing members of the House from the taint of undertaking. So too did Sir Dudley Digges, who confessed that he was almost an undertaker, and Sir Edwin Sandys, who grieved that worthy members should be traduced as undertakers. Sir Maurice Berkeley, who in 1612 applauded Sir Robert Phelips for treating with Neville, likewise favored such a message. Indeed, in a later debate, Phelips himself opposed a further inquiry into undertaking and favored a message clearing the House from all suspicion of it. These "ancient champions" of the House, as Chamberlain called them, carried the day. A committee was named, not to inquire into the undertaking, but to draw up a message clearing the House of the charge of it. Sir Henry Neville was named to the committee, thus making the chief poacher one of the gamekeepers.[70]

Then on 2 May, Sir Roger Owen, the chairman of the committee, reported to the House. The committee generally condemned the undertaking, he declared, and desired the House to continue an order made the Parliament before that no member of the House should confer with the King about Parliament but the Speaker. Sir Henry Poole then moved that there be no more debate concerning the business of undertaking. Sir Robert Phelips supported the motion, but the irrepressible John Hoskyns, probably a dupe of the Earl of Northampton, demanded a recommitment and further inquiry. Sir Dudley Digges and Sir Herbert Croft then suggested that the rumors of an undertaking were false, and urged an inquiry into those who had spread these false rumors. The debate ended in an order empowering the committee to examine the undertakers.[71]

Duly empowered, the committee met on 5 May, but to little purpose. Digges stated, "It was thought that particular men went to the King and in hope to merit favour [offered] to betray their country." Francis Ashley declared that when he first came to town he was greeted by bills of grace and that Sir John Sammes had once told him that Prince Henry had expostulated with Overbury for being so great with men who answered to do the King good service in the next Parliament.[72] Since Prince Henry died in late 1612, Ashley's testimony only proved the existence of an undertaking in early 1612.

But though the committee met to little purpose, the continuing turmoil over undertaking revealed the nature of men's objections to the practice. Sir John Holles, sulking for want of preferment, voiced his objections in a letter to Lord Norris. The undertakers, he wrote, "have promised that the Parliament shall supply the King's wants to his contentment." Thereby they proclaim their omnipotence and their fellow members' "weakness and obedience to their will."[73] Sir Richard Weston put it succinctly: "A House of Commons [is] not to suffer their counsels to be led by any private man."[74]

Sir Thomas Wentworth, later to become the Earl of Strafford, urged a remonstrance to the King stating that "they were not to be drawn on by the vain hopes of any man's preferment whosoever."[75] Sir Francis Bacon echoed these sentiments: "That private men should undertake for the Commons of England! why a man might as well undertake for the four elements." Men come to the House open to reason. A member does not know how he will vote himself, much less how someone else will vote. The undertakers treat the House like a flock of sheep; they hold that men, however wise as individuals, are to be guided in an assembly by a few. This is "to make Parliament vile and servile in the eyes of the Sovereign."[76]

But Bacon voiced other sentiments in this same speech, sentiments that were to lead to Neville's acquittal a week later. Any man, urged Bacon, was to be commended who advised the King to meet Parliament; commended too if he gave the King his opinion of the minds of Parliament men and whether they would meet the King's wants liberally. Nor should a man be blamed if he revives propositions from an earlier Parliament and adds new ones "for comforting the hearts of the people." Such a man, he concluded, "hath sown good seed."[77] And so the Commons concluded on 14 May, when Sir Roger Owen, reporting from the committee to inquire into rumors of undertaking, laid before the House a paper distributed before the meeting of Parliament. Sir Henry Neville at once owned himself to be its author. Neville explained that the King at Windsor, in July 1612, had asked his advice about a Parliament. He had taken the occasion to divert the King from projects and to persuade him instead to rely upon the love of his subjects. He had told His Majesty what various gentlemen desired. Most of the graces contained in the memorial had already been desired by the last Parliament. He had not included everything in the memorial, but what he had included was of much value to the people and of little prejudice to the King. He concluded with a declaration, which was certainly false, that he was no undertaker to lead a Parliament. The House accepted his excuses and applauded his efforts.[78] He acquitted himself, wrote the Reverend Lorkin, "with so much satisfaction to the House and honour to himself, as they presently superseded from all farther search, declaring in favour and justification of him, that he had done nothing which became not a good subject and an honest man."[79]

The differing fates of Parry and Neville have a significance that transcends their personal fortunes. Parry's expulsion revealed the deep resentment felt toward packing, toward Bacon's strategy of creating, through electoral influence and patronage, a court party in the House. Neville's vindication showed that there was no similar resentment against those who would urge the King to meet Parliament and offer graces to it. But the outcry against those who had contracted for the House did contain a lesson for future undertakers. The House of Commons was jealous of its independence. It was likewise wedded to the Elizabethan ideal of government in which the monarch ruled and the House of Commons sought the redress of grievances, an ideal incompatible with a parliamentary undertaking. If undertakers were to wrest office from a monarch on the basis of their power in the House of Commons, they had better make certain of that power. They had better allow for the discredit into which they would fall when knowledge of the undertaking became known. Neville had no solution to this problem; indeed, he had probably not forseen that such a problem would arise. Herein lay a fatal defect in his proposal to manage Parliament for the King. The Commons were not yet ready to be directed by a few, no matter how virtuous they were.

There was a second defect in Neville's undertaking. James did not need Neville's help in managing Parliament because he had no need of Parliament. He proclaimed this to the world by dissolving the Addled Parliament in June and not meeting another Parliament until 1621. What precipitated the dissolution was not the row over undertaking, for that had been settled by the middle of May. What precipitated it was the furious attack by the House of Commons on impositions. The Commons saw in the King's right to levy impositions a threat to its control over taxation; the King saw in the surrender of that right a threat to his financial independence.

Rather than see that independence impaired, he sent Parliament home and governed England by selling crown lands and running deeper into debt.[80]

Upon the dissolution of Parliament, Neville returned to Billingbeare, a lonely, disappointed man. The undertaking he had offered the King at Windsor had been rejected by the King, taken up and cast down by Rochester, scorned by Bacon, exploited by Suffolk, and repudiated by Parliament. Only by prevarication had he survived condemnation. It was a sad moment for Sir Henry, who had known greater triumphs and finer hours. There had been the day he received Elizabeth's praise for his stout replies to Henry IV, the day James singled him out to speak for the Commons of England, the happy days at Fulham conversing with Bodley and Savile, the June day in 1610 when he gave two (of his five) daughters away in marriage, amidst great feasting and much company, and that splendid summer day in 1608 when he traveled with the King to Oxford to receive, amidst much pomp, his master of arts degree. These triumphant moments were now part of the past. The future presented a bleaker face. Discredited, ill, in debt, out of favor, Neville had little to live for. Yet he was ever resilient, ever the projector. He immediately sued at court for the right to prosecute spoilers of the woods. But his suit was crushed in February 1615. Five months later, on 10 July, he died.

John Pym wrote that he died of a broken heart at not getting the secretaryship, but more likely he died of jaundice, scurvy, and edema.[81] He died disappointed but not uncelebrated. Ben Jonson, the sovereign wit of his age, wrote an epitaph praising Neville for seeking true honor, not the appearance of it; for desiring the public good, not personal gain; for pursuing virtue, not fame or title.[82] Jonson promised Neville that posterity would not forget him now that he, Jonson, had sung his fame, but ensuing ages did largely forget him. But though his fame died, the expedient upon which he stumbled survived. There were to be other parliamentary undertakers, as the history of the seventeenth century bears witness.

Chapter II

The Earl of Bedford and the Parliamentary Undertaking of 1641

F RANCIS RUSSELL, fourth Earl of Bedford, possessed greater lands than Sir Henry Neville and enjoyed a more exalted title, but in many other ways he resembled the Berkshire knight. Both men enlisted themselves among the patriots in Parliament, not among the courtiers. Both men remained men of the middle, seeking not to subvert government but to reconcile the prerogatives of the crown with the rights of the people. Though favoring moderate policies, they both associated with men of more extreme views. As a result an angry Queen sent Neville to the Tower and an angry King brought Bedford before the Star Chamber. Both men were projectors—bold, enterprising, ingenious. Neville organized the ordnance industry in Surrey and promoted a plan to trade with Persia through Muscovy; Bedford began the development of Covent Garden and undertook to drain the Fens. Both men aspired to high office; neither attained it. Both men won a reputation for wisdom: Neville was called "our English Tacitus," Bedford, "the wise Earl." And both won the affections of their contemporaries: in 1614 the House of Commons applauded Neville; in May 1641 three hundred coaches rolled down the Strand to Bedford House for the Earl's funeral.[1]

But the most striking parallel lies in the efforts of each to mediate between King and Parliament. In the spring of 1641, the Earl of Bedford proposed an undertaking similar to Neville's in 1614. In return for office, he and his friends would undertake to manage Parliament and to secure for the King an adequate revenue. There is no evidence that Bedford modeled his undertaking on Neville's. He never spoke of the 1614 undertaking—possibly because men remembered that undertaking only as a thing of infamy.

Bacon himself did his best to give Neville's undertaking an infamous character. In the autumn of 1615 he castigated it in a memorial to James I. The undertakers, he wrote, were "merely empirics of Parliament," unversed in the rules of statecraft, oversanguine about their strength. He admitted that they acted out of a zeal to do well, even that they were the best voices in the House; but they had revived the old course of merchandising with the King, of offering supply in return for graces. Even worse, it became known abroad that they "had undertaken to value themselves with the King by the service of preparing and inducing a Parliament to pay his debts and supply his wants." This had angered the honest members of the House, who were indignant that a House of Commons should become "the followers of a few." Falling thus into discredit, the undertakers had sought to recover their reputation by forwarding popular causes. They soon discovered that though they were able to row with the stream, they "had no arms or power to row against it." This being true, James should lay aside all thoughts of an undertaking.[2]

Bacon's private censure in 1615 was followed by James's public condemnation in 1621. Opening the first Parliament to meet since 1614, he reminded the members that at the last Parliament there came up "a strange kind of Beast, called Undertakers, a name which in my nature I abhor." Some principal men about him were content to believe it, but he never had. Now, however, he summoned them of his own free motion and would trust solely in their good offices toward him.[3]

James's abhorrence of the Beast called Undertakers marked the last royal mention of Neville's undertaking, but the memory of it lingered on among parliamentarians. In 1624 Sir John Eliot, still vice-admiral of Devon and not yet the popular orator he was to become, reminded the House of Commons that in 1614 "there was an aspersion of undertaking cast upon the service of some members of that House, from whence there grew a jealousy, in the rest, that the whole business was compounded by those principals who had before-hand given the King assurance of what he desired." From this jealousy sprang up opposition, and from this opposition, faction. But Eliot doubted that there had been any substance to the "unknown and vain reports of undertakers." He doubted that the King intended "by a secret practice with a few to undermine the rest." Neither could those few, "for themselves have assumed so much power above others to undertake for all."[4] In 1626 Sir Dudley Digges remembered the undertaking in similar terms. In an advice to Charles on the summoning of Parliament, he urged him not to trouble himself with the propositions "of such parliament men as desire too much to seem to do your service." "Plain open and old ways are best, without these fancies of offering bills of Grace . . . or like novelties, which serve but to make [men] wanton, and were invented for men's private ends."[5] If the memory of Neville's undertaking survived at all into the 1630s, it survived as a buoy marking a shoal to be avoided, not a channel to be entered upon.

Whether the memory of Neville's undertaking survived is, however, of little matter, for both Bedford's undertaking and Neville's were responses to the dictates of the moment. Like circumstances brought forth like responses. In fact, these same circumstances operated in the tempestuous Parliaments of the 1620s. The basic pressure then was an insatiable need for money—money for the recovery of the Palatinate, money for the war against Spain, money for the attack on the Isle of Rhé. Benevolences and forced loans having failed, there was no recourse but to meet Parliament; and the need to meet Parliament meant a need to manage it. This presented the King with three options: to rely solely upon the Elizabethan arts of management, to add to them the arts of canvassing and bridling, or to embark upon an undertaking with those who led in Parliament.

In 1620 Bacon urged upon James the second option. The King should maintain unity in the council, should prepare measures for Parliament, should secure the election of fit persons to the Commons, and should bridle or win over the lawyers.[6] James paid little heed to his advice. Factions continued to divide the council, and no great effort was made to elect courtiers. Parliament met and proceeded on its wayward course. But when its pursuit of monopolies led to the great Duke of Buckingham, the royal favorite turned to Bishop Williams for advice. "Swim with the Tide," urged the bishop, "and you cannot be drowned." "Trust me and your servants that have some credit with the most active members to keep you clear from the strife of tongues." But do not obstruct the course of justice by breaking the Parliament. Buckingham acted upon the Bishop's advice and survived unscathed.[7] It is doubtful that Williams had that credit with the Parliament men that he thought he had, but his advice to swim with the stream proved effective.

In 1624 pressures for an undertaking with the leaders of the House of Commons surfaced even more clearly than in 1621. Buckingham and the Prince needed money with which to wage war against Spain. Since Parliament alone could furnish the money, writs went out for a Parliament. The King sought to secure the return of his creatures, but his efforts failed. The Prince and the Duke preferred to court the popular leaders in both Houses. Eliot was released from prison, Oxford freed from the Tower, Hertford readmitted to the Lords, and Coke and Sandys excused from going to Ireland. The Prince and the Duke supped with Oxford, Southampton, and Say; and they reconciled themselves with the Earl of Pembroke, who controlled twenty seats in the Commons.[8] The Duke begged James to agree to break with Spain if Parliament voted six subsidies and fifteenths; he also begged the King to allow him "to assure some of them underhand" that Parliament would not be prorogued before abuses were reformed and grievances redressed.[9]

Thanks to the thorough research of Conrad Russell, documentary evidence now confirms what rumor alone once reported. In his *Parliaments and English Politics, 1621–1629*, Russell argues that "a Discourse by way of dialogue between a Counsellor of State and a Country gentleman who served in the last assembly of the estates in the yeare 1621" probably represents an undertaking reached between Sir Robert Phelips and the Duke of Buckingham in October 1623. According to the terms of that undertaking, the Duke promised to persuade the King and council to call a Parliament, to break off the Spanish negotiations, to enter into a war with Spain, to leave members of Parliament free to attack recusancy, and to protect those who debated matters of state. Sir Robert, on his part, undertook to prevent any dispute about the imprisonment of members of Parliament in 1621, to pass over in silence the dissolution of Parliament in 1621, to let sleep the question of impositions, and to secure a vote of supply sufficient to carry out military preparations against Spain. "It cannot be proved," writes Russsell, "that these undertakings are the exact words of Buckingham and Phelips, but it can be proved that, if Chamberlain is right that there was an undertaking between Buckingham and Phelips, its terms very closely resembled these."[10]

Acting upon these undertakings, Parliament met and voted the money needed for military preparations. In return James agreed not to make peace without Parliament's consent and to allow it to name the treasurers to handle the money voted. Buckingham also sought Parliament's aid in destroying Lionel Cranfield, Earl of Middlesex. Parliament, on its side, demanded the enforcement of the penal laws. Phelips duly opposed raising the issue of the imprisonment of members in 1621 and declaimed against the spread of recusancy. Whether one regards these underhand agreements as an undertaking or merely as an understanding, they succeeded. Of all the Parliaments of the 1620s, this Parliament alone was harmonious and productive.[11] The subsidies were voted, the treasurers named, Middlesex impeached, and a proclamation issued against priests. All that suffered was the reputation of the popular leaders. Though they speak well, wrote Chamberlain, "yet it is not so well taken at their hands for still they suspect them to prevaricate, and hold them for undertakers." Bishop Williams, now lord keeper, put it this way to James: though matters are carried by the whole vote of Parliament, "yet they that walk in Westminster Hall call this the Prince's undertaking."[12]

The 1625 Parliament marked a turning point in the court's strategy. Confronted in July with the need for £293,000 to set out the fleet, Buckingham proposed that Parliament, which had already voted two subsidies, be asked to vote an additional supply when it met again in August. Lord Keeper Williams, with his finger ever on the pulse of the people, opposed this act of folly. He urged Charles instead to adjourn Parliament until Christmas. "For," he said, "I hope to give such account by that time, by undertaking with the chief sticklers, that they shall supersede from their bitterness against your great Servant, and that passage to your weighty Councils shall be made smooth and peaceable."[13] But Charles and Buckingham declined the lord keeper's undertaking. They met Parliament in August, at Oxford, but with no success. Within a week the Duke was in deep trouble, from which his friends sought to extricate him on 6 August. Led by Sir Nathaniel Rich, a man often seen in the Duke's chamber, they offered an accommodation. If the King would renounce impositions and rely upon grave councillors, Parliament would vote supplies. This was, Rich added, no bargaining with the King, but an ordinary parliamentary course. Had Bacon been alive, he would have shuddered at these words, for he had ever denounced merchandising with the King in this manner. As it turned out, there was to be no merchandising, for Buckingham spurned the advice of his own friends, as he had earlier spurned the advice of Lord Keeper Williams. Six days later Charles dissolved Parliament; a month later he dismissed the lord keeper.[14]

The dismissal of the lord keeper marked a turn from a Nevillian policy to a Baconian one, from attempts to reach an accommodation with the popular party to attempts to build up a court party. The new tactics were straightforward: root out the leaders of the popular party in Parliament by naming them sheriffs, look to the Cinque ports and Cornish boroughs, and win over those elected with promises and menaces. The appeal was not to argument, but to material rewards. Buckingham hoped to win Pembroke with the offer of the white staff of steward; Pembroke's brother would become chamberlain. Those who supported Buckingham in Parliament—Dorset, Salisbury, and Bridgewater—were admitted to the Privy Council. Those who spoke against the Duke were thrown out of Commissions of the Peace.[13] In May 1626 Charles banished three of his servants from court for speaking against Buckingham.[14] But though there were celebrated coups, such as the winning of Sir John Savile by place, the resort to canvassing and corruption failed. The King's party in the Commons grew ever smaller. In 1628 Charles spared no pains to get a loyal Parliament, but the courtiers in the House were fewer than ever.[15] A Remonstrance against Buckingham carried by more than one hundred votes. The same Parliament met again in 1629, with even more disastrous results. The Parliaments of 1626, 1628, and 1629 proved conclusively that packing and patronage could not prevail against a nation angered at the incompetence of the Duke of Buckingham and frightened by the high prerogative notions of the King himself.

Unable to prevail in Parliament, Charles governed without Parliament. From 1629 to 1640 his power rested firmly on his financial independence, but that independence was only won by anticipating future revenues and selling royal lands.[16] Even had he not stumbled into war with Scotland, he would have had to turn to Parliament again—unless, that is, he found some extraparliamentary tax acceptable to Englishmen. But he found no such tax, and he did stumble into war. The two Scottish wars brought down the whole edifice of prerogative government. To find the means to wage the second Scottish war, Charles summoned Parliament in April 1640, but the lure of a Spanish loan led him to dissolve the Short Parliament when it demanded the redress of grievances before the vote of supply. The Spanish loan proved illusory, and so did the voluntary contributions of Englishmen. The Scots invaded the realm, the crown faced bankruptcy, and Charles could do little but summon Parliament. The court labored to bring in its friends, but those who were most favored at court were the most opposed in the country. Few were chosen. There were only 27 officials and 22 courtiers in the House of Commons that met in November 1640.[19]

Charles now found himself in circumstances far different from those he had faced in the 1620s. His army was defeated at Newburn, his Exchequer was empty, his servants in the

Commons were few, and he had no choice but to reach some accommodation with those who prevailed in Parliament. This being true, it is not surprising that rumors of an undertaking soon appeared. On 3 December, Lady Carlisle wrote to Lady Leicester in Paris: "What you hear concerning my Lord of Bedford is certainly the news of the town, and nothing of it either true or possible without such a change as I dare not think of. They have disposed and changed all the officers of this Kingdom. The King makes himself merry at it, though I believe there is not much cause for that."[20]

During December talk of Bedford as lord treasurer increased. On 31 December Northumberland reported: "Hertford, as well as Bedford, is nominated to the Treasurer's Staff; the first of these hath hopes given him from the Court, the other is wished unto that office by the ruling party in this Parliament."[21] But it was not until 21 January 1641 that the scheme of the ruling party burst into full view. On that day the gossips at Whitehall were buzzing with talk of impending changes at court. Bedford would become lord treasurer. Lord Cottington would resign, leaving the office of master of the wards to Lord Say and the office of chancellor of the Exchequer to John Pym. Essex would go to Ireland and St. John become Recorder of London. Many observers reported the rumors, but none so fully as Sir John Temple. "I understand," he wrote, "the King is brought into a dislike of those counsels that he hath formerly followed, and therefore resolves to steer another course." He then reported the rumored appointments of Bedford, Pym, and Say. "These preparatives," he continued, "make us now hope for a happy success of this Parliament, and I do believe some ways are laid, upon the bringing in of these new men, to make up an entire union between the King and his people, and so moderate their demands, as well as the height of that power which hath been lately used in the government."[22]

But it no more lay in the power of the Earl of Bedford to persuade Charles to steer another course than it lay in Neville's power to persuade James to do so. Neither man served at court, nor found a welcome there. They needed a broker at court to plead their cause. Neville relied upon Overbury and

Rochester. It is uncertain upon whom Bedford relied, but it is clear that Henry Jermyn, the Queen's master of the horse, and the Marquis of Hamilton, the King's chief Scottish adviser, favored his scheme. "Hamilton and Jermyn," wrote Temple on the twenty-first, "have deeply contributed to this change [of counsels]." And six days later, he reported that Jermyn, who is often alone with the King and Queen for many hours, holds "secret intelligence with the new officers that shall be made."[23] Dr. Baillie, the Scotsman, gave more credit to the Marquis of Hamilton. Commenting on the King's recent appointment of Littleton to be lord keeper and Bankes to be chief justice of the Common Pleas, both of them men who had once advocated ship money, he observed: "Few are pleased with their promotions; the men are none of them beloved. . . . It is expected the King, by the Marquis's advice, shall make a better choice of his other officers; that Bedford shall be Treasurer, etc."[24] On the very day Baillie wrote this, the twenty-ninth, his prediction came partially true when Charles named Oliver St. John his solicitor general. Clarendon states that Bedford prevailed upon the King to name St. John solicitor. He probably did, but he surely did so through a broker at court, through Jermyn or Hamilton or both.[25]

Bedford must have regarded St. John's appointment as the prelude to his own, for on 1 February he conferred a messenger's place at the Treasury on Mr. Stockdale. Sir John Coke forwarded this news to his father, along with a story told him by the Popish party, that Bedford, Pym, and Say attended upon the Queen in private. "If these men come in by the Queen's side," he remarked, "there is art enough somewhere."[26] Art there certainly was, for on 4 February the Queen sent a message to the Commons promising to do them all good offices: the Commons, said Temple, "were much taken with it."[27] These secret negotiations finally bore fruit on 19 February when seven popular peers—Bedford, Hertford, Essex, Bristol, Savile, Mandeville, and Say—were sworn as councillors. Charles bitterly opposed the initial suggestion that he bring these men into his council, but the Marquis of Hamilton persuaded him to do so.[28] The Marquis may have had several motives for his actions. He may have sought to save his own head by appeasing his enemies in the popular party. On the other hand, he may have acted from a larger realism. Only three days before, on the sixteenth, Charles had assented to the Triennial Act, an act that would require him to meet Parliament every three years. "Having assented to this bill," wrote the French envoy, "the King can refuse nothing."[29] The Venetian ambassador concurred: it will "ruin his authority entirely."[30] This being the case, realism dictated that Charles reach an accommodation with those who led in Parliament. And those who led in Parliament were eager for an accommodation. "The King," wrote Count Rossetti, the Papal envoy, "has brought into his Council six of the principal puritans . . . and they promise to do great things in Parliament for his Majesty's service."[31]

Rossetti's dispatch contains the earliest mention of an actual undertaking by Bedford and his friends to serve the King in Parliament, but later accounts—Heylyn's, Whitelocke's, Nicholas's, Digby's, and Clarendon's—also describe it. From these accounts it is possible to piece together the puzzle, to discover what "the governing and undertaking party" (the words are Clarendon's) demanded and what they offered. What they demanded was high office. Peter Heylyn, Laud's chaplain and biographer, and Bulstrode Whitelocke, lawyer and parliamentarian, agreed with Clarendon that the party designed Bedford to be lord treasurer, Pym to be chancellor of the Exchequer, Say to be master of the wards, and Holles to be secretary of state. Clarendon adds that they also sought preferment for Hampden, Essex, and others; furthermore, none was to enter into office until the others were provided for. Heylyn is more specific: Essex should become governor of the Prince, Hampden the Prince's tutor, and Warwick have a command in the navy. In return for these promotions, writes Clarendon, they "engaged to procure the King's revenue to be liberally provided for and honourably increased and settled." Edward Nicholas, the King's secretary of state, tells a similar story. Their design, he wrote in 1644, was to gain all the powerful offices of the court. "And to effect this, they made overtures to the King, claiming that if such and such were one time received in Council of State, in office, and in the management of affairs, he will see at once the end of all his troubles, his debts paid, his revenues established and increased, and his royal dignity carried and affirmed to the highest point of glory and luster." Lord Digby summed it up this way: the prime actors in the late reformation were to have the chief places at court, in return for which they would promote the King's honor and plenty.[32]

The Earl of Bedford's inquiries into the condition of the King's finances in the spring of 1641 prove the seriousness of his purpose. In response to his inquiries, an unknown official in the Exchequer prepared a memorandum for the Earl. In it he recommended that the Earl should determine what the King's revenues and expenditures were, should make all pensions payable in the Exchequer, and should retrench the King's expenses wherever possible. But even with these retrenchments, the King could not, because of the great anticipations on his revenues, live on those revenues. Parliament must vote subsidies that would allow the King to take off those anticipations and restore his credit. And there must be no anticipations in the future. The unknown official then descended to details about monthly payments from the customs to the Household, details which suggest that he believed Bedford would soon be treasurer.[33] The Earl also entered into discussions with a leading farmer of the customs, Sir John Harrison. Harrison had prepared his own scheme for retiring the King's debts. He proposed that the King should sell all his forests, chases, and parks, except those surrounding his mansions. Harrison presented the plan to Cottington, who turned it over to Bedford.[34]

Meanwhile, Bedford, Pym, and St. John had put their own minds to work on the problem of paying the King's debts and increasing his revenues. Their plan included a new method of calculating subsidies, the confiscation of the lands of delinquents, increased fines on Catholic recusants, the seizure of a third of the rents of the lands of deans and chapters, and the abolition of wardship.[35] The comprehensiveness of their plans testifies to the seriousness of their purpose to pay off the King's debts and increase his revenues. But Bedford and his friends were also aware of the dangers of making the King independent of Parliament. It was a central part of their scheme to vote tunnage and poundage to the King for only three years. A triennial revenue should put teeth into the triennial act.[36]

Francis Russell, the fourth Earl of Bedford, was the principal architect of this undertaking. He was a man of austere habits and few words, a man who tempered his love of liberty with a love of moderation, and leavened his idealism with an appreciation of the practical. He was born in 1593, and inherited from his ancestors great wealth and an ardent Protestant faith. He enjoyed an income of about £15,000 a year, drawn mostly from those abbey lands—Tavistock, Thorney, Woburn, Covent Garden— that Henry VIII showered upon John Russell, the first Earl and the founder of the family's fortune.[37] The fourth Earl entered the political arena early, taking a seat in the Commons in 1610 and entering the Lords in 1614. His political apprenticeship was one of opposition. In 1621 he opposed James's lavish grants of Irish and Scottish titles to Englishmen; in 1628 he supported the Petition of Right; in the Short Parliament, he favored the redress of grievances before the vote of supply. His intimacy with the opposition led in 1629 to a brush with the Star Chamber. Oliver St. John gave him a copy of a discourse on "Bridling Parliaments"; he passed it on to Somerset, who gave it to Clare, who gave it to Cotton, who let it fall into the King's hands. Angered by the imputations contained in the discourse, Charles prosecuted those who had circulated it. Only when he discovered that Robert Dudley, twenty years earlier, had drawn up the discourse, did he release the defendants from a too hasty prosecution.[38]

The Earl's practical bent of mind emerged in the 1630s, when he became the principal undertaker in a scheme to drain the Fens. He entered into the undertaking not only for the public service he could perform but for the profit he could make. He hoped to turn a capital investment of £100,000 into an income of £60,000 a year. His energy and care, allied with Vermuyden's skill, met with partial success. In 1637 the commissioners of sewers declared the Bedford Level to be drained and awarded the Earl his 43,000 acres, but his associates protested against the award and began a prosecution in Star Chamber. Complaints likewise poured in from the inhabitants of the Fens. The King himself intervened, persuading a new commission to declare the Bedford Level undrained and to name him, the King, the new undertaker. Charles promised the Earl 40,000 acres in recompense for the £100,000 he had spent hitherto, but death removed the Earl and civil war interrupted the engineering. Eleven years later, however, in 1649, Parliament declared the fifth Earl to be the undertaker for the enterprise his father had begun.[39]

Bedford's love of projects and profit also led him in 1631 to build a square at Covent Garden. Handsome houses rose on the north and east sides, a stately church to the west, and the gardens of Bedford House to the south. In a grotto of trees on the south side, the future fruit and vegetable market had its beginnings. As he had engaged Vermuyden, the greatest of engineers, to drain the Bedford Level, so he chose Inigo Jones, the greatest of architects, to design the church and piazza of Covent Garden. The ground rents meanwhile rose from £500 to £1000 a year.[40]

The crisis of 1640 turned Bedford's mind back to politics, where he soon found himself at the center of affairs. In July he joined five other peers in a letter to the Scots, offering to stand by them in a legal way, though refusing to support them militarily. In August, to the consternation of the King, he conferred regularly with Warwick, Say, Brooke, Pym, Hampden, and St. John.[41] These men, who gathered at Warwick's house, were by no means strangers to one another. The third Earl of Bedford had found John Pym a place in the Exchequer; the fourth Earl regularly returned him to Parliament from Tavistock. St. John had served Bedford as a lawyer since 1629 and lived in intimate trust with him. Lord Brooke married the Earl's daughter, Katherine.[42] When Parliament met in November these men—Bedford, Say, and Mandeville in the Lords, Pym, Hampden, and St. John in the Commons—proved to be, in Clarendon's words, "the engine that moved all the rest."[43]

In August their purpose was to secure the meeting of Parliament. To this end Pym and St. John drafted a petition to the King asking that he summon Parliament; Bedford and eleven other peers signed the petition. Bedford and Hertford then boldly took the petition before the council at Whitehall to ask their support for it. From Windebanke's account of the meeting (and from Van Dyke's portrait of the fourth Earl), one can form a picture of the scene: the Earl standing erect before the council, proud in bearing, severe in countenance, dressed austerely in black with no jewelry or ornaments, only a broad white collar and cuffs, a reticent and shy man, but capable of quick outbursts of passion. Hertford presented the petition to the council, which then deputized four of its members to confer more particularly with the two Earls. Professing great loyalty to the King and denying any knowledge of the Scottish invasion, Bedford and Hertford urged that there were many grievances that lay heavy upon the people, grievances that hindered them from being able to serve His Majesty. They desired that Parliament should meet so that these impediments to His Majesty's service might be removed. When asked about their own intentions, they protested "that they were employed by those that did put them in trust, only to present the petition to the Lords." When asked who these were that employed them, they replied, "many other Noblemen and most of the Gentry in several parts of the Kingdom." As Neville in 1610 suddenly found himself speaking for the Commons of England before James, so Bedford in 1640 suddenly found himself speaking for the noblemen and gentry of England before the council. Events had catapulted both men into the role of spokesman for an aggrieved nation.[44]

Bedford desired the meeting of Parliament, but what he desired beyond that is more difficult to determine. The redress of grievances he assuredly sought, and the punishment of notorious offenders. He undoubtedly wished to see the abolition of Star Chamber and ship money, for he had suffered more than once in that court and his friend St. John was the great opponent of ship money. Nor is it likely that he approved of the harrying of Puritans out of the church. He himself had confided to ten folio volumes his religious meditations, and Cornelius Burgess, a Puritan divine, had dedicated

Baptismal Regeneration to him.[45] But though he sought the redress of grievances, he did not seek the subversion of the existing government in church and state. He had too great a fortune to desire that, commented Clarendon. He also had a temper too disposed to accommodation. He found no difficulty in both countenancing Puritans and dining with Archbishop Laud.[46] Government by a King advised by self-seeking courtiers he surely opposed. Nor did he favor government by a King advised by the nobility alone. When Arundel asked his opinion concerning a meeting of the Council of Peers at York, he replied that it might be useful, but not "if it should be intended exclusive to the Commons, or to raise monies any other way than by a Parliament."[47] A King governing according to the law, seeking advice from a grave council, meeting Parliament frequently, this was his ideal of good government. And if the King was badly advised, advised to invade the law, then Parliament should remove those councillors. But who, once they were removed, should replace them? It was the need to find a solution to this problem that led Bedford and his friends to undertake to serve the King in Parliament in return for office.

Negotiations to bring Bedford and his friends into office proceeded fitfully during the winter of 1641. Charles demanded, as had James before him, that men earn their preferment by first serving him in Parliament. The new councillors were not slow to do so. They favored granting Strafford another week in which to answer the articles of impeachment brought against him. They urged the vote of two additional subsidies. They labored to prevent the prosecution of Hamilton. They even defended the queen's right to keep her Catholic servants.[48] Preferments, however, were not forthcoming; they remained a matter of rumor. On 26 March, Rossetti wrote that Newcastle would be removed as governor of the Prince, and Bishop Duppa as his tutor, "it being desired by Parliament." Two weeks later he reported that Essex, a Puritan, would be vice-roy of Ireland.[49]

Then, on 12 April, came the revelation that Lord Cottington had, a year before in council, slandered the House of Commons and given pernicious advice to the King. The

Commons at once demanded that he be removed from court and his person secured. Cottington, however, escaped impeachment. By the means of the Earl of Bedford, the charge designed against him was dropped—but only upon the condition that he resign all his offices.[50] He immediately laid them at the King's feet. He offered to resign his places, wrote John Coke, "for the use of Lord Say and Mr. Pym."[51] Bedford's scheme appeared closer to fruition than at any time since February. Pym himself met twice with the King in the next fortnight, and the Queen, alone, candle in hand, went to a chamber of one of her ladies to speak with the rebels.[52] On 27 April the King named Warwick to the council. But all this perturbation led nowhere. Within a fortnight the undertaking collapsed, Strafford lost his head, and Bedford died of small pox.

The immediate cause of the failure of Bedford's undertaking is not hard to find: it was the difference of opinion that arose over the fate of the Earl of Strafford, "the great remora to all matters," said Robert Baillie.[53] Whether the saving of Strafford's life was part of Bedford's undertaking is one of the minor mysteries surrounding it. In the King's mind, it was certainly part of the undertaking. He named the seven peers to the council because he believed that step would help save the Earl. And two years later, he issued a declaration in which he asserted that the faction knew "what great services should be done for us, and what other undertakings were (even to have saved the life of the Earl of Strafford) if we would confer such offices upon them."[54] But did the Earl of Bedford and his confederates in fact promise to save Strafford's life? Whitelocke, Heylyn, and Clarendon state that this promise was part of the undertaking, but Nicholas and Digby make no mention of it.[55] There probably existed more misunderstanding than understanding on the subject. Sir John Coke wrote his father that those lords who hope to win place by making "a show" on Strafford's behalf "design that the rigour against him shall be the work of the House of Commons."[56]

The course of events confirmed Sir John Coke's speculation. When Strafford requested a week's delay in answering his impeachment, Bedford and the other lords newly named to the council favored granting the delay. Their apostasy convinced Daniel O'Neil that Strafford would escape conviction in the House of Lords.[57] But several weeks later, on 9 March, Bedford, Say, Essex, Mandeville, and Brooke, to the great anger of Bristol and Savile, who had gone over to the court, supported the House of Commons in their pursuit of Strafford.[58] Robert Baillie explained the course of events in a like manner. In order to please the King, the Marquis of Hamilton had, through his friends in the Lords, secured a delay in Strafford's answer. By doing this, he had made the King believe that his power in both Houses was so great that he could, if he endeavored, save Strafford's life. But in fact he only placed himself in a dilemma: "if he denied to deal for Strafford he should offend the King, if he assayed to deal farther for him, he should lose the Parliament and us all."[59]

The prosecution of Strafford proceeded remorselessly, though Bedford did not live to see its fateful end. He died of smallpox on Sunday morning, 9 May, the same Sunday upon which Charles agreed to sign the Earl of Strafford's attainder. Strafford lost his head on the scaffold the following Wednesday. Clarendon and Heylyn offer two opposite explanations of why the King and the undertakers fell out over the fate of Strafford. Clarendon asserts that "the continued and renewed violence in the prosecution of the Earl of Strafford" made the King well contented that these promotions be suspended.[60] Heylyn declares: "But before all things were fully settled and agreed on, the King's mind was altered, which so exasperated them who were concerned in this designation, that they pursued the Earl of Strafford with greater eagerness."[61] Where the fault truly lay the historian will probably never know. But this fact matters little, for, though the assigning of responsibility is a legitimate task for a historian, it is not always a fruitful one. In the case of Bedford's undertaking, it is not fruitful since there is no reason to believe that the undertaking could have succeeded even had the King given Bedford and his confederates office. Nor is there any reason to believe that Bedford and his confederates could have saved Strafford's life even had they tried.

At bottom Bedford's undertaking failed for two reasons.

The first was Charles's determination not to give offices of power and trust to those who had opposed him in the past. The second was the inability of Bedford and his friends to govern Parliament.

Charles never sought a true reconciliation with the leaders of the popular party. He never truly intended to follow their counsels, to entrust them with the management of affairs, to give them offices of power. He bitterly rejected the first motion to bring the seven peers into the council.[62] He clung, lamented Clarendon, to the rule that a person should first perform some service for him before being preferred.[63] And if he granted them a lucrative office here, an honorary one there, it was "to win them over," "to take them off," "to mitigate their displeasure." Faced with the deepest crisis of his reign, he fell back upon the stratagem of "winning men by place."[64] But the power of patronage proved a frail reed when divorced from any change in policy. The credit won by naming St. John solicitor was lost by the grant of a reprieve to a Catholic priest. The hopes raised by the appointment of the seven new councillors were extinguished by Charles's personally attending Strafford's trial and conversing long and secretly with him. On 27 April, Charles named Warwick to the council, but this act was lost in the furor caused by his refusal the next day to disband the Irish army.[65] Indeed, it was the refusal to disband the Irish army that probably proved the breaking point for John Pym. Until then he had negotiated with the King; thereafter he opposed such negotiations and demanded the parliamentary nomination of the King's ministers.[66]

Charles could not have been blind to the futility of the policy of winning men by place. That he did not desert such a policy for a wholehearted reconciliation with Bedford and his allies can probably be attributed to his infatuation with a third solution, a military solution. As early as 1 April, Colonel Goring had informed Bedford, who in turn informed Pym, of the existence of the Army Plot. By late April there was talk of the Queen's going to Portsmouth and of the King's posting to the army in the north. Then came Charles's attempt to rescue Strafford from the Tower, further revelations of the Army

Plot, the flight of Jermyn, Percy, Suckling, and Davenant, and the refusal to disband the Irish army. To Charles the throw of the dice in war seemed preferable to a surrender to the leaders of the ruling party in Parliament.[67]

But even had he entrusted power to those leaders and forgone a resort to force, there is no reason to believe that those leaders could have succeeded in their undertaking. In the first place, there was not the slightest chance that they could have secured that which was closest to the King's heart, the saving of Strafford's life. Bedford appears to have sincerely sought to save the Earl, but the tide running against Strafford was too great to be stemmed by one man.[68] The Commons would not vote subsidies, the Scottish army would not leave the kingdom, the City would not loan money, the populace would not remain quiet unless "justice" was done against Strafford—a euphemism for his death.[69] The passions of the moment overwhelmed all the calculations of reason and all the dictates of compromise. Either Strafford will be destroyed, wrote the French ambassador, or one will destroy England to save him.[70] Twenty thousand citizens petitioned for his death; upon his execution the crowds surged out into the countryside, shouting, "He is dead! He is dead!", as a modern crowd might celebrate victory in a cup final.[71] Pym himself, who wished to continue by way of impeachment, lost control of the House on 15 April, when the inflexible party carried a vote for an attainder.[72] The King was not the only enemy to moderation in 1641.

Nor could Bedford and his confederates have, as they promised, paid off the King's debts and increased his revenues. Bedford had resolved not to enter the Treasury until tunnage and poundage had been settled upon the King, but the Commons showed no signs of a willingness to settle tunnage and poundage upon the King, either for life or for three years.[73] They persisted in voting it for only two months at a time. Furthermore, they diminished its value by voting on 25 March that tunnage and poundage, not a new subsidy, should be used to equip twenty ships of war. In June the debt still stood at £800,000, with no prospect for its reduction.[74]

It might be argued that the bestowal of high office on

Bedford, Pym, and Say might have given them the authority they needed to manage Parliament for the King, but the very reverse seems to be the case. Admittedly, the nomination of the seven peers to the council momentarily pleased the public; but the moment the peers pleaded for a delay in Strafford's trial, the public turned against them.[75] The new councillors regained some reputation by issuing a proclamation banishing priests from the realm and by changing the day of the council meeting from Sunday to Monday.[76] But they lost ground the next Saturday when their allies in the Commons spoke for granting two additional subsidies. This, reported Salvetti, the Tuscan envoy, "makes the Puritan faction very jealous, who show much disgust at those newly advanced to honour."[77] In truth, the putative leaders of the ruling party could only, as Bacon had predicted, row with the stream, not against it. Oliver St. John on one occasion did seek to row against the stream. In late May he urged that tunnage and poundage be voted to the King himself and not to commissioners who would spend it in his name. His advocacy of the royal cause appears to have aroused considerable anger at servants of the King sitting in the House of Commons. Six days later the Commons gave a first reading to a bill that would debar any member of the House from serving the King unless he first obtained the leave of both Houses of Parliament to do so.[78] It was the first of many self-denying bills that suspicious country members were to introduce into the House during the next century. Bedford had not solved any better than Neville the problem of retaining the confidence of the Commons. He and his friends could neither save Strafford's life nor secure the King a settled revenue. The Earl of Bedford died, reports Clarendon, in despair that he could not stem the fury of his party.[79]

Two years later, in the summer of 1643, the King advanced with his army into Bedfordshire. There, at Woburn Abbey, he told the Countess Dowager of Bedford that he would not now be troubled with this work—the civil war—had her husband lived.[80] It was a gallant remark, but poor history. Charles had never given the Earl the confidence he needed, when alive, to make his undertaking succeed. And even had the King given him that confidence, the rooted aversion of the country gentlemen for all courtiers guaranteed its failure.

The Earl of Bedford's death did not, in fact, end endeavors at an undertaking. "As soon as the Earl of Bedford was dead," wrote Clarendon, "the Lord Say (hoping to receive the reward of the Treasurership) succeeded him in his undertaking."[81] The linkage between Bedford's undertaking in February and Lord Say's in May, however, was less that of a son inheriting an estate than that of a politician rushing in to fill a vacuum. Lord Say, though more intransigent and puritanical than Bedford, pursued preferment at court with equal zeal. He met with little success. He had neither the authority with his allies that Bedford had nor the credit with the King.[82] Charles now paid less heed than ever to the wishes of the popular party. On the day after Strafford's execution, he gave the mastership of the wards, an office long destined for Lord Say, to Sir Robert Heath, the prosecutor of Eliot and Holles in 1629. The appointment, however, did not stick. On 17 May, Charles, probably yielding to a threat to resume the prosecution of Cottington, named Lord Say master of the wards.[83]

But Charles's discountenancing of the undertakers continued. When Bishop Juxon resigned as treasurer on 19 May, he placed the office in a commission headed by the unpopular Littleton. On 2 June he named the Earl of Leicester lord deputy of Ireland, to the anger of Parliament, who wanted that kingdom in the hands of one of their own.[84] When Newcastle, to avoid an attack in Parliament, resigned as governor of the Prince, Charles replaced him that very afternoon with Lord Hertford, now a courtier.[85] Not even the nomination of Essex as lord chamberlain can be regarded as a triumph for the undertakers, for they wished Pembroke to keep the white staff and believed he was dismissed only because he voted against Strafford.[86]

Then suddenly, in the last week of July, there was a spate of rumors that Lord Say should be treasurer, Pym chancellor of the Exchequer, Holles secretary of state, and Hampden chancellor of the duchy.[87] It is most unlikely that the cause of these rumors was the conversion of the King to the merits of an undertaking, even though Bishop Williams, the perennial advocate of such schemes, was now at his side, urging him to mitigate "the Grand Contrivers with some Preferments."[88] The more likely cause of these rumors was the Queen's determination to prevent the impeachment for treason of Percy and Jermyn. Four days before an accusation against them was to be brought into the House, the Queen was all sweetness and light toward the members of the Commons and hinted that Pym should soon be chancellor of the Exchequer. "They are in hopes at Court and have some reason to believe," wrote Temple on 5 August, "that what concerns Mr. Percy and Mr. Jermyn will not be declared treason by the Parliament."[89] Lord Finch concurred: "I doubt not," he wrote, but the Queen's "desire to satisfy the Parliament in all things will give her a return of much affection from them."[90] But Charles would have none of it. He crushed all such hopes on 8 August by naming the hated Lord Digby as ambassador to France, by making the Earl of Bristol (Digby's father) a gentleman of the bedchamber, by appointing three of Bristol's nominees to the council, and by promising Savile the post of comptroller of the Household. Charles then hurried off to Scotland in search of an army. The next day, 12 August, the House impeached Percy and Jermyn for treason. "It is admirable," wrote Temple, "to see what an alteration one week hath produced amongst us."[91]

The appointments made on 8 August mark the final collapse of Bedford's undertaking, an undertaking that Lord Say had sought to carry through the summer. Parliament now turned for guidance to John Pym, a realist, who saw that power resided in the two Houses themselves, not in those who would undertake to manage Parliament for the King. Pym's strategy was direct: the two Houses should demand that the King name councillors in whom the kingdom could confide. This strategy lay behind the Ten Propositions of June, behind the address in August that Charles name Salisbury to be lord treasurer and Pembroke lord steward, and behind the Grand Remonstrance in November.[92]

Charles, who faced his powerlessness with an insouciance born of blindness, replied in December by dismissing from

office those in whom the popular party confided and by naming to office those whom they most distrusted. He removed
the elder Vane from the secretaryship and from the treasurership of the Household. He dismissed the younger Vane from
his post of treasurer of the navy. The massacre of the Puritan
innocents even extended to officers of the Green Cloth and to
cart-takers.[93] To the offices thus made vacant Charles named
courtiers and clerks. John Nicholas, not Denzil Holles, became secretary. Mr. Pennyman, a former Star Chamber clerk,
became treasurer of the navy. The Duke of Richmond became
steward of the Household, though Parliament asked Charles
to name Pembroke. The "good party," reported William
Montagu, "is certainly tottering."[94]

But the "good party," though tottering at court, fought
back with the one weapon it had: the power of the purse. On
18 December the Commons ordered a committee to find a fit
way to ensure the continuance of the younger Vane as treasurer of the navy. On the twenty-seventh, John Pym reported for
the committee. It is the opinion of the committee, he said,
that this House do declare that they will take into consideration the case of Sir Henry Vane and the office of the treasurer
of the navy when they next consider the Bill for Tunnage and
Poundage. The full House, upon the question being put,
assented to the order. This was not the first time that the
Commons had fallen back on the power of the purse. Both
Parliament and the City had refused money for disbanding the
armies until justice was done against Strafford. And after
Strafford's death, Parliament had preserved the power of the
purse by voting Tunnage and Poundage for only a few months
at a time. But it was the first time that the Commons had
nakedly used the power of the purse to force upon the King
officers of their choice.[95]

Charles would not surrender. He replied to the power of the
purse with the power of the sword. To prevent Parliament
from stripping him of his faithful servants, not to speak of his
Queen, he sought to arrest the five leading members of the
House of Commons. That attempt not only failed, it destroyed utterly confidence in the King. The struggle now was
for the control of the Tower, of Hull, of Portsmouth, of the

militia. In the midst of this turmoil, however, there were still some who believed that the King could regain all by a vigorous use of the power of patronage. The Prince of Orange in January 1642 instructed his ambassador, Heenvliet, to act as an intermediary between the King and Parliament. Suggest to the King, wrote the prince, that he win back the peers by presents, gifts, offices, and honors. That being done, he continued, "I do not doubt but that, by their authority and credit, they will be able to persuade the Commons to embrace a good reconciliation."[96]

But Charles knew better, and rejected Heenvliet's advice. He took up the sword, and he justified his actions by publishing a declaration on 12 August 1642. In it he described how he had admitted to his Privy Council those in most esteem with the people, in hopes that they would be instruments in a blessed reformation and confirmation in church and state. They themselves, he continued, know what overtures were made by them for offices and preferments, "what great services should be done for us, and what other undertakings were (even to have saved the life of the Earl of Strafford) if we would confer such offices upon them." But they sought, he declared, only their private ends and to alter religion and the laws. Nothing seems to have angered Charles more than their attempt to capture for themselves the power of patronage. He cited the insolent speech of Mr. Pym to the Earl of Dover, that if he "looked for any preferment, he must comply with them in their ways, and not hope to have it by serving" the King. Charles took up the sword for many reasons, not the least among them a determination not to surrender the power of patronage to those who led in Parliament.[97]

The decline of his military fortunes caused Charles to turn once again to the stratagem of winning men by place. During the peace negotiations at Oxford in February 1643, a rumor arose that the Duke of Northumberland would be reinstated as lord admiral and that Denzil Holles would be named secretary of state.[98] At the Treaty of Uxbridge in 1645, Charles empowered Secretary Nicholas to win over persons by promising "them rewards for performed services, not sparing to engage for places, so they be not of great trust."[99] Irrevocable defeat in battle led Charles to drop the qualification that the places must not be of great trust. In the autumn of 1648, a prisoner on the Isle of Wight, he entered into a personal treaty with those two irrepressible undertakers Lord Say and Denzil Holles. Of all the parliamentary commissioners, Lord Say was the most inward with the King and undertook most to carry the two Houses to serve him. So confident was he of success that he designed himself to be lord treasurer. Lord Say held intelligence with the King through the Duke of Richmond; Denzil Holles's broker with the King was the Earl of Lindsey. Through Lindsey, Holles sought to secure the office of secretary of state for himself and another great office for Mr. Pierrepoint. "The King," reported Thomas Coke, "was often in conference how he should dispose the offices to please them all."[100] But the army put an end to all such schemes by purging the Commons, abolishing the Lords, and executing the King.

During the Commonwealth, the stratagem of winning men by place fell into disrepute, especially with ardent royalists. Brooding over past events, they denounced the stratagem as a grave error. Among those royalists were the Marquis of Newcastle (once general of the Royalist Forces in the North), Sir Edward Walker (formerly Charles's secretary of war), Francis Osborne (a friend of monarchy and the church), and the nameless author of a royalist tract entitled "A Confutation of Two Paradoxes." Their indictment, allowing for some variation in sentiments, reads as follows: One of the greatest errors of state committed by the last two kings—and the principal reason for the usurpation of the Commons in these years—was the taking off by preferment of those who opposed the King in Parliament. These kings rewarded their enemies and neglected their friends. They would say of one man, he is a shrewd man, we must please him, reward him, give him office; but of another, he is a friend, he will do us no harm. By this means Parliament grew refractory, everyone opposing, thinking thereby to be raised. When Parliament meets, it commonly falls out that about a dozen of the boldest and best voices do knot together and carry the House. These plausible men aim to become courtiers and officers, whereof the last two reigns could produce a grand jury of examples. What man almost has been raised these two last reigns that did not oppose the King?[101]

The authors of these indictments egregiously overstated their case. Most men won office by serving the King, not by opposing him; and those who opposed him usually did so from conscience and policy, not ambition. Nor did these authors perceive the fundamental difference between Bacon's strategy of winning men over to the King's policies by the offer of place and Neville's strategy of persuading the King to embrace the policies of those who led in Parliament. But at the center of their exaggerated claims lay a genuine sense of outrage at the preferment of those who had opposed the King in Parliament.

But what was the remedy? The Marquis of Newcastle had no doubt what it was. It was the repudiation of all such stratagems as a Bacon might advise and of all such undertakings as a Neville might propose. "The remedy is very easy," he told Charles II in 1658, "reward your friends and punish your enemies."[102]

Chapter III

Sir Richard Temple and the Anti-Clarendonians

I T WAS A TRUTH widely acknowledged in Stuart England that a man deeply in debt might repair his fortune by securing employment at court. In 1660 Sir Richard Temple, of Stowe, Buckinghamshire, was deeply in debt. Obligations totalling £12,000 encumbered an estate worth only £3,500 a year. Sir Richard owned lands in Warwickshire and Buckinghamshire, lands that Peter Temple had amassed during Elizabeth's reign. Peter and his son, John, had established the family's fortune by enclosing arable land for pasture, securing favorable leases, and selling sheep, cattle, and wool on a rising market. But the estate that they built up was wasted by Sir Thomas and Sir Peter, grandfather and father to Sir Richard. The need to provide settlements for nine daughters drove Thomas into debt; Peter was simply a spendthrift. As a result, Sir Richard, at age nineteen, upon his father's death in 1653 came into an estate burdened with a debt of £19,468. Through a favorable settlement with his creditors, he reduced that debt in 1656 to £12,000; but the weight of that £12,000 ensured that at the Restoration Sir Richard should seek profitable employment at court.[1]

To secure employment at court, one needed a patron. Sir Richard found his in Sir William Morice, kinsman of General Monck and secretary of state. But the event proved discouraging, as Morice's letter to Temple on 30 August 1660 makes clear:

> . . . I waited a fit opportunity to move his Majesty in your behalf, and represented to him yourself according to that character which I suppose you wish and your desires according to what your letter intimate[s]. And I wish I could give you such an account of the transaction as might suit with our desires, and

correspond with that affection I have for you, but I find that umbrage wherein you stand toward his Majesty is neither easily nor suddenly to be removed or cleared. Time may do much and your patient and silent submission, but especially your readiness and diligence in acting in whatsoever may occur for the King's service may dissipate the cloud and set you in a better light.[2]

Charles, it seems, had not forgotten that Sir Richard had sat in two Protectorate Parliaments and had helped the Rump and the army govern Buckinghamshire in 1659.[3] Nor was he willing to accept Temple's sudden conversion to royalism in January 1660 as a sufficient requital. In that month Sir Richard, at the head of the gentlemen of Buckinghamshire, presented to General Monck at Stony Stratford a petition for a free parliament. One of the soldiers present threatened to sequester him for his audacity, but a second soldier warned that such an action might provoke the people to rise. Sir Richard returned safely to Stowe.[4]

The presentation of the petition did not end Temple's services to the King, if his own boasts may be credited. He declared later that he had opposed placing conditions on the King at the Restoration, and had opposed it in so high a manner that General Monck warned him that it was more than the time would bear.[5] He also boasted of performing other services for the King in the Convention Parliament, but in fact he seems to have been more active as a lieutenant of the Presbyterian party, who were for placing conditions on the restored King, than as a member of the Cavalier party, who were opposed to conditions.[6] Secretary Morice probably had good reason to admonish Sir Richard to serve the King more diligently.

By refusing office to Sir Richard Temple, Charles seems to have embraced the principles of the Marquis of Newcastle, that the King should reward his friends and punish his enemies. But in that same year of 1660, he violated that maxim by bestowing offices of honor and profit upon the Presbyterian lords. Herein he acted out of respect for their power, rather than from fidelity to any principle. Indeed, at one moment in April those Presbyterians who caballed at Suffolk House— Northumberland, Manchester, Pierrepoint, and St. John—

became so infatuated with their supposed power in Parliament that they divided up the chief offices of state among themselves. Northumberland was to be admiral, Manchester treasurer, and Holles secretary. On this basis they proposed to open negotiations with Charles for his restoration.[7] But their grand design collapsed when it became manifest that they did not have that credit in the new Parliament that they believed they had. The admission of the royalist peers to the Lords and the victory of the Cavaliers at the polls destroyed their hoped-for omnipotency.

Yet Charles did grant offices to the Presbyterians—to the grandees he gave places at court and in the council, to the clergy, chaplaincies and prebends. He did so in part because they had worked for his restoration, but also because he needed their support in Parliament. They had lost their ascendancy there but not their credit, and the management of Parliament now became the King's chief concern. This task he entrusted to Edward Hyde, whom he created Earl of Clarendon and named lord chancellor. Clarendon had definite views about how Parliament should be managed, views that were essentially conservative in character, views that would not have caused Lord Burleigh to raise an eyebrow. Ministers of the crown should have measures ready, should meet regularly with a few members of the Commons, and should make known through these few the wishes of the King.[8]

For three years these principles of management met with success—a permanent revenue was settled, an Act of Uniformity passed—but in 1663 those who spoke a different dialect gained the King's ear. This new dialect was one of recompense and rewards, a dialect that Sir Francis Bacon would readily have understood. Among the courtiers who spoke in this manner, two were preeminent: Sir Henry Bennet and Sir Thomas Clifford. They advised the King to secure the election of his servants to Parliament, to win men over with preferments, and to invite more members to meet with his ministers. Clarendon looked upon these practices with contempt and predicted that men would not meet with the King's ministers for fear of the "odious name of Undertakers, which in all parliaments hath been a brand." But Charles compelled Clarendon to invite Bennet and others to his meetings; and Clarendon, whether on his own initiative or at Bennet's urging, drew up a list of 167 members of the House of Commons who held office or received royal favors.[9]

But the most bizarre assault on the Clarendonian system came from a different quarter, from the Earl of Bristol and from Sir Richard Temple (who found Morice's advice to be patient and submissive more than his froward spirit could endure). Clarendon's management of Parliament was Elizabethan; Bennet's and Clifford's reflected a Baconian reliance upon patronage; Bristol's and Temple's scheme represented a revival of parliamentary undertaking. The House of Commons first heard of the scheme on 13 June 1663. On that day Charles informed the House that he had received a message from Sir Richard Temple in which Temple declared that "he was sorry his Majesty was offended with him that he could not go along with them that had undertaken his business in the House of Commons: But, if his Majesty would take his advice, and intrust him and his friends, he would undertake his business should be effected, and Revenue settled, better than he could desire; if the courtiers did not hinder it."[10]

The Commons at once asked who had delivered the message from Sir Richard Temple. The King named the Earl of Bristol, whereupon the former Lord Digby, the quondam Straffordian and a recent convert to Catholicism, hurried to the House to explain his actions. In a florid speech, filled with Latin, law, eloquence, and comedy, he cleared Temple and took all upon himself.[11] But if Daniel O'Neil, who was intimate with the King, can be believed, Temple talked the Earl into the project. "This fellow," wrote O'Neil of Temple, "fastens a great friendship upon my Lord of Bristol and being a nimble-tongued fellow overcame my Lord's easy nature so far as to believe he was able to carry anything in our House, upon which confidence he was brought to the King at the beginning of this session." At that meeting Charles received him well, and Temple undertook to secure the passage of a Declaration of Indulgence.[12]

The Earl of Bristol and Sir Richard Temple had this in

common: each sought a greater role in public affairs than Clarendon would grant them, and both sought by their knowledge of Parliament, and their credit there, to win office. Thus it came about that in early February 1663, Bristol discoursed with Charles about the coming Parliament. He urged the King not to press for supplies this session, so that he might win the love of his people. But if supplies were needed, he should accompany his request for money with acts of grace, with wholesome laws, with the reformation of abuses.[13] It was advice such as Neville had given to James in 1612, and Charles II found it no more palatable than had James I.

Simultaneously with their overtures at court, Temple and Bristol launched a campaign to win credit in Parliament and the country. Gentlemen in the counties, acting upon instructions from Temple, whispered to discontented Cavaliers that Clarendon was not well affected to their interests. Other agents gave hopes of liberty of conscience to papists and sectaries.[14] Temple boasted that he could get a Declaration of Indulgence through the House.[15] He found, wrote O'Neil, no occasion to disturb His Majesty's service or blast his ministers but he laid hold of it.[16] He moved for a committee to inquire into those who had sold offices, and was named its chairman. The investigation was aimed at Clarendon, wrote Nathaniel Hodges, "that by his fall such a stream of preferment would happen that all their friends might be satisfied."[17]

With the courtiers in the House, Temple's strategy backfired. They were displeased that the King should make use of such a man. The King also grew angry with Temple, complaining to Bristol about the opposition that Temple made to his affairs. Bristol at once sought out Temple to discuss the matter. He then returned to the King with a message from Temple. He, Temple, could "not go along with those that managed his business in the House but that if his Majesty would leave the business to him and his friends, he should not only have a large supply to put him out of his present wanting condition but his established revenue should be augmented."[18] Bristol then added his own sentiments. There could be no hope of obtaining supply unless accompanied by acts of grace and by measures to ensure that the money voted was better spent than before. But it was a loyal House, such a House that he and others could undertake that the Commons would vote the supplies needed. Charles's reply was instant: he scorned private undertakings, either by courtiers or others, and would rely upon the affections of the whole House—an answer, Bristol declared later, to put an end "to the vain proposals of all pickthank undertakers."[19]

This second meeting between Charles and Bristol probably occurred in May. It was not, however, until 13 June that Charles lost his temper and informed the House of Temple's undertaking. The day before, Charles had summoned the Commons to Whitehall, where he had made a long, skillfull, earnest appeal for an immediate supply. The Commons then returned to their House, where they voted, by only 159 to 111, to proceed to an immediate supply. Of the two Tellers for the Noes, one was Sir Richard Temple. This was more than the amiable Charles could swallow. He at once informed the Commons of Sir Richard's proffered undertaking.[20]

Charles's message led to Bristol's florid speech on 1 July. Sir William Batten thought the speech "comedian like", but Charles was not amused. He found it mutinous, seditious, and false.[21] Bristol then moved from comedy to farce by bringing into the House of Lords an impeachment against the Earl of Clarendon, an impeachment that the Lords rejected. The King thereupon ordered the arrest of Bristol, who promptly went into hiding.[22] But Bristol's folly should not blind the historian to the fate of Sir Richard Temple. Though the manifest author of the undertaking and the linchpin in the Commons, he escaped condemnation there. His fellow members voted that he had not broken any privilege of the House.[23] As with Neville in 1614, so with Temple now, the House condemned the undertaking but not the undertaker. The undertaking threatened their independence; the undertaker merely sought to persuade the King to redress their grievances.

But it was not so easy to escape the wrath of the court. To the King, Sir Richard at once sent a petition, in which he protested that he had never harbored an undutiful thought toward His Majesty or used any undutiful expression to hinder his service. If he erred, he continued, it was from weakness, not ill intentions, and he implored His Majesty that he might be restored to his good opinion.[24] The petition seems to have done little good, for Temple, fearing arrest, went into hiding.[25] The King meanwhile dismissed him from the office of deputy lieutenant of Buckinghamshire.[26]

In this precarious position, Temple appealed to the rising star at court, Sir Henry Bennet, now secretary of state and soon to be the Earl of Arlington. He wrote to him on 18 August. Bennet replied on 3 September:

> What I promise again is to do my utmost to leave you at your whim to London, and in the mean time to take occasion of representing to his Majesty with how much submission and duty you have attended his pleasure, which I hope you will have no cause to repent. I assure you it would trouble me much you should, not only for the good I wish you and that value I have for your good parts, but for the part I suppose I may have had in advising you to this patience.[27]

But submission and patience seem to have been no part of the temperament of Sir Richard Temple. He heeded Bennet's warning no better than Morice's. In March 1664 Charles summoned Parliament with the sole aim of repealing the Triennial Act of 1641, an act that made the summoning of Parliament every three years mandatory. Temple not only opposed its repeal but urged that the King meet Parliaments annually, as required by a law passed in Edward III's reign.[28] Temple failed to carry the House of Commons with him in 1664, but when he next championed a popular cause, in the autumn of 1665, he found more support. On 18 October he introduced into the House a bill to prohibit the importation of Irish cattle into England. This struck a responsive chord in members upset by falling cattle prices. Despite opposition from the court, the bill passed, though by only 13 votes.[29]

When Parliament next met, in the autumn of 1666, a formed opposition appeared against the court, led by Edward Seymour, Sir Thomas Littleton, Sir Robert Howard, William Garroway, and Sir Richard Temple. "Sir Richard and his friends," John Nicholas called them.[30] These mutineers, these neglected men of talent, sought preferment at court by making themselves considerable in Parliament. The source of their power was their ability to give voice to the sullen discontents of the country members, of men grown weary of the profligacy of the court, of the waste of public money, of the embezzlement of prize goods, and of the ill success of the war.[31] To gain credit in the House, they exploited whatever grievances arose. Temple again introduced a bill against Irish cattle (the Lords' having rejected the 1665 bill); Garroway proposed the parliamentary examination of public accounts; Seymour attacked the monopoly enjoyed by the Canary Company.[32] "Parliament driving," contemporaries called it; and Sir Richard, in part because he shared the country member's outrage at these grievances, was one of its ablest practitioners.[33]

The success of the opposition was made easier by the ineptness of the court. The Court party was often unprepared, and the King's servants frequently crossed each other's purposes. It was not a courtier but Sir Richard Temple himself who moved that Parliament grant the King £1,600,000 for carrying on the war against the Dutch, a sum that the court thought too little. But the court could act when stung. Charles regarded the parliamentary examination of the public accounts as an invasion of his prerogative. When the House attached such a proviso to the poll bill, he ordered his servants to separate the proviso from the bill. On 11 December the court marshalled its forces and succeeded in separating the two. One reason for the court's success was the growing number of placemen in the House, a number variously estimated at 100, 140, and 178 (though nowhere near that number ever appeared at one time at a division).[34] Emboldened by these numbers, the court fell upon a stratagem for carrying the supply bill through both Houses in advance of the Irish cattle bill, which could then be defeated by a prorogation. As the Christmas season approached, the country members, as always, trickled home, leaving the courtiers with a majority in a thin House. In this depleted House, the court sought to drive through the supply bill. The Country party first suspected such a maneuver when Charles announced that there would be no Christmas recess. This galvanized Temple and his friends: they ordered absentee members to return; they introduced new business only for delay; they postponed the supply bill by objecting to every trifle in it. Their tactics succeeded. The supply bill was still in the House when the country members returned in January.[35]

Having failed in its stratagem, the court was forced to negotiate with the leaders of the House of Commons. The intermediary in these negotiations was Henry Bennet, now the Earl of Arlington. He undertook to secure the passage of the Irish cattle bill in the Lords if Temple and his friends would pass the supply bill in the Commons. The undertaking proved a success; both bills became law. Arlington later regretted the role he played in these events, probably because he saw that the court had yielded more to the opposition than the opposition had to the court.[36]

Before Parliament met again, a series of disasters overwhelmed England, making the management of Parliament more difficult than ever. In June 1667 the Dutch captured Sheerness, raided the Medway, burned three men-of-war, and captured the *Royal Charles*. Faced with these calamities, Charles turned to a policy of concessions. He dismissed Clarendon, turned Catholics out of the court, cancelled the Canary patent, and issued a Declaration against the Smuggling of Irish Cattle.[37]

But it was not enough merely to mollify Parliament; someone had to manage it. Here Charles faced a difficult problem for the chancellor was gone and Arlington was discredited. He therefore turned to the opposition, above all to its leader in the House of Lords, George Villiers, the second Duke of Buckingham. In the 1666–67 session of Parliament, Buckingham had worked closely with Temple and his friends. For doing so (and for allegedly casting the King's horoscope), Charles threw him into the Tower. Now he restored the Duke to liberty, office, and royal favor. The explanation for the Duke's swift restoration is not hard to find. Lord Conway put it succinctly on 22 October: "his undertaking that the Parliament shall give money makes him continue very acceptable at Court."[38] John Nicholas confirmed Conway's explanation: "The Duke of Bucks is the great man who carries all before him, and hath, as it's said, undertaken to his Majesty by his interest in the House of Commons to make them do whatsoever he shall desire."[39]

The precise terms of the undertaking offered by Buckingham are hard to discern, for it was not so much an engagement as an understanding. Certainly it encompassed the impeachment of Clarendon; probably it also included the preferment to office of the undertakers (soon to be called the Anti-Clarendonians); and undoubtedly it meant a supply for the King. Three years later Sir Richard Temple described the undertakers in these words: "A number of Country Gentlemen who after they had a long time headed the House as to the public and national interest embarked themselves in the charge against the Chancellor, in full confidence that the King would have made a considerable change both in measures and persons upon his remove. . . . "[40] Though the undertaking was only an understanding, it is possible to describe it in greater detail than Temple does. The King, on his part, agreed to leave his servants to the justice of Parliament, to place the fleet in different hands, to dismiss the Clarendonians from court and council, and to put in their places Buckingham's friends. In return the Anti-Clarendonians agreed to win for Charles the money needed to set out a fleet, to secure the passage of a bill of comprehension, and to prevent the impeachments of the Earl of Arlington and Sir William Coventry. Particular offices were spoken of. Lord Berkeley should replace the Duke of Ormond in Ireland, and Buckingham should have Ormond's place as lord steward. Sir Thomas Osborne and Sir Thomas Littleton should replace Anglesey as treasurer of the navy. And the King should dismiss Clarendon's two sons from their places at court.[41]

Why Charles listened to the siren songs of the undertakers must be a matter of conjecture. He had assuredly grown tired of the imperious and censorious sermons of the Earl of Clarendon, and he had certainly fallen under the sway of the agreeable and libertine Duke. But it is more likely that he acted out of desperation: he was in debt, his navy was unready, his neighbors were arming. "Parliament has the power," wrote the French ambassador in November, "and the Duke of Buckingham has the credit there."[42] That credit was exercised through his lieutenants, the chief of whom were Sir Richard Temple, Edward Seymour, Sir Thomas Osborne, and Sir Robert Howard. They managed the impeachment of the Earl of Clarendon. They drove on the inquiry into the division of the fleet, into the disaster at Chatham, into the waste of public money. They recited again and again in the House of Commons Clarendon's unfortunate remark that 400 country gentlemen were only fit to give money.[43]

The Anti-Clarendonians triumphed in the House of Commons, but not in the Lords, even though Charles acted as their chief whip there. Sir Richard Temple in 1663 had undertaken to manage the Commons only "if the Courtiers did not hinder it."[44] In 1667 he had his wish. Charles did all he could to bring the courtiers in line behind the impeachment of Clarendon. And though the Lords obdurately refused to imprison the Earl on a general charge of treason, the Commons did force him to flee to France; and both Houses passed a bill banishing him from the realm.

This success emboldened Buckingham in late December to endeavor to drive from council, court, and chapel all who had favored Clarendon. It was a continuation and elaboration of the undertaking entered into in October. Anglesey, Ashley, and Holles should be removed from the council. Clarendon's sons must lose their places at court. The bishop of Winchester should cease to be dean of the chapel, and the bishop of Rochester should no longer serve as clerk of the closet. Those stalwart Anti-Clarendonians Sir Thomas Osborne and Sir Thomas Littleton, should replace Lord Anglesey as joint treasurers of the navy. And Secretary Morice, who had shown sympathy for Clarendon, should surrender his place to John Trevor, who had not. To persuade the notoriously humane and irresolute Charles to make these changes, Buckingham waited on him on 29 December 1667, assuring him that he would never receive satisfaction from Parliament unless he dismissed from office those thought unworthy. Charles promised he would dismiss them.[45]

But he did not. The Clarendonian lords remained in the council, Anglesey remained treasurer of the navy, Secretary Morice kept the seals, and Clarendon's two sons kept their offices. Charles did throw some crumbs to the Anti-Clarendonians. He named Sir Richard Temple, Sir Thomas Littleton, and Sir Thomas Osborne to be commissioners for settling trade with Scotland, and he sent John Trevor to France as envoy extraordinaire. But this was not the rout of the Clarendonians that Buckingham and his lieutenants had expected.[46]

Samuel Pepys believed that Charles forbore dismissing these men because, though he could gratify some House of Commons men with their places, he would anger the rest who were not provided for.[47] But Charles may have held back for another reason. He may have wished to see whether the Anti-Clarendonians had as much talent for doing good as they had capacity for doing harm. Could they secure him a bill of comprehension and a vote of supply?

By the time Parliament met in February, the undertakers had a bill of comprehension in readiness, a carefully drawn bill, supported by Tillotson and Stillingfleet among Anglicans and by Baxter and Bates among Presbyterians.[48] They intended to introduce it into the House on the first day of the sessions, the sixth, but the Church party forestalled them by securing an order that no new business be introduced for a week. On 10 February, Charles addressed both Houses, urging them to take some course to promote a better union among his Protestant subjects. Some applauded, but most stood silent. When the Commons returned to their House, they declined to vote an address of thanks for the speech; instead they voted an address asking that the laws be enforced against nonconformists.[49] The Anti-Clarendonians were routed, their weakness revealed, their measures broken. In part their defeat arose from the fact that the Cavalier Parliament possessed an Anglican majority. But their defeat also arose from the discredit into which they fell as "undertakers." Arlington, it was said, had bribed members of the Commons to spread the rumor that Buckingham had boasted to the King that Parliament was as wax in his hands. Others whispered that the Duke's cabal sought to win places at court by persuading the King that they governed in Parliament.[50] In 1614 the Earl of Northampton had discredited Neville by spreading rumors that he had undertaken to manage the House for the King. Like rumors now undermined the Anti-Clarendonians. The House, wrote Pepys, is "now quite mad at the undertakers."[51]

Sir Richard Temple was the chief actor in the next move by the Anti-Clarendonians, though it was a move arising more out of country prejudices than political calculations. On 18 February he introduced into the House of Commons a triennial bill as severe as that of 1641. He was seconded, observed John Nicholas, by "those called undertakers." But the scorn of the House against the bill forced Temple to withdraw it.[52] Temple was not the most esteemed of the Anti-Clarendonians—Seymour and Howard were better heard by the House—but he was surely the boldest, the most persistent, the most resilient, and the most extravagant.

The reputation of the Anti-Clarendonians steadily declined. "My Lord of Buckingham's friends that are called the undertakers," wrote Lord Ossory, "do daily lose ground, and did the King withdraw his countenance from them would be very insignificant."[53] Lose ground they assuredly did. They failed in further attempts to gain either a comprehension or a toleration. They failed to prevent an address against conventicles. They failed to prevent the passage of the Bill to Continue the Existing Act against Conventicles. The passage of this bill prompted John Nicholas to write: "The King if he pleases may take a right measure of our temper by this, and leave off crediting the Undertakers who persuade him that the generality of the Kingdom, and of our House too, is inclined to a toleration."[54]

It soon appeared, therefore, that their talent for doing good did not equal their capacity for doing harm. Indeed, the undertakers soon set out, as Bacon had predicted they invariably would, to repair their credit in the House by doing harm. They demanded inquiries into the miscarriages of the war, and they attacked evil councillors. Seymour managed the attack upon Ormond, Howard the impeachment of Sir William Penn. Temple's particular contribution was the pursuit of Sir William Coventry for selling offices in the navy. To this end he set Captain Tatnall to work digging out the dirt. He occasionally dined with the captain, whom he greatly impressed. Temple, the captain boasted, "made the Chancellor fly his country and so he would make the rest, or else their necks must &c."[55] The House never impeached Coventry (he had already resigned as secretary to the Duke of York), but the undertakers did manage to secure, by narrow margins, the condemnation of past miscarriages. At "parliament driving" they were singularly adept; at helping the King, remarkably maladroit.

For Charles the critical question was supply, and here the undertakers let him down totally. Far from helping him secure a generous supply, they appeared to place obstacles in the way of his receiving any at all. In January, Charles had entered into an alliance with Sweden and the United Provinces, a triple alliance, that obliged him to put fifty ships to sea that spring. Temple and Howard thereupon demanded that the House examine that treaty before voting money. Seymour boldly declared, "We may date our misery from our bounty here." The Commons did not ask to see the treaty, but on 26 February it held a crucial debate on supply, the House sitting until seven in the evening. Sir Richard Temple made a long, querulous speech, urging that before they vote money they inquire into the necessity for it, where the money was to be found, and into whose hands it should be entrusted. As the day wore on and as the House grew thin, it appeared that the party opposed to supply would carry the day; but then the loyal Cavaliers came flowing back into the House, and the royal party prevalied. They voted to grant the King £300,000.[56]

Nor were the Anti-Clarendonians any more helpful when it came to ways and means. Howard spoke for an excise and against a customs duty; Temple spoke for a customs duty and against an excise. Others advocated the sale of dean and chapter lands. "We have to our shame," wrote Nicholas, "made as yet but inconsiderable progress towards the raising the £300,000 for the summer fleet, all our undertakers making it their business to oppose all the propositions that are made for it."[57]

In April the Anti-Clarendonians sought to hold up the supply bill until they had taken revenge upon the authors of the late miscarriages, upon Penn and Coventry and Carteret and Brounker. But the power of the purse no longer lay in their hands. They could not prevent the House from perfecting the supply bill. On 1 May, Seymour and Howard made a last attempt to clog the bill with a clause appropriating part of the customs to the cost of setting out a fleet, but their attempt failed, by 139 to 93. On 4 May the Commons sent the supply bill, now worth £310,000, to the Lords, who passed it on the fifth. On the ninth Charles adjourned Parliament.[58]

Shortly after the adjournment of Parliament, Sir Richard Temple journeyed to the south of France in order to recover his health, which had not survived the vicissitudes of a hectic session. In France he drank the waters of Bourbon and settled down in the town of Montpellier, where his archenemy the Earl of Clarendon also resided. Sir Richard left neither his venom nor his vanity behind when he crossed the Channel. He ostentatiously refused to visit Clarendon and dissuaded other Englishmen from doing so. And he openly called himself (if Clarendon can be believed) "the Premier President of the Parliament of England."[59] But such boasts neither paid off his debts nor brought him office.

In January 1669 his brother-in-law, John Doddington, wrote him a long letter, recounting a conversation he had had with the Duke of Buckingham. The Duke, he wrote, "was still resolute to bring in all his friends, and most particularly yourself." He therefore urges you not to go for Italy, but to return toward Paris at the beginning of March, for the intended alterations should happen then. But there is another reason why the Duke would have you return, the dissolution of Parliament. True, the King starts at the word *dissolution*, though heard only in his laboratory, but the Duke "doth not doubt of inclining or forcing his reason to it." And so he wishes you would return to Paris, "that you may not be left out." Doddington then observed, "He assents to what you say, as touching his having no foundation until he hath brought in all his friends, whom he assureth you, he will tender as himself."[60]

But the Duke of Buckingham, though he could persuade Charles to replace Anglesey with Osborne and Littleton in

November 1668 and to remove Ormond in March 1669, could not prevail with the King to dissolve the Cavalier Parliament. To secure the dissolution of Parliament had been Buckingham's purpose ever since he discovered in May that he had no credit in the present Parliament. In order to persuade Charles to dissolve it, he and his confederates had sought to exacerbate a quarrel between the two Houses over the Lords' assertion of an original jurisdiction in a civil case, the case of Skinner versus the East India Company. No doubt the Commons had good reason to resent the Lords' action, but the zealous exploitation of the issue by the Anti-Clarendonians was rather more cynical. As John Nicholas observed, "The Undertakers in ours and the Duke of Buckingham and some of the Presbyterians in the Lords House are most passionate in it; which makes it be looked on by sober men as a design to break this Parliament, which all factions are desirous to accomplish."[61]

Faced with a loss of power in the Commons, Buckingham and his confederates turned to a radically new strategy, one not dreamed of by Neville or Bedford. They would appeal from the knights and burgesses in Parliament to the electorate in the country. Their strategy, however, failed, for Charles's political instincts told him that he was not likely to meet a Parliament more favorable to him than the Cavalier Parliament. As a result, when Sir Richard Temple landed at Dover on 19 October 1669, he did not face the election of a new Parliament but rather the stale intrigues of the old one.

Karl Marx once observed that every historical event occurs twice, once as tragedy, again as farce. He could well have illustrated this dictum with the fate of the undertakers in 1668 and 1669. The word *tragic* may be too exalted an expression to describe their failure in 1668, but their failure in 1669 was surely farcical. Buckingham once again urged Charles to rely upon him to manage Parliament. Permit the two Houses to look into the public accounts, delay the consideration of supply, offer measures to guarantee liberty of conscience, then Parliament would be his.[62] And though Charles refused to commit himself wholly to the Duke, the Anti-Clarendonians pursued this strategy. Temple, Howard, and Seymour—the great triumvirate of this Parliament—urged on the investigation of accounts, attacked Carteret for misapplying the King's revenues, demanded that grievances be discussed before supply, and opposed the bill against conventicles (introduced again because the 1668 bill had died in the Lords). This time, however, the Clarendonians retaliated in kind. They introduced articles of impeachment against the Earl of Orrery, a leading AntiClarendonian. The Anti-Clarendonians replied by threatening to impeach Ormond, a leading Clarendonian. The Clarendonians then demanded that witnesses against Orrery be brought over from Ireland. The Anti-Clarendonians opposed the demand. Charles ended the farce on 11 December by proroguing Parliament.[63]

Shortly after the prorogation, Sir Richard Temple wrote "A Discourse Endeavouring to Penetrate into the Reasons of the Ill Success of the Last Sessions." He found that there had been both sins of omission and of commission. The King had, in the first place, erred by not espousing popular measures (in other words, measures to guarantee liberty of conscience), by not disciplining the Court party, and by not entirely entrusting some persons about him (he probably meant the Duke of Buckingham) to conduct his affairs, to whom those that were willing to be gained might apply and with whom eminent members of the House might meet to frame matters. Then there were those actions of the King that were repugnant, such as frequent discourses on behalf of Carteret, messages for overhastening supply, not sufficiently resenting the bill of conventicles, and not espousing one party there, who would engage to give money. Because of these actions, the Anti-Clarendonians and Presbyterians were offended, and in truth did not concur vigorously in matters of money. The Anti-Clarendonians, he added, justify themselves in this by their ill usage—by their being rendered suspect as undertakers yet not entrusted with office. Furthermore, their counsel for a new Parliament was not embraced, and this Parliament was called at the instance, "and upon the undertaking," of the Clarendonian party, whereby if money were obtained the Clarendonians would reap the honor and the Anti-Clarendonians be rendered useless. Sir Richard then urged the King to trust the Anti-Clarendonians in the next sessions, for the Clarendonians have only two things to gratify the country gentlemen—the persecution of fanatics and the favor of the duke of York—whereas the Anti-Clarendonians had "three prevalent charms to induce the House to give money": the punishment of all miscarriages, a change of hands and better management of the King's affairs, and the national interest of moderation.[64]

Rarely has a politician written a discourse filled with more mistakes, special pleading, and self-revelations. Temple was quite wrong to believe that toleration was a popular measure or that inquiries into past miscarriages was still a prevalent charm. His justification of the refusal of the Anti-Clarendonians to concur in matters of money was lame. But most revealing of all was the statement that the Anti-Clarendonians would not concur in the vote of money if such a vote redounded to the honor of the Clarendonians and rendered the Anti-Clarendonians useless. This was a confession that the chief end of their management of Parliament was to wrest office from the King.

For Charles the 1669 session proved a great awakening. He now discovered that the Anti-Clarendonians could not win him a supply, indeed, worked against it. He therefore turned from the undertakers and the cause of toleration to the courtiers and the cause of persecution. Chief among the courtiers was the Earl of Arlington, silent and thoughtful where Buckingham was voluble and heedless. Arlington saw that a policy of concessions must be directed to the Anglican majority in the Commons. He therefore ended his long, uneasy alliance with Buckingham, an alliance into which he entered in September 1667 largely to prevent his own impeachment. He now allied himself with the Duke of York, and through him with those Cavaliers and Churchmen who had proved so formidable in the 1668 session.[65]

But Arlington had another trump card in his deck. He had built up, with the help of Sir Thomas Clifford and Joseph Williamson, a sizeable Court party in the House, a party numbering (according to Sir Thomas Osborne) 92 members.[66] This was widely known, or at least it was after Buckingham and his allies distributed the pamphlet "The Alarum" throughout the precincts of Westminister in the autumn of 1669. "The Alarum" was an attack on placemen and on those who would distribute place, money, and loans to corrupt Parliament. The great instrument of this distribution, asserted the author of "The Alarum," was Lord Arlington, next in rank was his man, Clifford. As an example of a man silenced by place, the author pointed to Sir Thomas Littleton, "that angry man against the Court until silenced by a good place."[67]

When Parliament met on 14 February 1670, a well-disciplined Court party, allied with a zealous Church party, carried all before it. On 18 February they voted that the consideration of supply should take precedence over the examination of public accounts, whereupon 80 irate country gentlemen, well coached by Sir Robert Howard, walked out of the House. The courtiers and the Church party went on to vote the King an additional revenue of £300,000 a year for eight years, and to pass the Act against Conventicles—"the price of money," said Andrew Marvell. Sir Richard Temple spoke in vain against the conventicle act, which carried by a vote of 138 to 78.[68]

For Temple the 1670 session proved the great awakening. He now saw that advancement could not be gained by adherence to the Duke of Buckingham, whose party in the Commons had shrunk to some 60 members. He therefore resolved to go over to the court, and did so in the autumn session of Parliament. He took leave of his former party on 1 December 1670, when he defended a land tax of £70,000 a month ("a mark of our chains," said Garroway, still loyal to the country interest). He went on during that session to favor raising money by a subsidy and by an additional excise on beef. The reward for his apostasy was not long in coming. In May 1671 Charles named him to the Council for Foreign Plantations; in 1672 he named him a commissioner of the Customs at £2,000 a year.[69]

Sir Richard used the money well. By 1675 he had repaid £9,660 of the £13,660 he had borrowed by mortgage from 1656 to 1667. In the following years he extricated his estates from financial difficulty, rebuilt Stowe House in "the grand manner," purchased pictures, and formed a library.[70] But he paid a price in the loss of reputation. In a debate in February 1673, the Speaker had to tell Sir Richard that it was not in his power to persuade the House to hear him.[71] Sir William Temple, a distant cousin, wrote in October 1673 that the court's unofficial spokesmen in the House were Sir Robert Carr and Sir Richard Temple, "who are the worst heard that can be in the House, especially the last."[72]

Sir Richard Temple was not the only Anti-Clarendonian who came to enjoy the emoluments of office. Sir Thomas Littleton and Sir Thomas Osborne became joint treasurers of the navy, and Osborne later became a commissioner of the Treasury. Sir John Trevor received the seals as secretary of state. The King named Sir Robert Howard secretary of the treasury in 1671 and Edward Seymour treasurer of the navy in 1673. Sir Robert Carr became chancellor of the duchy of Lancaster. These appointments did not go unnoticed, but they elicited different responses from different men.

Country party stalwarts like Andrew Marvell threw up their hands in horror at these apostate patriots. They saw the emergence of a Court party that would destroy the independence of Parliament. In a pamphlet entitled *A Seasonable Argument to Persuade All the Grand Juries in England to Petition for a New Parliament*, they listed 215 members of parliament corrupted by the court, a list shown by modern scholarship not to be wholly fanciful.[73] There is, indeed, a large measure of truth in the analysis of the political scene presented in *A Seasonable Argument*. Temple himself saw by 1670 that power lay with Arlington, Clifford, and the Court party, not with Buckingham and the undertakers. In 1666 and 1667, the Anti-Clarendonians proved that they could win control of the House of Commons by denouncing waste, mismanagement, monopolies, and the importation of Irish cattle, but they were quite unable to turn a talent for opposition into a capacity for serving the court. In part this inability arose from the discredit they won as undertakers. A House jealous of its independence and suspicious of those who joined with the court was not likely to hearken to them. But it also arose from a misreading of the composition of the House of Commons. Most members did not favor toleration or triennial bills. They favored the church and the prerogative, as Charles discovered in 1670. It was not the power of patronage alone, or even principally, that explains the court's success in 1670; it was the strength of the Anglican party, with which the King momentarily allied himself.[74]

Though useful to the court, the power of patronage also presented dangers, especially when used to win over opponents of the court. "Those who most declaim against the government," wrote Colbert de Croissy, "and for the destruction of Clarendon were recompensed with office, which led others openly to say, 'As the most factious were rewarded, so they must speak against the government'; so that where five or six were won over, now many more are in opposition."[75] Gilbert Burnet noted the same phenomenon, and reduced it to a law: "As a man rose in credit, he raised his price, and expected to be treated accordingly."[76] And the chief means to raise one's credit was to oppose the court. As Thomas Baker put it, "Seeing preferment came by thwarting the King's party, the whole nation, I mean their representatives, made it their constant trade."[77]

Chapter IV

Parliamentary Undertaking during the Exclusion Crisis

I N FEBRUARY 1675 the first Earl of Shaftesbury, small of stature but great in ambition, once lord chancellor but now out of office, wrote to the Earl of Carlisle that they need not fear to be accounted undertakers at the next meeting of Parliament. Shaftesbury was the first English politician to accept publicly the odious name of undertaker, though a close reading of his letter shows that by "undertaker" he merely meant a lord who gave the King his opinion in private. In this sense Neville in 1614 had confessed to being an undertaker and had won applause for it (though Neville did not limit to peers alone, as did Shaftesbury, those who might advise the King privately). In the same letter to Carlisle, however, Shaftesbury heaped scorn on those who sought to gain office at the expense of their principles. In this sense of the word, he was no undertaker. He vowed that all the great places at court together could not buy him from his principles. But neither did he repudiate altogether the possibility of taking office. He would accept office, only it would be on his terms. And he made clear what they were: the dissolution of this Parliament and the King's commitment to frequent Parliaments.[1]

The circumstances that occasioned Shaftesbury's letter of 3 February 1675 help reveal its meaning. Early in January the Duke of York had met with a number of lords opposed to the court: Carlisle, Bedford, Holles, Salisbury, Falconbridge, and Newport. The Duke declared he would favor any law passed by Parliament to secure religion, property, and government. Furthermore, he would not oppose in council those lords who favored the meeting of Parliament. In return he asked that he be left to the freedom of his own thoughts (he was now a declared Catholic) and that nothing be undertaken in Parliament against him.[2] Rumor embellished these negotiations with talk of Shaftesbury's appointment as lord lieutenant of Ireland, or even as vicar general for ecclesiastical affairs. Lord Mordaunt's visit to Shaftesbury's country seat at St. Giles gave some semblance of reality to these rumors. Some said that the court sent him; others, that he was sent by the opposition lords; most likely he was sent by the Duke of York and the opposition lords to report on their negotiations.[3] What is certainly known is Shaftesbury's response to Lord Mordaunt's visit. It was contained in a letter to Lord Carlisle, a letter widely circulated in manuscript and later published. In that letter Shaftesbury expressly approved of what Carlisle and Mordaunt were doing. He did not repudiate their negotiations, he did not shrink from the name of undertaker. At the same time, he declared that he would only return to court on his terms, terms that included the dissolution of the present Parliament.[4]

The negotiations that took place in January 1675 between York and the opposition lords (and perhaps between the court and Shaftesbury) arose out of the court's total failure to manage Parliament successfully in the years 1673 and 1674. That failure is the more startling when contrasted with the remarkable success of Charles's parliamentary management in 1670 and 1671. The two earlier sessions mark the zenith of Charles's career as a parliamentary manager, the two latter sessions its nadir.

The explanation for this descent into failure can be found in Charles's pursuit of his personal predilections at the expense of the national will. In 1668 he had advertised his opposition to France by forming the Triple Alliance, and in 1670 he had shown his support for the church by favoring the Act against Conventicles. A grateful Parliament voted him the additional revenues he requested. But in the next three years he yielded to personal impulses, signed the Treaty of Dover, allied with France, declared war against the Dutch, and issued a Declaration of Indulgence that excused Catholic as well as Protestant dissenters from the operation of the penal laws. It was a path that no Elizabethan statesman would have taken, and it was a path that led to an unmanageable Parliament in the spring of 1675.[5]

In the course of the seventeenth century, three strategies for the management of Parliament emerged. Though no contemporary would have used the terms, it is a convenient form of shorthand to refer to them as the Elizabethan, the Baconian, and the Nevillian. The essence of the Elizabethan strategy was to lead Parliament in the direction it wished to go. It was the peculiar genius of Queen Elizabeth to sense the national impulse, and it was the peculiar talent of her ministers to be able to seize the initiative in the two Houses. The second strategy emerged when the first broke down in 1610, and may fairly be called the Baconian because Sir Francis Bacon was one of the first to suggest to the King that he win men over to his policies by the offer of place. At the same time, Sir Henry Neville suggested that James entrust the management of Parliament to those who had opposed him in recent Parliaments. This strategy envisaged the King not only giving office to the opposition but embracing their policies as well.

In the year 1673, the Nevillian strategy was discredited. Bristol's folly, Buckingham's failure, and Temple's defection to the court had left parliamentary undertakings in a bad odor. As a result Charles and his ministers had either to rely upon a court party in the two Houses, the Baconian strategy, or to yield to the policies demanded by the political nation, the Elizabethan strategy. Early in the year 1673, the King's ministers made an attempt to strengthen the Court party in the House of Commons, but that attempt boomeranged. Shaftesbury, as lord chancellor, issued writs for the election of members for 36 vacant seats; he issued the writs even though the Speaker had not requested him to do so. The great majority of those returned in the ensuing by elections were courtiers and could be relied upon to vote the King supplies, but their numbers could not outweigh the resentment of the House at the lord chancellor's high-handed action. Men spoke of impeaching him for issuing the writs.[6] More serious still were the divisions within the Court party. Clifford, as lord treasurer, was the chief corrupter of the pensionary Parliament; but his efforts, never very systematic, foundered when Arlington and Shaftesbury broke from Clifford and York. The dependents of Clifford intrigued against Shaftesbury, and Shaftesbury entered into negotiations with the opponents of Clifford.[7]

It was the war against the Dutch, expensive as all wars are, that occasioned the summoning of Parliament in the spring of 1673. And the success of that Parliament can best be measured by the success of the court in securing the money needed to wage war. At the opening of Parliament, the opposition, led by Garroway and Lee, surprisingly supported the court's demand for some £1,200,000 to pay for the war. Bishop Burnet attributes this to the court's buying off Garroway and Lee, but Denis Witcombe is probably nearer the truth when he suggests that the opposition sought to secure the revocation of the Declaration of Indulgence by holding out the hope of a large supply.[8] The intriguing question is whether this bargain was implicit or explicit. Alberti, the Venetian ambassador, wrote, "The King relies greatly upon the promises of the leaders of the House of Commons and hopes to obtain money as well for the war as the payment of his debts."[9] And Burnet declares that Arlington and Shaftesbury pressed the King to give Parliament full content and undertook, if he did so, to procure him money for carrying on the war.[10] Whether implicit or explicit, it was a bargain. The opposition held back the supply bill until the King revoked the Declaration of Indulgence and passed the Test Act. The King won the supply he sought, but only by yielding to the clamor of the nation against popery and the suspending power.

The Parliaments that met in the autumn of 1673 and the winter of 1674 witnessed the entire collapse of the court's efforts to manage Parliament. The great men at court threatened to impeach each other, and the leading ministers had contending parties in Parliament.[11] The King gave no directions to his friends how to govern themselves, and spokesmen for the court were few. Only one member of the House spoke for supply in the 1674 session.[12] Sir Robert Howard, a leading placeman, took the lead in attacking the King's ministers. The Duke of York begged his brother to dismiss Howard—and some fifty others who deserted the court—but

Charles could not summon up the resolution to do so.[13] Nor could he maintain amity among his ministers, who in January 1674 introduced impeachments and addresses against each other. It was a picture of total confusion.

Charles hoped to escape from this confusion by redressing the greatest of all grievances: the war against the Dutch and the alliance with France. The House of Commons, wrote the Earl of Conway on 17 January, "is well assured the King leaves all things to their disposal. He will have money and we shall have peace, but how far the reformation will go no man can tell."[14] The King did give his subjects peace, a peace whose terms he presented to Parliament on 26 January. But Charles never received his money, for the House demanded more reforms. The moderates, led by Sir William Coventry, lost control of the House to the extremists in the southeast corner, men allied to Shaftesbury in the Lords.[15] On 10 February, Conway saw no appearance that Parliament would give money. "Fear of the Duke," he wrote, "makes them every day fetter the Crown."[16] Rather than suffer the prerogative to be further diminished, Charles prorogued Parliament.

Charles in 1673 won supply by reversing his religious policy; in 1674 he sought to win supply by reversing his foreign policy, but before he could reap the rewards of that concession the Exclusion Crisis arose to wreck his plans. Indeed, as far as the history of parliamentary undertaking is concerned, the Exclusion Crisis arose in November 1673 when the Earl of Shaftesbury (according to the Venetian ambassador) offered to secure money from Parliament if Charles would divorce the Queen and make a second marriage. The King refused the Earl's undertaking.[17]

Charles preferred to entrust his affairs to Sir Thomas Osborne, a Yorkshire gentleman, once an Anti-Clarendonian and now a courtier, whom he named lord treasurer in June 1673 and Earl of Danby in 1674. Danby's first purpose was to order the King's finances so that he would be independent of Parliament. "I hear from very good hands," wrote William Harbord in February 1674, "that Osborne hath proposed a way or method not to want parliaments any more."[18] But the financial problem proved intractable. By January 1675 payments were stopped, the fleet was in decay, and the King longed for thirty ships with which to make England the equal to her neighbors.[19] Fortunately Danby had a second string to his bow: a method to give the King control of the House of Commons. This method comprehended both the pursuit of Anglican policies and the creation of a vigorous Court party. Danby met with the bishops at Lambeth in January 1675 and devised a program for the conviction of recusants and the suppression of conventicles. At the same time, he gave place, pensions, and bribes to loyal members of Parliament—to the rank and file as well as to the leaders. Thus equipped he undertook to manage Parliament for the King. "Treasurer hath undertaken with the King," wrote Harbord, "to help him to money this session."[20] A politician could preserve his hold on an office, as well as gain it, by undertaking to secure the King a vote of supply.

The session opened in April with an assault on the power of patronage itself. Sir William Coventry, the most incorruptible man in the House, introduced a bill that would compel members of Parliament who were appointed to office either to refuse the office or to resign from the Commons (though they could seek reelection). Sir William defended his bill with warmth, pointing out that whereas there were 40 pensioners and placemen in the House in 1661 there were now 200, and predicting that soon Parliament would only register edicts, as did the Parlement of Paris.[21] But Sir William was answered by an equally powerful speech from Daniel Finch, who shrewdly observed that this bill would force the King to bestow all offices and employments upon the Lords. Why, he asked, should their abilities alone be rewarded? His argument appears to have carried the day, for the House rejected the bill by 145 to 113.[22]

The 1675 session of Parliament put to a test Danby's methods of parliamentary management. In part those methods proved successful, for Coventry's bill went down in defeat and Danby survived an impeachment brought against him by the followers of Arlington. But in a deeper sense they were a failure, for Danby was unable to secure for Charles the £300,000 he sought. Even worse, the Commons, not unmindful of the power of the purse, condemned the practice of anticipating revenues and asked that the customs be appropriated to the maintenance of the navy.[23]

The causes of Danby's failure were many—Arlington's division of the Court party, the anger of the Commons that English forces served in France, and the Shirley-Fagg dispute between the two Houses (a dispute fomented by Shaftesbury in order to provoke a dissolution).[24] But the fundamental cause was the untimeliness of Danby's appeal to narrow Anglicanism. As the Earl of Orrery explained to Danby during a long night of talk in July 1675, the Church party was once numerous, and having no fear of popery, "all our edge was set against Non-Conformists." But the fear of popery had now grown so great that an appeal to the church will not work. He urged Danby to scrap the new oath that he and the bishops had devised, by which men must swear not to seek to alter the existing government in the church and the state.[25]

Danby's reply is significant. He told Orrery that the King could rest with safety on no other party than the Church party, and that it was the most dangerous condition imaginable for the King to be left without a party.[26] Lord Burleigh would have been shocked to have been told that the Queen must rely upon a party, but Danby lived in a different age, an age in which Parliament was riven by the struggle of parties. And in that struggle, Danby was determined that the Court party should prevail. To ensure that it did, he was resolved to pursue a Protestant foreign policy and to adopt an Anglican ecclesiastical policy. And to ensure that it prevailed, he was prepared to use corruption and resort to energetic management. In the summer of 1675, he began the systematic organization of the Excise pensioners; by autumn some 30 members had pensions on the Excise.[27] That same autumn the ministers met to prepare business for Parliament, letters were sent out urging the attendance of loyal members at Parliament, and these same loyal members were instructed how to behave in the House of Commons.[28]

A Court party serving the King was Danby's alternative to the King's entering into an undertaking with the leaders of the opposition. Such an undertaking still seemed possible to some men in June 1675. The appearance of Shaftesbury and Winchester at court led to a flurry of rumors that the lord treasurer would be thrown out and the opposition lords brought in.[29] But Charles chose to stick with Danby's strategy of creating a powerful Court party, a strategy that was put to the test, with varying success, in the next three Parliaments.

In the autumn of 1675, Danby prepared more carefully for Parliament than he had that spring, but he failed once again to secure for the King the money he needed. It is true that the Commons voted £300,000 to build 20 ships, but they tacked that sum, an inadequate sum to begin with, to a bill appropriating the customs to the maintenance of the navy. This was quite unacceptable to the King, who prorogued Parliament without receiving any supply. There were two reasons for Danby's failure, both forseen by the Earl of Orrery. To begin with, the Nonconformists, vexed at the failure of all negotiations for liberty of conscience, joined with the party of the opposition lords to carry most votes in Parliament.[30] Secondly, fear of corruption led members, even royalist members, to oppose the measures of the court. In October, Sir Nicholas Carew moved that every member, upon taking his seat, swear that he had not taken money or place from King or minister; in November a committee was named to determine what acts constituted bribery in the election of members to Parliament.[31] As Kenneth Haley observes, "Danby's pensions had not, after all, been sufficient to sway the 'Pensionary Parliament'"[32]

In 1677 they nearly were. The Danbean system never came closer to success. Parliament voted £600,000 for the building of 30 ships and rejected a motion to appropriate the customs to the use of the navy. It also renewed the Additional Excise for three years. "The Lord Treasurer did so order the matter," wrote his Yorkshire neighbor, Sir John Reresby, "that the King's party increased rather than the other; but it was much feared that some votes were gained more by purchase than affection."[33] Yet at the very moment of success, a cloud appeared on the horizon that threatened failure. On 4 April

1677, Danby warned the King that men's fears at the success of French arms had grown so great that he and his ministers would lose all credit unless some action was taken.[34]

Danby's tragedy was that he could not persuade Charles to take that action. The closing weeks of the 1677 session and the whole of the spring session of 1678 offer testimony enough to men's fears that Charles did not mean to check the growing power of France. Their fears redoubled when Charles raised an army, ostensibly to be employed against France, but actually, thought the Country party, to be employed in the government of England. These mounting fears led on 11 May 1678 to a vote in the Commons to condemn the King's ministers. This vote provoked Charles and Danby to take action—action to discipline the Court party, not to alter their foreign policy. Charles banished Henry Savile from court, dismissed Sir William Lowther from the Customs for opposing the court, and warned all other courtiers that the same fate awaited them should they oppose royal policies. Danby brought all his creatures up to London to ensure a majority for the court. The mustermasters of the other party followed suit. Recruits arrived by every coach. The House soon numbered 403 members.[35] "The Lord Treasurer," reported the French ambassador, "has won more voices in Parliament."[36] But these votes were only sufficient to prevent further addresses against ministers and to secure £200,000 for disbanding the army. They were not sufficient to secure money for the support of troops in Flanders or an additional revenue for the crown. The final weeks of the 1678 session illustrate what might be called, after its author Sir William Temple, Temple's Law: when the court falls into the true interest of the nation, it can, through corruption, carry the House; when it does not, it cannot.[37]

It was of the nature of parliamentary undertakings in the seventeenth century that they only occurred at moments of crisis. It was the collapse of the Elizabethan system in 1610 that led to Sir Henry Neville's undertaking. It was the deepest crisis of the century, that of 1640, that led to Bedford's, and it was the disaster at Chatham in 1667 that led to Buckingham's. It is therefore not surprising that the crisis engendered by the Popish Plot and the impeachment of Danby led to renewed attempts at parliamentary undertaking. The leaders of the opposition stood ready to rescue the King. Indeed, it was a constant complaint that they opposed the government only to make themselves the more indispensable. In 1675 the Earl of Lindsey complained to Danby about those who affected popularity merely to gain preferment. And Sir Francis North later observed, "Men are chosen into great assemblies because they have no offices, and in the assembly are never satisfied till they have offices and advantages either in immediate profit, or strength, which, after confusion entered in, is to bring in profit."[38] But Charles had no mind to bring the leaders of the opposition into office. The crisis having not yet broken, he was able in January 1676 to dismiss Holles and Halifax from the council and in February 1676 to order Shaftesbury to leave town. He was then riding the crest of his power, hopeful of aid from France and promised by Danby financial support from Parliament. The next two years transformed the scene.

It was the Popish Plot and the letter produced by Ralph Montagu that undermined the Danbean citadel in the autumn of 1678. Until then Danby had kept the Court party level with the Country party; after 1678 it shrank to a mere fraction of its former self. It was not the plot itself that brought Danby down, but the pervasive fear of a popish successor, a fear that the plot exploited. Nor was it Danby's letter of 25 March 1678 alone that destroyed him, but rather the growing suspicion, confirmed by the letter, that the court intended to set aside the use of Parliaments. In September, Titus Oates told his portentous tale of a plot by the Jesuits to assassinate Charles in order to place his Catholic brother on the throne. It was pure fiction, but such was the fear of popery in England that there was no stopping Parliament, when it met in October, from investigating the plot and demanding the removal of the Duke from the King's presence and councils. The courtiers joined in the prosecution of the plot. When the contest was merely one of court or country, observed Narcissus Luttrell, the courtiers were numerous enough to carry some issues by four or five votes, or to lose others by four or five; but in this session, the courtiers applied "themselves earnestly to the prosecution of the Popish Plot." They went on very unanimously and came even to consider "excluding the Duke of York from the Crown as a Papist."[39]

A similar majority appeared when Ralph Montagu, on 19 December, read to the House a letter that Danby had written to him on 25 March 1678. In that letter Danby ordered Montagu, then ambassador to France, to negotiate a French subsidy, so that Charles need not meet Parliament for three years. Those who had been uncertain were now convinced that the court sought to govern by a standing army, not by Parliaments.[40] Two days later the Commons, by a vote of 179 to 116, voted to impeach the Earl of Danby for high treason. Among the 179 were many placemen, a fact that infuriated Charles. He promptly suspended from office Sir Stephen Fox, Sir Francis Winnington, Sir Robert Holmes, and Sir John Holmes.[41] But these draconian measures had no effect. The anger of the House at the lord treasurer continued unabated. To save Danby from the vehemence of his enemies, Charles prorogued Parliament on 30 December.[42] The significance of the autumn 1678 session of the Pensionary Parliament is manifest: it showed that in a crisis the power of place and pension was no match for the dictates of passion and principle.

It was not simply the practice of corruption that fell, but the whole Danbean edifice—the appeal to the church, the pursuit of a Protestant foreign policy, the creation of a Court party that was the King's own party. During the autumn session, Danby had sought popularity by driving on the investigation of the plot and by proposing in the Lords that the King should become the head of the Protestants in Europe.[43] But it now rang hollow. Men no longer trusted a lord treasurer who would sell his country to France for six million livres. A second path of escape from the present crisis was not to meet Parliament at all. But the need for money to disband the troops was too insistent, and all efforts to secure the money from France or from the Orphan's Fund or by retrenching expenses failed.[44]

It was during this crisis, with his life in peril and with all hope of securing money gone, that Danby turned to negotiations with the opposition and entered into an undertaking with them. He turned, however, not to Shaftesbury and his lieutenants but to Lord Holles and the Presbyterian wing of the Country party. Lord Holles, the Denzil Holles of 1641, was now an elder statesman, moderate in his opinions, a pragmatic man, who would even deal with the Duke of York. Since January 1674 his house in London had been the meeting place of those opposition lords who sought employment at court through negotiations with the Duke. Holles had an unrivaled record as a parliamentary undertaker. In 1641 he had joined with Lord Say in his abortive undertaking—he was expected to enter office as secretary of state. Again in 1643 he was spoken of as a possible secretary. In April 1660 he sought to come into office with the Suffolk House cabal.[45] Thus in 1679, when Danby sought him out, he was quite ready to do business. They soon reached an understanding. Danby was to persuade the King to dissolve Parliament, disband the troops, and send away the Duke. Holles, on his part, undertook, if Danby would resign from office and retire from affairs, to turn his impeachment into a mild censure and to secure the money needed to disband the troops.[46] By 20 January the negotiations were completed; on the twenty-fourth, the King dissolved Parliament. The court had now met the chief condition laid down in Shaftesbury's celebrated letter of 1675 for the opposition lords to enter the court. Shaftesbury had not negotiated the dissolution, but he was exultant that it had been negotiated.[47]

"'Tis said," reported a newsletter of 24 January, "that the Non-Conformists and malcontents to dissolve the Parliament offered to do great service to the King in the next. But probably both are deceived."[48] Deceived they were. The intense joy displayed by the opposition at the dissolution gave advertisement to the court that they had miscalculated. In the ensuing elections, the King remained indifferent, not concerning himself with the results. A few courtiers struggled valiantly against the tide of county sentiment. The opposition won 302 seats in the new Parliament; the number of courtiers fell to 158.[49] But Lord Holles and his allies in the Commons—Boscawen, Littleton, and Hampden—were likewise deceived. When Parliament met in March, they were unable to exercise any control over it. The Commons drove on the impeachment of Danby and demanded the exclusion of the Duke of York. The reasons for the failure of the undertakers were many. In the first place, the aged Holles and his Nonconformist allies in the House of Commons had nothing approaching a majority in the old House; their problems were doubly compounded in the new House, where there were more than 200 new members, members filled with hatred for the lord treasurer and fear of a popish successor. In fact, a year later Lord Holles confessed to Charles his disappointment and anger at the conduct of the new Parliament.[50] It would be unfair to Lord Holles to believe that he ever thought that he and his allies could control the new House of Commons. Rather, like Neville and Bedford before him, he believed he understood the House. He believed that the dissolution of Parliament and the resignation of the lord treasurer would lead the Commons to mitigate its severity against Danby. Herein he miscalculated.[51]

Lord Holles's undertaking presents a puzzle: why was nothing heard of it after 30 January 1679? Having entered upon the undertaking, Lord Holles seems to have deserted it. The letters, memoirs, and debates of the time record no effort to organize the House, no attempt to save Danby, no resulting outcry against undertakers. There is no sign of an undertaking in February or March—with one possible exception. When Parliament met in March, the court sought to secure the election of Sir Thomas Meres as Speaker. It was an odd choice, for Meres had long been an enemy of Danby. On the other hand, Meres hoped to become a commissioner of the Treasury and was an ally of Sir Thomas Littleton, whom Gilbert Burnet names as one of Lord Holles's lieutenants.[52] It is possible that the nomination of Meres was the first step in the execution of Holles's design and that the Commons's rejection of Meres as Speaker was the decisive step in its final death. After a week of controversy, the Commons settled upon William Gregory as Speaker, a man nominated, not by the court, but by Lord Russell, a lieutenant of the Earl of Shaftesbury.

In truth, it was the Earl of Shaftesbury and his wing of the Country party who were in the ascendant, not Lord Holles and his friends. And it was the undertaking entered into by Shaftesbury and Essex in the spring of 1679 that pushed Holles's scheme aside. Or perhaps it would be more accurate to say that the scheme of Shaftesbury and Essex merged with Holles's, for both the French and the Dutch ambassadors attribute to Holles the concept, if not the carrying out, of those remarkable changes that occurred in April.[53]

As early as 22 February, the Duke of Monmouth, the King's son by Lucy Walters, entered into conversations with the Earls of Shaftesbury and Essex. The Duke of York stood amazed to see Monmouth whisper with them and yet go unpunished.[54] Upon an assurance brought by Monmouth from the leaders of the House of Commons that the King would have money if he removed Danby, Charles dismissed the Earl on 16 March.[55] But the commissioners named to replace Danby at the Treasury were unacceptable to the opposition.[56] Negotiations continued, abetted by the Earl of Sunderland, an ambitious courtier who was well placed to play both sides of the street, for he was both secretary of state and Shaftesbury's nephew. Monmouth and Sunderland now opened negotiations with the Earl of Essex, whom Charles named first commissioner of the Treasury on 26 March. Essex, who had served as lord lieutenant of Ireland and who was a pillar of the Country party, earned considerable obloquy by coming into office before the rest. He answered that he did so in order to promote further changes at court.[57]

Those changes proceeded slowly. On 14 April, Lord Robartes, a Presbyterian peer, met privately with the King for two hours, giving rise to the rumor that Charles would soon name him lord treasurer or lord privy seal.[58] Three days later, Barillon, the French ambassador, wrote:

> I am informed that there has been a secret negotiation for some days between the principal leaders of the cabals in Parliament and the King of England. They treat of an entire change in the Privy Council and in the direction of finances, as also about placing the chief offices and the management of affairs in the hands of men who until now have been the most opposed to the Court. They

promise on their part to insure that his Majesty has sufficient money for the needs of the state, as well as for his own personal needs. I believe that the terms of this agreement are concluded, though one must assume nothing in this country until it happens.[59]

Two days after Barillon had sent off this dispatch, Sir Robert Southwell sent similar news to the Duke of Ormond. He had learned that night at Whitehall that Shaftesbury, Robartes, and Halifax were to enter the council, that a select committee, both for foreign and home affairs, should sit in the Council Chamber, and that the Ordnance, the Treasury, and the Treasury of the Navy should be put in commission.[60]

These anticipated changes burst upon the political world on 21 April 1679, though disguised by Sir William Temple's elaborate scheme for an all-party government, functioning through a revamped Privy Council.[61] But for this bit of constitutional jugglery, the changes announced by Charles on 21 April might have been seen for what they were, an undertaking by Essex and Shaftesbury to serve the King in Parliament.

What the undertaking consisted of can never be known for certain. One has only the rumors reported by Barillon and Southwell, and what did occur. The changes that did occur were three in number: (1) Charles promised to rely upon the advice of a Privy Council, over half of whose members were of the opposition and whose lord president was the Earl of Shaftesbury.[62] (2) The Treasury was placed in a commission of five, which the Earl of Essex headed and which contained four other members acceptable to the Country party.[63] (3) The Admiralty was placed in a commission of seven, headed by Sir Henry Capel, the Earl of Essex's brother, and containing three other men who had opposed the court in the past.[64] It is difficult, wrote Barillon, to conceive of a greater change in the government; affairs will now be in the hands of those who have opposed the court in the past.[65]

Charles conceded more to Shaftesbury and Essex than James I ever conceded to Neville or Charles I to Bedford or Charles himself to Buckingham. He brought the leaders of the opposition into office as well as the council. Invincible necessity, not a careless regard for the prerogative, drove him to it. Only Parliament could vote him the £200,000 he needed to disband the army, and those who led in Parliament were not going to vote that money as long as Danby or his dependents were at the Treasury.[66] The leaders of the House of Commons were not unmindful of the power of the purse. On 15 April they had denounced Sir Stephen Fox for offering to advance the King the money he needed to disband the army. "They are very much displeased," wrote Charles Hatton, "that his Majesty should be able to raise any money but by them."[67]

The motives of Shaftesbury and Essex and their friends are harder to untangle than Charles's. The royalists, of course, had no doubt what their motives were: these men sought the power and profit that office brings. "Men that have tasted power and profit and are ousted," observed Lord Guilford, "are the most eager to overturn all to make way for themselves again."[68] Yet it is likely that these men desired office more for the power it gave them than for the profit. Shaftesbury was no careerist, as J. R. Jones has observed.[69] He and his confederates feared that the Earl of Danby and the Duke of York designed to introduce a military and arbitrary government.[70] They entered the council in April 1679 not merely to enjoy the honor it conferred but also to be in a position to defend the liberties of England.

The undertaking into which Shaftesbury and Essex entered had a short and disastrous career. "Whether we are landing upon New Atlantis or only in view of old Brazil," wrote Edward Harley, "time will show."[71] Time soon showed that they were only in view of old Brazil; no new continent appeared. The brave, new undertaking failed, and failed for three substantial reasons. To begin with, the undertakers lost all credit in the House of Commons. Then the Exclusion Crisis wrecked whatever harmony existed between King and Commons. Finally, it soon became evident that Charles had no intention of surrendering power to his new ministers.

Shaftesbury and Essex now faced the same problem that Neville, Bedford, and Temple had faced: how to put on the livery of the court and still retain one's virtue. Merely being preferred made them suspect. Those who gained preferment, wrote the Duke of York, "have already quite lost their credit."[72] Within a fortnight suspicious country squires joined with disappointed office-seekers to introduce a self-denying ordinance, a bill requiring the resignation of any member who accepted an office or a place of profit.[73]

But it was not this bill (which died with the session) that marked the real failure of the undertakers. That failure came when they sought to secure Charles the money he needed to equip the fleet. In early May, Lord Russell, one of the new councillors, asked the Commons to proceed to a bill for raising money for the navy. His speech made little impression. Then on 14 May, the King sent a message to the Commons asking for money for the fleet. In the ensuing debate, Henry Powle, also recently named to the council, spoke for supply. His former colleagues in opposition taunted him for changing his opinions because he had won preferment. The House showed itself to be in no mood to vote money for the fleet until justice was done to Danby, the popish lords in the Tower were tried, Lauderdale was removed, and the Protestant succession secured.[74] The very day before they voted such a resolution, the Earl of Danby, imprisoned in the Tower, wrote the King that the late changes could only be justified if the new ministers secured him money, and he predicted that they would not be able to secure money for setting out the fleet until the Commons had "everything they wanted."[75]

And what they wanted was the condemnation of Danby's pardon and the exclusion of the Duke of York. It is doubtful whether in the best of times the undertaking entered into by Shaftesbury and Essex could have succeeded, but it is certain that the passions unleashed by the pardon of Danby and the possible succession of a papist wrecked it totally. These two issues created an unbridgeable gap between King and Commons. Charles, though he was willing to yield in many things, was not willing to yield in these.[76] It was a hopeless endeavor for the new councillors to seek to persuade the Commons to accept the pardon, for the pardon undermined the power of impeachment. But they did seek to persuade the House to accept limitations upon a popish successor rather than his exclusion. The critical debates occurred on 30 April, when the new councillors supported limitations, and on 11 May, when they opposed exclusion. Capel, Littleton, Cavendish, Powle, Vaughan, Lee, Meres, all named either to the council or the Admiralty, all once counted the greatest of patriots, now spoke for limitations and against exclusion. But they could not sway the House, which voted, 207 to 128, to exclude the Duke of York from the succession.[77]

Sir William Temple believed that the Earl of Shaftesbury had caused the Commons to reject limitations, but therein he erred. It is true that Shafftesbury was opposed to limitations, but he had no control over the House of Commons. No politician did until the emergence of political parties, whose very gestation was now in progress. Meanwhile, however, the House was out of control. The heads of the cabal, wrote Barillon, do not know where they are for the great number of new members whom no one dares contradict.[78]

Even had there been no Exclusion Crisis, no pardon to Danby, the undertaking would have failed. It would have failed because Charles had no intention of granting real power to those whom he brought into office and the council. This became evident almost at once, when he refused to proceed to further changes in the government. It was widely rumored that the new scheme of administration would include not only a new Admiralty commission but new commissions for the Ordnance, the Chancery, and the Treasury of the Navy. Furthermore, the lord lieutenancies, commissions of the peace, and the governors of ports were to be purged of adherents of the Duke of York. Men spoke of Lord Russell as Colonel Legg's replacement at Portsmouth and whispered that Shaftesbury should become lord chancellor and Essex either lord treasurer or lord lieutenant of Ireland.[79] But Charles had other ideas. He told the Earl of Arlington that "the new ministers he had got were for jostling out his old faithful servants, but they should never gain that point of him."[80] Nor did he heed their counsel when they advised him to dismiss the Earl of Lauderdale in Scotland. For Charles the entire scheme of a Treasury commission headed by Essex, of a new Privy Council, and of a new Admiralty commission was but a stratagem to win time and gain advantage. He played his cards skillfully, and he won a vote of supply for disbanding the army. But he did not fool Shaftesbury, or Country party stalwarts like Colonel Birch. "Are we come here to give money for some few new men being put into the Privy Council?" asked Birch. "It must not be the addition of four or five persons to the Council that will do it, it must be thoroughly done."[81] And the House of Commons did refuse further supply. It was their riposte to Charles's artifice.

All hopes of money being gone and only the prospect of further violent remonstrances remaining, Charles prorogued Parliament on 27 May 1679. His manner of doing so made a mockery of his promise to follow the advice of the Privy Council in all his weighty and important affairs. He prorogued Parliament on the advice of Sunderland, Halifax, and Essex alone, without consulting the Privy Council. Shaftesbury was furious, but there was little he could do, for the lords of the treasury had told Charles that they had the money needed to pay off the Mediterranean fleet.[82] Charles for the next eighteen months was not a powerful King, but he was a solvent King, and therefore need not meet Parliament.

Charles prorogued Parliament without consulting the Privy Council; in July he dissolved Parliament against the Privy Council's advice. On Thursday the third of July, at Hampton Court, the council met. Shaftesbury and all the others who spoke opposed the dissolution, but Charles ordered it nevertheless. "I have just freed myself," he later told some assembled courtiers, "from the burden which weighed upon me. How they have deceived themselves, if they imagined that want of money would force me to extremities! But I shall find means to pay the fleet, and to manage economically; it will be difficult and uncomfortable for me, but I will rather submit to anything than endure the gentlemen of the Commons any longer."[83]

The new ministers responded in various ways to Charles's conduct. The moderates—Essex and Halifax in particular—continued to work with the King. But the extremists, led by Shaftesbury, raged against him for refusing to heed the Council's advice. They threw themselves with great energy into the parliamentary elections held in August and September 1679.

The result was a Parliament more hostile to the court than ever.[84] Charles therefore prorogued it, and at the same time dismissed his turbulent lord president from office. Shaftesbury's dismissal in October was followed by Essex's resignation in November. Essex lay down his staff as first lord of the Treasury because the King would give no assurances that he would again meet Parliament.[85] Then in January 1680, Lord Russell, Lord Cavendish, Sir Henry Capel, and Henry Powle, acting in concert and upon Shaftesbury's advice, resigned from the Privy Council. A few weeks later Capel, Vaughan, and Lee resigned from the Admiralty. Only by resignation, Shaftesbury wrote the four councillors, could they restore their reputations, which now suffered for being thought the authors of the counsel to dissolve the last Parliament and of the advice to pursue good husbandry now, so that the King might live without Parliaments.[86]

The resignations of the four councillors and the three commissioners marked the final demise of a once hopeful undertaking. Essex's dream of reconciling King and nation had led only to a King and nation more deeply divided than ever. Charles now resolved to govern without consulting the despised gentlemen of the Commons. Yet the experiment of governing without Parliament might fail, and the King might find it necessary or useful to meet Parliament again. For that reason Charles, infinitely flexible, ever the opportunist, unbounded by scruples, had entered into negotiations with Shaftesbury in November 1679. Edmund Warcup, a magistrate, served as intermediary between the King and the Earl. The King laid down his conditions for Shaftesbury's return to court: that he agree with His Majesty on the question of the validity of Danby's pardon and on the right of the bishops to vote on its validity. Sunderland meanwhile sought to persuade Shaftesbury to take Essex's position at the Treasury. But the negotiations foundered upon Shaftesbury's insistence that Charles agree to divorce the Queen and consent to the exclusion of his brother from the succession. Knowing that Charles would not accept these conditions, Shaftesbury declined to attend a meeting with the King arranged for the afternoon of 5 November, in Chiffinch's chambers.[87] This episode, though a minor one, illustrates a curious truth about the politics of these times: parliamentary undertakings were both hopeless and unavoidable. They were hopeless because the King did not intend to surrender to the undertakers. They were unavoidable because he dared not meet Parliament without trying to come to some understanding with its leaders.

This truth was illustrated once again in May 1680, when Charles and his ministers contemplated the meeting of Parliament. On this occasion a most unlikely parliamentary undertaker appeared on the scene, Horatio Lord Townshend. As a young man, in 1659, Townshend had been elected to the Council of State by the Rump Parliament. In the 1670s he became an enemy of Danby and an ally of Shaftesbury. He was the original leader of the Whigs in Norfolk, but he adhered rather to the moderate wing of the party than to the extreme.[88] In early May 1680, he urged the King to meet Parliament and to inform the two Houses that he would leave all matters to them but the matter of the Queen and the Duke. If the King would do this, he, Townshend, "would undertake for a good Session."[89] The undertaking strikes one as improbable because Townshend had never been a prominent leader in Parliament. But there was an explanation for his sudden prominence now. It lay in the death of the venerable and much respected Lord Holles in February 1680. Lord Townshend now took his place as the leader of the moderates. Lord Holles had always worked closely with Sir John Baber, a wealthy Presbyterian merchant in the City; Lord Townshend now entered into a similar alliance with Baber.[90] In February, Baber held out hopes of managing a new farm of the excise that would increase that revenue by £200,000, though by March these hopes vanished. During these negotiations, however, Baber met frequently with the King, with Sunderland, with the Duke—so frequently that the clergy began to fear that the court was treating with the Presbyterians.[91] At the same time, Shaftesbury's influence declined, even among members of Parliament.[92] It was from these circumstances that Lord Townshend's undertaking was born. But it was still-born. The King declined it, and so did Shaftesbury. It was Shaftesbury's strategy at this time to put off the meeting of

Parliament until the 9d Excise and the Additional Duty on Wine expired, that thereby the King might be forced into a greater compliance with Parliament.[93]

Charles was able to reject Lord Townshend's undertaking because the commissioners of the Customs in April promised him that he could subsist without meeting Parliament.[94] Subsist he could, but only as a feeble, inglorious monarch. The Admiralty Board asked for £350,000 to set out the Straits Fleet and convoys; the King could give them only £200,000. Tangier, for want of men and supplies, stood in imminent danger of being lost. Charles desired to enter into an alliance with the Dutch, but could not for want of money to furnish the 10,000 men the alliance called for.[95] The cost of governing without Parliament was weakness abroad. Charles's ministers—Sunderland, Laurence Hyde, and Sidney Godolphin—were not satisfied with so ignominious a role for a King of England. In the spring and summer of 1680, they therefore sought to negotiate treaties with Spain, the Dutch, and the Emperor, but the Spanish and the Dutch insisted that such alliances were worthless unless the King met Parliament. In June, therefore, Charles signed a treaty with Spain that called for the meeting of Parliament in the autumn.[96]

Charles's ministers hoped that these alliances would win them the friends they needed in Parliament, but they did not rely solely upon the credit these alliances would bring them. They also opened negotiations with the leaders of Parliament. In June there was a great meeting at Althorp, Sunderland's country seat in Northamptonshire. At the meeting Sunderland succeeded in winning Halifax's support for his scheme of management in the next Parliament.[97] But Halifax had little credit in the House of Commons, where the real problem lay. Sunderland therefore opened negotiations with the leaders of the House of Commons, negotiations that led in the autumn of 1680 to three separate undertakings, one by Sir Henry Capel, another by the Earl of Shaftesbury, and a third by a group of Whigs called the Southamptons.

A month before Parliament assembled, which was on 21 October, Sir Henry Capel, brother of the Earl of Essex and former head of the Admiralty, proposed that the Duke of York retire from court, that limitations be placed upon a Catholic successor, that Parliament give sufficient money to equip the fleet, and that such money be administered by commissioners named by Parliament.[98] Capel's proposals were acceptable to the court—indeed, Sunderland may have prompted them. They also represented the wishes of the moderates—of Essex, who had been lord lieutenant of Ireland; of Halifax, who had entered into like measures at Althorp; of Sir William Temple, with whom Capel was visiting at Sheen when Sunderland dropped by one September evening.[99] But their scheme for the management of the Commons ran up against the same insuperable obstacle that Lord Holles's had, and Townshend's. It did not provide for the exclusion of the Duke of York from the succession, and the leaders of the House of Commons would accept nothing less. Capel soon discovered this and dropped the proposal. In fact, when the House met, he himself made the first motion to exclude a popish successor.[100]

The failure of Capel's scheme caused Sunderland to turn to Shaftesbury, who exercised a far greater sway over the House of Commons than did Capel. Since his dismissal the previous October, the Earl had opposed the court with characteristic audacity, courage, intelligence, vehemence, and lack of scruple. He and his followers promoted petitions for the meeting of Parliament, presented the Duke as a recusant, defended the truth of the Popish Plot, and claimed to have discovered a like plot in Ireland. No man was more bitterly hated at court than Shaftesbury. Thus it is not surprising that in June 1680 the court negotiated with all segments of the opposition but the followers of Shaftesbury.[101] Then suddenly in mid-August, there were rumors that Shaftesbury was to be made treasurer, that he was privately reconciled to the court, that there were to be other alterations, that several things were to be done to make the meeting of Parliament in October a happy session.[102] Early in September, Barillon promised Louis XIV that he would endeavor to discover how far Shaftesbury would allow himself to be tempted by the offers that the court made him. Eleven days later he reported that Sunderland employed all his authority and all his industry to persuade Shaftesbury to enter into an accommodation.[103]

In early October, Sunderland's authority and industry met with success. On the seventh Henry Sidney wrote to the Prince of Orange: "The Duke of Monmouth, my Lord Shaftesbury, my Lord Russell, and several others, do undertake to do great matters for the King, if he will part with the Duke, and I believe there may be a good session, if that be, though the people are very angry at this time."[104] On the same day, Barillon reported that Sunderland and Shaftesbury "do reciprocally promise one another, so much as they can, to conciliate the King and Parliament." "The exclusion of the Duke of York," he added a few days later, "will be the first condition, though I believe that the leaders of the cabal, not trusting the King or his ministers, will wish to place the government, in some fashion, in their hands." They wished, he continued, to change the governors of fortified places, to remove Ormond from Ireland, to have the management of any money voted the King, and to exclude the Duke of Lauderdale from Scottish affairs.[105]

In this undertaking to do great matters for the King, there was no mention of offices for the undertakers. This was not an accidental oversight; it was a deliberate omission. Shaftesbury knew that their credit in the House would be destroyed within three days if they made a particular accommodation.[106] But as the negotiations progressed, talk of particular offices arose. A few days after Parliament opened, Sunderland promised Shaftesbury that the King would grant all that Parliament demanded, provided that Parliament gave the King the money he needed. There was also a secret proviso: Parliament should give the King the power to name his successor. Monmouth naturally flattered himself that he would be named, and Sunderland humored him in this belief. Furthermore, in the execution of this undertaking Monmouth should resume his old offices, Shaftesbury become chancellor or lord treasurer, and Lord Russell be given a great office. But none of these steps should be taken until the Duke of York had been excluded from the succession.[107]

The undertaking failed, as all previous undertakings had failed, but for a different reason. The undertakers suffered no discredit in the Commons. Indeed, they carried their favorite measure, exclusion, through the House in nine days. Rather, their broker at court failed them. Sunderland played the same role in this undertaking that Rochester played in Neville's, Hamilton in Bedford's, and Bristol in Temple's; he was the intermediary at court for those who undertook to manage the Commons. But he could not persuade the King to consent to exclusion, as the tumultuous events of this session bore witness. The court, through its influence in the House of Lords and through the eloquence of Lord Halifax, secured the defeat of the exclusion bill. The initial response of the Commons was to vote a violent address against the Earl of Halifax, who had led the forces in the Lords against exclusion, but its more sober response was to seek to bargain with the King. On 21 December the House of Commons told the King that they would vote the money needed for Tangiers and the fleet if he would consent to the exclusion of the Duke of York, accept an act of association to guarantee the Duke's exclusion, purge the courts of ill judges, reform the deputy lieutenancies and commissions of the peace, and put the navy and militia into such hands as may be trusted.[108]

To this public bargain some of the principal leaders of the House of Commons sought to add a private accommodation. They were led by Ralph Montagu, who had long sought the office of secretary of state and who had no hopes, once he had produced Danby's letter in the Commons, of securing it through favor at court. Others among them were Sir William Jones, learned in the law, eloquent in speech, once attorney general, recently elected to the House of Commons where he at once established his ascendancy; Sir Francis Winnington, formerly solicitor general, the eloquent opponent of the pardoning power, now out of office and anxious to return; Lord Russell, less brilliant than the others but more respected for his honesty, openess, and steadfastness to the cause; William Harbord, a careerist who had sought the year before to climb to office in the Admiralty over the wrecked career of Samuel Pepys.[109] With the exception of Lord Russell, these men had in common a desire for office, experience in matters of state, and a reputation that prevented them from securing office through court favor. Because two of these men, Ralph Montagu and Lord Russell, owned splendid houses on Southampton Square, they were called the Southamptons.[110]

In late December they opened negotiations with the King through Sunderland and Portsmouth. They had the full support of Monmouth but not of Shaftesbury, who continued to believe that to seek office before exclusion was gained would ruin their cause. The immediate purpose of the negotiations was to explain the last paragraph of the Commons' address of 21 December, in which certain sums of money were promised the King if he should accept the demands of the House of Commons.[111] But the bargaining soon turned to the bestowal of high office upon the leaders of the House of Commons. Sir William Jones should become chief justice of the Common Pleas; Sir Francis Winnington, attorney general; Lord Russell, governor of Portsmouth; William Harbord, treasurer of the navy; and Colonel Titus, secretary of state. Daniel Finch believed that Ralph Montagu was to become Marquis of Chichester, but Barillon was of the opinion that Montagu sought Sir Leoline Jenkins's office of secretary of state. For Shaftesbury, at least before he denounced the scheme, they sought the office of lord chancellor or lord treasurer, believing it too dangerous to leave him out. Their intrigues had progressed far enough by Monday, 27 December, for someone, perhaps the Duchess of Portsmouth, to arrange a supper that evening with the King at Lord St. Alban's lodgings. Ralph Montagu and William Harbord came that evening, but the King did not.[112]

News of the negotiations soon spread through London and the provinces. "There hath been a universal discourse throughout the City," reported the Nonconformist minister Roger Morrice, "that all things would be healed betwixt the King and Parliament; and that a dozen or more [of the] Commons were to come into places of honour and trust."[113] A newsletter to Warwickshire reported the same: "There is a discourse that several eminent men are like to be found tardy in endeavouring to get preferment by under-practices, which if true you shall hear more of it by the next, for the persons are of such quality that they ought not to be mentioned till the truth is confirmed."[114] Sir Edward Harley wrote home of "the common buzz of some bargain striking up with the Court," and Sir Leoline Jenkins told Henry Sidney on 31 December: "The bargain which all wished might be struck up is somewhat doubted at this time."[115]

It was somewhat doubted of with good reason. The King refused to countenance it, Shaftesbury raged against it, and the House of Commons appeared to repudiate it. On the day before Jenkins wrote to Sidney, the House of Commons voted unanimously, "That no Member of this House shall accept of any Office, or Place of Profit, from the Crown, without the leave of this House; or any promise of any such Office, or Place of Profit, during such time as he shall continue a Member of this House; and that all offenders herein shall be expelled this House."[116] It was the negotiation at St. Albans's lodgings that occasioned this vote, but the vote was not the total repudiation of the undertakers that it might seem to be, nor were Winnington, Titus, Harbord, and Jones hypocrites for introducing and supporting the resolution. Winnington, at the conclusion of a long philippic against placemen and pensionary parliaments, introduced the resolution, and carefully placed in it the words "without the leave of this House." Sir Thomas Lee proposed that they omit these words, but Winnington replied: "I believe the people will be satisfied with any of your members having places whom the House thinks well of." Sir William Jones agreed: "Shall the world say, 'you will make a Vote, be the occasion ever so great, or the man ever so fit, that he must not accept of an office?'" The House left the words in the vote, and Winnington and Jones continued to exercise the same leadership in the House that they had exercised in November and December.[117] The vote of 30 December was rather a condemnation of court pensioners than a censure of parliamentary undertakers.

No man understood better than Shaftesbury what distinguished the two. He who entered the court on the court's terms was a pensioner, a placeman, he was "bought off"; but he who insisted that the court meet his terms, be it the dissolution of Parliament or the exclusion of the Duke of York, was a parliamentary undertaker. This was the message that he proclaimed in his letter to Lord Carlisle in 1675, and this was the policy he pursued in the following five years. When Sir Francis Winnington on 30 December condemned those who "are promised great places to sell their country." he implied the same distinction.[118] The fault lay in selling one's country, not in taking office, and the Southamptons were not going to be bought off. "They will maintain their credit in the House," wrote Barillon, "by agreeing to anything that will please it."[119]

Loss of credit in the House of Commons, therefore, did not wreck the undertaking into which the Southamptons wished to enter. What wrecked it was the King's message of 4 January 1681, refusing the public demands of 21 December. To the bitter end, Sunderland held out the hope that the King would be prevailed upon to accept exclusion, but the King made it clear on the fourth that he would not. The Commons answered by voting several inflammatory addresses against the King's ministers. Charles replied by proroguing and then dissolving Parliament.[120] Though Charles met a new Parliament briefly at Oxford in March 1681, the prorogation in January ended the story of parliamentary undertaking during the Exclusion Crisis.

During that crisis Charles often made use of undertakers. He toyed with them, he deceived them, he used them to divide the opposition, he negotiated with them to win time, but he never surrendered real power to them. That he was not compelled to do so cannot be explained by his skill at parliamentary management. True, under the tutelage of the Earl of Danby, he did seek to build up in the House of Commons a Court party equal to that in the Lords, a party that would allow him to govern through Parliament, not independently of it. Therein he failed. The power of patronage, given the court's suspect policies and the presence of a popish heir in the wings, proved unequal to the task. From 1675 to 1681, Charles exhibited considerable political acumen, but it is an incontrovertible fact that he failed to win control of the House of Commons. He therefore fell back upon the prorogation and dissolution of the House. In May 1679, again in October 1679, throughout the spring of 1680, once again in January 1681, he was able to deny real power to the leaders of the opposition only because he could find the money to govern without having to meet Parliament.[121] A sufficient revenue, not the corrupting power of place and pension, gave Charles his victory. His brother James enjoyed an even greater revenue as James II of England, but his inglorious reign led to a Revolution Settlement that denied to the kings of England a revenue that would allow them to live "of their own." In these changed circumstances, the history of parliamentary undertaking took a very different course.

Chapter V

The Two Faces of
Parliamentary Management: 1689–1697

O
N 13 FEBRUARY 1689, in the exquisitely proportioned splendor of the Banqueting Hall, a grateful nation bestowed upon the Prince and Princess of Orange the crown of England. But that nation did not see fit, in the ensuing months, to bestow upon Their Majesties the same full revenues that their predecessors had enjoyed. For a year Parliament delayed settling the revenue, and then in March 1690 it voted Their Majesties a revenue that was inadequate, encumbered, and temporary. It voted the customs for only four years, and encumbered both it and the excise with loans to pay for the war. The total revenues voted— including the customs—fell short of the cost of governing the realm in time of peace. All this Parliament did deliberately, for it meant the King to be financially dependent on Parliament. "When Princes have not needed money," declared Sir Joseph Williamson, once secretary of state to Charles II, "they have not needed us."[1]

Denied the ability to live "of his own," William had to govern through Parliament, not outside it. This fact raised in an urgent and inescapable fashion the problem of parliamentary management. Ever since the breakdown of the Elizabethan system in 1610, it had been a critical problem, but the Stuarts had possessed a fail-safe system in their ability to prorogue Parliament and live "of their own." William possessed no such system. He must manage the two Houses of Parliament successfully, or they would not vote him the supplies he needed to govern at home and wage war abroad. Nor was it merely a matter of winning supply; it was also a matter of winning supply early in the year, of preventing violent addresses against ministers of state, of defending the prerogative from further erosion, and of securing the laws needed to govern well. Such, then, was the problem. The solution lay in a resort to all the arts of parliamentary management. By no means were these arts simple—a matter of buying off this man or winning that one. On the contrary, these arts were many and complex, though among them one can distinguish five that deserve special notice.

The first of these comprehended the daily management of the business of the two Houses. This was "management" as Thomas Cromwell and Lord Burleigh understood it. Ministers should have bills ready for introduction into the two Houses. The King's councillors, united, loyal, and instructed, should second and support such measures. These same councillors should work closely with the Speaker to ensure that the King's business advanced. No mere country gentleman should be allowed to propose the amount of supply to be given in a session; spokesmen for the court should forestall him. To vigilance and initiative, the court managers should add procedural finesse. They should know when to amend a measure, when to divide the House, when to move for an adjournment, when to call for candles (a procedural tactic first used in the 1690s). It was to these daily arts of management that the second Earl of Sunderland referred when in 1693 he cried out at the "want of management." But he was in error if he thought they would, by themselves, solve very much.[2]

The keenest vigilance and the subtlest procedural finesse were of no use if the government pursued policies anathema to Parliament and the nation. The second art of parliamentary management was the pursuit of policies acceptable to Englishmen. Charles II's greatest triumph in the management of Parliament came in 1670 and 1671 when, publicly at least, he embraced Anglican policies popular in the nation. His greatest failure came when he stood against the wishes of the nation to exclude the Duke of York from the succession. Management did not occur in a vacuum, and one of the essential ingredients of successful management was the pursuit of national policies.

A third ingredient was the successful conduct of the affairs of the realm. To an alarming degree, defeat in war, losses at sea, incompetence in administration, and miscarriages of justice meant ruin to the ministers responsible. Victory made management easier; defeat made it hopeless, as Clarendon discovered after Chatham. Englishmen believed that executive power belonged to the crown, but they wanted that power to be well used. If it was badly used, a clamor would arise that not even the most skillful manager could silence. If it was well used, not all the party spite in the House could dislodge the ministers responsible. Marlborough's victories in Queen Anne's reign must have been worth fourscore placemen to the managers of the two Houses.

With the growth of political parties in Parliament, the problems of parliamentary management multiplied. They multiplied because of the growing willingness of men to oppose the King because they were not entrusted with office—and because their enemies were. To counter this divisive spirit, the Kings of England fell back on what must have been their strongest weapon, stronger even than the power of patronage: an appeal to the loyalty and awe and reverence men owed to the crown. Charles II unwittingly stumbled upon a corollary to this appeal, the idea of an all-party government. The Privy Council of 1679 was an attempt to balance both parties in one government, to pursue a moderate path between the extremes of court and country. William III, more consciously than Charles, sought to balance both parties in a royal government. The pursuit of balanced counsels and the creation of mixed ministries became a fourth art of parliamentary management. William gave office to the leaders of both the Whigs and Tories, and hoped thereby to win the support of their adherents in the two Houses—and so to escape the domination of a single party.

The fifth art of parliamentary management is the one to which historians usually refer when they speak of "parliamentary management," namely, the use of the power of patronage to create a Court party in both Houses of Parliament. The appeal was not to loyalty or principle but to self-interest. The King would win men over by the offer of place, pension, and title. Sir Francis Bacon proposed this course of action to James I; Lord Clifford in Charles II's reign added downright bribery to it; and the earl of Danby raised it to a fine art. Country members cried out against corruption, but the kings of England continued to employ it.

One cannot understand the complexity and subtlety of the politics of William's reign—why one measure carried and another met defeat, why one ministry prospered and another collapsed, without taking into consideration all five of these arts of parliamentary management. But the problem of parliamentary management can be looked at in a different way, one that illuminates more profoundly the sources of power in William's reign. In the management of Parliament, the King sought by his influence, particularly by the discreet use of patronage, to persuade Parliament to support men and measures of his choice. At other times, however, in order to win supply, he yielded to the men and measures demanded by Parliament. These are the two faces of parliamentary management. They may be called the Baconian and the Nevillian, for Sir Francis Bacon first proposed the one and Sir Henry Neville the other. What makes it difficult to understand the politics of William's reign is that one and the same political maneuver—Somers's appointment or Nottingham's removal—could embody both faces of parliamentary management, both the use of patronage to buy men off and the grant of concessions to win supply. It all depended upon whether the King moved toward Parliament or Parliament toward the King, whether Mohammed went to the mountain or the mountain to Mohammed.

In his struggle with the politicians in Parliament, the King possessed many trump cards. Through his councillors, through the Speaker, through the lord keeper, he could take the initiative in the daily management of the two Houses. His exercise of the executive power gave him an unrivaled knowledge of affairs, a knowledge denied to those out of power. He was the recipient of the reverence that men felt for the crown. And he was the cornucopia of all good things, of titles, honors, gifts, office, place, and pensions. These powers added together made William far more than a doge of Venice.

But those politicians who sought to wrest office from the King by their power in the House of Commons possessed their trump cards too. As tribunes of the people, as defenders of the liberties of Englishmen against arbitrary government, they were applauded and cheered in the House. Furthermore, they enjoyed the luxury of being critics of the government. They could denounce miscarriages recklessly, for they bore no responsibility for them. To this one may add their knowledge of the House, of its procedures, of its temper, of its customs, of its quirks and vagaries, a knowledge gained from constant attendance over many years. Finally, there was party. Men denounced the distinction of Whig and Tory, but that distinction inevitably appeared. The leaders of a party found themselves more powerful in the two Houses because they had a party behind them.

The politician who took office, however, faced a serious problem. He discovered that putting on the livery of the court destroyed much of his popularity in the House of Commons. He found that elevation to the Lords—a concomitant of the highest office—took him from the House he knew so well. His power in Parliament eroded. To this problem there was a solution, and the politicians soon stumbled upon it. The solution was reliance upon a party that would support its leaders, in office as well as out.

Behind all these trump cards held by the politician lay one supreme power, the power of the purse. For William there were three sovereign reasons for meeting Parliaments: money, money, and money. He needed a supply to carry on the war, a revenue that could be anticipated, and money for the civil list. Given William's desperate need for money, it is surprising that the Commons never used this lever to wrest from him the right to name his ministers. But they never did. In 1689 they declined William's offer that they nominate the commissioners to send supplies to Ireland. In 1691 they rejected a motion that Parliament name the officers of the navy. In 1696 they drew back from a proposal for the parliamentary nomination of the Board of Trade.[3] In part they declined to nominate the king's ministers because they wanted no responsibility for the administration of the realm, but they also declined because they did not wish to offend a king whose undoubted prerogative it was to name his ministers of state. A frontal attack

[111]

upon his prerogative would be fiercely resisted by William, who was as jealous to preserve the prerogative intact as any Stuart monarch. Therefore any limitations upon his power to name his own servants would have to be oblique and disguised, couched in the language of the court and whispered in the privacy of the closet.

There has been some debate among the Whigs, reported Roger Morrice in December 1689, whether the House of Commons should address the King to employ faithful persons in his great affairs and to give them leave to nominate such to him. But two objections were made to such an address, continued Morrice. In the first place, if the House of Commons should fall into the ill humor it was in the last session, it would name men worse than those now employed. Secondly, "It were an intrenching upon the Prerogative the law has given him, and therefore it might be uneasy to him, though he should grant it." "Hereupon," declared Morrice, "the present resolution is that these particulars above mentioned shall be by private persons humbly offered unto him, and imprinted as far as they can upon him."[4]

From this resolve to employ private persons rather than public addresses to secure the nomination of ministers pleasing to Parliament, the politicians of William's reign did not retreat. They steadfastly refused to demand the formal nomination of ministers of state by Parliament, but they were quite willing to resort to parliamentary undertakings to force themselves into office. William resisted all such importunities. He preferred to name ministers of his own choice and to win support for them in Parliament by all the arts of management at his disposal. As a result there followed a prolonged struggle between a King who would name his own ministers and find support for them in Parliament and the politicians who would use their popularity in Parliament to wrest office from the King. This struggle not only dominated William's reign, it dominated the entire eighteenth century, not to be resolved until the politicians triumphed over the crown in the Age of Reform.

The first chapter in this long story is the formation of the Junto ministry between 1693 and 1697. But that story is only explicable in terms of the failure of balanced counsels in 1689, and the collapse of the Tory ministry of 1690–93.

I must "absolutely go upon the bottom of the trimmers," declared William to the Marquis of Halifax, "that is the good foot."[5] And he meant what he said, for he dreaded surrendering himself to one extreme or the other. Only by balancing diverse interests could he remain in command, and he was determined to remain in command. "He would have men come to his humour," he declared, "not he to theirs."[6] Guided by these calculations, William named ministers who represented all the interests of the nation. The Whigs had done the most to bring him to the throne, so he named leading Whigs to the Treasury and Admiralty commissions. The Earl of Danby had raised the North to his cause, so he named this restless politician lord president and created him Marquis of Carmarthen. The Earl of Halifax, a keen rival of Carmarthen, he named lord privy seal and made a marquis. To win the church interest, he named as secretary of state the stern and unbending Earl of Nottingham, but he balanced this appointment by naming a Whig, the Earl of Shrewsbury, to the other secretaryship. With these ministers, chosen more for their political interests than their administrative abilities, he set out to manage Parliament and govern the realm.

The experiment proved a failure. The council met only for form's sake, ministers dared not speak freely in front of one another, and the privy councillors in Parliament gave only an uncertain lead.[7] Confusion and delay in the government soon gave rise to miscarriages: Londonderry nearly fell for want of prompt relief, Schomberg's army in Ireland lacked supplies, the victualling of the navy was inefficient, and the fleet tarried in Portsmouth while French cruisers preyed on English shipping. The government might have survived these miscarriages had not the Whigs in the House of Commons seized upon them as a weapon for driving Carmarthen and Halifax and Nottingham from office.

But even more fatal to the experiment in balanced counsels was the determination of the Whigs to rake into the faults of past years. They now sought revenge for the years of proscription and disgrace that they had suffered after the dissolution of the Oxford Parliament. In June they moved that all those who stood impeached—the target was Carmarthen—be removed. In November they named committees in both Houses to search out the authors of the "murders" of Russell and Sidney. And during the entire year they obstructed the passage of a bill of indemnity that would have buried the quarrels of the past.[8] Nor were the extreme Whigs the least bit abashed in demanding the removal of the Tories. The Earl of Monmouth continually urged William to throw all Tories out of employment.[9] Thomas Wharton, comptroller of the Household and a manager in the Commons for the King, told William that "trimming between Parties is beneath you and your cause" and urged His Majesty to employ only those "whose principles have brought them to your service and interest."[10]

The extreme Whigs never wanted a mixed ministry to succeed, but the Earl of Shrewsbury did. Yet even the Earl had to admit by December that it had failed. "I wish you could have established your party upon the moderate and honest principled men of both factions," he told William, "but as there be a necessity of declaring, I shall make no difficulty to own my sense, that your Majesty and the government are much more safe depending upon the Whigs, whose designs, if any against, are improbable and remoter than with the Tories, who many of them, questionless, would bring in King James. . . ."[11] William eventually came to agree that trimming had failed, but, deeply offended by the rudeness and arrogance of the Whigs, he was not persuaded that he ought to declare for them. He was the more hesitant because the leaders of the Church party made him such fair promises in the autumn and winter of 1689 and 1690.

The two great spokesmen for the Church party were the Marquis of Carmarthen and the Earl of Nottingham. In the autumn of 1689, they besieged William with their advice. They told him that the Church party was the strongest in Parliament and the nation, that the Church party would remain loyal to him, that the Church party would maintain his prerogative, not tear it down as the Commonwealth party did, and would unite his subjects by promoting an act of indemnity, not divide them as the Whigs did.[12] In December the

Tories made more particular promises. If the King would dissolve Parliament and change the lieutenancy of London, they would undertake to settle a revenue upon him, a revenue that should be an immediate fund of credit.[13] "Your Majesty has no other course nor remedy under Heaven," wrote Sir John Trevor, "unless you will absolutely throw yourself and your Crown upon the Dissenters."[14]

The Dissenters, or the Whigs, as they were coming to be called, pleaded their cause with a like fervor. They had placed William on the throne. They had invaded no part of his lawful prerogative. They had raised him a supply of £2,000,000, despite efforts by the Church party to divert it. They had demonstrated their strength in the Commons by defeating an effort to settle an independent revenue upon Princess Anne.[15] These arguments contained enough truth to cause William to delay a decision to dissolve Parliament until he saw whether the Whigs, in January, would make up the deficiency in the supply bill. Parliament met in January, and the Commons promptly voted to add another shilling in the pound to the two shillings already voted. "It is a good business," William wrote, "but the Whigs are so proud to have triumphed that they undertake everything."[16] Indeed they did, to William's fury. They sought to add to the corporation bill a clause that would proscribe many Tories from political life. They threatened to hold back the supply bill if William balked at accepting the corporation bill.[17] They added a bill of pains and penalties to the bill of indemnity, thus transforming a bill to unite Englishmen into a bill to divide them. And they threatened to address the King against his going in person to Ireland.[18] The consequence of their presumption was to drive William into the hands of the Tories. On 5 February he told Halifax that "he wished he could trim a little longer, but things pressed so, he could not."[19] On the sixth he dissolved Parliament.

William now placed the direction of affairs at home in the hands of the Church party. He had already altered the Admiralty commission in their favor; in March he did the same to the Treasury commission, naming to it men of substance, honest churchmen, men to whom the Tories in the City would lend money. Churchmen, observed Constantijn Huygens, would provide no money as long as the Treasury was in the hands of the Whigs.[20] With the resignation of the Earl of Shrewsbury as secretary in June, a resignation quite unwelcome to William, the ascendancy of the Church party was complete. The conduct of affairs and the management of Parliament now rested in the hands of Carmarthen and Nottingham.

For the next three years, they exercised that power with considerable success. The newly elected Parliament promptly settled a regular revenue upon Their Majesties, declared it to be a fund of credit, and voted an additional supply of £200,000. In the autumn of 1690, Parliament acted with more zeal for the King's service than it had ever done before: it voted him an unprecedented supply of £4,600,000. In 1691–92 Parliament voted him three and a half million and in 1692–93 nearly five million.[21] Nor did the Commons seek to tear the King's ministers from him by impeachments and violent addresses. In time, after three years, the ministry collapsed; but before examining that collapse, it is worth asking why Carmarthen and Nottingham were able to manage Parliament successfully for three years.

They succeeded in the first place because they had behind them what neither Neville nor Bedford nor the Anti-Clarendonians nor the Southamptons had: a political party, or, as Carmarthen called it, "a particular interest." William had clear advertisement of this fact even before he dissolved Parliament, for on 29 January 150 Tory members of Parliament crowded into the Apollo room of the Devil Tavern, where they voted to send a message to the King assuring him of their services.[22] Upon the dissolution these same churchmen, and others of the same opinion, fought with great warmth for seats in the new House. William, though he publicly espoused their cause, did not interfere in the elections themselves, not even in those held in the Cinque Ports. The King, lamented Carmarthen, "does us no good in this chief business of the elections."[23] What did the Church party the most good was the extravagance of the extreme Whigs, which drove moderate men into the Tory camp. When the new

Parliament met, the Church party, as a result of its exertions during the elections, found itself stronger than it had been in the Convention Parliament, but it had no certain majority over the Whigs. In votes on purely party issues, it sometimes won by one or two or three votes, sometimes lost by a similar margin. The same narrow margin prevailed in the Lords.[24] Clearly, the successful management of Parliament required more than a reliance upon "a particular interest," or party.

To the Marquis of Carmarthen, the solution was evident: to the power of party should be added the power of patronage. And not patronage alone, but a formed management. The King's ministers, working with the Speaker, should speak for supply, have measures ready, count votes, secure the attendance of the King's friends, and speak to those in their interest. With the help of Sir John Trevor, a bold, skillfull man, whom the court and the Church party elected Speaker, Carmarthen organized such a management. An essential part of it, especially in Trevor's mind, was the winning of men by place, pension, and bribe.[25] The number of placemen in the House of Commons rose from 101 in 1689, to 119 in 1690, to 131 in January 1693. In the Lords even a greater proportion probably held some office of profit under the crown.[26]

But these numbers are deceptive, for placemen did not invariably vote with the court. A juster estimate of the power of the court can be formed by examining the actual divisions that occurred during these years. Such an examination shows that the court could not carry measures that affronted the principles or prejudices or fears of the House. In 1690 the court was unable to secure Their Majesties a sufficient revenue for their lives or to suspend the Habeas Corpus Act; in 1692 it could not (because the Whig placemen deserted) prevent the passage through the Commons of a popular place bill. But the court interest did allow the managers to swing the balance in close votes, as the progress of the abjuration bill in April 1690 illustrates. Early in the month, the court favored the bill, and it progressed smoothly through the House; then the King, persuaded by Nottingham, turned against it. Churchmen and placemen now joined to defeat the bill by 23 votes. Yet a like bill in 1692, introduced by the court, met defeat by 25 votes because those placemen who were also churchmen opposed it. In the House of Lords, the court had the strength in 1693 to defeat the place bill but not the triennial bill, which was equally abhorrent to it. No one can say precisely what role this phalanx of placemen played in the management of Parliament, but it would be as wrong to deny it a role as to exaggerate its importance.[27]

Where Carmarthen looked instinctively to patronage for help in the management of Parliament, William looked instinctively to trimming. "He was still a Trimmer," he told Halifax upon Shrewsbury's resignation, "and would continue so."[28] Thus, he retained the services of the ministerial Whigs, of Devonshire and Dorset in the Household, of Wharton as comptroller, of the elder Hampden at the Treasury. And though in 1691 and 1692 he brought Godolphin into the Treasury and Seymour and Rochester into the council, all of them Tories, he also gave Edward Russell command of the fleet, named John Somers attorney general, and made Charles Montagu a commissioner of the Treasury, all of them Whigs. And the ministerial Whigs proved useful in the management of Parliament—Wharton seconded the demand for a supply of £1,500,000 in 1690, and Montagu cut off an inquiry into miscarriages in the fleet in 1691 by a timely motion that Mr. Grey leave the Chair.[29] "What," complained a Whig pamphleteer in 1692, "can more satisfy it [the court] than the present construction of Whig and Tory in Parliament? Is there any thing that the Court cannot carry? Whereas, if one party were declared for, it would not be so."[30]

Churchmen, placemen, ministerial Whigs, these formed that confederation of interests which voted supply each year, but more important than any one group were those in both Houses who belonged to no party or were only nominally attached to a party. To retain their support, the government must govern successfully, which in time of war meant winning battles and avoiding defeats. The King's ministers understood this well. Henry Sidney and Thomas Coningsby hoped that victory at the Battle of the Boyne would persuade moderate people on both sides to refuse the King nothing.[31] Carmarthen in 1691 was ready to retire from office until news of the capitulation of Limerick improved the political situation.[32] And Nottingham became obsessed with the belief that only a successful descent on the coast of France could induce the Commons to vote money to continue the war abroad.[33] As Henry Horwitz remarks, "The course of the war was to be the principal determinant of the ministers' fate."[34]

In 1691 and 1692, the course of the war went badly, and the fate of the government suffered accordingly. In 1691 the fleet was inactive, even allowing French reinforcements to reach Ireland.[35] In 1692 the fleet failed to follow up its victory at La Hogue by carrying out a descent on the French coast. On land there was a costly and inconclusive battle at Steenkirk. In the government there was waste, incompetence, inaction, venality, and great expense. French privateers, among them the famous Jean Bart, preyed on English shipping in the channel.[36] "To be plain," said a Whig to his Tory friend, "a Ministry from Wapping could not have made worse work on't than yours have done."[37] Weariness with heavy taxes at home and anger at ill successes abroad reached a critical mass in the autumn of 1692 and exploded. Parliament launched inquiries into the conduct of the Admiralty, into the want of convoys, into the failure to carry out a descent. The Whigs initiated and promoted these inquiries. Among their motives certainly was a desire to see a thorough reformation of abuses in government, but they had other motives. They attacked the Earl of Nottingham with a special fury, believing that through him they could drive the Tories from office and succeed to their places.[38] The ultra Whigs had always harbored such purposes, but now the ministerial Whigs, impatient at William's neglect of them, defected from the government coalition. They now sought that popularity which ever comes to the critic of government and the tribune of the people. They were the most vigilant in the House and commanded a majority there on all popular issues.[39] Even the placemen deserted the government; on the third reading of the triennial bill, 34 Whig placemen voted for the bill.[40] The weakness of the government extended even into the City, where Carmarthen and Godolphin had difficulty raising a loan funded on the supply voted that session.[41]

The situation cried out for a remedy, for the government could hardly stagger on, as weak and disunited as it was. One remedy was to yield to the clamor for Nottingham's dismissal and to entrust the government to the Whigs. But William was not prepared to deliver himself into the hands of the Whigs. He preferred to trim the ship rather than change the crew. He therefore kept Nottingham as secretary of state and named three Tories—Killigrew, Delaval, and Shovell—to command the fleet in Russell's place. But he balanced these appointments by naming Sir John Trenchard, a Whig and a skillful manager in the House, as the other secretary, and by promoting Sir John Somers to the office of lord keeper.[42] With the government thus patched and trimmed, William departed for the Continent in April.

Who advised the King to this patching cannot be known for certain, but it was probably the Earl of Sunderland. This resilient politician, this quondam exclusionist, this former broker for the Southamptons, this notorious servant of James II, crept back to England in 1690. He soon, to the astonishment of many, found his way into the inner councils of the King. What advice he gave William during the years 1691 and 1692 cannot be known, but from April through June of 1693, he bombarded the Earl of Portland with advice for His Majesty. These letters and memorials are extant and breathe the same shrewd, cynical spirit found in Sir Francis Bacon's memorials to James I in 1612. Both men appreciated the need for careful management, early preparation, unity of counsels, and firmness. "The whole government is loose," complained Sunderland "No respect paid to it. No order in any of the counsells. Nor care of anything."[43] But to this realistic appreciation of the need for careful management, Sunderland, like Bacon, added a remarkably cynical view of human nature. Parliament men were to be "fixed," "gained," "engaged," granted "terms," and "bought." The Earl of Mulgrave was to be won by a marquisate, Lord Brandon by a regiment of horse, and the Earl of Bath by favors to his sons. "The Earl of Stamford and other lords must have money."[44] Money was also to be used to win men in the House of Commons:

Speaker, Guy, and myself have done a great deal in order to persuade men to serve the King, and I think with good success. They have acted with great industry, diligence, and skill. Most of those we named to you being fixed. I have talked to many of the principal, and doubt not but they will do well. I need not tell you the particulars of what will suffice, such as are to have money, but I can assure you it will come within compass.[45]

The whole scheme—"our great project," Sunderland called it— reveals in all its nakedness the first face of parliamentary management, the use of place, favor, and bribes to win men to the court.

But Sunderland was not so blind as to think that the power of patronage alone would suffice. He entered into negotiations not only with the Speaker and Henry Guy, the corrupters-general of the Parliament, but also with Somers and Trenchard, the leaders of the Whigs. With them he looked over the list of Parliament men and "agreed upon the best means of persuading them to be reasonable."[46] The Earl of Sunderland, reported Robert Harley, was "setting up to be premier at winter; in order to it driving barters with several."[47] But though the Earl sought the help of Somers and Trenchard, he told them that "the strongest argument" for persuading men to be reasonable must not be used.[48] What he meant by that gnomic remark can only be guessed at, but it is not unreasonable to suggest that he meant that no promises should be made that the King would bring more Whigs into the government. As he put it to Portland on 10 July:

If under all the ill circumstances of the King's affairs his business can be set right, without doing anything dishonourable, anything that interferes between Whig and Tory, or that shall lessen the prerogative, I think he ought to be satisfied, and approve of all. I hope to keep within these bounds and yet propose what shall give a new life and spirit to the government, which must be done as I have often said, or it cannot hold.[49]

But other men had other plans. The Earl of Shrewsbury, the king of hearts, a man esteemed by all, had grown angry at William's turning away from those who had placed him on the throne. He formed an alliance with the Earl of Marlborough, whose opposition to the government, arising from the King's reliance upon Dutchmen, was even more vehement. In October 1692 they were seen leaving the house of Comptroller Wharton, the ebullient leader of the Whigs.[50] In the summer of 1693, their meetings became more frequent. On 8 July, Shrewsbury wrote Wharton urging him to come to town, pleading that Marlborough believed his presence necessary and that Mr. Montagu and his friends would be unable to visit him at Winchenden next week, as planned.[51] Wharton came to town on the thirteenth, to his house in Chelsea, newly planted with orange trees. There the Whigs met and drew up their scheme of management for the next year. No one put down on paper the nature of that scheme, but Sir Robert Howard, years ago a leading Anti-Clarendonian and now auditor of the Exchequer, revealed the scope of it in a letter to Wharton on 27 July:

> Yesterday I was with my Lord Keeper and debated all our matters fully with him. I found him perfectly clear with us and possessed in some measure of our Northampton friend's [Sunderland's] mind, that the King would come to those matters, but he was also of opinion since we had gone so far in the knowledge of one another's minds, that now all things should be kept in silence till the King came, and then to agree to have it laid open. . . . [52]

Sir Robert Howard, who some weeks before had enjoyed the peace and quiet of Winchendon, then added his opinion that "no good can come of anything unless it pleases God it come by some great Alteration." Sir John Trenchard, the Whig secretary of state, fully concurred. He wrote Portland on 1 August, "I assure Your Lordship, it will be very requisite to do some things in order to dispose people to be in a good temper, and I really believe the King will find the men of interest ready to do their utmost to support the government, if reasonable terms be proposed to them. . . . "[53] "If reasonable terms be proposed to them"—the Whigs were now laying down terms for supporting the government, as Shaftesbury had in 1675. Nottingham had warned William in June 1692 that the Whigs would never let slip an opportunity "of imposing terms" upon him.[54]

What those terms might be rumor soon reported, but not very distinctly. "Our great men here," reported Robert Harley, "are talking of their new Scheme, which nobody yet gives a perfect account of."[55] That there should be great alterations, everyone agreed. That the Earl of Nottingham should be dismissed won a like assent.[56] But there was disagreement whether the Earl of Sunderland should replace him. Many men thought he would, but John Isham, a prudent and observant civil servant, thought Sunderland would be unacceptable to the generality of both parties.[57] The earl of Sunderland no doubt agreed with Isham, and so chose to remain a minister behind the curtain.

But his advice as minister behind the curtain changed during the summer. In June he was a court manager, directing his lieutenants, Guy and Trevor, and setting up to be a premier minister. Such a scheme of management, he knew, would succeed only if there were no miscarriages that summer. But miscarriages there were, disastrous ones, such as the French attack upon the Smyrna fleet in the Bay of Lagos, where the French captured 32 ships and burned 27. And shortly thereafter the English lost four merchantmen at Gibraltar. The merchants in the City drew up remonstrances and spoke of taking the management of naval affairs into their hands. Sunderland saw the handwriting on the wall. "I think," he wrote Portland on 2 August, "that the measures which were resolved upon before you went away must be pursued, and shall be; they grow more necessary every day . . . with this difference, that the King must do abundance more than if these dismall accidents had not happened." A fortnight later he urged upon Portland that the King might still cure all if he pleased. "But it must not be by patching, but by a thorough good administration, and employing men firm to this government and thought to be so."[58] From a manager exercising the power of patronage, he became a broker for those who would impose terms upon the King.

The actual brokerage took place at a celebrated meeting at Althorp in the middle of August. "Several great men," wrote the author of a newsletter on August 24, "as the Earl of Shrewsbury, Mr. Comptroller Wharton, the Earl of Sunderland, etc. are gone together into the country, but their per-ambulation is variously discoursed of as to concert matters relating to the Government. . . . "[59] Among the Whigs who came were Shrewsbury, Sir Edward Russell, Sir Thomas Wharton, and Sunderland's Northamptonshire neighbor, Lord Montagu. Marlborough and Godolophin also attended, as did the Duke of Bolton. These politicians assembled among the oaks and beeches and limes of Althorp Park about the eighteenth of August and broke up on the twentieth or twenty-first. The meeting caused much talk in the coffee-houses, but time has drawn a veil over what happened there. The only event known for certain to have occurred at Althorp was a quarrel between one Mompesson and the Duke of Bolton; provoked by the Duke's spitting in his face, Mompesson spoke rudely to His Grace.[60] But several days after the meet-ing, Shrewsbury wrote an enigmatical letter to Wharton, a letter which suggests that Shrewsbury was initially dis-appointed with the results of the meeting, but later changed his mind. "I think," wrote Shrewsbury, "you have considered very discreetly, and there are ways enough of disobliging great men without going so far for it; I should not have been sorry for the journey if it had not been for the consequences, but they are not in my opinion so slight as at time they appear. . . . "[61] What these consequences were Shrewsbury did not say, but "every politician," wrote one observer, "is making his reflections about it."[62] They spoke mostly of great changes at court. The Dutch ambassador heard that Pem-broke would become admiral, Shrewsbury, lord privy seal, and Sunderland, secretary in Nottingham's place.[63] John Isham, hoping that diligence, fidelity, and zeal to the government would protect him in his place at the secretary's office, did not believe that Sunderland would replace Nottingham. He admitted that Sunderland had taken a great house in St. James's Square, that he might come into the court, perhaps even into the council; but "if that Party prevails and there is a thorough change, I would think it most likely that my Lord Shrewsbury will come into his old post."[64]

What happened at Althorp must be a matter of conjecture, but it seems likely, from the subsequent course of events, that

Lord Sunderland sounded out the Whigs as to the terms they would demand for supporting the government. It seems likely that the Whigs made the dismissal of Nottingham the first of their demands.[65] They probably also suggested that Russell be named admiral.[66] Shrewsbury may well have demanded the King's assent to a triennial bill, a demand to which Sunderland may have raised objections—hence Shrewsbury's expression of disappointment in his letter to Wharton. What was said about replacing Nottingham is much harder to guess at, for the position was not filled until March of 1694. Wharton may have subtly suggested that he be offered the position, for he was known to seek it. If he did, Sunderland probably countered with Shrewsbury's name, knowing he was the only Whig acceptable to William.[67] Throughout November political observers as diverse as John Isham, Robert Harley, Narcissus Luttrell, Charles Hatton, Bonnet, and L'Hermitage reported that Shrewsbury would succeed Nottingham.[68] Then in late November William offered the place to Shrewsbury, who refused it. His refusal, wrote Humphrey Prideaux, dean of Norwich, "put the King out of all his measures and much exasperated him against that party who assured him that the Earl would accept of the place."[69] It seems likely that Shrewsbury's becoming secretary was at least discussed at Althorp.

Whatever the details, it is almost certain that the politicians assembled at Althorp negotiated about the entry of the Whigs into the government. Althorp presents the second face of parliamentary management: the politicians' using their influence in Parliament to wrest office from the King.

William, exhausted from a campaign that had ended in defeat at Landen, arrived at Kensington late on the evening of 30 October. One week later he dismissed the Earl of Nottingham from office and named Edward Russell admiral of the fleet. A few weeks later, he offered the vacated seals to Shrewsbury; but the Earl, who balanced an ability to charm with a penchant for being difficult, refused unless William agreed to accept a triennial bill.[70]

William did not make these changes from choice, but from necessity. "It is only from necessity," he told Nottingham, "that I part with you."[71] Queen Mary was equally blunt. The

King, she wrote, was forced "to part with Lord Nottingham to please a party whom he cannot trust."[72] From the beginning of his reign, William had resisted all proposals that Parliament name his ministers of state. He no doubt still would resist such proposals if made to him explicitly, but the Earl of Sunderland possessed the address to present these changes to William in a manner that seemed to do the least injury to his prerogative. William was simply bringing into office men who could better serve him in the management of Parliament and in the conduct of his affairs. The element of duress that Sunderland certainly sought to conceal was clearly seen, however, by the Earl of Nottingham. French victories abroad, he wrote, and the need to raise great sums of money for the army drove the King to the Whigs, who promised "to extricate him out of all his difficulties if he would put his affairs into their hands, and he yielded to their importunity."[73]

In the ensuing Parliament, the Whigs fulfilled their undertaking to extricate the King from his difficulties. The new scheme of administration worked smoothly. Parliament voted the King not only £2,000,000 for the fleet, not only £500,000 to pay the arrears of wages owed to the seamen, but also £2,500,000 to maintain land forces that were increased by six new regiments of horse, four of dragoons, and fifteen of foot.[74] And when the opposition sought to obstruct the ways and means for raising this supply, the new managers carried a land tax, a poll tax, an excise on salt, and duties on leather, soap, paper, and the tonnage carried by ships; in addition they secured a loan of £1,000,000 from the newly created Bank of England.[75]

The new managers likewise steered skillfully through those crises that seemed an inescapable part of parliamentary life in William's reign. When the King vetoed a place bill passed by both Houses, there was an eruption of anger at the King's ministers. The Commons voted an address asking the King to harken to the advice of Parliament and not to the secret advice of particular persons. To this address William gave a courteous but vacuous answer, which led to a motion for a further address. But at this point the managers marshalled their forces, defeated the motion, and turned the House back to the consideration of supply.[76]

The success of the new managers had several explanations. To begin with, there were no great issues, such as the attainder of Strafford in 1641 or the exclusion of the Duke of York in 1680, to divide the new managers from the King. In the second place, Somers, Trenchard, and Russell—"the governing men," Sir Charles Lyttleton called them—did not lose their credit in the House because they served at court.[77] Neither did Wharton and Montagu, who were equally active as managers. These men did not lose their credit because, unlike Neville and Bedford and Temple, they had a political party behind them. Robert Harley and Paul Foley took only a few Whigs with them into the new Country party. The bulk of the Whigs remained loyal to their leaders.[78] But those leaders could not have managed Parliament solely on the basis of the Whig interest. They needed also the support of the court. When they lacked that support, as with the triennial bill, or when the issue was purely Whig against Tory, as with the condemnation of the admirals, they met defeat. Yet when the Tory placemen, led by Sir John Lowther, joined with them, they could carry a duty on wine or impose a license fee on hackney coaches.[79]

The Whigs not only needed the support of the court interest, they sought to capture control of it. Not satisfied with the profits of high office, they also sought the patronage that came with it. In March, William had named Somers lord keeper but had denied him the right to recommend the new attorney general. Somers protested angrily, insisting that the recommendation of men to offices of law belonged to the lord keeper.[80] In December the Whigs pressed William to declare yet further in their favor by removing Jacobites (a Whig euphemism for Tories) from the commissions of peace throughout the country, by reforming the lieutenancy of London in a similar fashion, and by naming a Whig to the vacant secretaryship.[81] William yielded to their demands. In February he removed some forty Tories from the London militia and named Whigs in their place. In March he named Shrewsbury secretary of state, who finally gave way to the importunities of his fellow Whigs and accepted.[82] In April, William took yet further steps toward entrusting power to the Whigs. He named Montagu chancellor of the Exchequer, he placed Russell at the head of a new Admiralty commission, and he removed Edward Seymour from the Treasury. Honors, too, he bestowed upon the Whigs, elevating the Earls of Devonshire and Bedford to dukedoms.[83]

But the fiercest battle for the control of patronage came in the summer of 1694. William named Somers, Trenchard, Shrewsbury, and Godolphin to be a committee to recommend to him changes in the customs and excise commissions. Godolphin, a civil servant at heart, not a politician, protested that the Whig members of the committee sought to remove men of one party merely to bring in those of another. Trenchard answered that men were needed who would not only administer the revenue efficiently but would support the King's affairs in Parliament. Somers likewise urged that men be named to the commission who could explain to the House whatever related to their office. He also observed that Excise commissioners named inferior officers throughout the country, who exercised a great influence upon the people. Shrewsbury was even more candidly political. He urged William to name Robert Molesworth to the Excise Commission, "for if he be desperate of your favour, I forsee he will be a very troublesome popular speaker."[84] William did not name Molesworth to any commission, but he accepted, to the great mortification of Godolphin, all the other recommendations made by Somers, Trenchard, and Shrewsbury.[85] William's sympathies undoubtedly lay with Godolphin, who merely wished to name good administrators to the commissions, but he dared not ignore Sunderland's warning in August 1694 that the world expected these changes and that the government could not be right without them.[86] In August of 1694, the second face of parliamentary management was more visible than ever: the politician was seen to be more powerful than the court manager.

The government's management of the 1694–95 Parliament proved as calm and successful as the year before. Parliament voted nearly £5,000,000 for the fleet and the land forces, and all attempts to embarrass the government, as over its prosecution of the Lancashire plot, failed. The success of the government arose from the same amalgam of causes: military success abroad,[87] a strong Whig interest in the House, and the support of the court. A Tory attack upon Secretary Trenchard for his handling of the Lancashire plot offered an excellent test of party strength. The Whigs were able to carry a vote (117 to 102) to examine not only the accused but also those who alleged there was such a plot against the government.[88] On one crucial issue the Whigs allied with the Country party, not the court. Shrewsbury in October met frequently with Robert Harley, who in November introduced a triennial bill into the House.[89] The bill was less injurious to the prerogative than earlier bills, and swept through Parliament with the support of the Whigs and of the Harley-Foley interest there. Indeed, fifty placemen deserted the court to vote for the bill.[90] William this time accepted the bill, probably because Shrewsbury made his continuance in office conditional upon it. On the chief constitutional issue before Parliament this session, the King moved toward Parliament, not Parliament toward the King.

Lord Coningsby, a former lord justice of Ireland, was quick to advise William how he could regain his freedom of action. He should set up a party of his own and should let all people see that if they expected favor they must serve him, not a faction.[91] It was the same advice that the Earl of Newcastle gave Charles II, the same advice that Danby made the center of his political strategy, the same advice that Sunderland in the spring of 1693 gave to William—manage Parliament through a Court party. But in the year 1695 it was more impracticable than ever, for during that spring the practitioners of "the Carmarthen art" (as one pamphleteer called it) fell into disrepute.[92] Henry Guy, paymaster of the secret service, was sent to the Tower for taking a bribe of 200 guineas. Sir John Trevor, the captain of the pensioners, resigned as Speaker when a committee of the House discovered he had accepted a thousand guineas for helping to pass the Orphans Bill. The Marquis of Normanby, the man who was to sway the Lords in return for a marquisate, was accused, though cleared, of taking money for passing the Lantern patent. Even Carmarthen himself, now Duke of Leeds, fell from grace for having allegedly accepted 5,000 guineas for his service to the East India Company.[93] For the moment the Court party lay in shambles. It could not even secure the election of its candidate, Sir Thomas Littleton, as the new Speaker; the House elected Thomas Foley, a country Whig on his way to becoming a country Tory.[94]

The fall of the court managers, like a strong wine, went to the heads of Montagu and Wharton, and robbed them for a moment of their senses. They came to believe that they no longer needed a broker at court, that they could do without Sunderland, both in relation to the King and to the Whig party.[95] But the ever resilient Sunderland loved politics too much to bow out of affairs. Through Henry Guy he opened negotiations with Paul Foley and Robert Harley, and through them sought to detach the Whig party from the leadership of the rambunctious Montagu and Wharton.[96] Wharton replied by boasting that he had the power to keep the Harleys and Foleys, and some eighty other members, out of the new Parliament, whose election men soon expected.[97] Montagu and Wharton, however, soon came to their senses. Perceiving their isolation, they drew closer to Somers and Shrewsbury,[98] through whom a reconciliation with Sunderland was reached in August. The festivities celebrating this reunion occurred in October when Wharton and Montagu joined the King himself in a progress to Althorp. But though Sunderland displayed once again his genius for reconciling men, the corrupters-general of Parliament did not return to power. William ordered Trevor not to seek a seat in the new House of Commons, and he commanded Leeds to stay away from council meetings. The leading men at court were now Somers and Shrewsbury, both of them Whigs.[99]

In October of 1695, William dissolved the "officers" Parliament, as it had come to be called. Wharton and Montagu at once set to work to win those majorities that they had boasted they could win and that alone could support their undertaking to manage Parliament for the King. But the results of the elections disappointed their expectations. In the new House of Commons, there were 248 members for the court, 247 in opposition, and 9 whose allegiances were uncertain.[100] The court did not have the numbers to challenge Foley's reelection as Speaker. They also suffered defeat on disputed election returns and failed by one vote to prevent the parliamentary nomination of the new Council of Trade. When they moved to prohibit MPs from serving on the new council, they lost by 209 to 188.[101] The root cause of these defeats was the strength of the new Country party, composed largely of Tories, but led by two former Whigs, Robert Harley and Paul Foley. The most important fact about the new Country party was not that two former Whigs led it but that a party once devoted to defending the prerogative now opposed it. In 1689 the Earl of Nottingham had boasted to William that the Tories sought to defend his prerogative, the Whigs to tear it down. Now the Earl himself, and his party, espoused a measure— the parliamentary nomination of the Council of Trade—that would rob the King of one of the chief flowers of his prerogative.[102] They were probably led to this act by the spirit of opposition. They were now the "outs," the Whigs were the "ins." They now sought that popularity which a stout defense of country principles brings to a member of Parliament. In January 1695 Nottingham had promoted a trial for treason bill that was popular with the country and opposed by the court.[103] In 1696 he favored the parliamentary nomination of councillors to a Board of Trade. He would probably have opposed both in 1689. Few practices proved more injurious to the King's independence than the willingness of politicians to oppose the government because they were not of it. "Popular opposition," Abel Boyer called it.[104]

Despite the strength of the opposition, however, the Whigs managed the 1695–96 Parliament with success. Though they failed to elect Littleton as Speaker, they did elect him chairman of the Committee on Supply, a post second only to the Speaker in importance. They won the King a supply of nearly £5,000,000 to carry on the war. In December they carried eleven resolutions concerning the recoinage of England's currency. But in January everything seemed to go wrong—defeat over the trial for treason bill, defeat over the new Council of Trade, defeat over the qualification of members bill. Littleton and Montagu, the court managers, lost all credit.[105] There was a profound uneasiness at court, even talk of Nottingham's becoming lord chancellor.[106] Then in late February, the court revealed that there had been a plot, fortunately discovered, to assassinate the King at Turnham Green, as he returned home from Richmond. The Whigs immediately exploited the Turnham Green plot, just as Carmarthen had exploited the Preston plot in 1691.[107] They drew up an association in defense of His Majesty's person and government, an association that was to be tendered to all officeholders and that contained a declaration that William was "rightful and lawful King." There followed a substantial purging from the magistracy and militia of England of those who would not subscribe to the association.[108] In March a loyal Parliament voted the King a civil list of £500,000 a year and a relief of £15,000 to the Huguenot refugees, a favorite cause of the Whigs. In April the court defeated by 212 to 70 a motion to censure those who advised the King to veto the qualification of members bill.[109] Abetted by the wave of loyalty that followed the assassination plot, the Whig ministers proved to William that they could successfully manage his affairs in Parliament, even though they had lost that odor of sanctity that they had won during the years in opposition.

The success of the Whigs whetted their appetite for office. Stop trimming and trust none but those who are faithful to your cause, wrote Lord Capel to William.[110] But William, as always, was guarded in his bestowal of office. He named Whigs to the Council of Trade, among them John Locke, and he named Littleton to the Treasury, but he kept Godolphin at the head of the Treasury. Littleton's promotion carried a particular significance, for the Whigs had sought for over a year to bring him to the treasury, during which time Henry Guy struggled to secure the place for Charles Duncombe.[111] Littleton's nomination offers one more sign that patronage was falling into the hands of the politicians who governed in Parliament and out of the hands of the managers who were well heard at court. Indeed, before the summer was over,

Sunderland, who for the past year had negotiated with Harley and Foley, now returned to his accustomed role as broker for the Whigs at court. But he found that he was less needed than ever before, for Shrewsbury and Somers had established themselves in the good graces of the King.[112]

Sunderland returned to the Whigs not only because they had proved their ability to manage Parliament but also because they had proved their ability to manage the finances of the kingdom. Power in Williamite England resided not only in those who could secure a vote of supply but also in those who could raise an immediate loan based upon that supply. William turned to the Tories in 1690 in part because they could secure him a loan in the City. In the autumn of 1693, he turned to the Whigs in part because Somers and Trenchard had secured him an advance upon the poll tax of £50,000.[113] The greatest coup of all, that which cemented the Whig interest, was the creation of the Bank of England in 1694 and its loan of £1,000,000 to the government. To counter this Whig money machine, the Tories sought in 1696 to establish a land bank. The scheme was ambitious. Harley and Foley labored hard to make it succeed, but it failed in the summer of 1696. Unable to borrow the money he needed from the land bank, a King of England, resolved that his army should not starve, turned to the Bank of England, which lent him £200,000. "William was now," observes Stephen Baxter, "by the logic of the financial situation, delivered over to the rabid Whigs bound hand and foot."[114]

With Sunderland once more serving them at court and vowing that all jealousies were buried, the Whigs proceeded with high hopes to the management of Parliament in 1696 and 1697. Only one event disturbed the mood of euphoria: Sir John Fenwick, one of the conspirators in the assassination plot, had accused Shrewsbury, Russell, Marlborough, and Godolphin of plotting to secure the return of James II. This presented a delicate problem in parliamentary management, for some Whigs would have Fenwick believed in order to injure Godolphin, and others would have him disbelieved in order to save Shrewsbury and Russell. With great finesse, the Whigs steered a Bill of Attainder against Fenwick through both Houses, while at the same time clearing the names of Shrewsbury and Russell. Meanwhile Sunderland persuaded Godolphin that safety lay in offering to resign, an offer that William would then refuse, thereby demonstrating his confidence in Godolphin. Godolphin acted on Sunderland's suggestion, only to see himself "tricked" and "cozened," for William accepted his resignation.[115] In February 1697 William named Charles Montagu, the Whig financial wizard, first lord of the Treasury. There now remained not a Tory of any eminence in the government of England.

William had finally conceded to the Whigs that monopoly of office that they had sought. He did so because he believed they could carry his business through Parliament. In the 1696–97 session, he was not disappointed. Never was the Court party more united; never was the opposition feebler. Parliament voted a supply of £5,000,000, a civil list of £515,000, another £125,000 to assist in recoinage, and £840,000 to make up the deficiency in the funds voted the previous year. The opposition opposed, and as always they opposed not the vote of supply but the ways and means for raising supply. But the managers beat back all attempts to defeat the ways and means proposed for raising the supply. Their success was not accidental, for they carefully prepared for every session. In late November, Montagu and Littleton carefully explained to "the Club,"as James Vernon called the Whig caucus, the scheme for raising supply, and they then brought it before the House. These meetings, held the night before the meeting of Parliament, were frequent, almost nightly.

> They meet almost every night [wrote Vernon], and settle what they will propose, and how manage it. They did so last night to near the number of fifty, and agree to all the resolutions that were taken this day about the corn, so that it went on smoothly, notwithstanding Seymour, Temple, and Harley, would have offered some rubs.[116]

Upon the conclusion of this triumphant session, William showered honors and office upon the Whigs. Russell became Lord Orford and treasurer of the Navy. Somers became lord chancellor and a baron. Montagu now headed the Treasury. Only Wharton, whose libertine ways were distasteful to William, received no reward (other than the lord lieutenancy of Oxfordshire). But the Whigs' broker at court, the Earl of Sunderland, became lord chamberlain. Trimming now came to an end. It came to an end because William finally discovered that the strategy of balancing parties would not work—party jealousies were too fierce. Nor was William able to establish, through the bestowal of place, pension, and bribes (the first face of parliamentary management), a court party that would allow him to name ministers of his own choice and support them in Parliament. Carmarthen, Trevor, and Guy plied this art with considerable skill during the years 1691 and 1692, but they could not build up a party of placemen large enough to carry the King's business through the Commons by itself. The placemen had to ally with the prevailing party there, and the politicians who led the prevailing party, being politicians, sought to use their influence in Parliament to wrest office from the King. Through negotiations that were often implicit, always discreet, and suitably indirect, they undertook to manage Parliament for the King in return for office. This was the second face of parliamentary management—the King yielding to the demands of those who governed in Parliament. The profound significance of the first nine years of William's reign lies in the fact that the parliamentary undertaker, armed with the power of the purse and the power of party, proved to be stronger than the court manager, armed with place and pension. By 1697 the second face of parliamentary management had triumphed over the first.

Chapter VI

The Politics of Opposition: 1698–1701

I N LATE JUNE of the year 1700, James Vernon, the unobstrusive Whig secretary of state, met Robert Harley, the acknowledged leader of the Country party. The two men began to talk politics. Finding Harley exasperated with Lord Somers, Vernon expressed the hope that Harley and his friends would not fall upon him again next winter. Harley answered that the King ought long ago to have seen that the men whom he employed were not capable of carrying on his service. The King's business must miscarry, he said, "while blasted men had the conduct of it." The nation, he continued, "will rid themselves of such pilots one way or another." If the King did not ensure the right management of affairs, "a reformation would be wrought in a more disagreeable manner."[1]

Robert Harley's threats were not academic, for he and his friends had, for the past three years, blasted the reputations of the King's Whig ministers. The new Country party had opposed the King's government because they were not *of* it, and they were resolved to continue to oppose it until they were. This was, in essence, the politics of opposition. John Trenchard, author of A *History of Standing Armies*, traced the origins of the politics of opposition back to the reign of Charles I. Charles the First, he wrote, was the first King who "made an Opposition to himself in the House of Commons the Road to Preferment." And he instanced the bestowal of office on Strafford and Noy.[2] But Strafford and Noy did not oppose the King with a deliberate purpose to wrest office from him. The first Englishman to do this was probably Sir Richard Temple. He and other Anti-Clarendonians won popularity in the 1660s by attacking corruption and mismanagement at court. They then sought to use that popularity as a lever to prize office from the King. To make room for themselves at court, they sought to drive the King's ministers from him. Their success in winning office in the 1670s did not go unnoticed. All men seek for rewards by contradicting state policy, observed Henry Ball.[3] Men affect popularity, declared the Earl of Lindsey, merely to gain preferment. As the most factious were rewarded, wrote Colbert de Croissey, others resolved to speak against the government. Charles himself saw that men opposed him merely "to have their mouths stopped by places."[4]

The Glorious Revolution by no means put a stop to the politics of opposition. Thrown out of office in 1690, the Whigs went into opposition. They hammered away at Carmarthen. They attacked Nottingham. They denounced the Admiralty. As one pamphleteer observed in 1692, "They don't pry, but rake into the actions of great men, as if they had an interest they should be faulty, and were to share in the forfeiture or composition."[5] When the Tories in their turn were turned out in 1693, they became "grumbletonians." It is not difficult to divine their motives, concluded L'Hermitage in 1694; they have either lost office at court or desire to have one.[6]

The clamor of the opposition against the government, a gentle breeze in 1694, became a gale in 1697. The coming of peace made this possible, for as long as France threatened the shores of England, no member of Parliament dared vote against the supply that supported English arms. "Of what use are Parliaments," reflected the Earl of Nottingham in 1694. "if when there is war, everything that is asked is to be given."[7] The prodigal sums required by the war no doubt forced William to an unwelcome dependence upon Parliament, but at the same time, the exigencies of war dampened the fires of opposition. The Peace of Ryswick ended the exigencies of war, but not the dependence upon Parliament. The war came to an end, but the national debt went on. Peace also brought new political quarrels—the standing army, the examination of public accounts, the resumption of land grants—quarrels that heightened the passions of the country members against the court. The distinction of court and country soon threatened to extinguish that of Whig and Tory.[8] William further exacerbated matters by requiring his Whig ministers to advocate measures sure to win them infamy. The end of the war made opposition less unpatriotic; the new court-country polarity made it more popular; the juxtaposition of both made it formidable.

The strength of the opposition in the 1697–98 Parliament was resolute rather than formidable, though formidable it was in its first foray against the court. On 10 December, Robert Harley moved a resolution that all land forces raised since 1689 be disbanded, an action that would leave William with only 8,000 men. After a five-hour debate, the question was carried by a great cry on a voice vote. Many country gentlemen, observed Robert Price, fell off from the court on this question.[9] In the following weeks, goaded by William, the court managers sought to increase the number of men to be retained, but with each effort their reputation fell and the credit of their opponents rose.[10] There was no doubt a leaven of opportunism in the oppositions's denunciation of standing armies, but on the whole the campaign against the maintenance of 30,000 troops in time of peace arose from a genuine desire for lower taxes and from a real fear for the liberty of the subject. The leaders of the Country party in 1697, like the Earl of Shaftesbury in the 1670s, acted from mixed motives, some private and self-seeking, others public and patriotic.[11]

The private, self-seeking motives came to the fore during the remainder of the session. Led by Seymour and Musgrave, the Tories sought repeatedly to obstruct the King's business and to discredit his managers. In December they opposed going to supply before the consideration of the King's speech. Seymour then proposed an inquiry into the false endorsement of Exchequer bills, in the hope that some of the Treasury lords would be shown to be guilty. When this proved a blind alley, they—Seymour, Musgrave, and Harley—launched an attack upon the lords of the Treasury for directing that Exchequer bills be accepted in payment of bills of exchange originally drawn in milled money or gold.[12] The true object of these attacks was Charles Montagu, first lord of the Treasury, chancellor of the Exchequer, the premier manager of the House, and a Whig. In February the opposition sought to condemn him for accepting a grant of land from His Majesty, alleging that to accept such a grant was to violate his oath as a privy councillor. As Lord Somers observed, the opposing party turns their malice against our friend "because they are sensible how useful, and indeed, how necessary he is."[13] They have the greatest mind to lower him, remarked Vernon, because "he stands in their way."[14]

These attacks upon Montagu were persistent but not successful. The House defeated by 206 to 97 a motion to condemn him for accepting a grant of land from the King. It defeated by 177 to 88 a motion to censure the lords of the Treasury for directing that Exchequer bills be accepted in payment of bills of exchange.[15] These victories led the Earl of Portland to complain that the Whigs, if they would be of one mind on public business as they were on Montagu's, could do as they liked. But Portland showed little appreciation of the problems of managing a seventeenth-century Parliament. The success of any endeavor at management depended upon how popular or how obnoxious the measures were that the managers sought to promote. Montagu and his party could not secure His Majesty a standing army of 30,000 men, or even of 12,000, because such a measure was thoroughly obnoxious to the members of the House. But Montagu and his party could secure His Majesty a civil list for life, could persuade Parliament to vote taxes for the next year worth £3,000,000, and could drive through both Houses a bill for borrowing £2,000,000 from the new East India Company, because such measures were seen to be necessary. The success of Montagu's management arose from a medley of reasons. The Whig party, not wholly eclipsed by the new country-court polarity, stood behind him, more united than ever.[16] His own eloquence, quickness, and knowledge of affairs gave him a visible ascendancy in the House. He had the power of the court on his side, most notably in the struggle in the Lords to pass a bill creating the East India company.[17] And finally there was his own innocence and his opponents' guilt. The new Country party had hoped to use Charles Duncombe to expose Montagu's venality at the Treasury, but Duncombe soon discovered that those who live in glass houses should not throw rocks. In late January, Montagu successfully proved to the House that it was Duncombe, not he, who had falsely endorsed Exchequer bills. The attack upon Duncombe was done to a purpose, reported Vernon, "and 'tis certain the [Whig] party will be more considerable by it."[18]

All these successes the Whigs secured without the benefit of the Earl of Sunderland, for they had abandoned him in December. The occasion for their parting from the Earl illustrates graphically the growing struggle between the undertaker and the court manager for the control of patronage. In his heart of hearts, Sunderland was a court manager, surrounded by his instruments and protégés: Guy, Trevor, Duncombe, Methuen, and Trumbull. In December, Sir William Trumbull, ostracized by the Whigs, resigned as secretary of state. Before the Whigs could urge upon the King the appointment of Lord Wharton, Sunderland persuaded William to name James Vernon, Shrewsbury's chief clerk, to the office. It was a slap in the face to the Whigs, and they soon found their revenge. In late December the Tories, led by Dyke, Winnington, and How, threatened to impeach Sunderland, who promptly turned to the Whigs for support. They refused to support him. The Earl therefore resigned as lord chamberlain and fled to Althorp.[19] Revenge may have tasted sweet, but the retirement of Sunderland to Althorp left the Whigs with only one spokesman at court, Lord Somers, who was oftener found at the Chancery than at Kensington. The Whig leaders soon sensed their isolation from the court and sought to rectify it. In early February, Montagu, Somers, and Orford labored for an accommodation with Sunderland; but Lord Wharton, the most averse to Sunderland, opposed it, as did Jack Smith, a rising luminary in the party. Smith, indeed, threatened to resign from the Treasury if Sunderland returned.[20] His obstinacy ended the February negotiations, but the isolation of the Whigs continued, with the result that they resumed negotiations with the King in April. The King went to Newmarket for the races. Shrewsbury came over from Eyfort. At Woburn Abbey the King, Shrewsbury, Montagu, Smith, and Coningsby dined. The Whigs urged that Wharton be made secretary of state and Shrewsbury lord chamberlain. But in the midst of these negotiations, Shrewsbury fell ill, began to spit blood, and returned to Eyfort. The Whigs now proposed that Wharton be named lord chamberlain, a proposal that William found as abhorrent as naming him secretary. The Whigs told William that his affairs in Parliament would not proceed to his satisfaction unless he took Wharton into his service.[21] This was blunt language, not often heard by a King. But the Whigs were now acting upon a truth perceived by the ever observant James Vernon: "Those who are strongest in the House of Commons, and in possession of the management, methinks, should not be in danger of being discarded for the sake of any one man [meaning Sunderland]."[22] Sunderland remarked succinctly, they think "themselves so much masters as to need no help."[23]

But William remained adamant: he would not have Wharton forced upon him. And he won out, for though the Whigs in early May made a gesture of opposing the King's business in the Commons, [24] they thereafter managed both Houses for the King most successfully. William acknowledged as much. "This has been an intolerably long session," he wrote Heinsius in July, " . . . but God be thanked, it has ended better than I could have hoped."[25] In this buoyant mood, William sought once more to secure a reconciliation between Lord Sunderland and the Whigs. The Earl came to London, hoping, so rumor declared, to be named secretary. But the Whigs proved stubborn; they refused to take part in affairs if Sunderland either received office or resided in London. Sunderland returned to Althorp with disappointment written across his face.[26] Wharton's face probably registered a like disappointment, for his ambitions too had been thwarted. The power struggle that spring between the Whigs and the King ended in a standoff. The King refused high office to Wharton, the Whigs blocked Sunderland's return, and no new secretary was named. Count Tallard, the French ambassador, believed he knew why a new secretary was not named: "It is thought that the elections for the new Parliament will be waited for to see what party will prevail in them, in order to fill the office with a member of the predominant party."[27]

Count Tallard was a true prophet, for when the elections took place in July and August, William refused to declare himself in any manner—with the intent, thought Somers, of seeing "which faction would get the better upon the struggle."[28] The results of the elections were inconclusive. An anonymous contemporary observer estimated that the new House of Commons contained 241 who would support the court, 227 who would oppose, and 26 who were uncertain.[29] Because the new Country party could not agree on whom it wished to nominate as Speaker, the Whigs were able to secure the election of Sir Thomas Littleton. And because it was impossible to find a set of Tories who would unite together, the King could not piece together a government from the opposition.[30] William must stick with the Whigs, a decision that forced the Whigs to find some strategy for carrying on the King's business in the new Parliament. In ordinary times the problem of managing a new Parliament was daunting enough, but now there were three additional difficulties.

In the first place, William weakened his ministers by discountenancing them. In December, Lord Somers warned William that he did not have enough men of business about him and that his administration could not be strong until people saw that the ministers he employed had credit with him. Since Shrewsbury had just resigned the seals, Somers hinted that granting them to Lord Wharton would strengthen the government; but William kept them in his possession during the entire session.[31]

The second difficulty proved the most insurmountable of all: the King put his ministers upon measures certain to discredit them in the House. The managers knew very well that the first measures brought into the House tended to fix men in parties. Thus their despair was great when Robert Harley moved that the army be reduced to 7,000 men, and William commanded them to oppose this motion. They might have salvaged something from the quarrel had they been allowed to fight for 10,000 men, but William was passionately set on gaining more than that number and forbid them to offer 10,000. Either the ministers must remain silent and offend the court, or they must speak out against the disbanding bill and destroy their credit in the House. A "staggering dilemma," observed James Vernon.[32]

Had the insidious power of place and pension been what the Country party pamphleteers thought it to be, William could have relied upon the Court party to win him a large standing army. But the Court party was weak and discredited, a fact that presented the managers with a third difficulty. Sir Miles Cooke, himself a courtier, took some comfort from the fact that "the loaves and fishes were on our side," but then grew doubtful when he considered that "without a miracle four or five baskets full of preferment will be hardly able to feed five hundred persons."[33] More serious than the want of places was the disrepute that place brought. "All the young men that have places," observed James Lowther, "meet with the greatest discouragement that hardly any venture to speak."[34]

Faced with these staggering difficulties, the Whig managers in effect gave up management. They promoted the King's measures in a perfunctory manner. They remained silent in debates. They chose not to divide the House. Some of them—Thomas Pelham, for example—even deserted the King and voted with the opposition.[35] The result was a session deeply humiliating to the King. Parliament denied him the troops he needed, took his Dutch Guard from him, forced him to make retrenchments in Ireland, and denied him the supplies needed to sustain the government's credit.[36] Meanwhile, the ministers sought a safe refuge from the storm. Montagu had his brother hold the place of auditor of the Exchequer for him. Orford talked of leaving the Admiralty and remaining treasurer of the navy. Mr. Smith thought of securing a place as teller of the Exchequer. The emoluments of office they desired, but not the heat of the kitchen.[37]

That heat was the greater because the Country party had embarked upon an unremitting opposition to the present ministry. Harley and Foley launched the attack on 20 December by proposing an inquiry into mismanagements in the navy, mismanagements which, they declared, cost the kingdom a sum equal to the debts of the navy. They began with an inquiry into the passing of a victualling account without vouchers under a privy seal.[38] In January the Committee on the Admiralty inquired into the late sailing of the Straits squadron and the disposition of prizes taken in the Mediterranean. They dropped the matter of prizes when it appeared that Lord Orford had nothing to do with them, but a Committee of the Whole House, on 28 January, voted by 174 to 141 that not sending out the Streights squadron was a great prejudice and mismanagement. "This is the first successful attack," wrote Edward Harley, and added, "There are things of a much higher nature can be charged."[39]

In February and March, the committee searched for these higher matters, but in vain. They found that the Admiralty had paid one of its own members, Captain Priestman, back pay for service as a commander of a squadron in Charles II's reign, but the back pay came to only £400. They found that the paymaster had, without warrant, deducted one shilling in the pound from monies spent on tobacco, slop-clothes, chaplains, dead men's clothes, and the Chest at Chatham. They duly voted this a mismanagement. But when they sought to condemn Lord Orford for victualling the fleet without first securing proof of the prime cost of provisions, they failed by one vote to carry the question. And when, on 27 March, they sought to add to their address a clause requesting that the King place the Admiralty in other hands, they lost by four votes. On this occasion Foley and Winnington, moderate members of the Country party, joined with the court.[40] Great was the persistence of the opposition in their attack upon the Admiralty, but the filth in the Augean stables proved less deep than they expected.

But the opposition did not entirely fail in what Walter Moyle called the noble sport of "Ministry hunting."[41] They carried an address condemning mismanagement in the Admiralty, an address that the Commons presented to William on 3 April. Among the mismanagements complained of was the incompatibility of Lord Orford's being both treasurer of the navy and admiral. William gave a polite answer, but it was obvious that the political situation demanded more than a polite answer. The address of 3 April, joined to the general want of management during the session, made a reconstruction of the ministry necessary. To this end the Whig grandees met with William at Windsor in early May, surrounding him so closely, wrote Colonel Granville, "that no unfortunate Tory can be admitted into his presence."[42] But the Whigs failed of their purposes, for Shrewsbury refused to serve as lord chamberlain, William would not name Wharton secretary of state, and Orford suddenly resigned all his offices.[43] The congress at Windsor having failed, William in a more private manner reconstructed the ministry. He replaced the Duke of Leeds as lord president with the Earl of Pembroke and named Lord Lonsdale to succeed Pembroke as lord privy seal. To balance these two Tories, he named two inveterate Whigs, Jack Smith and Sir Thomas Littleton, to be chancellor of the Exchequer and treasurer of the navy respectively. He named Lord Tankerville to the Treasury and Lord Bridgewater to the Admiralty, both of them moderate Whigs. Perhaps it would be more accurate to call them *politiques*, for like Lord Jersey, whom William now named secretary of state, they espoused the King's cause more than that of any party. It was all an exercise in balancing and trimming, an exercise that William could now pursue because the Whigs were too discredited to resist and the Tories too disunited to protest.[44]

But the balancing and trimming in the spring of 1699 did not diminish the implacable resolve of the Tories to drive the Whigs from office. Not even Montagu's resignation from the Treasury in November lessened their determination. The three parliaments of 1697–98, 1698–99, and 1699–1700 saw the vehemence of the opposition mount in a crescendo of fury, each parliament angrier than the former. In 1697–98 Exchequer bills were the weapon and the Treasury the target; the next year the Admiralty was the target and mismanagement in the navy the weapon; in 1699–1700 the weapons were the piracy of Captain Kidd and the forfeited lands in Ireland, and the target was Lord Chancellor Somers.

The problems facing England in the autumn of 1699 were grave—an unpaid debt, a declining credit, soldier and seamen clamoring for pay—but the House of Commons no sooner assembled than it turned its attention to the affair of Captain Kidd. A consortium of Whig lords, among them Lord Somers, had commissioned William Kidd to hunt down pirates in the Indian Ocean. To their chagrin he turned pirate himself. The Country party now sought, even though Kidd had been captured, to declare that the letters patent granted to him were illegal and to place the chief blame for their being granted on Lord Somers. The House of Commons, however, defeated the motion by 56 votes.[45] Nothing daunted, the opposition launched inquiries into Lord Orford's taking a share in what the frigate *Dolphin* should recover from wrecks in the West Indies, into Lord Somers's accepting (as a gift from the King) lands set aside for the maintenance of Windsor, and Jack Smith's begging the reversion of a Welsh estate given to the King.[46] None of these inquiries led to the condemnation of a minister, but they weakened the ministry. Since they have "the power of the King's purse-strings," wrote one pamphleteer of the opposition, they will "puzzle his affairs; cross his politicks; tire him with troublesome tasks; confound his ministry with cross-purposes; deny him what they think he desires; advance whatever [they] think will displease him." They will not be satisfied, he concluded, until given office.[47]

The most artfully constructed machine to cross the King's purposes and confound his ministry was the bill for the resumption of forfeited lands in Ireland. William's grants of forfeited Irish lands were prodigious, and were made in violation of his promise not to dispose of those lands without consulting Parliament. Not even the Whigs would defend them, though they had often acquiesced in the grant of them. Indeed, it was their acquiescence in William's generosity to his Dutch favorites and to Lady Orkney that now gave the opposition the purchase with which to prize them from office. On 18 January 1700, the Country party persuaded the House to vote that the Irish grants had occasioned the nation's debts and that the advisers of them had acted dishonorably.[48]

But they had no proof that Somers had advised them. To find him guilty, they must also condemn the passing of the grants under the great seal. To this end Jack How, the boldest of the Tories, moved that the House debate the state of the nation on 13 February. As the day approached, the foreign ministers in London—Bonnet, L'Hermitage, Tallard—reported that the design was to attack the ministry under the guise of redressing grievances. "It is only a continuation," wrote Bonnet, "of that grand design about which one has spoken so often, which is to change the Ministry."[49] The opposition prepared carefully for the debate—rounding up absent members, winning over country members, annulling the election of those who spoke for the court. But these efforts proved of no avail. The House rejected by 52 votes a motion that the advising, procuring, and passing of the grants was dishonorable.[50] Most men attributed Somers's vindication to his reputation for probity and honesty; Edward Harley blamed it upon "the folly" of some who should have known better; but his vindication may well have arisen from Jack Smith's exposure of the blatant partiality of the proceedings. Edward Seymour had just employed all his eloquence to heighten Somers's conduct into a crime, when Smith rose to express his surprise that one who had approved the grants at the Treasury should condemn another for passing them at the Chancery. The hypocrisy revealed by Smith caused the House to fall silent.[51]

The baiting of the lord chancellor might have stopped there but for the blindness of the House of Lords and the persistence of the opposition. When the bill for the resumption of forfeited lands in Ireland reached the Lords, they amended it in three minor respects and sent it back to the Commons. This was like waving a red flag at a bull, for the Commons had tacked the resumption bill to a supply bill, and the Commons denied that the Lords could amend a supply bill: they could only reject or accept it. The Lords returned the amended bill to the Commons on 8 April. The next three days witnessed a political crisis unlike any seen for a decade. The Commons demanded that the Lords recede from their amendments. The Lords resolved to adhere to their amendments. William and his Dutch favorites worked for the defeat of the bill. Lady Orkney even sought to persuade the Tories to part with the bill upon condition the lord chancellor part with the seals. It was an unlikely bargain, yet one week earlier it had been rumored that the Tories would be content to lose the bill provided the Whigs were discarded.[52]

What the Tories really sought was both the passage of the bill and the discarding of the Whigs. They therefore stood adamantly behind the bill, while seizing the opportunity to attack Lord Somers. Seymour denounced him as a dangerous minister who had been bought by the court and was chiefly responsible for the present ill state of affairs. Others denounced the ministry as servile and corrupt. An inflamed House now passed the resolution that it had refused to pass in February; it voted that it was a high crime and misdemeanor for a privy councillor to procure or pass an exorbitant grant for his own use.[53] Two days later, on the tenth, it proceeded through a list of privy councillors, turning first to the name of Lord Somers. Sir John Leveson moved his impeachment, a motion that Sir Christopher Musgrave turned into an address requesting the King to remove Lord Somers from his councils and presence forever. But news having arrived that the Lords had passed the bill without any amendments, the fires of indignation died down. The Commons, by a vote of 167 to 106, rejected the address.[54] Some of the younger members then spoke of impeaching Portland and Albemarle, the King's Dutch favorites, but "they would not prosecute them to a question," observed James Lowther, "their business being, as they openly declared, to break the Ministry."[55]

The Commons, on that terrible Wednesday, did pass an address asking the King not to admit foreigners to his council. To prevent the Commons from presenting this address, William hurried to the House of Lords the next day, accepted 60 bills (among them the Irish forfeiture and the supply bill), and prorogued Parliament.[56] But prorogation did not solve the chief problem confronting William: whether to continue with his present ministers or turn to new ones.

It was not solely the fury of the attack on Somers that created the problem; it was also the complete collapse of the Whig management during the 1699–1700 session. At first matters moved auspiciously enough—numerous election petitions were decided in favor of the Whigs. Secretary Vernon was confident that the Whigs could "hold the government if not asked to do unpopular things."[57] But there was the rub: the King did ask them to do unpopular things. He asked them in January to seek to amend the Irish forfeiture bill so that the King might retain one-third of the lands. They made a feeble effort to this end, with no success other than to earn more obloquy.[58] Thereafter they remained silent, with the result that Robert Harley seized the management of the House from them. It was Harley who managed the business of supply. It was Harley who proposed that the land tax be reduced from three to two shillings in the pound and that the confiscated lands in Ireland be used to retire the debt. It was Harley who rallied the House behind the Irish forfeiture bill when spirits flagged in late March. It was Harley who opened the debate on 10 April with a speech depicting the deplorable state of the nation.[59] From February onward he and his confederates carried their measures with ease. They won disputed election returns, they excluded the Excise men from the House, they carried an address requesting the King to name men of quality and estates to the commissions of peace, and they established a commission to examine the accounts of all monies voted for the army and the navy since the revolution.[60] During the last weeks, Smith and Montagu, the great court spokesmen, remained silent; all the eloquence was on the other side. "There was not the appearance," wrote Burnet, "of a ministry at this time."[61]

In the politics of opposition, negotiation is the next step after opposition. Having demonstrated their power to obstruct His Majesty's government, the opposition had now to show its willingness to serve it. Sir Edward Seymour did so two days after the prorogation of Parliament by unexpectedly attending the King's dinner on Sunday, in order to ask leave to go into Ireland. William chastized him for his conduct in the last Parliament and expressed the hope that he would be a better friend in the next. Sir Edward replied, "Sir, I make no doubt of it."[62]

But the serious negotiations went on secretly, obliquely, obscurely, to the great puzzlement of historians since. "Several new schemes," wrote Harley on the twenty-fifth, "have been erected and vanished within these ten days. . . ."[63] One of these schemes may well have been that which Lord Jersey and Lord Albemarle, on behalf of the Tories, urged upon

William. It comprehended the dismissal of Lord Somers, further alteration in favor of the Tory party, and a new Parliament.[64] What Sunderland urged upon William will never be known for certain, but it appears that he advised him to yield to Parliament all that it asked. He may also have advised William to replace Lord Somers with John Methuen, the Irish lord chancellor. Such advice would be consonant with the Earl's love of the role of manager. The author of "The Present Disposition" observed: "It is well known, that if that noble Lord [Somers] had left the Great Seal behind him at Hampton Court, they had prepared for us an Irish successor [Methuen], whose Phiz and Conscience has no simily but that of his patron's [Sunderland's]."[65] Sunderland later denied that he had advised the dismissal of Lord Somers, but the Whigs did not believe him.[66]

The one rock-like fact is that William, whether on Albemarle's advice or Sunderland's, dismissed Lord Somers on 27 April 1700. Somers's dismissal, however, did not end the search for a new scheme of administration. It only made that search more imperative. The Tories, led by the Earl of Rochester, continued to urge their scheme upon the King. From the rumors attendant upon it, one can guess at its nature. Rochester was to enter the Cabinet, Sir Thomas Trevor would take the seals as lord keeper, Lord Jersey would become lord chamberlain, and preferment would be found for Harley and Harcourt, perhaps as secretary and solicitor.[67] The linchpin in this scheme was Trevor's appointment as lord keeper, but he refused the seals, despite a late-night visit from Rochester and daily importunities from Harley. The most that Rochester could secure for his party was the nomination of Nathan Wright, an unimportant Tory lawyer, as lord keeper.[68]

Meanwhile the Earl of Sunderland concocted an ambitious scheme that provided for Lord Somers's naming commissioners to retain the seals until he chose to resume them. The heart of this scheme was the reconciliation of the King with the Whigs through the instrumentality of Sunderland. But it came to nothing because of Montagu's and Wharton's and Orford's unconquerable distrust of Sunderland, whom they blamed for Vernon's preferment over Wharton in 1697 and for Somers's dismissal in the interest of John Methuen in 1700. The Earl always professed to be serving the Whigs, but he had a habit of recommending the appointment of courtiers—Trumbull, Vernon, Methuen—rather than Whigs. The effect was to produce a profound aversion in the Whigs to the Earl, and to wreck all his schemes.[69]

Neither Rochester's scheme for a new Tory ministry nor Sunderland's for a patched-up Whig ministry won the day. Instead, William, ever pursuing the ideal of a balanced ministry, resolved to govern with a mixture of Whigs, Tories, and neutrals. Shrewsbury should go to Ireland as lord lieutenant, Lord Jersey should become lord chamberlain in his place, and Lord Lexington should become secretary in Jersey's place. Those Whigs still in office (Lord Orford declared there were none) should remain in office. In pursuance of this strategy, William met with Charles Montagu, spoke freely with him about affairs, and assured him that he had no intention of turning the Whigs out of their employments.[70] At the same time, he met frequently with Rochester, to whom he offered the vice-royalty of Ireland (after Shrewsbury had refused it).[71] There was also talk of bringing Godolphin back to the Treasury. The King, observed Burnet, holds the middle between Whig and Tory, attempting to satisfy both equally.[72]

But William's balancing act only won time; it solved no problems. Because William had dismissed Somers and turned away from the Whigs, Shrewsbury (in bad health as always) refused to go to Ireland and resigned as lord chamberlain.[73] Because William had removed him from office, Somers refused to attend council meetings.[74] Because of his friendship for Somers, Lord Hartington refused the proferred appointment as gentleman of the bedchamber, though worth £1,000 a year.[75] The same querulous spirit animated the Tories. Because William would not commit himself to the Tories, Rochester in June refused the office of vice-roy of Ireland.[76] Because Tankerville sat at the Treasury, Godolphin would not meddle with it. Because Harcourt was not made solicitor general, Harley predicted that the House of Commons would be a cockpit the next session. Secretary Vernon concluded that the parties had grown so heated against one another that nothing but the destruction of the other would satisfy each.[77] Neither the Whigs nor the Tories, remarked Bonnet, will be satisfied unless they have all power in their hands.[78]

Before he left for Holland in July, William met for more than an hour with the Earl of Rochester, the younger son of the first Earl of Clarendon, a high churchman, a passionate Tory, a blunt man, a difficult one.[79] The understanding that emerged from that meeting formed the kernel of an undertaking by the Tories to manage Parliament for the King the next winter. This undertaking was not a neat package of demands and promises, presented at one time, but rather a long series of negotiations carried out over many months through the mediation of Sunderland and Henry Guy in London and the Earl of Jersey in Holland. The first step in this undertaking was the decision to give the government of Ireland to Rochester. By the middle of August, William had resolved upon this appointment, though it is unclear whether Rochester, who aspired to the chief direction of affairs in London, desired it. In July rumor made him lord privy seal and in November president of the Council. William finally resolved the problem by admitting Rochester to the cabinet on 7 December and by declaring him lord lieutenant of Ireland on 12 December—with the proviso that he need not go to Ireland until the spring.[80]

The second step in these negotiations was the nomination of a new lord privy seal, the former privy seal, Lord Lonsdale, having died in July. But on this question, the schemes of the courtiers and those of the politicians diverged. Lord Jersey, now the greatest schemer among the courtiers, favored giving the privy seal to the Whig earl of Tankerville, thereby removing him from the Treasury to make room for Godolphin. The politicians agreed that Tankerville should leave the Treasury to make room for Godolphin, but they wanted no Whigs in high office. Henry Guy, who constantly met or corresponded with Harley, Sunderland, Godolphin, Rochester, and Marlborough, believed Tankerville's receiving the privy seal would wreck all their measures and be tantamount to inviting Lord Somers back. He opposed offering the post to Tankerville.[81]

Sunderland was more sanguine. He was certain Tankerville would not accept it, even though the Whigs desired the post for him. Indeed, the Tory strategy seems to have been for the King to offer the privy seal to Tankerville, for him to refuse it, and for the King then to offer it to Sir Christopher Musgrave. But the best laid plans of mice and men go oft astray. When William on 29 October offered the privy seal to Tankerville, he accepted it.[82]

Upon the very day that William gave the privy seal to Tankerville, L'Hermitage heard that Marlborough was soon to be named secretary of state. During the following week, his appointment was the constant talk of the town. On 5 November the King held a great council at the Cockpit, where it was thought he would name Marlborough as secretary. But then, to the surprise of many, he called in Sir Charles Hedges and gave him the seals. Sir Charles, it is true, was a Tory, but a moderate Tory, a judge of the Admiralty, a courtier whose election to Parliament the year before had been successfully contested by the Country party. Men wondered who the author of this appointment might be. They might have noticed that the King dined that day with the Earl of Jersey.[83]

The heart of the new Tory scheme was Godolphin's return to the Treasury as the first commissioner, and to this end the Earl of Tankerville had been kicked upstairs. Yet Godolphin's appointment was delayed until 7 December. This delay did not arise from William's reluctance to name Godolphin; it arose from Godolphin's stiffness in laying down conditions for entering the Treasury. He insisted that the Whig Jack Smith be removed from the Treasury, he demanded that all orders for the expenditure of monies bear a privy seal, and he cavilled at William Lowndes's serving as secretary to the Treasury. But William held out, and Godolphin finally agreed to become first commissioner of the Treasury without these conditions being met.[84] William was prepared to entrust the Tories with the management of affairs, but not to capitulate to them totally.

It is of the nature of parliamentary undertakings that they concern measures as well as men. Thus Rochester and his allies not only asked that Tories be named to high office but also that William pursue measures they deemed necessary to their undertaking. Six measures in particular they sought: the meeting of Convocation, changes in the Ecclesiastical Commission, alterations in the lieutenancy of London, the removal of Charles Montagu to the Lords, the summoning of a new Parliament, and the election of Robert Harley as Speaker of the new House of Commons. Since Rochester would not agree to accept office unless Convocation was called, William in early December agreed to summon it.[85] In early December he also raised Montagu to the peerage as Lord Halifax. On 19 December, having first named new sheriffs to suit the Tories, William dissolved the Parliament, which the undertakers thought too Whiggish, and ordered the election of a new one.[86] When the new Parliament met in February, the court threw its weight behind the election of Robert Harley as Speaker.[87] The third Earl of Shaftesbury, a country Whig of pristine virtue, summed up the political situation thus: Godolphin, Rochester, and the rest of that party are now "esteemed the undertakers and to be the managers in a new Parliament chosen by their interest." All things are "put into their hands and pledges given to the Church party such as were desired."[88]

William did not turn to the Tories because he liked them. In fact, he found Rochester insufferable and was disenchanted with Godolphin. Harley, with whom he often conferred secretly, he respected, but he could hardly forget that Harley had opposed him on the treason bill, the standing army, and the forfeited lands in Ireland. It was from necessity, not choice, that he turned to the Tories; he needed their help in the management of Parliament.[89] This need became even more acute upon the death in July of the Duke of Gloucester, the only surviving child of Princess Anne. To prevent the return of the House of Stuart, it became imperative to establish the succession in the House of Hanover. The Tories readily undertook to establish the succession in Hanover, so William turned to them.[90]

The need to turn to the Tories was the greater because the Whigs were in total disarray. In August the Whig politicians met in a great conclave at Boughton, the Earl of Montagu's house in Northamptonshire, but that meeting did not check the disintegration of their party. Sunderland, who was now serving the Tories, did not attend. Vernon, who had concluded that the Tories were too strong to be ignored and the Whigs too weak to be trusted, leaned toward a moderate Tory scheme. Shrewsbury, the premier Whig, fled to Montpellier, in France. Montagu gladly accepted a peerage. For William the choice was either no management at all or a Tory management.[91]

The Tories undertook to manage Parliament for William, but what particular measures they promised to carry for him are unclear. The succession of the House of Hanover was certainly part of the undertaking, as the correspondence of Henry Guy and the memoir of Edward Harley make clear.[92] The Tories probably also undertook to win the King a vote of supply, though it is doubtful whether that supply would be sufficient to begin to repay the government's debts. Colonel Granville, who knew the genius of the Tory party well, declared in August that the next Parliament would give no more than two shillings in the pound, merely enough to pay for the fleet, the guards, and the garrisons.[93]

More perplexing to the historian is the attitude of the Tories toward the Spanish Succession. In November, Charles II, King of Spain, died, leaving his sprawling domains to Philip, Duke of Anjou. Louis XIV, ignoring the treaty he had made with William for the partition of the Spanish domains, accepted the whole Spanish inheritance for his grandon. John Oldmixon, the historian, reports that the Church party, in return for employment, offered to support William in a war to preserve the balance of Europe.[94] Lord Coningsby, the politician, tells a similar story. The King, he writes, was now thrown into the hands of the Tories, that party having "the majority of the House of Commons." "And he was the rather induced to comply with this necessity, my Lord Rochester, Sir Edward Seymour, and that party having given him, as he told me, full assurances that they would . . . come in to the vigorous carrying on of the war against France. . . . "[95] But the story told by the historian and the politician seems most improbable, for most Tories preferred the will to partition and sought peace, not war. Furthermore, William's letters to Heinsius in February reveal no such undertaking. William confessed to Heinsius that he could not foresee what Parliament might do in relation to war against France.[96]

Whatever the exact terms, the Tories had undertaken to manage Parliament for the King and must now endeavor to do so successfully. Their chief reliance in that endeavor was upon a Tory party, a new Tory party that had emerged in the late 1690s and that now possessed a majority in the House of Commons.[97] For this reason the elections held in the winter of 1701 were crucial. The Tories began preparing for the elections even before Parliament was dissolved—new sheriffs were picked, new justices of the peace named, circular letters sent to Tory members, the clergy enlisted. The Whigs, crying "To your tents, O Israel," entered the campaign with equal warmth.[98] The result of this furious campaign was a House of Commons with a modest Tory majority—ten or twelve votes. A Tory Election Committee and a Tory House soon improved this majority by declaring invalid the election of some thirty Whigs.[99] Many Tories were angry at Rochester for not securing a greater triumph at the polls, but they probably exaggerated what the weight of the court could do for a party. Indeed, Herr Hoffman, the imperial envoy, thought that any party for which the King declared, be it ever so strong before, would be overwhelmed.[100] He exaggerated, too. In truth, the support of the court probably counted for less than politicians at the time and historians since have believed.

The Tories also relied upon those arts of parliamentary management that Robert Harley had mastered. Harley's participation was central to the Tory scheme of government. Without him Rochester and Godolphin probably could not have persuaded William to entertain their undertaking. In September, for example, when negotiations for a Tory scheme threatened to founder before Jersey's meddling hands, Henry Guy urged that all must be done by Harley, "for only he will have the power." He must meet with the King, "and must be positive and bold, and rely upon his strength, for that will be sufficiently able to do it thoroughly."[101] And so it proved to be. William met with Harley, listened to his proposals, and embraced the Tory scheme. Part of the scheme was the election of Harley as Speaker, for he had the respect of both parties and the skill to preside over the House. In the ensuing session, he did not act as impartially as some had imagined he would, but neither was there any complaint of a want of management.

Though the Tories had gained office by opposing the court, they sought its support in the management of Parliament. It was the support of the court that give Harley the handsome majority by which he became Speaker. It was the opposition of the court that prevented the Tories from carrying votes in favor of peace. With court support the Whigs were able to declare the commission granted to Captain Kidd to be lawful,[102] and with court support the Whigs were able to defeat a Tory attempt on 29 March to censure Lord Somers. This last act by the court proved the final straw to the Tories. That night they called a special meeting, where it was said that one could now see that the King had named Tory ministers only for appearance sake and that at heart he still sympathized with the Whigs. Until he separated wholly from that party, it was vowed, they would not vote him a farthing for the war.[103] Clearly, the Tories were now less interested in destroying the court interest than in capturing it. Over the applying of Mary of Modena's jointure to public use, Robert Harley, the former enemy of placemen, now chastised the King for not making his own servants stand firm.[104] There was yet other evidence that the Tories sought to capture, not destroy, the power of patronage. No sooner had Godolphin and Rochester entered the cabinet than they were advising the King whom he should name as chief justice of the Common Pleas (Sir Thomas Trevor), whom he should name clerk of the council (Musgrave's son), and whom he should make a Welsh judge (Harley's friend, Price).[105] Desiring to succeed Mr. Meesters as comptroller of the Ordnance, James Lowther paid his court to the Earl of Rochester.[106] It was not merely office that the undertakers sought, but control of patronage as well.

Putting on the livery of the court, however, had its drawbacks, as previous undertakers had discovered. The popularity that came from opposing the court receded before the odium that came from serving it. Robert Harley did not escape this dilemna. "His ten year opposition to the Court," wrote Edmund Gibson, "followed by such a sudden turn to that side, is made use of by enemies to his disadvantage."[107] But Robert Harley and his allies found an answer to this dilemma: the continued espousal of popular causes. In the 1701 session, they examined the accounts of the commissioners of the Prizes, threatened to examine Littleton's accounts, prohibited commissioners of the Customs from sitting in the House, and added to the bill of succession a long catalog of popular measures—against foreigners, against secret counsels, against placemen.[108]

It was only a small step from the espousal of popular causes back to the politics of opposition. The most astonishing fact about the 1701 session was the renewed attack that the Tories launched against William's former ministers, an attack whose fury marks the apotheosis of the politics of opposition. Opposition seems to have become a habit and hatred for the Whigs an obsession. Parliament had hardly met before the Tories whispered that they would have Lord Somers's neck for sealing the Partition Treaty.[109] In March both Houses voted addresses condemning the Partition Treaty and the manner in which it was made. Nottingham declared in the Lords that it was the worst treaty made since John Lackland sold the kingdom to the pope.[110] On 14 April the House of Commons impeached Lord Somers, Lord Halifax, and Lord Orford for advising the first Partition Treaty, whereby large territories of the King of Spain were delivered to France. The next day they asked William to remove the impeached lords from his councils and presence forever. They then delayed as long as possible the prosecution of their impeachments, knowing they could not justify them before the House of Lords. The motive behind these impeachments was less a desire to see justice done than a desire to abase, blast, crush, and ruin the Whig party, so that its leaders would never come into office again. The Tories wished to ensure that when war came the King would employ them, not the Whigs, in its management. Such was the testimony, not only of Tallard and Bonnet and L'Hermitage and Vernon, but also of Tories such as Matthew Prior and the Earl of Nottingham.[111]

The Tories failed in their vendetta against the Whig lords, and their failure says much about the locus of power in the English constitution. The House of Lords, in which the Whigs now had a majority, indisputably possessed the power of judicature in cases of impeachment. The King, determined that the Whigs should not be wholly proscribed, possessed the power to name his own councillors and ministers. Against the Lords determination to bring the impeached lords to trial and the King's refusal to dismiss them from the Privy Council, the Commons had only the power of the purse. It was a weapon that had allowed them in April 1700 to sweep aside the combined resistance of King and Lords in the matter of the resumption of Irish forfeited lands. But the situation was now altered. In the first place, the resumption bill had been tacked—not wholly unreasonably—to a supply bill, which made the operation of the power of the purse automatic. In the second place, the resumption of Irish forfeited lands was an immensely popular measure. This was not true of the impeachment of Lord Somers, which carried by only ten votes in a House with nearly four hundred members present. Nor were Orford and Halifax seen as threats to liberty, even though Harley declared that to fail to impeach them would be to put the ax to the roots of English liberty.[112] The Tories repeatedly spoke of delaying supply until the King had dismissed the impeached lords, but they did not dare do so because the progress of French troops across Flanders and into Milan created a mounting demand that Parliament vote the King the money he needed to sustain his allies.[113]

The politics of opposition was a game that others could play, as the Whigs now demonstrated by resorting to such tactics. In March they launched an inquiry into Rochester's and Godolphin's role in delaying the meeting of Parliament until February, thereby allowing France to seize Flanders. The Commons now examined the letters of Blathwayt to the Tory lords, just as they had examined the letters of Vernon to the Whig lords. And though these inquiries revealed nothing, the irrepressible Lord Wharton raised the matter in the House of

Lords.[114] The Whigs also left to the Tories the odium of introducing a supply bill that placed three shillings in the pound on land. The Whigs even opposed the rate of three shillings in order to show the King that he ought to rely upon them. They supported even more enthusiastically than the Tories limitations on the successor to the crown.[115] In the Lords they even resorted to the power of the purse, delaying the supply bill until the impeached lords had been tried and acquitted.[116]

When all these tactics failed to secure the Whigs the majority they sought, they resorted to the classic move of the opposition, classic since the days of the second duke of Buckingham: they appealed to the electorate, and they sought the dissolution of Parliament. Whigs on the Grand Jury of Kent, Whigs on the Common Council of London, Whigs in every county petitioned and wrote urging the Commons to end their divisions and to support the war.[117] Only by suddenly proroguing Parliament on 24 June could William prevent the House of Lords from framing an address asking him to dissolve Parliament.[118]

Having prorogued Parliament, William now had to decide whether to continue to rely upon the Tories or to return to the Whigs. Weighing in the balance for a continued reliance upon the Tories was the fact that they had largely succeeded in their undertaking. They had settled the succession. They had secured the King an adequate supply. They had persuaded the Commons to support those alliances that His Majesty thought fit to make to reduce the exorbitant power of France. Weighing against a reliance upon the Tories was their inability to restrain the extremists in their own party, their unwillingness to call off their civil war with the Whigs, and their obvious reluctance to see England enter into war against France. It was the hot party among the Tories, for example, who took £100,000 away from the King's civil list.

> This incident [wrote John Ellis] has put our Ministry into very great disorder, as tending much to the diminution of their credit with the King, since they have so little authority with their party as not to be able to restrain them from passing unreasonable and extravagant things only to lessen the King, and it is not doubted

but it will put the King upon employing the Whigs again, as they are usually called.[119]

The factiousness of the Tories cannot have pleased William. Their fierce attack upon the Whigs caused Jack Smith to resign from the Treasury and Lord Shaftesbury to write that had he a son, he would "sooner breed him a cobbler than a courtier, and a hangman than a statesman."[120] But what must have given William most alarm was the reluctance of the Tories to commit England to a war against France. True, they finally did, with the address of 12 June, but they did so largely from fear—from a fear of displeasing the court, from a fear of being replaced by the Whigs, from a fear of a dissolution and defeat at the polls, from a fear even, reported Bonnet, of being stoned to death on their return home.[121]

In the spring of 1700, James Vernon had predicted that there would be an auction for offices next winter, with offices going to the fairest bidder.[122] He proved wrong, for the Whigs were too bankrupt to bid for anything. But the auction that he predicted for the winter of 1701 did occur in the autumn of 1701. Both Whigs and Tories then sought to persuade William to employ them. To this end they each made promises and presented demands. The style of their undertakings, however, differed. The Tories were importunate, the Whigs polite.

Led by the overbearing Lord Rochester, the Tories pressed hard upon the King. They wanted the Ecclesiastical Commission altered in their favor; they wanted the commissions of the peace in the North changed; they wanted Whigs removed from lesser offices; they wanted the lieutenancy of London altered; they wanted the present Parliament continued. In return they gave the King great hopes and fair promises.[123] To some of these demands William yielded—he altered the commissions of the peace in the North and the London lieutenancy. But before he went further, he wanted a promise from the leaders of the Tory party that they would not renew their impeachments in the next session. He dreaded the prospect of entering a war against France only to see the supply bill lost because of a quarrel between the two Houses. He therefore called in the leading Tories and asked them if they would promise to lay aside their partisan quarrels. They refused.[124] They were bent, as St. John confessed he was, on the great work of destroying a dying party.[125]

At the very moment when the Tories were demonstrating a bitter intransigency, the Whigs exhibited a newfound diplomacy. Through the Earl of Sunderland, Lord Somers entered into negotiations with the King. The ensuing correspondence between the three men reveals more vividly than any other correspondence in William's reign the nature of a parliamentary undertaking. Lord Somers should, advised the Earl, tell the King "what he and his friends can do, and will do, and what they can expect, and the methods they would propose." But this must be done delicately. Somers should not insist on things that are not absolutely necessary. He should not ask for anything for himself or for the other impeached lords, but rather should make the King "find as much ease as may be; for if the main be agreed to, all the rest will follow." "The main," of course, was the dissolution of Parliament. Somers readily agreed to these tactics. He would ask nothing for himself or for any other Whig. These matters would be left to later "accidents," but this fact must be explained to his friends; otherwise he would be deprived of the only assistance he valued.[126]

Lord Somers then drew up arguments to induce the King to call a new Parliament, some of which he may have used when he met with William in November. In this paper he dwelled upon the Tories' disinclination for war, the number of Jacobites among them, the likelihood of their reviving the differences between the two Houses, and their inability to govern their own party. He then assured the King that if he dissolved Parliament and turned to the Whigs, they could win him a majority in Parliament (a fact that Harley assured the King the Whigs could not do). Furthermore, Somers continued, the Whigs would "leave him entirely to his own scheme on the plan of a new Parliament." But behind this generous offer lay a veiled threat. To set himself at ease, the King must "trust those whom the body of the people do not distrust." And if he did not, if he persisted in the uncertainties of a Tory ministry, then "it is in the power of one side to interrupt as well as the other."[127]

It is unlikely that Somers voiced this last threat to the King, for he shared with Sunderland an intuitive understanding of William's pride and sense of dignity. One might suggest to the King whom he should employ, but one should not tell him. The King might be forced by circumstances to accept one set of ministers, but he should not be *seen* to be forced. It is the quality of disguise that made the mechanism of a parliamentary undertaking so useful; it hid, perhaps even from the King himself, the insensible transfer of the prerogative to name ministers of state from the King to the party that governed in Parliament. Not all Englishmen were so anxious to disguise this transfer. In fact, there was probably never a time in the history of England—unless it was the years 1642 and 1643—when so many pamphleteers called for the formal nomination of the King's ministers by Parliament. John Toland did so, in *The Art of Governing by Parties*, as did the anonymous authors of *Limitations for the New Successor*, *The Dangers of Europe*, *The Claims of the People*, and *Lex Vera*.[128] But their voices were not heeded, for the substance of their demands were gained in ways less disruptive to the constitution and less insulting to the monarch.

On 11 November 1701, William dissolved Parliament and turned to the Whigs. The Tories attributed the decision to the secret machinations of Sunderland and to the nefarious advice of the Dutch, but it probably arose from their own refusal to end their civil war with the Whigs and the willingness of the Whigs to serve William without making unacceptable demands.[129] No sooner had the King announced the dissolution than Sunderland wrote Somers a long letter, filled with wise counsel. He desired "others to make the scheme for the ministry and the conduct of the Parliament." But having said this, he proceeded to give his advice freely. The King should, with all his power, support the Whigs in the elections. When Parliament met, it should be managed by those methods that proved so successful in the year 1696. The King's servants should be made to come up immediately, and should be told the King's intentions. Some measure upon which the Whigs could gain a majority should be put forth at the opening of the session. Lord Somers should help compose the King's speech, which should exhort the two Houses to end their divisions. The King should send an Act of Grace to the two Houses. Sunderland, though he disavowed such an intention, even fell to drawing up a scheme for the ministry. The King should name the Duke of Somerset lord chamberlain, should make the Earl of Carlisle first commissioner of the Treasury, should replace Sir Charles Hedges with Lord Wharton, and should bring Jack Smith into the Treasury.[130]

Toward this scheme of administration William took a hesitant step on 23 December, when he named the Earl of Carlisle to the Treasury in the place of Godolphin, who had resigned in a huff over the dissolution. He replaced Hedges with the Earl of Manchester in January. But here the changes stopped, for the Whigs did not win the majority they had hoped for. Once again the King's electoral support—admittedly half-hearted—had proved less effective than many, including Sunderland, thought it would be.[131] The weakness of the Whigs became evident when the combined forces of the Whigs and court were unable to elect Sir Thomas Littleton Speaker of the House of Commons. Robert Harley carried it by four votes. The incident also reveals how frail were the ties of place and how powerful were those of party. The Rookes and the Churchills at the Admiralty voted against Littleton, though he was the court nominee.[132]

From William's point of view, the nearly exact division of the House of Commons between Whig and Tory proved a blessing. He could now indulge in his beloved policy of trimming, for neither party had a majority so great as to imprison him.[133] He could govern with moderate Whigs at the Treasury and Secretary's office and moderate Tories at the Admiralty and Chancery. His independence of action was further enhanced by Louis XIV's recognition of the Pretender as King of England, for this act provoked an enthusiasm for the war that infected even the Tories. The Commons voted unanimously for the alliances and for the supplies needed to wage war against France.[134]

But the Tories, as they had shown over four turbulent

years, disliked a policy of trimming between two parties. They still sought to use their power in the House to drive the Whigs from office forever. To this end they proposed on 26 February that the House of Commons "had not right done them in the matter of the impeachments in the last Parliament." Robert Harley spoke passionately for it. The sick were carried into the House to vote for it. The debate raged for eight hours, with little civility and no decorum. The Whigs rallied their forces. When the House divided, at nine in the evening, the opponents of the motion found they had a majority of four-teen.[135] The Whigs and the court had blocked the Tories in their last, vindictive attack upon the leaders of the Whig party. William could live out his remaining days—hardly more than a week—in the confidence that this session would be harmonious and brief. The politics of opposition had been momentarily checked, but only momentarily, as the reign of Queen Anne was to show.

Chapter VII

The Whig Scheme of 1705–1709

TO THE FACT THAT Queen Anne was a woman, broken in health, slow of wit, bashful, and weak in understanding, historians have attributed the decline of the monarch's personal power in the early eighteenth century.[1] But much that is attributed to her weakness ought to be attributed to her situation. The England she sought to govern had changed profoundly from the England of a century before. To undertake to manage Parliament for the monarch was no longer the crime it had been in Neville's day. To accept office in return for such an undertaking was no longer the unpardonable sin it had been in the Earl of Bedford's time. To wear the livery of the court no longer rendered one powerless, for one could now rely upon a party for support. And the polarity of court and country, resurgent in 1698, gave way to that of Whig and Tory.[2] Nor was it any longer an unspeakable act, as Clarendon believed it to be, to oppose those in office merely to wrest office from them. Indeed, Clarendon's own son, the Earl of Rochester, had furiously assailed the Whig lords in order to win a monopoly of office for his party. And it was not simply the emoluments of office that each party sought but the power that went with it, particularly the power of patronage. To win office and to secure the power of patronage, men were quite willing to use their strength in Parliament; and though they were not willing to oppose a supply bill directly, they were willing to lessen it or to impair the ways and means to sustain it or to delay it until they had harassed the government. Nor could the monarch, financially dependent on Parliament as he or she was, long resist the importunities of those who governed there, particularly in the House of Commons. It was a very different world from that over which Queen Elizabeth governed.

At the opening of her reign, however, Queen Anne enjoyed as full a liberty to name her own servants as had any King or Queen before her. She nominated her favorite, Marlborough, as captain general of Her Majesty's forces and his close friend Godolphin as lord treasurer, and she entrusted to them the management of her affairs. She then revealed her predilection for the party that defended her beloved church by removing Whigs and naming Tories in their place. From Thomas Wharton, the most zealous of Whigs, she took the staff of comptroller of the Household, which she then gave to Sir Edward Seymour, the most redoubtable of Tories. She named the Earl of Nottingham, whom the Whigs had driven from office in 1693, her secretary of state, and made Sir Charles Hedges, whom Lord Jersey had brought into the government in 1700, his fellow secretary. Rochester became once again lord lieutenant of Ireland. Other Tories were brought into the Household, named to the council, placed on commissions, and promoted in the church. By the summer of 1702, there were only two Whigs left in high office—Devonshire and Somerset—and a small host of them in subaltern offices.[3]

Queen Anne enjoyed the liberty to name Tories to office for two reasons: because the Tories were willing to accept her terms for entering into office, and because the Tories won a majority of seats in the new Parliament elected in 1702.

The management of affairs in 1702 rested with Marlborough and Godolphin, and they had no intention of entrusting office to a party that would not support the war against France. They therefore secured an undertaking from the leaders of the Tory party that they would, if given office, carry on the war and maintain the alliances. The Tories gave such assurances and received office.[4]

The Tories could hardly have carried out their undertaking had they not won a majority of seats in the House of Commons. Their victory was a resounding one, a majority of 133 over the Whigs.[5] Their victory raises a central question about the politics of these years: Could a monarch name ministers of his or her choice and then secure for them a majority at the next election? The experience of the year 1702 suggests that it was possible, but one should look closely at the reasons for the court's victory in that year. In the first place, Marlborough and Godolphin, the managers, did not want a great Tory triumph. They feared it and made no effort to secure it.[6] The leaders of the Tory party soon complained that the law officers were not changed, that the Tories were not told earlier of the dissolution, and that Whigs were left in commissions of the peace.[7] "Trimming goes on at a great rate," wrote St. John.[8] Yet the Queen did, when proroguing the old Parliament, declare her favor for the Church party; and the lord keeper, advised by Seymour, did purge Whigs from the commissions of the peace in Devonshire and Worcestershire. Through his control over patronage, Lord Thanet won four seats for the Tories in Westmorland.[9] The picture is a confused one, but one hypothesis ought certainly to be entertained—the hypothesis that the Tories rode to victory, not on any changes in the commissions of the peace, but on that wave of enthusiasm that always greets a new monarch, whether it be a Henry VIII, a Charles I, or a James II.[10]

The Queen and her managers chose, then, to ally with the Tory party, and for two years that alliance proved fruitful. Tories in the House of Commons voted to send 40,000 men to wage war on the Continent, gave £50,000 in subsidies to England's allies, quashed an inquiry into the defeat at Cadiz, imposed four shillings in the pound on land, and gave the Earl of Nottingham a resounding vote of confidence when the Whigs attacked his handling of an alleged Jacobite plot in Scotland.[11] Yet this fruitful alliance between managers and party collapsed within two years.

It did not collapse because of the strength of the Whig opposition, though oppose the Whigs did, especially in the House of Lords, where they had a majority whenever party issues came before the House. The Whigs defended the bishop of Worcester, whom the Tories attacked, and cleared the reputations of Halifax and Orford, whose accounts the Tories questioned. They then carried the war into the enemies' camp by taking the investigation of the Jacobite plot out of the hands of the Earl of Nottingham and placing it in a committee of the House of Lords, a committee composed wholly of Whigs. In March the House of Lords censured the government for failing to prosecute a witness who had sought to discredit the plot. They also voted a series of addresses condemning the government in general, and Admiral Graydon in particular, for mismanagements in the Navy.[12] These censures proved a nuisance to the government and an affront to Nottingham, but, occurring in the House of Lords, they did not endanger that scheme of administration established in the spring of 1702.[13] What brought down that scheme was the Tory desertion of the alliance upon which it rested.

In truth, the managers and the politicians held very different views of the character and purposes of their alliance. The managers believed that the control of patronage and the shaping of policy should remain with them. A few Tories might sit in the Cabinet and other Tories might enjoy lesser employment, but they must not demand a monopoly of the Queen's favor. The leading Tories in the Commons might meet at Harley's house to plan strategy. They might decide how best to promote moderation, how to hasten money bills, and how to defend Her Majesty's ministers from attack, but they must not dictate to the Queen or her servants. I shall "be governed by neither party," vowed Marlborough, and Godolphin was of the same mind.[14] The managers had no illusion, of course, that they could manage the House of Commons solely through the placemen there: they were too few in number, only some 120, and of these only 60 were court dependents.[15] What they chiefly relied upon was prudent management, military success abroad, and the deference that Tory members ought to show to the Queen and her servants. In the last years of William's reign, Robert Harley had pursued a politics of opposition; now he advocated a politics of deference. The Tories should defer to the Queen and her managers, of whom he was one.[16]

But Nottingham and Rochester and Seymour had no intention of being junior partners in the firm. From the beginning they sought to purge all Whigs from the government and to prevent their return. To this end they persuaded the Commons to vote censures against the bishop of Worcester, Lord Ranelagh, the Victualling Office, and Halifax and Orford. To this end they urged Godolphin to remove all Whigs from the

Treasury. To this end they had the Commons declare to the Queen that the church could not be perfectly restored until those men be divested "of the power, who have shewn they want not the will, to destroy it."[17] And to this end they sought both in 1702 and 1703 to pass a bill against the practice of occasional conformity, a practice that allowed Dissenters to slip into offices of profit in the government.[18]

The alliance established in 1702 between the managers and the politicians collapsed the moment the Tories discovered that Godolophin did not intend to remove the remaining Whigs from the Treasury, that the High Fliers could not determine all ecclesiastical appointments, and that the court managers, however they might vote, worked surreptiously against the passage of the bill to prevent occasional conformity. The Earl of Rochester's patience snapped first; he resigned in February 1703 rather than obey the Queen's command to take up his duties in Ireland. Nottingham resigned the next year when the Queen not only refused his demand that Devonshire and Somerset be dismissed from the Cabinet, but took the occasion to dismiss Jersey and Seymour from their offices at court. Office without power is not what Rochester and Nottingham sought.[19]

"'Tis not taken that this is a change from Tories to Whigs," wrote Charles Davenant, once an extremist and now a moderate, "but from violence to Moderation."[20] Thus the managers who had engineered Rochester's resignation and provoked Nottingham's now turned to moderate Tories, not to Whigs. Godolphin persuaded the Queen to name Kent as lord chamberlain; Harley secured for Sir Thomas Mansell the office of comptroller, and Marlborough insisted on Harley's being named secretary. It was a moderate scheme, a nonparty scheme, a scheme that appealed to men's reason and to their loyalty to the Queen. But it was a precarious scheme, based on a small number of men, as even Davenant admitted.[21] And Daniel Defoe warned Harley that "now the two ends will be reconciled to overturn the middle," and will "easily put by all this scheme of management."[22]

As regards the Tories, Defoe proved a true prophet. Led by Bromley and Seymour, the Tories in November 1704 resolved

to oppose the government on the question of occasional conformity. They resolved further to tack their bill against occasional conformity to the supply bill. Against this divisive and
mischievous measure the managers brought all their forces to
bear, and defeated it by 251 votes to 134. Marlborough's great
triumph at Blenheim helped bring victory in the Commons,
but military success abroad, though a necessary cause, was not
a sufficient cause of political success at home. The defeat of
the "Tackers" was also the result of the consummate skill of
Harley and Godolphin in the management of the House.
Harley canvassed 90 moderate Tories; Godolphin drilled the
placemen into submission. In the final vote, some 100 Tories
left their party.[23]

But the Tories lost—as Defoe and St. John saw—because
they chose the worst possible issue upon which to challenge
the government.[24] The Whigs were bound to vote against the
bill, for it violated their principles and subverted their interests. Given a unanimous Whig vote against tacking, the
managers had only to detach the moderate Tories from the
true believers. The result was to divide the Tory party and to
enrage a major part of it. The split in the party made it less
useful to the court, and the rage of the High Church wing
made it a constant threat to the court. The ultimate effect was
to drive the government to an unwelcome reliance upon the
Whigs, a reliance whose extent was revealed to the political
world when Lord Haversham set off his bomb.

On 23 November, Lord Haversham rose in the House of
Lords and delivered an eloquent and telling speech against the
ministry, a speech in which he complained of the loss of coin,
of abuses in the Navy, and, above all, of the Queen's assent to
the Act of Security, an act that allowed the Scots, upon the
Queen's death, to settle the succession on a family other than
Hanover. Six days later the Lords resumed the debate on the
danger that the Act of Security presented to England, at
which time Nottingham and Rochester led the attack. Lord
Halifax then joined in the assault, threatening that "conjunction of extremes" feared by Defoe. But Lord Wharton whispered with Godolphin, then spoke to Somers, who then, with
Wharton, spoke to Halifax.[25] The Whig Lords thereupon

secured a postponement of the debate for a week, in order, wrote Roxburgh, "to get a thorough conjunction between the Lord Treasurer and the Whigs."[26] It was, wrote Lord Dartmouth, a crisis in Lord Godolphin's career. Until then he had played a double game, and now he had to choose; and he chose "to deliver himself entirely into their [the Whig's] management, provided they bring him off."[27] Bring him off they did, diverting in the Lords and defeating in the Commons votes of censure against Godolphin for advising the Queen to assent to the Act of Security.[28]

Four days after Godolphin's escape, in the dusk of early evening, Bishop Nicolson strolled from Gray's Inn to Swallow Street, where he visited with Colonel Graham. "The new Scheme of Alterations at Court," the Colonel told the Bishop, is "to run thus: Lord Pembroke to be Admiral; Lord Somers President of the Council; Lord Sunderland Secretary of State, &c."[29] Secretary Johnston heard a like report: "The Lord Treasurer . . . has now made up with the Whigs. Somers, Peterborough, &c. are to be in."[30] Four years later Pembroke was lord admiral, Somers, lord president, and Sunderland, secretary of state, just as Colonel Graham had predicted. But the triumph of "the new Scheme" did not come easily; it required four years of fierce political struggle and bitter negotiation.

Godolphin survived the parliamentary session of 1704–5 unscathed; but the Whigs, who had protected him, now asked for their reward, and it was slow in coming. True, the Queen did, on Godolphin's declaring that he could not otherwise answer for what Parliament might do, take the privy seal from the Tory Duke of Buckingham and give it to the Duke of Newcastle, a moderate Whig whom Harley sought to place at the center of a moderate scheme.[31] And she removed seven of the more notorious Tackers, replacing them with moderate men. She even named Peterborough to command in Spain. But this was not the major alteration that the Whig lords sought. As Herr Hoffmann observed: when one needed them to save Godolphin, "one promised them that there should be a full change and new appointments. This promise has been only partly kept." They intend, he continued, "to press for the full alteration."[32]

In April the Queen, as required by the Triennial Act, dissolved the old Parliament and sent out writs for the election of a new one. The Tories spared nothing to gain a superiority in the new Parliament, enlisting the clergy in their cause and crying out that the church was in danger. The Whigs exerted themselves with a like zeal, resting their hopes on an invincible alliance between Low Churchmen and Dissenters. The court favored neither party, but rather supported the moderates in each and opposed the extremists—the Tackers and the Junto Whigs. The court most certainly did not throw its weight on the side of the Whigs. Indeed, Lord Keeper Wright refused to remove Tackers from the commissions of peace and named several Tackers to be serjeants-at-law. The results of the election were both heartening and disheartening to the court—heartening because no party gained an overwhelming preponderance, disheartening because the extremists were not defeated (90 Tackers came back) and because each party emerged from the election, to Harley's dismay, more united than ever. The Whigs made substantial gains, securing 246 seats, 62 more than they held in the previous Parliament. The Tories saw the number of seats they held fall from 329 to 267. They now had a majority of only 21. The loyal placemen among both parties numbered about 80, which allowed the court to tip the balance either way. The managers now had that equilibrium of parties they desired, but it remained to be seen whether that equilibrium would give them the independence they sought.[33]

The managers saw immediately that in order to manage the next Parliament they must ally with one party or the other. In late June they resolved to work with the Whigs, which meant that the court would support the Whig John Smith for Speaker. The managers probably would have preferred to work with the moderate Tories, but the moderate Tories refused to rally behind Harcourt, the solicitor general. Instead they rallied behind Bromley, the proclaimed enemy of occasional conformity.[34] So the decision went to the Whigs, but the Whigs expected payment for their support: they expected the managers to name William Cowper, their most eloquent spokesman in the House, to be lord keeper of England. On 27 June it was confidently reported that Cowper would become lord keeper within a week.[35] But then the Queen objected. She told Godolphin in early July that she wished a moderate Tory might be found for the office, for she feared that if a few more Whigs were named, she would be put "insensibly into their power."[36] Robert Harley apparently agreed with her. Certainly he urged on Godolphin that "things which at other times would be reasonable will shock more persons than they will gain." He then enunciated what might be called the court manager's creed: "The foundation is persons or parties are to come in to the Queen, and not the Queen to them."[37] Meanwhile, however, the Whigs grew mutinous at Godolphin's neglect of them.[38] In September, Marlborough, displaying more realism than Harley, wrote the Queen that she must name Cowper lord keeper or turn to Rochester and Nottingham, "and let them take your business into their hands."[39] Marlborough's letter proved decisive: on 11 October the Queen named Cowper lord keeper.

What promises the Whig lords made to Godolphin the historical record does not reveal, but that promises were made the Queen herself avowed. She hoped, she wrote Marlborough, to have a good issue of the next Parliament, "if the Promises made were made good." Godolphin went out of his way to show this letter to Cowper and Halifax and Somers, since it was upon them—and their allies in the Commons—that he looked for the successful management of the coming Parliament.[40]

History not only fails to record what promises were made, but who made them. This is not surprising, for parliamentary undertakings were invariably informal, private, clandestine, and unwritten. One sees the tip of the iceberg—the resolution to appoint Cowper, the Queen's opposition, Marlborough's importunities, the final concessions—but who negotiated with whom about what remains hidden. One can, however, guess at the protagonists. Godolphin was surely the spokesman for the court. He probably negotiated with Halifax, and through Halifax, with Somers. As early as 21 June, Somers revealed a glimpse of his role in a letter to Portland. "According to our calculation," he wrote, "the Parliament now chosen may probably prove very good, especially if the Court see their interest, which we are told they do."[41] In July the Whig lords clubbed together, as a Tory newswriter promptly reported; and in August and September, Godolphin met often with Halifax and Somers, as Halifax's letters make clear. The number of those engaged in these negotiations were few; as late as early October, only Godolphin, Cowper, Halifax, and Somers knew of the decision to name Cowper lord keeper.[42]

The Whig lords, of course, could not make good their undertaking to manage Parliament without the support of their lieutenants in the House of Commons, Jack Smith, Spencer Compton, Robert Walpole, Thomas Conyers, and others. These lieutenants, as the event proved, were quite willing to work closely with the Whig lords. With the help of 81 placemen (27 of them Tories), the Whigs elected Jack Smith Speaker.[43] They then went on to vote all the supplies needed for the war, and to vote them before Christmas. Equally important to the nervous Godolphin was their success in parrying all Tory attacks upon the ministry. The embittered Tories sought to remove Godolphin from the list of lord justices provided in the bill of regency. They sought to declare that the church was in danger under the present ministry. They sought to invite the Hanoverian successor to England. They denounced those ministers who had advised the Queen to accept the Act of Security. All these attacks the Whigs repulsed. They went on to persuade the Commons to declare their confidence in Godolphin by voting that the public revenues had been prudently managed, to the advantage and honor of the nation.[44] Marlborough, upon the prorogation of Parliament in March, pronounced it "the best ever for England."[45]

On one notable occasion, however, the Whig lords nearly lost control of their party, and so of the House. During most of the session, the managers could count on some 245 votes, 160 of them Whigs, 85 of them placemen. The Tories could usually muster 205 votes.[46] It was obvious that if some thirty

Whigs deserted to the opposition, the managers would lose the division. This in fact occurred in January, when about thirty Whigs, called the Whimsicals, men of strict country principles and sworn enemies of placemen, joined with the Tories to remove from the regency bill a clause that would repeal a provision in the Act of Settlement that prohibited placemen from sitting in the House of Commons. In the place of total repeal, the Commons wrote into the bill a clause prohibiting all but 47 placemen from sitting in the Commons. This amendment was unacceptable to the Lords, who restored to the bill the outright repeal of the provision in the Act of Settlement. They did so far relent as to place in the bill a clause prohibiting the commissioners of the Prize Office from sitting in the Commons, or any holder of an office created after the dissolution of the present Parliament. But the Commons, on 5 February, by a vote of 205 to 183, refused to accept the Lords' amendment. It was a stalemate, a stalemate from which the managers could escape only by sedulously courting the Whimsicals. They met with them privately, and they sought to detach some of them from the rest. They finally offered a compromise, which provided that inferior officers other than those in the Prize Office should be disqualified from sitting in the House. Their efforts met with success, for some twenty Whimsicals accepted the compromise. On 18 February the Commons accepted the Lords' amendments, suitably altered. The regency bill passed swiftly through both Houses.[47]

This episode has a threefold significance. First, it demonstrated that those Whigs who had undertaken to serve the Queen could hold their party together and could do so even under adverse circumstances, even when long-cherished principles seemed to be violated. Secondly, the Whimsicals proved that they, as well as the placemen, could tip the balance. The managers had to make concessions to them; Mohammed had to move to the mountain. Sir John Cropley, the leader of the Whimsicals, no doubt exaggerated the submission that the court made to the Whimsicals, but there is some truth in his boast that our squadron is the most formidable now in the House (that is excepting the two great ones of Tory and Court) consisting of about thirty, sufficient to turn the scale, and for all we lost the day, 'tis visible what our power is by the court and by the submission made to us.[48]

Thirdly, it now became manifest that the majority of the Commons no longer desired to remove the principal officers of the crown from the House. "Do not exclude everyone," urged Mr. Lynes, for then there will be "none to inform on the state of the nation."[49] But at no time did the Commons propose to exclude everyone. They were willing that the 47 principal officers of the court and government be seated among them. It was the corruption of the House by the bestowal of inferior offices on the rank and file that they feared, not the grant of ministerial offices to their leaders.

The alliance between the court and the Whigs proved a success, but where in this alliance did real power reside, with the court or with the Whigs? One cannot look at the fate of measures to answer this question, for court and Whigs were usually of one mind. Both opposed bills against occasional conformity, both favored waging war on the Continent, both sought a union with Scotland, both opposed place bills that banished all officers from the House. It is no test of strength to push at a door that another is opening.

But over persons the Whigs and the court did engage in a prolonged tug-of-war. It is quite extraordinary the extent to which the control of patronage was the stuff of politics in the early eighteenth century. When a party won office, it grasped at the patronage that went with it. Lord Cowper frankly confessed this: "One of the greatest reasons inducing me to take my present post was the opportunity to promote such men only as I judged in the true interest of England."[50] And the office of lord keeper brought with it a formidable influence, both over judicial appointments and appointments to numerous benefices in the church. In the bestowal of the ecclesiastical patronage at his command, William Cowper worked closely with Thomas Tenison, the archbishop of Canterbury. Do not, warned the archbishop, leave to the Queen the awarding of valuable livings in your gift, for then they would depend "upon the importunity of the women and hangers on at Court."[51] The archbishop was a bit severe in his strictures, for it was not to the women and hangers-on at court that the Queen listened but to John Sharp, the Tory archbishop of York, and to Robert Harley, secretary of state. Initially Cowper deferred to the Queen's request that she might directly dispose of all his benefices, but in January 1706 the Whigs demanded, and the Queen and her managers conceded to them, greater control over ecclesiastical affairs.[52]

The greatest struggle over patronage in the year 1706 concerned not rectories in St. James or bishoprics at Winchester but the nomination of the Earl of Sunderland to the office of secretary of state. Sunderland was a Whig with a fiery temper and powerful friends. That the Whigs now demanded his nomination should have caused the managers no surprise; it was the price of their support for the ministry. As Lord Wharton jestingly told Godolphin upon the occasion of Cowper's appointment: "He was now got into the net and must either make his way through or else he might be in danger of being hanged in it."[53] That Sunderland would replace the Tory Hedges as secretary of state was rumored in January, requested in March, urged in June, and demanded in August. But the Queen remained obdurate. She objected that Sunderland was a party man and that there were already too many of his party in office. To name Sunderland would be to throw herself into the hands of a party, to place herself "in the power of one set of men," to deny herself the liberty of employing any man faithful to her, "be he Whig or Tory."[54]

Behind the Queen's stubborness lay the advice of Robert Harley. To both the Queen and Godolphin, he poured out his scorn for the Whigs. They were inferior in numbers and could never be a majority. The ordinary Whig resented the fury of his leaders and would not follow them. Nothing would satisfy those leaders until all power was given them. Their grasping at offices made other men who wished to serve the Queen desperate. The better course would be to increase the number of men from both parties who would serve the Queen loyally.

The Queen began her reign upon that footing and had met with success. Should she now set up another scheme?[55]

Godolphin and Marlborough concluded she should, for they found more rhetoric than sense in Harley's arguments. Godolphin told Harley bluntly that there were 160 Whigs and 190 Tories, and "for every one we are like to get from the 190 we shall lose two or three from the 160."[56] This might mean little to Harley, who could, and soon did, resume his correspondence with the Tory party, but Godolphin lived in constant fear of being torn to pieces by the Tory party. In September he addressed a poignant letter to the Queen in which he urged that it is "more than time that your Majesty would resolve upon some scheme for carrying on your affairs in the next sessions of Parliament." He then reminded her that the Whigs had ventured all their credit to serve her in the last Parliament, and expected some favor in return. If denied that favor,

> they would sit sullen in the Parliament, and silent at best, while the other party whose inveteracy is sufficiently known to yourself will have the satisfaction of tearing your government and ministers to pieces; but I am in the wrong to say Ministers, for it would really not affect any body but my self, and this is perhaps one reason why all your Majesty's servants are so very indifferent and unconcerned whether any thing be done, or not done to prevent these consequences.[57]

Godolphin favored a Whig scheme of management in order to survive; Marlborough favored it in order to carry on the war. It might be practicable, he wrote the Queen, to govern without making use of the heads of either party, "if both parties sought your favour."

> But, Madame, the truth is that the heads of one party have declared against you and your government, as far as it is possible, without going into open rebellion. Now should your Majesty disoblige the others, how is it possible to obtain the five millions for carrying on the war with vigour, without which all is undone.[58]

To Marlborough and Godolphin, a moderate scheme was impracticable: "The majority will be against us upon every occasion of consequence," and dependence on the Tories was impossible.[59]

This being so, the Whig threat to ruin the Ministry if the Queen did not name Sunderland secretary presented a terrifying prospect. And there was no doubting the reality of the threat. As early as June, Godolphin learned from Sarah Duchess of Marlborough that until the Whigs "have the power in their hands they will be against every thing that may be an assistance to the Queen and the government."[60] In September, Sunderland confirmed the resolve of the Whigs to desert the ministry if their demands were not met. As he wrote to the Duchess:

> Lord Somers, Lord Halifax, and I have talked very fully over all this matter, and we are come to our last resolution in it, that this [Sunderland's appointment] and what other things have been promised must be done, or we and the Lord Treasurer must have nothing more to do together about business; and that we must let all our friends know just how the matter stands between us and the Lord Treasurer, whatever the consequences of it.[61]

In distant Grametz, Marlborough heard of the same resolve to "vex and ruin Godolphin, because the Queen has not complied with what is desired for Sunderland."[62] Godolphin and Marlborough were practical men, for whom government meant the raising of revenues and the commanding of armies. They knew that the Whigs alone could win them the money and the supplies needed to defeat the armies of France. They therefore told the Queen that they must resign unless she named Sunderland as secretary of state.[63] The Queen might have withstood the Whigs alone; she was no match for the Whigs joined with the duumvirs. On the day Parliament met, she named Sunderland secretary of state.

The Whigs fully met their side of the bargain. With greater dispatch than ever, Parliament voted a greater supply than ever, a supply of six millions rather than five. On one occasion the Tories opposed a motion to vote £900,000 to pay for the German troops who had saved Turin the summer before.

The Whigs, angered that Godolphin sought and enjoyed Whig support and yet would not declare fully for them, remained silent as the debate raged back and forth. Finally they intervened on Godolphin's side, and carried by 254 to 105 a resolution that the money had been well used for the security and honor of the nation.[64] The Whigs also carried the Act of Union swiftly and easily through both Houses. There was not one Whig who voted against the Union, in either House, upon any question.[65] In February the Tories sought to prevent the continuance of the Bank, but the Whigs defeated this attempt by 25 votes. Harley's gloomy prognostication that the Whigs could neither hold their followers nor manage Parliament proved false. The best Parliament ever held, concluded the Duke of Somerset.[66]

But beneath the outward calm, beneath the seeming harmony, there raged a fierce tug-of-war over the control of patronage. The Whig lords were not political innocents; they expected payment for their services to the court. Lord Wharton desired to replace Ormond as lord lieutenant of Ireland, and men spoke of Lord Somers as the next president of the council.[67] But the court named Pembroke to replace Ormond and allowed Pembroke to retain his office of president of the council. The most they would give the Whigs were a few crumbs—four places at the Board of Trade and the office of solicitor general to Halifax's brother, Sir James Montagu.[68] Far worse followed in the summer, when Queen Anne announced her intention of naming Sir William Dawes and Dr. Blackall, two Tory clergymen, to the vacant sees of Chester and Exeter. The Whig lords foresaw the whole patronage of the church falling to the Queen's Tory counsellors, of whom they suspected Robert Harley to be the chief.[69]

Their reply was to go into opposition, to desert the managers. Opposition to the government of the day—or the threat of it—was the parliamentary undertaker's ultimate weapon, just as in modern times the strike is the trade unionist's. In late August 1707, the Whigs assembled at Althorp, where they resolved upon the measures to be pursued in the coming session of Parliament. Edmund Gibson wrote a discerning account of it:

The Lords Sunderland, Somers, Halifax, and (I think) Orford have been lately at Althorp, to fix measures for the approaching Parliament, as is believed, but as for the Whig-Commoners, they are shy, and will have the great ones know they are out of humour, and will have no dealings with them till they have good assurances that their services shall be better remembered, than they have been. Two days ago one of 'em bid me be assured, that there was not yet one step made towards concerting any one thing for the next Session.[70]

Robert Harley liked to believe that the ordinary Whig resented the fury of his leaders, but Edmund Gibson knew better: it was the ordinary Whig who demanded that "their services shall be remembered."

As Parliament approached, as September gave way to October, the Whigs refused to relent in their resolve to oppose the court if the Queen named Blackall and Dawes to the vacant bishoprics. If that step is taken, wrote Cowper, I am firmly persuaded, "that it would not be in the power of any leading men to bring the Parliament to act quickly and with good effect the next session."[71] For the bumptious Lord Wharton, it was not enough to sit by passively; he was for carrying the war into the enemy's camp. Shortly before Parliament assembled, he visited Lord Nottingham with a proposal that the High Tories and extreme Whigs join to humble the court.[72]

The anticipated attack came on 12 November. The House of Lords on that day met to consider an address of thanks to the Queen. But before such a motion could be moved, Lord Wharton rose to urge that the need to discuss the state of the nation was greater than the need to vote an address of thanks. He complained of the decay of trade and the scarcity of money. Lord Somers seconded him and enlarged upon the ill condition of the navy. The Tories then demanded that a day be set aside to debate the state of the nation, which led the Lords to set 19 November for the debate. When that day arrived, Lord Wharton was ready with a petition from the most eminent merchants of London, a petition complaining of the great losses caused by the want of convoys and cruisers.[73] There was reason enough behind their complaints.

The government had chosen to use the navy to pursue strate-
gic purposes rather than to protect trade, and the cost had
been the loss of 1,139 ships from the port of London alone
between 1703 and 1707. Furthermore, a series of disasters had
recently befallen the navy—seven warships lost in less than a
fortnight.[74] The Commons, on 27 November, joined in the
pursuit of the seemingly incompetent Admiralty. Godolphin's
prophecy that the government should be torn to pieces over
the management of sea affairs, with no friends to support it
but some few placemen, appeared to be fulfilling itself.[75]

But then there occurred a remarkable *volte-face*. On 19
November, when the debate in the House of Lords grew high
and sharp and Lord Haversham began to lay it on the ministry, the Whigs came to the rescue of Godolphin and Marlborough. Lord Halifax diverted a vote of censure by proposing
the creation of a committee to receive proposals for encouraging trade. The lord treasurer supported the motion, and the
House passed it, upon which Wharton moved the adjournment of the debate. The Whigs in the House of Commons
pursued similar tactics. On 13 December they prevented a
vote on the merchants' complaints against the Admiralty by
moving that the chairman leave the chair, which the House
duly voted.[76] The Whigs came to the support of the ministry
once again on 19 December, when Lord Nottingham proposed that 20,000 men be sent from Flanders to the Spanish
theater of war. Marlborough passionately opposed the motion, and was supported by the Whigs. Wharton praised the
government for its conduct of the war and declared that a
Queen who placed her civil administration in such wise men
and her military affairs in so great a general would certainly
recover England's fortunes in Spain. Lord Somers then
moved, and the House voted, that no peace should be made
with France until the House of Bourbon was removed from
Spain.[77]

There were several reasons for this *volte-face*. The Whigs in
the Lords wished to use the miscarriages at sea as a weapon to
discredit the Admiralty, not the ministry. When Haversham
diverted the attack from the Admiralty to the ministry, they
deserted him. In the Commons it was the Tories who deserted

the Whigs, suspecting that the Whigs were attacking the Admiralty merely to drive the Tories there from it and to place Lord Orford in it.[78] But there was a deeper reason for the turnabout of the Whig Junto (as Halifax, Somers, Wharton, Orford, and Sunderland were now beginning to be called). It lay in the fact that the real occasion of the quarrel between the court and the Junto was not mismanagement at sea but the Queen's insistence upon naming two Tory clergymen to the vacant bishoprics.[79] It was a struggle for the control of patronage. The Junto opposed the Ministry in order to demonstrate their strength, to prove their usefulness, perhaps even to terrify Godolphin and frighten Marlborough. But they were also aware that such violent tactics, pursued too far, might alienate the court irremediably and cause their own friends in both Houses to fall off. They therefore sought, wrote James Brydges, "to gain by submission what they say they could not by direct opposition."[80]

The more cynical observers of the times thought that the Whigs had been bought off by concessions, but they were mistaken. The court refused any concessions to the Whigs. This does not mean that the court did not seek a reconciliation with the Whigs, for it did. In October, and again in December, Queen Anne told the Whigs that she was bound by her word and honor to name Dawes and Blackall to the two vacant bishoprics, but that she desired to heal the breach and would engage that preferments in the future should be such as they would approve of. In January she finally named Dawes and Blackall to their sees, but softened the blow by naming Whigs to the bishopric of Norwich and the deanery of Peterborough. These promises, however, did not satisfy the Junto, who wanted power and place, not promises.[81]

The Whigs now resumed their cat-and-mouse tactics. They opposed the ministry in order to demonstrate their capacity for doing ill, and came to its rescue to prove their talent for doing good. On Scottish affairs they demonstrated their capacity for doing ill. The ministry wanted to continue the Scottish Privy Council, in part as an instrument for controlling parliamentary elections. But on 29 November the Junto and Country Whigs in the Commons joined with the Tories, who were mostly silent, to carry a motion to abolish the council. This formidable alliance then went on to carry a motion, over the court's protest, to give Scottish justices of the peace the same powers as English justices. In January 1708 they defeated an attempt by the court to give the Scottish council a reprieve until October.[82] When the Scottish bill reached the Lords, the court made a final attempt to save the council, but the Junto lords joined with Rochester and Nottingham to confound their efforts. The court likewise failed to remove the clause granting authority to the Scottish justices of the peace, authority that invaded the heritable jurisdiction of Scottish lords. Unamended, the Scottish bill passed through the Lords, a stinging defeat for the ministry.[83]

The failure to amend the Scottish bill was not the only defeat suffered by the ministry during that winter of discontent. In January 1708 it brought in a measure to improve the methods by which the government recruited soldiers, a measure vital to the government's resolve to wage war both in Flanders and Spain. Henry Boyle, the chancellor of the Exchequer, commended the bill; but Peter King, the champion of the Country Whigs, opposed it. An alliance of Junto Whigs, Country Whigs, and Tories defeated the bill by eight votes.[84] Worse was to follow. On 29 January the House debated a motion by Sir Thomas Hanmer, a Tory, that censured the government for having only 8,660 men at the Battle of Almanza, though money had been voted for 29,395. The Tories grew warm during the debate; then the Country Whigs, led by Peter King, joined the attack. But on this occasion, the Junto Whigs came forward, late in the night, to rescue the ministry; at 3:00 A.M. Sir Joseph Jeckyll, one of their spokesmen, moved that the debate be adjourned so that clearer information might be secured about the number of troops at Almanza. The motion carried by 15 votes.[85] The Junto Whigs, however, were not prepared to let the ministry off the hook so easily. On 3 February they joined to oppose the court. Sir Joseph Jeckyll moved an address to Her Majesty desiring her to order that an account be presented to the House explaining why there were not more troops in Spain. The House passed the motion without a division. The court now faced a vote of censure that could prove devastating to its fortunes.

The root cause of the court's miseries lay in the want of a scheme for the management of Parliament. As early as October 1707, Marlborough had complained to Godolphin that "there is really no such thing as a scheme, or any thing like it from any body else."[86] But politics, like nature, abhors a vacuum, and before long there were a number of schemes proposed, four at least. They can usefully be designated as a Whig scheme, the Queen's scheme, Godolphin's, and Harley's.

The Whig scheme was straightforward: the court and the Whigs should continue that alliance which had proved so successful in the management of Parliament the year before. For the continuance of this alliance, they demanded a price: that Dawes and Blackall not be named to Chester and Exeter, that Robert Harley, whose tricks they distrusted, should be removed from office, and that George Churchill be removed from the Admiralty. This was very much laying down the law to the managers, and though Marlborough and Godolphin might have swallowed such demands, the Queen would not.[87]

Queen Anne knew with equal clarity what she wanted. She wanted to be dictated to by neither the Tackers nor the Junto, by neither Rochester nor Sunderland. In early December she offered to heal the breach with the Whigs by promising (in return for Whig acquiescence in the nomination of Dawes and Blackall) to make such preferments in the future as should content them. But to this conciliatory gesture, she coupled a threat. If they refused, she would never again consult them— just as she had earlier vowed never again to consult Lord Rochester. She would, as Sir John Cropley reported, "ever after trust herself in the hands of such as have never been on [the] stage of either party."[88] A week later she gave Robert Harley authority to say that she was firmly resolved to side neither with the violent Whigs nor with the violent Tories, that she would never make bargains with a party to persuade it to do what a sense of duty alone ought to lead it to do. She would henceforth favor those who, without laying down terms, voluntarily promoted her service.[89]

In December, to the great delight of the Queen, Lord Godolphin and Robert Harley joined together to promote such a scheme of management. But the secretary and the lord treasurer were not dreamers. They knew that the Queen's servants, only about a hundred in number and subject to desertion from the court when party passions were aroused, could not carry matters by themselves in Parliament. Harley and Godolphin also knew that the moderates of each party were not going to come flooding into the Queen's service voluntarily. They must be wooed, courted, and detached from the violent men of their party. Lord Godolphin was inclined to look for these moderate men in the Whig party. For many months he had sedulously wooed the moderate Whigs, men like Devonshire, Somerset, and Newcastle in the Lords, and Walpole, Compton, and Smith in the Commons. They were called the Lord Treasurer's Whigs, and they regularly met, along with other of the government's managers in the Commons, at Chancellor Boyle's house to plan their tactics for the next day in Parliament.[90] But Godolphin knew that these Whigs, even when joined by the placemen, were too few in number to ensure a majority for the ministry—too few, that is, unless the Country Whigs could be persuaded to join with them. To this improbable enterprise, Godolphin devoted all his efforts. He courted Sir John Cropley, a leading Whimsical. He hinted at a secretaryship for Lord Shaftesbury, the purest of Country Whigs. He enlisted Robert Molesworth, the publicist of the old Whig cause. He promised that the ministry would not intervene in the forthcoming elections.[91] Molesworth grew enthusiastic about this possible union between the ministry and the Country Whigs. It would be splendid for Great Britain, he wrote Shaftesbury, "if a Scheme could be made of laying the foundation of our future happiness on a set who have not yet bowed their knees to the Baals of either extremes."[92] But the course of events showed that Godolphin's subtle scheme of management was as impracticable as the Queen's simpler one. Cropley, Shaftesbury, and Molesworth did not govern the Country Whigs, Peter King did. And the Country Whigs now joined with the Junto Whigs to defeat the ministry on the Scottish bill, the recruitment bill, and the inquiry into Almanza. "The Court," wrote Jonathan Swift on 5 February 1708, "hath not been fortunate in their questions this session."[93]

Where Godolphin looked to the Whigs for support, Harley looked to the Tories, which proved his undoing. As early as September 1707, Marlborough became convinced that Harley and his friends had a "scheme," a scheme that would destroy his and Godolphin's credit and that boded ill for England's allies.[94] Godolphin denied that there was any such scheme, but by 5 December there clearly was, at least in the mind of Robert Harley. Late that evening Harley wrote to Newcastle:

> I am just come from the two great men [Marlborough and Godolphin]. I believe they are fully sensible of their danger, and that there are a number of men, enough to support them, who are ready and willing to do it, if they will but create a confidence in them; I was not willing to be thought an undertaker, and therefore would not name the method which is obvious enough if they please to make use of it.[95]

Harley's reluctance to name "the method" hardly arose from an unwillingness to be thought an undertaker, for the world knew him to be one of the greatest of undertakers. More likely it arose from his unwillingness to reveal to the two great men the extent to which his scheme rested upon the Tories.

In December 1707 Harley still envisaged working with Godolphin, but in late January 1708, meeting with obstruction from Godolphin, he devised a scheme that had no place in it for the lord treasurer. "It is said," wrote Swift on 12 February, "that Harley had laid a scheme for an entire new Ministry, and the men are named to whom the several employments were to be given."[96] Other contemporaries, in later weeks, were willing to guess at the names. Harley himself was to replace Godolphin, initially as first commissioner, then, with a peerage, as lord high treasurer. Henry St. John and Earl Poulett were to be secretaries of state. Lord Harcourt would be lord chancellor, and the Duke of Buckingham would come in as lord privy seal.[97] It was a bold undertaking that had the entire support of the Queen and the somewhat suspicious support of the Tories.[98] But it came to nothing, for

Marlborough threatened to resign, Somerset to leave the Cabinet, the Commons to delay the money bill, and the Whigs to impeach Harley should the Queen continue to listen to Harley. Marlborough's threat was decisive, for had he acquiesced in the removal of Godolphin, Harley might well have succeeded in his venture. But the debates on Spain had made it clear to Marlborough that the Tories would not support the war in Flanders. There could be no depending upon them for the £6,000,000 needed for the war. He and Godolphin therefore demanded the dismissal of Robert Harley, whose resignation the Queen reluctantly accepted on 11 February.[99]

Nothing illustrates more graphically the reluctance of the court managers—and the Queen behind them—to surrender power than their refusal to bring the Whigs into office upon the fall of Harley. Because St. John, Mansell, and Harcourt, all of them Tories, chose to resign upon Harley's dismissal, four offices became vacant. These offices the duumvirs either left vacant or filled with Lord Treasurer's Whigs. Henry Boyle, a Treasurer's Whig, became secretary of state; Jack Smith, once he had stepped down from being Speaker, replaced Boyle as chancellor of the Exchequer; Robert Walpole, who had stoutly defended the Admiralty in the Commons, became secretary of war in St. John's place. Mansell's place as comptroller and Harcourt's as attorney general were left vacant. The Junto Whigs, who had no hand in, or knowledge of, these changes, were furious that creatures of the court, and not their men, were brought into office.[100] They vented their anger in the Lords by supporting an address to the Queen cataloging and condemning the mismanagements of the Admiralty. "England must be undone," declared Lord Somers, "if the sea affairs stood longer on the present foot; England could bear it no longer." The extremes of Whig and Tory thereupon joined to carry the address, which the Lords presented to the Queen, all twenty-five sheets of it, on 1 March.[101]

Though the Whigs wished to condemn the Admiralty, they did not wish to bring down Godolphin, the very minister whose removal Harley had sought. The fall of Harley had filled the Whigs with delight and united them as they had not been united for months.[102] Thus when the Tories, now in open opposition to all measures of the government, moved in the Commons that the want of men at Almanza arose from "the want of timely and effectual recruits being sent thither," the Whigs rallied to the government's defense. They defeated this manifest censure by 230 to 175, and went on to commend Her Majesty for the measures she had taken to recover Spain.[103] Joseph Addison, the fledging essayist, believed that this vote "has fixed all men in their proper parties, and thoroughly established the present ministry."[104] But Addison was mistaken, for the present ministry was not thoroughly established. This became evident in March when Godolphin sought to persuade the Whigs to support the recruitment bill, a bill essential to the government's efforts to secure more soldiers. He held a great meeting of Whigs at Boyle's house, where he informed them that only 1,000 men had been raised of the 15,000 needed. But the Country Whigs ignored his plea and remained opposed to the bill. This being so—and all the money bills having passed through Parliament—Godolphin advised the Queen to prorogue Parliament, which she did on 1 April.[105]

Prorogation did not end the importunity of the Whigs. "They press hard for the whole game," observed Cropley in February; and by early March, rumor reported that the whole game consisted of the nomination of Pembroke as admiral, Somers as president of the council, and Wharton as viceroy of Ireland.[106] The Whigs, however, had more sense than to believe that they could gain the whole game at a blow. They began by demanding the appointment of Sir James Montagu as attorney general and Lord Somers as president of the council. It was Somers's appointment they particularly desired, to which end they brought pressure upon Godolphin, who in turn brought pressure upon the Queen. The Queen, however, remained as unyielding as granite. She would not name Lord Somers president of the council. The Whigs therefore proposed that Somers enter the Cabinet without office, and the two great Whig dukes, Devonshire and Newcastle, accordingly waited upon Her Majesty with this proposal. She again refused, declaring that to bring Somers into her service would mean her "utter destruction."[107] Queen Anne might have been slow of thought and inarticulate, but she was not blind. She saw with great clarity where her power lay and that it was slipping from her. To give the seals to Cowper, she had said in 1705, would tip the balance in favor of the Whigs; to name Sunderland secretary, she had urged in 1706, would make her a prisoner of a party; to bring Somers into her service, she now declared, would be destructive to her independence. All this she had seen, and now saw, clearly, but Godolphin saw with equal clarity that ruin must follow if Somers was not appointed.[108]

The previous session had taught Godolphin and Marlborough four lessons: the hazards of embarking upon a session without a firm scheme of management, the imprudence of relying upon the Lord Treasurer's Whigs alone, the difficulties of winning over the Country Whigs, and the dangers of seeking to divide the Whig party. Ruin must unavoidably ensue, wrote Godolphin to Marlborough in April, from divisions. Marlborough echoed these sentiments in May: "I am impatient to hear," he wrote Sarah, "of the success my letters to the Queen may have had concerning Lord Somers." He then added, "I am of the opinion of the Lord Treasurer, that any thing else will be but of little use, for if the body of men that must serve be divided, how can it be other than confusion."[109] Marlborough soon learned that his letters had met with no success. In late May the Queen refused to name Somers president or Montagu attorney.[110]

In this struggle for place and power, the ultimate weapon of the Whigs was their numbers in Parliament. The dissolution of Parliament in April, made necessary by the Triennial Act, gave them an opportunity in May and June to increase those numbers. They made good use of the opportunity. They won a majority of 69 voices in the new Parliament, a far cry from the previous one where they had thirty fewer seats than the Tories, and where the court party held the balance.[111] The Whigs did not win this majority because they enjoyed the support of the court, for the court feared (in Cropley's words) "an overgrown Whig Parliament."[112] The managers preferred

a Parliament in which the placemen held the balance between the two parties, thus giving the court some leverage in
bargaining with both. The court therefore remained neutral
in the elections, except in Scotland, where it supported
Queensbury and his friends against Hamilton and his, who
were allied with the Junto.[113] What really gave the Whigs
their victory was the anti-Jacobite sentiment created by the
Pretender's attempted invasion of Scotland in March. The
scare which that invasion caused, skillfully exploited by Whig
propaganda, seriously harmed the Tories, many of whom were
suspected of wishing success to the attempt.[114] The result was
a tide of Whig sentiment that carried a Whig majority into
Parliament.

It is astonishing that in the face of this Whig majority
Godolphin should embark on a strategy of creating a composite party out of Whigs and Tories, yet this is the policy that he
pursued in the summer of 1708. In early June, upon the advice
of Smith and Compton, he put forward Sir Richard Onslow as
the court candidate for Speaker in the coming Parliament. In
late June he sought to name a client of the Duke of Devonshire as attorney general and a Country Whig as solicitor
general. In July, if rumor can be believed, he employed
Somerset to detach the Earl of Wharton from the Junto. In
late July he opened negotiations with William Bromley, the
premier Tory in the House of Commons, with a design to win
Tory support for a composite ministry.[115] In part he pursued
this strategy because of the advice of John Smith and Henry
Boyle, in part because a court victory in Scotland had given
the court some forty obedient members, but principally, one
suspects, because the Queen's implacable resolve not to admit
Somers to the Cabinet left him no choice. When Marlborough chided the Queen for her unwillingness to forgive
and forget, she replied that Christian principles did not require her to put herself "into the hands of any one party."[116]
The lord treasurer was like a man caught between an irresistible force and an immoveable object.

The irresistible force was the Whig party, not only vic-
torious at the polls but united as never before. Devonshire,
Cowper, and others who had left the Junto the year before

now returned to the party fold.[117] To Somerset's invitation to make a private bargain with the court, Lord Wharton replied that if he had ever been of service to the nation, "it was chiefly owing to the assistance of those friends, from whom he would never divide." He then suggested that it would be wiser for the ministers "to put themselves at the head of the whole party, which would make them strong and carry them through all their present difficulties, than to think of dividing them again, which would only increase their troubles of last year. . . . "[118] Wharton's undertaking to carry the ministers "through all their present difficulties" was made also by Halifax. Those that have a majority, he wrote Marlborough in July, will support and assist you, and defend you from all enemies, if "your Grace and the Lord Treasurer are contented to carry on the administration by such measures and in such hands, as you declare to like."[119]

To these offers of service should they be given office, the Junto added threats of opposition should they not. They refused to support Onslow for Speaker because he was put forward on a court bottom. They empowered Sunderland to tell the Duchess of Marlborough that they would withdraw their support from the ministers if Somers was not made lord president and law officers more agreeable to the party appointed.[120] They let it be known that they would rather join with the Tories than support the lord treasurer any longer. Nathaniel Hooke, a Jacobite agent of the French crown, saw the ultimate source of their power. The lord treasurer and the general, he wrote, are obliged to throw themselves into the hands of the Whig party "because this party holds the purse in the present conjuncture."[121]

The Whigs were not, however, about to exercise the power of the purse in so naked a manner. A parliamentary undertaking should be negotiated in a more positive and courteous manner, as Lord Somers saw. Among the papers of Lord Somers collected by the Earl of Hardwicke is "A sketch for the conduct of the Whigs, by Lord Somers, and some Rules for their conjunction with Lord Godolphin," a sketch composed in 1708. Among the rules that Lord Somers sets forth are these: (1) that the ministers and the Whigs concert measures together for carrying on the public business, (2) that something be done to quiet people's minds about the Protestant Succession, (3) that the sea administration be put on a better footing, (4) that persons who behave well be countenanced in employment in church and state, and (5) that provision be made for securing "our constitution and Liberties and restoring and enlarging Trade in case God shall grant us peace." In this delicate manner did Lord Somers suggest that Jacobites be condemned, Orford brought to the Admiralty, Whigs employed, and trade with the Spanish Empire secured. All this was to be done in conjunction with Lord Godolphin, but Lord Somers left unsaid what should be done if Godolphin would not join in these measures or could not persuade the Queen to do so. It would hardly be consonant with the respect men owed the prerogative to say that they would go into opposition if denied the offices and measures they sought, but it is exactly that which they did in the autumn of 1708.[122]

In October of that year, the Whigs entered upon an opposition to the court that was more explicit, formal, resolute, and self-serving than any seen in England before. The Earl of Sunderland was the chief whip in this opposition, and working with him were the Dukes of Devonshire and Bolton, the Marquess of Dorchester, the Earls of Orford and Wharton, and Lords Townshend, Somers, and Halifax. Early in October they planned to meet with the lord treasurer at Newmarket, but the meeting was postponed because the Queen refused to offer any terms to the Whig lords. Godolphin pleaded with her, threatened to resign, and sent Somerset to woo her, but she remained adamant. On 15 October, or very close to that day, Godolphin did meet with the Whig lords. They declared that they could no longer, with any reputation, continue to support the court, for there were mismanagements everywhere—in the fleet, in Ireland, in Scotland, in the disposal of church preferments. Those Whigs who had places had so little credit that it was no different from Lords Rochester and Nottingham's being in power. They then proposed that Pembroke be made lord high admiral, Somers president of the council, and Ireland be left vacant (presumably for Wharton later). If this was not done, they would and must oppose the court in the choice of Speaker. Like many another chief whip, Sunderland had counted his votes and knew where he stood.[123] To Montrose he wrote, "We have the best Parliament that has been chosen these many years, and greatest union of men of reputation among us, those that differed last year being now entirely united, so that if one does fail of doing right, it's entirely our own fault."[124]

Godolphin's reply to this ultimatum was to persuade the Queen to name Sir James Montagu as attorney general and Robert Eyre as solicitor general, but this concession only persuaded Sunderland that if vigor and spirit could win this concession, greater vigor and greater spirit could win further concessions.[125] The great stumbling block to an accord between the court and the Whigs was, of course, the Queen's husband, the good-natured but bungling Prince George. The Whigs demanded his removal from the Admiralty; the Queen would not countenance it. At this critical moment, death, like some *deus ex machina*, stepped in to resolve the drama. On 28 October the Prince died. A few days later Godolphin informed Sunderland and his friends that the Queen had agreed to make Pembroke lord high admiral, Somers president of the council, and Wharton lord lieutenant of Ireland.[126] The Junto lords and their allies in the Commons immediately dropped the candidacy of Sir Peter King for Speaker. On 5 November an affable Dr. Garth met Lord Wharton. "My Lord," said the Doctor, "I hear the Lord Treasurer has beat the Chammado and I hope your Lordship will give him honourable terms."[127]

Whether the terms were honorable or not is hard to say; they were certainly successful. The day before Parliament met on 16 November, Wharton and Somers kissed the Queen's hands for their offices. A week later Pembroke became lord high admiral. The authors of this new scheme of administration then set out to make good their undertaking to serve the court in Parliament. They elected Sir Richard Onslow as Speaker. They secured the vote of £7,000,000 for the war, a sum sufficient not only to maintain the existing forces but to augment them by 7,000 foot and 3,000 horse. The estimates, usually hotly disputed, were agreed upon before Thanksgiving. The Commons sent up the land tax to the Lords before Christmas, and in January they continued the duty on malt and provided a fund to support the circulation of three millions in Exchequer bills.[128] Parliament also passed bills for the naturalization of foreign Protestants and for imposing on Scotland the English law of treason. And when the Tories sought to censure Lord Godolphin, the Whigs parried all their blows. They turned a motion censuring the government for its tardy conduct in meeting the attempted invasion of Scotland into a vote of thanks for the timely and effectual care it took to defend the realm. When the Tories criticized Godolphin by name for permitting arrears in the collection of the land tax, they secured the deletion of his name from the motion.[129] During the entire session, the court met with only one setback; an alliance of Tories and Country Whigs modified a court measure for raising recruits, altering it so that recruits were to be raised by parishes, not counties.[130] But this minor defeat aside, it was a quiet, harmonious, triumphant session; "Much better in all respects," wrote Godolphin in April 1709, "then we had reason to hope for."[131]

It was shortly before Christmas in 1704 that Colonel Graham told Bishop Nicolson about the new scheme of alterations at court: "Lord Pembroke to be Admiral; Lord Somers President of the Council; Lord Sunderland Secretary of State, &c."[132] It took the Junto four years and countless fierce political struggles to make that scheme a reality. The managers conceded as little power as possible to the Junto, and the Queen clung as obstinately as she could to her prerogative to choose her own servants; but on every occasion, with Cowper in 1705, with Sunderland in 1706, with Somers and Wharton in 1708, the Whigs proved too powerful for the Queen and her managers. They expressed their power in two ways: as a threat and as an undertaking. If denied office, they would go into opposition; if given office, they would manage the Queen's affairs for her in Parliament.

The final episode in the formation of a totally Whig scheme of administration—the nomination of Lord Orford to the Admiralty in 1709—offers yet another example of the simultaneous employment of the carrot and the stick. From the beginning the Junto had regarded Pembroke's nomination as lord high admiral as a stopgap measure, as merely a means to persuade the Earl, who was a Tory, to resign as president of the council and as lord lieutenant of Ireland, both of which offices he held in 1708. The Junto's ultimate design was to bring Lord Orford, the hero of La Hogue, into the Admiralty. In the spring of 1709, they launched their attack. They let Marlborough and Godolphin know that they could not carry on the Queen's business in Parliament if Orford was not named to the Admiralty. The Whig majority in the House of Commons, they declared, would not be easy if the Admiralty was not of one piece with the rest of the government. The House might run into inquisitions and create more trouble than it had ever done before. Seeing that they could not be of use to the public, the ministers themselves would have to resign. But if Lord Orford was named to the Admiralty, the war might be wound up quietly and honorably and the Queen's reign made perfectly happy for the future. The Whigs would then do everything in Parliament that could be desired of them.[133]

Marlborough and Godolphin, to Somers's great delight, saw the reasonableness of this request, but the Queen did not. She was willing that a commission replace Pembroke, but not that Orford be a member of that commission. There then followed a battle redolent of those waged in 1705, 1706, and 1708. The Queen obstinately refused to appoint Orford; the Whigs as stubbornly insisted on his appointment. If the Queen would not name Orford, threatened Sunderland, the Whig ministers would resign in a body just before Parliament met. Marlborough, as in the past, urged the Queen to yield to the demands of the Junto. Two months later, in October, she did. But even this concession did not end the struggle, for the Junto lords had never sought office merely for its emoluments; they also sought the patronage and the power that went with it. Lord Orford now demanded that Admirals Byng and Jennings, both of them Whigs, be named to the board that he would head. The Queen objected, and Godolphin had once again to labor like a slave in a galley to resolve the dispute. With the help of Lord Somers, he finally did so:

Byng came in, Jennings stayed out. On 10 November 1709, Lord Orford, as first lord of the Admiralty, took his seat at the cabinet table.[134]

The Whigs now possessed four of the five great departments of state: the Chancery, the Secretariat, the Admiralty, and the lord lieutenancy of Ireland. At the Treasury, the greatest of departments, sat an uneasy ally, Lord Godolphin. In the Cabinet they enjoyed a preponderant voice. This accession to power had not come to the Whigs because they enjoyed favor at court, for the court had continually opposed them. Nor had they secured it because the managers favored them, for the managers had struggled to keep power in their own hands. The true source of the Junto's power lay neither in court favor nor ministerial support; it lay in their ability to manage Parliament successfully for the crown—to defend Godolphin from parliamentary censure, to carry Acts of Union, to pass recruitment bills, and, above all, to secure for Marlborough the six millions he needed each year to wage war victoriously abroad. It was as parliamentary undertakers that they were able to fashion a Whig scheme of administration that assumed its final form in 1709.

Chapter VIII

The Tory Scheme of 1710–1714

I N DECEMBER 1707 Robert Harley, with his custom-
ary guile, told the Duke of Newcastle that he did not
want "to be thought an undertaker."[1] No doubt he did
not want to be *thought* an undertaker, but in the next three
years he proved himself to be a supremely gifted one, and
thereby proved able to rescue the Queen from the tyranny of
the Whigs. It was not as a courtier that in the year 1710 he
rescued the Queen from the Junto; it was as a politician who
could undertake to manage her affairs successfully in Parliament. He enjoyed the Queen's personal favor, assuredly, but
her favor had not allowed him to succeed in his efforts in
February 1708 to free her from the Whigs. In 1708 he failed
because he had not perfected his scheme of administration; in
1710 he succeeded because he had. The purpose of the 1710
scheme—as also of that in 1708—was not merely to free the
Queen from the Whigs but to free her from the tyranny of all
parties. Parties were to serve the Queen, not the Queen,
parties. Men of all parties, men loyal to the Queen, should
form her government and manage her Parliament. With remarkable tactical ingenuity and with great tenacity of purpose, Robert Harley pursued this goal for four years, only to
find himself increasingly caught in the toils of party. The
political history of these four years is largely the story of how a
scheme of administration designed to free the Queen from
party made her finally dependent upon a party, upon the Tory
party, the party of the gentlemen of England.

A major defect in Harley's scheme in February 1708 was the
want of firm support from the Tories. Soon after his fall from
office, Harley set out to remedy this defect. In August 1708 he
welcomed a tentative offer from William Bromley, the great
champion of the Tory cause, to enter into negotiations with

him. He soon promised to act frankly and in concert with Bromley, and their alliance was cemented in October when Harley actively canvassed for Bromley's election as Speaker.[2] Then, in January 1709, he joined the Tories in an attack upon the ministry for its conduct of the war in Spain.[3] In August of that year, Bromley declared himself fully determined to act in concert with Harley.[4] During these negotiations the ebullient Henry St. John urged Harley on. "There is no hope," he wrote Harley, "but in the Church of England party." Gain Bromley: by governing him, you influence them. You broke the party, unite it again. The fallen secretary hardly needed this advice, for he saw as clearly as did St. John that he needed the Tories. And Bromley for his part saw that the Tories needed Harley. The Tory gentlemen of England, he argued, were a natural majority in the country, but they could exploit that majority only if countenanced by the court.[6] Harley was the one man who could win them favor at court.

But it was not Harley's purpose to free the Queen from the tyranny of the Whigs only to subject her to the oppression of the Tories. In private notes hastily scribbled in these years, he made it plain that he had given up the politics of opposition for the politics of deference. Ministers should not "press and overpower" the Queen, they should not deprecate her understanding or lessen her credit; they should tell her the truth, see that she is not deceived, and carry out her will. "The power of the Crown," wrote Harley, "ought to protect against the violence of men or party, now the power of the Crown is given to a party to destroy others." The real key to the political career of Robert Harley is not that from being a Whig he became a Tory but that from being a country party politician he became a court favorite.[7]

The court favorite now set out to save the Queen from the tyranny of a single party by fashioning a scheme of administration based upon both parties. Thus he not only wooed Bromley and his Tory followers but also courted those independent Whig lords who could be detached from the Junto— Shrewsbury, Rivers, Newcastle, Somerset, Queensberry, and Argyle. His assiduity and skill in winning them to his scheme

[200]

was astonishing. In May of 1708, he entered into cordial relations with the charming Duke of Shrewsbury, recently returned from Italy with an eccentric Italian wife. In the next two years, the Duke often invited Harley to his country home in Oxfordshire, insisting that it was too mysterious to meet in a third place. Lord Rivers, on the other hand, found more congenial Harley's love of mystery: he arranged in July 1708 to arrive at Harley's house after dark[8] That same summer Harley resumed his intimate correspondence with the Duke of Newcastle, the powerful electoral magnate in the North. It was in 1709 that he won over the Duke of Somerset, a pompous and self-important politician who had turned against the Junto.[9] Queensberry was easily gained, for the Duke had entered into negotiations to wed his son to Harley's daughter. Hopes of a Garter were placed before Argyle.[10]

To succeed in his designs, Harley needed the favor of the Queen and access to her. Her favor he had won when secretary of state, won in many a private conference in the royal closet, won by flattering her and defending her prerogative. How deep that favor ran the crisis of February 1708 revealed: the Queen was ready to defy all—the Junto, the duumvirs, even Parliament—to keep her beloved secretary in office. It was Harley himself who had to persuade her to accept his resignation. Access to the Queen, once he had resigned, presented greater difficulties. It is unlikely that he paid her secret visits in her little garden house at Windsor, though the Duchess of Marlborough entertained this romantic idea.[11] What certainly did arise was a correspondence between Robert Harley and Abigail Masham, the Queen's favorite and a servant in the bedchamber. Lady Masham's letters to Harley in 1708, 1709, and early 1710 show her repeatedly urging Harley's counsels upon the Queen.[12] Harley found other intermediaries at court, the Duke of Shrewsbury for one, and the Duke of Somerset, whom Godolphin found spending more hours a day with the Queen than without her. In April 1710 Somerset was expelled from the Whig Kit Kat Club for having held conference with Robin the Trickster. Somerset looked upon himself as the head of a Juntilla composed of himself, Shrewsbury, Argyle, Rivers, Poulett, and Harley, but, reported the

Savoyard, Massei, they used him "only because he had the ear of the Queen."[13] By April, Somerset's intercession was unnecessary, for Harley was now meeting secretly with the Queen.[14] Thus Harley in 1710 had advantages—the Queen's favor and access to court—that were not vouchsafed to the Whigs in 1705, which no doubt explains why he accomplished in six months what they took four years to accomplish.

Harley soon discovered, however, that the Queen's warm regard was not enough. The Queen repeatedly, to Lady Masham's fury, rejected Harley's counsels and accepted Godolphin's.[15] This was quite understandable, for she had suffered deep mortification in February 1708 by following Harley's advice when he had not the strength to support it. She had no wish to be burned a second time. Robert Harley therefore set out to prove to the Queen that the gentlemen of England were loyal to her and to the church and to the monarchy. In November 1709, probably at Oxford, he met with Bromley and St. John to concert a plan for flooding the Queen with loyal addresses. "I remember," wrote the Tory George Lockhardt, "sometime before this session of Parliament met, the Tories, beginning to have some hopes from Mr. Harley's negotiations, procured from all parts wherein they had interest addresses full of loyalty and respect to her Majesty."[16]

The Whigs then committed the egregious blunder of impeaching an obscure clergyman, William Sacheverell, for preaching a sermon against revolutionary principles. That his impeachment was a blunder became evident as the trial progressed and the comfortable Whig majority in the Lords melted away. That majority disappeared altogether on 21 March 1710 when the Lords defeated a Whig proposal to send Sacheverell to prison for three months. Instead they merely suspended him from preaching for three years. The Harleian lords—Argyle, Somerset, Shrewsbury—joined with the Tories to defeat the Whig proposal.[17]

The addresses from the counties and the light punishment meted out to Sacheverell undoubtedly bolstered the Queen's courage, which Lady Masham found so wanting. So too did the division of the Whigs in January 1710. In that month the Queen, pursuant to Harley's advice and without consulting Marlborough, named Lord Rivers lieutenant of the Tower and gave a regiment of dragoons to Colonel Hill, Lady Masham's brother.[18] Marlborough, who saw his power of patronage rudely invaded, was furious. He wrote a letter to the Queen, never actually sent, threatening to resign unless the regiment were taken from Hill and Lady Masham dismissed from court. Sunderland began to engineer an address in Parliament calling for Lady Masham's removal. But Godolphin, who had served the Queen long and intimately, and Somers, who had recently won her favor, were too courtly to tear a servant of the bedchamber from the Queen. They persuaded all the Whig lords but Sunderland to support a compromise: Hill should lose his regiment, but Lady Masham should remain at court. The Queen herself actively and successfully canvassed against the address that Sunderland promoted.[19] The vigor of the Queen and the division among the Whigs forced Marlborough to accept the compromise. Lord Rivers became lieutenant of the Tower, Lady Masham remained at the Queen's side, the Queen took courage, and the Whigs stood exposed as divided.

At what exact point in time Robert Harley first fashioned a scheme of administration is difficult to ascertain. Schemes of administration, like Proteus, changed their shape through time. It is doubtful that Harley had one clearly in mind in January, when he advised the Queen to name Lord Rivers lieutenant of the Tower. By early March, however, he was certainly fashioning a scheme with the Duke of Shrewsbury; for on the morning of 8 March, he recounted to Henry St. John what had passed earlier between himself and Shrewsbury. The scheme that he then outlined to St. John gave that ambitious politician a fright, for he was not to become secretary of state. St. John wrote that very afternoon to protest. The next day he again wrote Harley, this time to report the alarm among the Tories that the Queen should name Sir Thomas Parker, one of Sacheverell's ablest prosecutors, to be chief justice of the Queen's Bench and should propose two moderate men for vacant bishoprics. "A Chief Justice whom we are jealous of," he wrote, "and two Bishops who will, we are sure, be against us, must turn all our schemes, and those who go on with them, into a jest."[20] The Earl of Orrery shared St. John's unease. He regretted that Parker had been named chief justice and wished that Argyle might have the Garter. "I wish that were done," he wrote Harley, "and the scheme finished and agreed to, that we might go out of town with satisfaction."[21]

Whether the scheme was finished before the Queen prorogued Parliament on 5 April cannot be known. What is known is that Godolphin went off to Newmarket to race his horses and the Queen, without asking his advice, decided to give the office of lord chamberlain to the Duke of Shrewsbury, a man who had voted regularly with the Tories in Sacheverell's trial. On the thirteenth she wrote Godolphin of her intentions, on the fourteenth she took the key and staff from the Marquis of Kent and gave them to Shrewsbury, and on the sixteenth she admitted him to the Cabinet. "Her Majesty," wrote Sir John Cropley, "has begun her new scheme of government."[22]

Now, if ever, was the time for Godolphin and the Whigs to strike, to threaten to resign unless the Queen sought and heeded their advice. But they did not. They did not because they feared that such united action would drive the Queen to dissolve Parliament. As the Earl of Sunderland remarked to the Duchess of Marlborough, " . . . I think the Lord Treasurer is perfectly in the right, that we must endeavour to weather it as well as we can, in order to preserve the Parliament from being dissolved."[23] Sir John Cropley deplored this cowardice. The only result, he wrote, will be that they will put "the Queen to the trouble of turning them directly out and not do what was both expected and wished for, laying down themselves." But he understood their dilemma. "Everybody saw the Queen was fully determined to dismiss all [who] should desire it" and to take such an affront as the occasion to dissolve Parliament. This would have brought "inevitable ruin," given the distractions in the kingdom caused by "the fruitless trial of the Dog Doctor." He then observed that "addresses of a sad nature are coming from all parts, which is the thing that has made some venture so soon and on such hazard to [the] whole of this scheme."[24]

Not only the numerous addresses but the prospect of peace emboldened Harley to venture upon this scheme. The Whigs had long used Marlborough's indispensability abroad as a lever to maintain themselves in power at home. But the Tories and the bulk of the nation were now determined on a peace, on a peace that would put an end to the Duke's indispensability. Harley, who knew how deep throughout the land ran the revulsion against the war, had already begun a correspondence with the peace party in Holland.[25] In April his emissary, Somerset, persuaded the Cabinet to strike from the Queen's speech proroguing Parliament the word "just" in the expression, "a just and necessary peace." In her speech the Queen also distinguished between the letter and the spirit of England's obligations. No wonder that the despondent Whigs confessed that they could not hinder the turn toward peace.[26]

In May, Harley and his allies resolved upon the second step in their ministerial revolution: they resolved to ask the Queen to remove the Earl of Sunderland from office. It was a prudent choice, for the Queen had never liked the tactless, brash secretary whom the Whigs had forced upon her in 1706. And she was the more easily persuaded to the step because Godolphin and the Junto lords had acquiesced in Shrewsbury's appointment. She told her physician, Sir David Hamilton, that she had made Shrewsbury lord chamberlain with less trouble than she had expected.[27] But the question of whom to name secretary in Sunderland's place proved a knottier one. To resolve it Harley invited Lord Rivers, Lord Poulet, and others to meet at his house in York Buildings. He then proposed that the Earl of Anglesey replace Sunderland, a proposal that Lord Rivers and Lord Poulett enthusiastically seconded. Lord Poulett hurried off to alert the Earl of his impending promotion. But Anglesey, a High Tory with Jacobite sympathies, was anathema to the Whigs. During the next week, Harley's Whig allies, led by Newcastle, voiced their determined opposition to Anglesey's appointment.[28]

The ensuing row over the nomination revealed that there were two divergent schemes in men's minds. James Brydges reported one of them on 20 May: "Matters run very high at Court and the new scheme of administration grows very fast." Sunderland will be out in five days, and Anglesey will succeed him. Harley and St. John are to be the most considerable persons in the scheme. Lord Marlborough and the lord treasurer are to be comprehended in it, but there is great uncertainty whether they will agree to enter the scheme. "If they do they must quit the Junto."[29] Lord Poulett was the strongest advocate of this scheme. In a heated letter to Harley, he defended Anglesey, complained of Newcastle, and expounded his view of the scheme. "Is not the division to be among the Whigs of consequence, must not the Tories be united to that, must not the Queen for her own security do something substantial to engage them so as to be depended upon, and must not that appear to be obtained by your credit?"[30] This view of the new scheme was clearly a Tory view. The Queen was to win over, and depend upon, the Tories.

But Robert Harley had a different scheme in mind. He wished to ally with the Whig lords, whom he would detach from Marlborough and Godolphin. In late May he jotted down a memorandum, "Graft the Whigs to the bulk of the Church party."[31] The Earl of Dartmouth later observed, "The scheme at that time went no further than for removing the Marlborough family."[32] James Brydges concurred, writing in September 1710 that the original "scheme was only, as I am informed, level'd at my Lord Duke of Marlborough & my Lord Godolphin, but would have had every thing else gone upon the foot of Whig measures. . . ."[33] Pursuant to this strategy, Harley courted Halifax and wooed Somers; and pursuant to this strategy, he yielded to Newcastle's insistence that the Earl of Anglesey not be named secretary.[34]

Anglesey being unacceptable, Harley turned to Lord Poulett, who pondered the offer and then refused it. In part he refused because his friends, angry that the alterations at court did not go further, urged him to refuse. But he also refused because Lord Godolphin told him that he, Godolphin, would resign as lord treasurer if Sunderland was dismissed. Upon hearing this, Lord Poulett sent the Queen his final refusal.[35] Harley therefore turned to a compromise candidate, the Earl of Dartmouth, an inoffensive Tory whom the Whig lords could stomach. On 14 June the Queen took the seals from the Earl of Sunderland and gave them to the Earl of Dartmouth.

At the first rumor of Sunderland's dismissal, the Whigs spit fire and fury: a direct attack upon the Whigs, cried Walpole. Now the mask is off, wrote Marlborough. Godolphin threatened to resign, as did the most considerable Whigs. Even the toadying James Brydges offered to lay down if Godolphin did.[36] But the Whigs never resigned; they never resigned because they were totally disarmed by the fear of a dissolution of Parliament. "As long as the Whigs fear an ill Parliament," wrote the Duchess of Marlborough to her husband, "nothing can be done, but by gaining Shrewsbury, which I believe is impossible." Marlborough, however, was of the same mind as the Whigs, believing that nothing would be worth managing if Parliament was not preserved.[37] And the Whigs had good reason to fear a dissolution. "I will be bold to forsee," wrote James Craggs, "as the common people are now set, they [the Tories] will get at least three for one."[38] So when the blow finally fell on 14 June, the Whig lords quickly assembled at Devonshire's house, not to resign, but to send a letter to Marlborough urging him not to resign. "This," they wrote, "we look upon as the most necessary step that can be taken to prevent the dissolution of this Parliament."[39]

The Tories, meanwhile, displayed a concomitant enthusiasm for a dissolution. Almost every day delegations from the counties arrived to present the Queen addresses urging the dissolution of Parliament. Bromley fell despondent that these addresses did not have a more immediate effect, and St. John ranted at the slowness of Harley; but more neutral observers were certain that a dissolution must follow Sunderland's dismissal.[40] Such a change, observed Hoffmann, "cannot be undertaken without dissolving Parliament."[41]

Indeed, the most remarkable fact about the ministerial revolution of 1710 was the widespread belief, the nearly unanimous belief, that a new ministry meant a new Parliament. They say a new Parliament is a necessity, reported Peter Wentworth, for the present one will fall upon the new ministers and prove very troublesome.[42] Our governors, wrote

Godolphin, have given such offense to the present Parliament that there is no safety but in a new one.[43] When it is known who contrived this mischief, predicted Maynwaring, a severe account will be demanded, and therefore a dissolution is violently pressed.[44] The dullest among us, concluded Sir Thomas Hanmer, can see that without new elections nothing can go on, "for a new ministry with an old Parliament will be worse than the Gospel absurdity of a piece of new cloth in an old garment, or a new wine in old bottles."[45] This fatal blow, wrote Sir John Cropley of Sunderland's dismissal, must occasion a new Parliament.[46] Sir James Brydges agreed: "Those who have credit enough with the Queen to persuade her to the measures she has taken, will hardly think themselves safe in a House of Commons where the majority is against them, and where by a dissolution they think they shall have as considerable a one on their side."[47] Abel Boyer, the publicist, summed it up this way: if Her Majesty changes her ministry, she ought to dissolve Parliament, "for in our Political Constitution, if the Ministerial Part of the Government and the Parliament be not of a-piece, nothing can be expected from them but continual jars and misunderstandings, each contending to put the other in the Wrong, and obstructing what the other moves for the public good."[48]

Given the fact that they possessed a majority in the present Parliament and feared they would lose that majority in elections for a new Parliament, it is not surprising that the Whigs and the duumvirs strove with all their might to prevent a dissolution. Marlborough, as acute a strategist in politics as in war, sent off a stream of letters to Sunderland, Godolphin, the Duchess, Somers, Cowper, and Orford, urging them to temporize, to work with Shrewsbury, to keep their tempers, to do everything to preserve the Parliament, for all depended upon its continuance.[49] To this end the Whigs and the duumvirs drew upon all the sources of power at their command. During the reign of Queen Anne, it had become apparent that they drew their power from three sources: from the ability of the Whigs to secure six millions a year from Parliament, from the ability of Godolphin to raise several millions in the City on the public credit, and from the ability of Marlborough to lead the armies of the Allies to victory. Now that a dissolution threatened the first of these sources of power, the Whigs resorted to the other two. They cried out that a change of the ministry and the dissolution of Parliament would sink the public credit, upon which the supply of the troops depended. To support their contention, they led a delegation from the Bank to the Queen, a delegation that warned her that public credit would sink and stocks fall if she further altered the Ministry and if she dissolved Parliament.[50] And during the weeks that followed, M. Vryberge for the States General and Count Gallas for the Emperor presented memorials warning the Queen that further changes in the ministry and a dissolution of Parliament would shake the confidence of her allies in her determination to wage war.[51]

The Whigs feared a dissolution, the Tories longed for it, and most observers regarded it as inevitable. But the man at the center of the ministerial revolution, Robert Harley, did not, in fact, seek a dissolution. James Lowther and Johann Hoffmann sensed why. Given the ferment in the nation, wrote Lowther on 8 June, the Tories, rightly or wrongly, would win a majority.[52] And Hoffmann remarked on 13 June that if the Tories gain a dissolution, they will become "masters of the Ministry," for "then it will no longer be in the power of the Queen to choose moderate men of both parties."[53] And it was just this power to choose moderate men of both parties that Harley sought for the Queen. The heart of his new scheme was a mixed ministry, headed by Harley himself, loyal to the Queen, governing Parliament through moderate men. What was inevitable in the summer of 1710 was not a new Parliament but the need to find some way to manage Parliament, whether old or new. The age when a favorite, a Carr or a Villiers, could gain power solely by winning favor at court had long gone by. Harley enjoyed the Queen's confidence to the fullest; but only if he could manage her affairs successfully in Parliament could he continue to serve her. This he undertook to do in the spring of 1710. It was as a parliamentary undertaker as well as a court favorite that he won office and power in 1710.

Robert Harley spent the month of July in treaty with the

moderate Whigs. The self-appointed intermediary was Lord Halifax. It was at Halifax's house that the conferences were held—between Shrewsbury and Harley on one side and Halifax and Somers on the other.[54] On Friday, 14 July, the two sides reached a tentative compromise: Parliament should not be dissolved and the lord treasurer should not be dismissed, though Mr. Smith and other underofficers in the Treasury should be removed to make room for others.[55] For a week the town buzzed with reports that the leading men on both sides had reached agreement. The public credit rose. It was even said that the Duchess of Marlborough had met with Harley to compose all differences. But in the next fortnight, the treaty collapsed.[56] It collapsed in the first place because the Whig lords would not descend to particulars, would not give assurances that past quarrels would be forgotten, would not guarantee the safety of the new ministers, would not say how the present Parliament could be made practicable and how the public interest could be carried on.[57]

But the compromise also collapsed because Robert Harley was determined to wrest power from Lord Godolphin. When Marlborough heard of the compromise, he observed that the ministers were now to have no power, were to watch their friends be thrown out of office, were to be rendered contemptible. In fact, Harley and Shrewsbury had already rendered Godolphin contemptible. They had sent Cressett to Hanover and Lord Portmore to Portugal without consulting Godolphin. They had ignored the lord treasurer's recommendations that Lord Raby be named to the Board of Trade and Lord Dorchester be given a peerage. They had removed Lord Coningsby, Godolphin's spokesman in the Commons, from a lucrative post in Ireland in order to give it to Anglesey.[58] They had become, in fact, the managers at court, an office that Marlborough and Godolphin had exercised since 1702. But Harley had to exercise that role in an awkward and surreptitious manner. From the first of July onward, he waited on the Queen almost daily, but had to come after nine in the evening, to the back stairs, upon Somerset's summons. It was an arrangement that could not last.[59] Godolphin grew ruder and more ill-tempered every day and Harley more eager to be at the Treasury, directing affairs. By 22 July, Shrewsbury and Harley had resolved upon the dismissal of Godolphin.[60] On 8 August the Queen asked the Earl to break his staff as lord treasurer. The same day she named Robert Harley one of the five new commissioners of the Treasury and two days later named him chancellor of the Exchequer.

It was not, as Herr Hoffmann thought, the need to prepare for a new Parliament that led the Queen to dismiss Godolphin, for Harley had not yet resolved upon a new Parliament. Nor was it, as James Brydges thought, the Queen's anger at Godolphin for presenting to her a representation from the Bank (in which the Bank threatened to lend no money should the ministry be changed and Parliament dissolved), for the decision to remove Godolphin was taken before the representation was made.[61] There is no need to resort to such explanations, for Godolphin's dismissal was inevitable the day Harley embarked upon his scheme. That scheme provided for a mixed ministry, for the bestowal of offices on both Whigs and Tories, but it did not provide for a mixed management at court. That management had to be of one piece, and Harley, whose malice toward Godolphin and Marlborough was but thinly disguised, was determined that it should be in his hands.[62]

Robert Harley now appeared openly at court, sat in the Cabinet, and met with his fellow Treasury commissioners at the Treasury. He and Shrewsbury were, in Defoe's words, "the new managers."[63] But they could retain that management only if they maintained the public credit, kept the confidence of the Allies (or made peace), and won the support of Parliament.

When Sir David Hamilton in August asked the Queen whether she did not fear that the Bank would refuse to support credit, she replied, "They [who say that] only frighted the people to put a stop to what was doing."[64] Subsequent events proved her right. By careful management, by hard work, by reliance on Tory bankers such as Sir Charles Duncombe, and with the assistance of victories in Spain, Robert Harley was able to find the money needed to pay the armies in Flanders until Christmas. Bank stock rose to 111. The vaunted Whig money power in the City proved less formidable than thought.[65]

Nor was an immediate peace as necessary to the new scheme as had once been believed. In July the negotiations at Gertruydenberg broke down, but the new managers at home found the means to retain the confidence of England's allies. That means was the retention of the Duke of Marlborough as commander-in-chief to the allied armies. The more rabid Tories would have liked to have removed him and to have offered the command to the Electoral Prince, but Robert Harley had more sense. Though he sent Lord Rivers to Hanover to reassure that court that the Protestant succession was not in danger, he sent no offer of command with Lord Rivers.[66] That command should remain with the one man whom the Allies trusted.

To maintain the public credit and to carry on the war proved far easier than men had imagined, but to create a mixed ministry that would free the Queen from the tyranny of party proved far more difficult than Harley had thought. That this was Harley's purpose there can be no doubt. Late on the night of 8 August, James Lowther wrote, "I hear that there is a new Scheme of a mixture at Court and that the Parliament will not be dissolved, God send it be true."[67] So spoke a Whig, but the Tories told the same story. As Lady Roxburgh declared to the Earl of Nottingham, " . . . 'Twas never to be thought of to bring the leaders of High Tories, such as yourself and my Lord Rochester, into the administration, for that would be as contrary to their rule of moderation as to keep in the violent Whigs."[68]

Harley's conduct was fully consonant with this assessment of his purposes. He offered places on the Treasury commission to two Whigs, Richard Hampden and Jack Smith. He prevented Arthur Moore from forcing out James Brydges. He advised the Queen to make Lord Cowper lord lieutenant of Hertfordshire. He talked freely and late into the night with a Treasury Whig, probably Henry Boyle. He even sought to win over the Earl of Shaftesbury through the good offices of Sir John Cropley.[69]

But the most bizarre effort at coalition-building was Harley's efforts to win over the Dissenters through the instrumentality of Dr. Daniel Williams. Through Edward Harley, his brother, and by means of several letters, Robert Harley laid his new scheme before Dr. Williams, along with an offer of £1,000 for the repair of meeting houses. On 4 August, Dr. Williams, in a long, closely reasoned letter, declined to have any part in it. "I can't see," he wrote, "that any mixed party distinct from the two extreme bodies, can be sufficient to accomplish those things, which I mentioned as the cause I must serve in my station." The "cause" he must serve he declared to be "the Christian Protestant religion, the Protestant Succession, civil rights, and our Toleration." Now though a mixed party might at first honestly seek those ends, he continued, the necessity of affairs would soon cause men to fall into one or the other of the extreme parties. Fear of revenge will deter the new ministers from joining with the Whigs, so they will probably join with the High Tories, "among whom the papist nonjurors and swearing Jacobite make so great a figure." If these good purposes—the Protestant succession and toleration—are truly to be pursued, why are men removed who adhere to them and replaced with those who were for the occasional conformity bill and assisted Doctor Sacheverell? "I durst not," he concluded, "give the Low Church such a ground of suspecting unsteadiness on our part," for the safety of our religious and civil rights depends "upon the union between the body of the Low Church men and Protestant dissenters."[70]

From the eighth of August to the eighteenth, Harley sought, though without much vigor, to reach an accommodation with the Whigs based on the continuance of the present Parliament. On the evening of the ninth, the Junto Lords delivered to Lord Rivers, who had been active in the July conferences, new proposals for an accommodation. Rivers gave the proposals to Harley, who immediately wrote Newcastle that he would do all he could to reach an accommodation.[71] Newcastle, in lonely retreat at Welbeck Abbey, now became the center of the negotiations. He urged upon Harley that it was in his interest to preserve the Whigs in the government, otherwise he would be thrown entirely into the hands of the Tories, who would soon make their former resentment felt against him. Newcastle then wrote Lord Somers that the only way to prevent the dissolution of Parliament was to convince the ministry that all former heats will be laid aside and that the Whigs, in concurrence with the Queen's servants, could carry on the business of the nation. To Halifax he expressed the hope that Godolphin's dismissal will cause our friends to treat more effectually than they have hitherto.[72] Halifax replied that since the lord treasurer's power now resides in the ministers' hands, "it lies upon them to demand what further security they require of us in recompense for saving the Parliament."[73] Harley did not, however, tell Halifax what security he required, for he had decided that the old Parliment was wholly impracticable. As he wrote later to Newcastle, " . . . It is impossible to carry on Parliament without intolerable heats, and even the party itself [the Whigs] will not be governed by their rules, as they profess to several others that they [the rank and file] will go their own way if they meet again."[74] The Duke of Somerset's abrupt departure to his country seat signaled Harley's decision to dissolve Parliament, for Somerset wished to be absent from court when the dissolution that he had always opposed was declared.[75]

Given the Tory demand for a new Parliament, it is doubtful that Harley could have continued the present one had he wished to. From the moment the Queen dismissed Sunderland, both parties had begun to prepare for new elections. The triumphant reception of Dr. Sacheverell in Worcester encouraged the Tories greatly. By July the Tory "understrappers" in the counties were as busy as if the writs had been issued. Harley's own son-in-law wrote him that the people thought him too slow. Godolphin's dismissal led both Whigs and Tories to redouble their efforts to win seats in the new Parliament. By 18 August, Peter Wentworth was persuaded that the Tories had already spent so much on the elections that it would be a base act to disappoint them.[76]

The decision to meet a new Parliament forced Harley to move toward the Tories. They had long been restive at his moderation. The nomination of Sir Richard Onslow to the

Privy Council, the composition of the new Treasury commission, the naming of Cowper as lord lieutenant of Hertfordshire, the delay in dissolving Parliament, all had filled them with disgust.[77] A number of them sent Dr. Atterbury to Harley to express their indignation that Parliament was not dissolved and more Whigs turned out.[78] Harley broke out in a passion at this intervention in his efforts to serve the Queen, but he soon changed his tune. The change was marked by the admission of the Earl of Rochester to the inner deliberations of "the Schemists" (as Robert Monckton called them).[79] As late as 18 August, Rochester was highly disgusted with Harley, but in the last week of August he was meeting with him and Shrewsbury. The world first heard of the new alliance when the Queen replaced Godolphin with Rochester as lord lieutenant of Cornwall, a county that returned 44 members to Parliament.[80] In the ensuing weeks, Harley, consulting with Rochester, fashioned a scheme of administration that satisfied the impatient Bromley, delighted the Queen, and pleased the zealous Tories who gathered at Dr. Stratford's house in Oxford.[81] Harcourt would be attorney general; St. John, secretary of state; Rochester, president of the council; and the Duke of Buckingham, lord steward. On the twelfth of September, the scheme was prepared; on the sixteenth the Queen named Harcourt attorney general; on the twentieth she named the others to office, and on the twenty-first she dissolved Parliament. Such a mortality among ministers of state, so universal an alteration, so entire a change of ministry, had rarely been seen in the history of England.[82]

This universal change was not forced upon Harley by the Tories alone; the Whigs by their refusal to serve with Tories drove him to it. In August, Richard Hampden and Jack Smith declined to serve on the new Treasury commission; Hampden told the Queen that he could not serve with those who were for dissolving the Parliament.[83] And in September, Harley implored Boyle, Cowper, and Newcastle to continue in office, but only the Duke of Newcastle chose to do so; the other two resigned. Harley brought the greatest possible pressure to bear upon Cowper. On 18 September he paid him a visit, assured him that at bottom a Whig game was intended, and enumerated those Whigs still in office. Cowper answered that "things were plainly put into Tory hands, a Whig game, either in whole or in part, impracticable; that to keep in, when all my friends were out, would be infamous."[84] Cowper resigned on the twenty-third, Wharton and Orford the next day. Thus did the passions of party wreck Harley's scheme of a mixed ministry, of a ministry that would place service to the Queen above service to party.[85] But even now the ever resilient Harley did not desert the cause of rescuing the Queen from the tyranny of party. To Newcastle he wrote on 14 September, "As soon as the Queen has shewn strength and ability to give the law to both sides, then will moderation be truly shewn in the exercise of power without regard to parties only."[86]

The irreverent Lord Wharton held a different view of English politics. Upon hearing of the intended dissolution, he told Lord Dartmouth, "If you have the majority we are undone, if we have the majority, you are broke."[87] But Harley's difficulties were greater than even Lord Wharton imagined, for if the Queen were to give the law to both sides, it was essential that no party win a substantial majority in the new Parliament. The Queen's servants must hold the balance there, and High Flying Tories and violent Whigs must be replaced by men of moderation, by men whose first loyalty was to the Queen, not party. Such clearly was Harley's purpose. In early October he wrote a Whig lord (possibly Halifax), begging his interest in the elections and declaring, "Is there danger to be apprehended but on one side, and do not both sides treat the Queen and her ministers ill. . . . I have no partiality to one side more than another. . . . I have endeavoured to justify the Whigs. I would not have them have any jealousy that anyone would rival them in places."[88] To the public at large, he proclaimed these sentiments in a pamphlet entitled *Faults on Both Sides*. In it he declared that the Queen was resolved to pursue moderate measures, to bury in oblivion the very name of parties, and to govern through a coalition of the honest men of both parties.[89] And he showed in action as well as in words his intent to pursue a moderate scheme. He brought the changes at court to a halt, left Walpole in his place as treasurer of the navy, and even gave a teller's place to Jack Smith and a pension to Sir James Montagu. He brought the changes to a halt, wrote Swift, because he feared too great a majority for the Tories in the new Parliament.[90]

It did not, however, lie in the power of the court to shape the House of Commons to its desires. The impeachment of Sacheverell unleashed passions that swept away moderation. The doctor himself increased the ferment by triumphantly touring the island. High Churchmen everywhere threw themselves into the election. More seats were contested than ever before during the Queen's reign. As a result the electors of England gave to the Tory party a majority of 151 in the new House of Commons.[91]

To support his scheme of administration in a Tory Parliament now became Harley's chief task. By undertaking to manage Parliament successfully for her, he had freed the Queen from the tyranny of the Whigs. He must now make good that undertaking. As it turned out, he did so with considerable skill. When the Queen prorogued Parliament in June 1711, she prorogued a Parliament that had voted six and a half millions for the war, had renewed the land tax of four shillings in the pound, had continued the duties on malt, had funded two lotteries worth three and a half millions, had granted a supply for building fifty churches in London and Westminster, and had consolidated the floating debt by launching the South Sea Company. By any standard Harley's parliamentary management was a success.

What explanation can be given for his success? To begin with, command of a Court party in the two Houses was not the key. The Queen's servants were too few and their discipline too lax to give Harley such power. When the Commons read a place bill for the third time, "all who have had, or now have, or are in hopes to have places" divided against it, only to go down in defeat by 235 to 143.[92] Nor did the key reside in an alliance between the court and the Whigs, for on those occasions when they did join together, the Tories handily defeated them.[93] Neither did it lie in an alliance between the court and the moderates of both parties, for the court and the Tories soon embarked upon a vendetta against the old ministry that precluded such an alliance. They condemned Godolphin for leaving £35,000,000 unaccounted for. They branded Sunderland an enemy of the nation for bringing in the Palatines. They reflected upon Lord Cowper for granting an allegedly illegal charter to the borough of Bewdley. They expelled from the Commons Thomas Ridge, a Whig and a victualler of the navy, for abuses that had been practiced since the Restoration. They resolved that the want of troops in Spain arose from the great neglect of the ministry.[94]

In these attacks upon the old ministry, the court merely acquiesced. The High Tories, led by the Earl of Nottingham, were the driving force behind them. Indeed, Nottingham met with Harley and Dartmouth and others to insist upon the prosecution of errant Whigs, and he later drew up a memorandum in which he set forth the plan of attack to be pursued. It was a remarkable memorandum, for it explicitly calls for a politics of opposition. To establish the present ministry, the Tories must expose the shameful proceedings of the last ministry. If they did not, the Whigs would not fail to boast at the next election that no faults could be found in their conduct. Nothing will rivet members to us more certainly than exposing the faults of the previous ministers. In the search for faults, they must not be too "nice," nor be diverted by long and difficult examinations; instead they should swiftly gather together all matters of maladministration and present them to the Queen in several addresses.[95]

Whatever else these attacks accomplished, they certainly helped cement the alliance between the court and the Tories, and that alliance was the key to Robert Harley's successful management of Parliament. As one anonymous correspondent rudely informed Harley in January, "You have mounted the backs of the High Church coursers to ride upon to place of honour and preferment. . . . "[96] That the Tories entered into that alliance, though denied the many places of profit and honor they sought, must be attributed largely to the Earl of Rochester. He now displayed a probity and reasonableness, a good sense and charm, a moderation and firmness, that held the party together (and won over many a Scottish lord).[97] Rochester probably remembered, as surely other Tories did, the disasters that had befallen their party in 1704, when they thought they could govern the managers. Experience had taught them that if they broke from the managers they would be cast into outer darkness. This gave Harley his greatest strength. Knowing the Tories had nowhere else to go, he was emboldened to resist their demands for office and place.

The Tories needed Harley; but so too did Harley need the Tories. It was an alliance much like that between Godolphin and the Whigs in 1705, or like that between two allies in a war. In such alliances the terms of it are a matter for bargaining, threats, and final agreement. The Tories soon declared that the price of their support was an end to all balancing schemes and motley ministries. A ministry independent of party is unworkable, Rochester told the Queen. "A Coalition-scheme is impracticable," wrote Nottingham in March.[98] The High Tories soon gained the imprimatur of the House of Commons itself for their new doctorine. In their address to the Queen in June 1711, the Commons condemned those ministers who had "framed to themselves wild and unwarrantable schemes of balancing parties."[99]

But to gain their ends, to put an end to balancing schemes and motley ministries, the High-Flying Tories needed power; and power, they soon realized, lay in the control of the House of Commons through a tightly disciplined, well-organized party. In early February 1711, they formed such a party, the October Club, 150 members strong, mostly country gentlemen, meeting every Wednesday night at the Bell Tavern in King Street. Its members agreed to support in the Commons whatever was carried by the majority in the club. What they sought was a strict inquiry into all mismanagements and the purging of all Whigs from the court, the government, the army, the navy, from the meanest employments. Their purpose was (in Sir Arthur Kaye's words) "to make the ministry in a great measure come in to us," a purpose diametrically opposed to Robert Harley's maxim, first proclaimed in 1705, that parties should come into the Queen, not the Queen into parties.[100]

The October Club soon demonstrated its strength in the House of Commons. Against the wishes of the court, they passed a bill repealing the Naturalization Act of 1709, another bill establishing a Commission of Accounts, and a third to resume crown grants. But Robert Harley was able in the House of Lords, where the court and the Whigs possessed a majority, to defeat the naturalization and resumption bills.[101] The Octobrists thereby discovered that the only effective way to frighten a ministry was either to oppose a supply bill or to threaten to tack an unwanted measure to a supply bill. Harley talked the Octobrists out of tacking the resumption bill to a money bill, but, lying wounded from the knife-blows of the Marquis de Guiscard, he was unable to prevent them from opposing a supply bill late in March. The October Club carefully planned their assault. They urged their members to attend the House on Monday, 26 March, upon which day they spoke against placing a duty on leather. The court, thunderstruck, called for the question anyway, certain that they could carry it. But the House rejected the measure by 136 votes to 95. The ministry the next day, by declaring that no other fund could be found, that without it the armies could not take the field and the campaign would be lost and credit sunk, recovered the duty. The appeal to necessity and patriotism carried the day by 181 to 76. But it was the Whigs who reversed themselves and supported the duty; the Octobrists remained sullenly opposed.[102]

The death of the Earl of Rochester and the prorogation of Parliament gave Robert Harley, now Earl of Oxford and lord treasurer, an opportunity to make several changes in the government. The October Club, naturally enough, clamored for a thorough change, and would have rejoiced to see Nottingham made president of the council. Against this step the Earl Poulett sent Harley an urgent warning. To name Nottingham lord president would be to invite the extravagances of the past, to bring party divorced from reason into the Cabinet, to upset the balance, to reduce the crown yet lower. He then recommended that the innocuous and useful Duke of Buckingham be made lord president and that Nottingham's interest be held by giving office to his relatives.[103] Harley readily accepted this advice. The Tory Buckingham became president of the council, and the Queen named Nottingham's nephew as master of the Jewell House, his son-in-law as paymaster of the marines, and his cousin as a commissioner of the Board of Trade. Two moderate Tories (William Benson and Henry Paget) and two High Tories (John Ward and James Bruce) received office. Poulet himself became lord steward. The October men complained that the lord treasurer had not thrown out every person suspected of being a Whig, but the lord treasurer had moved substantially closer to a Tory ministry.[104]

In August he took yet another step toward a ministry that was all of one piece. He prevailed upon the Queen to give the privy seal, vacated by the death of the Duke of Newcastle, to the bishop of Bristol, a moderate Tory and Churchman. The death of Newcastle left only one Whig in the Cabinet, the Duke of Somerset, who withdrew in late August when St. John refused to sit there if Somerset was present. It was now a wholly Tory Cabinet.[105]

A wholly Tory Cabinet, however, did not satisfy the October Club. They wanted a thorough reformation of the administration and threatened to make the ministry uneasy the next winter if it was not carried out.[106] But their threats came to nought, at least in the House of Commons, where the ministry the next winter carried all its measures by large majorities—the Preliminaries of the Peace by 232 to 106, the condemnation of Marlborough by 270 to 165, the Restraining Orders by 203 to 73, the final Approval of the Peace *nemine contradicente*. In part this triumph arose from careful management, with Bromley and his lieutenants making a superb effort to secure the attendance of Tories at debates and votes.[107] In part it arose from the politics of opposition, for the ministry invited the backbenchers to condemn Walpole for bribery, Townshend for the Barrier Treaty, and Marlborough for peculation. But the chief reason for the ministry's success was the passionate desire of Englishmen for peace. Oxford's success in gaining a peace brought his government that applause which Marlborough earned by victories. It ran even deeper than a longing for peace: the Tories in the House of Commons, even the Octobrists, feared that if Oxford failed to win a peace the Whigs would return to manage the war.[108]

The peace strengthened the ministry in the House of Commons; in the House of Lords it weakened it. This fact became evident on 7 December, when the Lords, by a margin of one vote and against the wishes of the court, resolved that no peace could be safe or honorable that left Spain and the West Indies in any branch of the House of Bourbon. The Earl of Nottingham's decision to oppose the peace certainly contributed to the defeat of the court, but he carried almost no other Tory with him. What actually caused the court's defeat was the collapse of that coalition of court Whigs and Tory lords that had allowed Harley to manage the Lords successfully the previous winter.[109] It was the issue of peace, of a peace without Spain, that broke the coalition. The court Whigs, some thirty in number, could not stomach a peace that left Spain in the hands of the House of Bourbon. Halifax sought to save the coalition by proposing to Oxford that the Queen merely transmit the preliminaries to the Allies, but Oxford persuaded the Queen to reject this proposal.[110] Somerset was particularly piqued, since he had assured his friends that Halifax's proposal was acceptable to the Queen.[111]

In January 1711 Lord Cowper observed that "the scheme lords, the necessitous lords, and the Scots lords voted according to the Ministry, but the wise and independent voted according to judgment."[112] The scheme lords, such as Halifax and Somerset, deserted Oxford because they could not accept the peace he had made, but there were still the necessitous lords and the Scots lords to depend upon. Unfortunately for Oxford, through carelessness, tardiness, and niggardliness, many of these were lost. Lord Mar received his notice too late to arrive before 12 December. The Duke of Atholl was not inclined to come to London unless he received employment in the Queen's service. The Marquis of Annandale sulked in his tent for want of an office more dignified than that of a commissioner of trade. Earl Home had difficulty finding the £100 to bring him to London. When the great crisis came on 7 December, there were only four or five Scottish lords present, the Earl of Anglesey was still in Ireland, and Lord Cornwallis was in a tavern.[113] But the fault lay deeper than in careless management: it lay in the weakness of the power of patronage itself. On that critical seventh of December, lords who enjoyed pensions, favors, and place—lords such as Chomondeley and St. Albans and Somerset— voted against the court. Between 40 and 50 percent of the House of Lords were servants of the Queen, yet on this vote, as also on other votes (such as Hamilton's patent as an English peer and the resumption bill), the court could not rely upon them.[114] The dictates of party, the demands of conscience, and the sway of prejudice too often proved more powerful than the claims of office.

The shock of defeat in the Lords drove the Earl of Oxford to ask the Queen to name twelve new peers. She did, all of them Tories. When they entered the House in January, Lord Wharton asked if they were going to vote through a foreman. It was a good jest, but in fact the twelve peers gave Oxford the votes he needed to secure the Lords' approval of the Restraining Orders sent to Ormond and of the Queen's endeavors to negotiate a peace.[115] The creation of the twelve peers marked a definite turning to the Tories, but it was not the only sign of such a turning. Oxford now ceased to talk of moderating schemes and mixed ministries. He now made promises to the October Club that there would be further changes in office. In January he named new commissioners of the Customs, all of them Tories. Henry St. John rejoiced, and Lord Halifax grew despondent at the prospect of a thorough reformation.[116]

This turn toward the Tories did not arise solely from the shock of defeat in the Lords; it arose also from the unremitting pressure of the Tories on Oxford. Oxford responded with promises and delays. Trying desperately to prevent the Commons from tacking the resumption bill to the lottery bill, William Bromley, the Speaker, wrote to Oxford in April, "Should I not succeed, I must impute it to my own want of credit with our friends, which I fear suffers from my having assured them a great deal more would be done before this time for serving and establishing our common interest, than they have yet seen performed, and in this I have never exceeded what you gave me reason to expect."[117] In the event Bromley defeated the tack, and Oxford in June and July granted a few more offices to the Tories. Sir William Wyndham became secretary-at-war, Lord Mansell replaced Jack Smith at the Exchequer, John Price was added to the Excise Commission, and Lord Guilford, Thomas Foley, and John Cotton were named to the Board of Trade. These changes did not add up to the total purge of all Whigs that the insatiable Octobrists sought, but it ended all pretense that Oxford could govern through balanced counsels. As the Earl of Strafford observed to Princess Sophia: "The Queen saw that reigning by one party was but being a slave to the heads of that party; and therefore when she first made her change, it was positively resolved not to stick to parties, but to those who served her best. However, the other party's opposition and violence may have made her change her mind, for the mere necessity, at this conjuncture."[118]

The lord treasurer's increasing dependence upon the Tories aggravated that constant tugging between court manager and party zealot that was ever a part of such arrangements. In the autumn of 1712, the party zealots, the October men, objected that men who publicly opposed the government were continued in office, that the promises that the lord treasurer had so often made were not kept, that most places of honor and profit were still in the hands of the Whigs, that now was the time to strike home and carry out a thorough reformation.[119] William Oldisworth in the *Examiner* thundered against a coalition with the Whigs. "If false hopes and chimerical fears prevail upon the easy temper of a statesmen, to attempt a Coalition of Friends and Foes, if he pays his deserters better than his regular troops, and beats up for volunteers in the enemy's country; fidelity will be made a jest, treachery become meritorious, and men of abilities will find their interest in opposing the government, and promoting faction as a step to preferment."[120] But Daniel Defoe, the most prolific publicist of the age, declaimed with equal fervor against the October men, against their "principles of absolute government," against their endeavors to establish "their Party in a power or capacity of governing." To this end they separated themselves from the new ministry, "pretended to act upon Schemes of their own," and sought "to influence things by their numbers."[121] Between the ideas of Oldisworth and those of

Defoe, Lord Oxford clearly preferred Defoe's. In the winter of 1713, he warned the October men that their demands for a proscription of all Whigs might turn the voters against the Tories, just as the impeachment of Sacheverell had turned the voters against the Whigs. He urged them to be patient, to wait for the ratification of the Articles of Peace in the coming Parliament. And just before the opening of Parliament, he publicly dined with Lord Halifax, through whom he hoped to win the support of the Whigs for the peace. The Tories immediately cried out that a coalition was intended.[122]

Parliament met in April 1713, and the court (as Ralph Bridges wrote in June) carried everything before it.[123] It defeated an attempt to tack a place bill to the malt bill. It fought off an attempt by the Whigs and the Scots in the House of Lords to dissolve the union with Scotland. It rescued the civil list from a debt of £500,000. In large part the success of the court can be attributed to two prevalent charms: the peace, which a grateful nation celebrated with bonfires, and a reduction in the land tax of two shillings in the pound. But the lord treasurer's success must also be attributed to the solid support of the Tories in both Houses and to Bolingbroke's entreaties to the October men not now to fly in the face of the ministry.[124]

The success of the court was not unalloyed. In the House of Commons, the country gentlemen defeated an attempt by the court to reduce the tax that Scotsmen should pay on malt. Nor could the court prevent the Lords from voting an address to the Queen asking what equivalent England had received in return for the demolition of the fortifications at Dunkirk and another address asking Her Majesty to take effectual care to remove the Pretender from Lorraine. But the most serious defeat suffered by the court occurred on 18 June, when the Commons rejected, by 194 to 185, a bill to give effect to a treaty of commerce recently negotiated with France. "In this," wrote the lord treasurer's brother, "was seen the folly of depending upon any Party, many of the leaders of the Tories in both Houses falling into the measures of the Whigs. . . . "[125] William Bishop, of Grey's Inn, concluded quite otherwise. "You see," he wrote Dr. Charlett in Oxford, "what becomes of Trimming it betwixt two parties: neither cares for you."[126]

There is no question but that the bill met defeat because Sir Thomas Hanmer and some eighty Tories deserted the government.[127] The uncertainty lies in why they deserted. One reason was the unpopularity of the treaty itself. A persuasive number of merchants testified that it would endanger the manufacture of silks and woolens in England, and members were reluctant to endanger those trades, particularly in an election year. Yet Sir Thomas Hanmer assured Jonathan Swift that he was perfectly satisfied with the treaty.[128] A second reason was the lord treasurer's indifference toward its passage; yet when his friends urged him to drop the bill, he refused, depending on the court majority to carry it.[129]

Though the unpopularity of the treaty and the indifference of the treasurer undoubtedly contributed to the defection of the eighty Tories, there was a more fundamental reason for their conduct. They were angry at Oxford for his slowness in throwing out Whigs and bringing in Tories. It is confidently reported, wrote William Bishop, "that the Lord Anglesey and Sir Thomas Hanmer are disobliged and that they did it out of pique to the Lord Treasurer."[130] They gave up their country, complained Swift, "out of pique."[131] Those who voted against the bill, wrote Ralph Wingate,

> do own it was to make the Treasurer shake at root. The truth is, he acts as if he was absolute, and as if he thought that everybody ought to be content and highly pleased with all his actings. The loyal party have complained many times of his not altering the greatest part of the Whig lieutenancy, and almost all the Justices of the Peace in the kingdom, and all the employments, offices, and collectors of the Customs, Excise, &c. These, he had promised twenty times to remove, but had never done anything in it. So now, they say, in general they will force him to act like an honest man, though there is not a word to be trusted to what he ever said; so that if there is not a clean house of all the Whigs, before next Parliament, it will go hard with him.[132]

Edward Harley's opinion that the defeat of the commerce bill showed the folly of depending upon one party was very wide of the mark. The defeat in fact showed the folly of disregarding the party upon whose support one depended.

The Earl of Oxford, as he had done the previous year, chose to run before the storm. In August he brought more Tories into the government. William Bromley, the most revered of Tories, became secretary of state in the place of Lord Dartmouth, who became lord privy seal. William Wyndham, a close friend of Bolingbroke's, was given the office of chancellor of the Exchequer, his former place as secretary-at-war being given to Francis Gwyn. Lord Lansdowne replaced Lord Cholmondeley (dismissed for opposing the peace in the Privy Council) as treasurer of the Household, and Sir John Stonehouse (a protégé of Bolingbroke's) took Lord Lansdowne's place as comptroller of the Household. Thomas Foley became an auditor of the Imprest and Lord Denbigh a teller of the Exchequer. Lord Delaware became treasurer of the Chamber, and Thomas Moore, Arthur's brother, replaced James Brydges in the lucrative office of paymaster to the land forces abroad. Sir Thomas Hanmer was promised the Speakership in the next Parliament, and Francis Atterbury became bishop of Rochester.[133] These preferments fell short of the thorough reformation that Goerge Lockhart cried out for and that Viscount Bolingbroke schemed to effect,[134] but one fact about them deserves attention: not one of the men preferred was a Whig. This was likewise true of the men preferred to office in 1711 and 1712. The power of patronage still resided in the hands of the Queen and her first minister, to the great grief of the October Club, but the Queen and her minister had to exercise that power within the limits set by party. In August 1711 the Duke of Somerset sought to persuade the Queen to give the Privy Seal, vacated by Newcastle's death, to Lord Somers.[135] She did not, for had she, the outcry from the Tories would have made the management of Parliament impossible. The lord treasurer might refuse to purge the remaining Whigs from office, but he dared not name Whigs to offices that fell vacant. To that extent party had captured patronage, and the Queen had become a prisoner of party.

When the Earl of Oxford in February 1714 met his fourth Parliament as the Queen's first minister, he enjoyed a larger majority than he had ever enjoyed before, for the Tories had triumphed in the elections held in the autumn of 1713. They had won 363 seats to the Whigs 150, a majority of 213. They had also won the 16 seats in the House of Lords for which the Scottish peers contested.[136] Yet the 1714 session was one of the most hectic, acrimonious, desperate, and mismanaged sessions of the Queen's reign. The government had to prorogue Parliament swiftly in July to prevent it from censuring a leading member of the administration. Why a ministry possessed of so great a majority should make so great a shambles of the management of Parliament is an important question, but, oddly enough, not a difficult one to answer. The ministry simply failed for want of unity within its ranks. The Tories themselves knew as well as any man the importance of unity; without it they could not manage Parliament successfully for the Queen. Oldisworth in the *Examiner*, Bolingbroke in letters to his friends, Dr. Stratford in letters to Lord Harley, and Oxford in his private memorandums, all called for unity.[137] But the more they called for it, the less they seemed able to achieve it. The cause of their failure lay in two great impediments to unity: the devious character of the Earl of Oxford and the political ambitions of Viscount Bolingbroke.

Throughout his political career, the Earl of Oxford had shown a love of dark counsels, devious ways, adroit management, and unkept promises. "Robin, the Trickster" they called him. He had also shown a firm resolve to be the sole manager—above party, guiding the Queen, pursuing moderation, and distributing patronage as he saw fit. To these devious ways and to this love of power, he now added a lethargy and an isolation that threatened all management. In the autumn of 1713, he withdrew from affairs, saw the Queen infrequently, talked of laying down his staff, yet clung to it. He ignored repeated pleas from court peers for the fulfillment of promises made to them.[138] Lord Harcourt found it almost impossible to see him for half an hour.[139] Shall we, cried out Bolingbroke, lose by mismanagement what we have won by our majority.[140] The demands of Oxford's fellow Cabinet ministers for a greater share in management and the demands of the rank and file for more places of honor and profit reached a climax in late March 1714. Oxford, feeling the weight of these pressures, waited upon the Queen and offered to resign from office. But at the same time (according to Herr Schutz, the Hanoverian envoy), he sent a friend to the Queen (Schutz does not say whom) to warn her that if she dismissed Oxford the Tory party would be ruined and she would fall again into the hands of the Whigs.[141] To save his place as lord treasurer, Oxford now posed as the leader of a party, not the minister who would save the Queen from party. His own letters and memorandums show the shift in his thought. On 26 March he scribbled, " . . . The complaint is he will not be head of the Tories. Does he expect quarter from the Whigs? Who hinders him from heading the Tories but those who complain and who would have all list under their colors?"[142] And to Harcourt he wrote, "I have found myself a burden to my friends and to the only party I ever have or will act with."[143]

It was not Oxford alone who deserted the ideal of a mixed ministry: the Queen herself abandoned it. In December she fell ill, and the Whigs too openly showed their delight. This led her, wrote Swift, "to lay aside all her schemes of reconciling the two opposite Interests." Her one purpose now was to keep from ever falling again into the hands of the Whigs.[144] To this purpose she strove with all her might to reconcile Oxford with the rest of her ministers. She succeeded, momentarily. "We flatter ourselves," wrote Erasmus Lewis on 29 March, "that during this short recess our friends are so far reconciled to one another that they will go on cheerfully and unanimously with the public business, which has proceeded slowly. . . ."[145] And Bolingbroke assured Oxford that he desired to see him forever "at the head of the Queen's affairs and of the Church of England party."[146] Within a week the Queen purged Whigs and errant Tories from the Admiralty and the Guards and took from Argyle all his employments.[147] That same week Oxford and Bolingbroke met with thirty backbenchers at Secretary Bromley's house, where they promised to meet twice a week to establish a mutual confidence and to work to prevent their majority in Parliament from slipping out of their hands. Bolingbroke added that he would not leave a Whig in office.[148] The compass had swung about, and a scheme of administration designed to rescue the Queen from a party had become a scheme to tie her to a party.

The patching that the Queen's ministers so assiduously performed in March became unglued during the next four months, but the new crisis arose less from anger at Oxford than from fear of the Pretender. Early in April the leading Hanoverian Tories—men like Hanmer, Anglesey, and the archbishop of York, men called "the Whimsicals"—met with Argyle and Nottingham, who were empowered to speak for the Whigs. The Whigs agreed that the Whimsicals might distribute offices as they wished, provided that they would secure the Protestant Succession, renew those alliances that the present ministry had broken, and protect English commerce.[149] On the basis of this alliance, the Whigs and the Whimsicals repeatedly attacked the ministry during the next four months. They came within 14 votes in the Lords and 48 votes in the Commons of declaring the Protestant Succession to be in danger under the present administration, and they did carry an address in the Lords asking the Queen to renew her requests that the Pretender be removed out of Lorraine.[150] But the Tories still had the strength to carry votes in both Houses declaring the treaties of Peace and Commerce with France and Spain to be safe, honorable, and advantageous. In the Commons the Tories would hardly suffer a debate to be held on the merits of the treaties but, knowing they had the votes, bawled out for the question.[151] Whigs and Whimsicals together were no match for the Court party.

Then came an irreparable and costly division within the Court party itself. Bolingbroke, without consulting or informing Oxford, persuaded Sir William Wyndham on 12 May to introduce into the House of Commons a bill to prohibit Dissenters from educating their children in their own academies.[152] The schism bill, as it came to be called, was Bolingbroke's bid for the leadership of the Church party. To secure that leadership, he was also willing to placate the Jacobites. Daniel Steingens, the Palatine resident, for one, believed that the enemies of the Earl of Oxford sought more than a share of the Queen's favor; they sought also to bring in the Pretender.[153] The lord treasurer's counterstroke was to carry in the Cabinet, before a stunned and speechless Bolingbroke, a proclamation offering £5,000 to any person who should apprehend the Pretender within Great Britain.[154]

Far more dangerous to Bolingbroke was an inquiry launched in the House of Lords into the three Explanatory Articles that accompanied the Treaty of Commerce with Spain. Witnesses before the Lords suggested that Arthur Moore, the author of the articles, may have been bribed by the Spanish, and that English courtiers, among them Arthur Moore, Lady Masham, and Bolingbroke, were to have the Queen's share of the Asiento contract.[155] At this moment in early July, Oxford, having lost the Queen's favor, could only have survived by accusing Bolingbroke of having added the Explanatory Articles to the Treaty of Commerce without the authority or knowledge of the Cabinet. He promised the Whigs, with whom he was now conspiring, that he would do so, but, devious to the last, he did not. His silence allowed Bolingbroke to rush the last money bill through the Lords and the Queen to prorogue Parliament on 9 July.[156]

During these last frantic weeks of Parliament, rumors of a new scheme of administration spread through England. "If the new scheme prevails," wrote Dr. Stratford on 17 June, "I hear the Bishop of Rochester is to be Lord Privy Seal."[157] Peter Wentworth on 25 June gave an even more complete account of the new scheme. It was to be entirely Tory, without the least mixture of Whigs. Bolingbroke was to be lord treasurer, Sir William Wyndham secretary of state, Henry Campion chancellor of the Exchequer, and Sir Constantine Phipps attorney general.[158] Ralph Bridges on 5 July summed it up in this way:

> Lord Bolingbroke, Lord Chancellor, and the Bishop of Rochester are the men chiefly concerned in what they call the new Scheme, and Bolingbroke is to have the Staff and be Premier Minister. This the Tories pretty unanimously talk. On the other hand the Treasurer [Oxford] is trying to retrieve himself with the Whigs, and is, they say, a courting them in order to save himself in that herd. The Lord knows what will be the issue; but sure the Church Party do not enough imbibe and consider that maxim, *divide & impera*.[159]

With these sentiments Dean Swift, who rushed off to Berkshire to avoid a storm he was powerless to prevent, would surely have concurred. On 22 July he wrote John Arbuthnot, who had remained at court, "What can be your new scheme, what are your new provocations? Are you sure of a Majority?"[160] The clear answer is that Bolingbroke was not sure of a majority— indeed, he feared that he would be impeached in the next session for want of one. Fearing an impeachment, he designed (so wrote Bothmar) to bring over the Pretender, "to save himself and to finish his grand scheme."[161]

The Queen took what seemed to be the first step toward the execution of this grand scheme on 27 July 1714, when she took the white staff from the lord treasurer. But if it was the first step, it was also the last, for the Queen died four days later and the accession of the House of Hanover broke forever all the schemes of Viscount Bolingbroke.

The twenty-seventh of July marked the last day of Robert Harley's scheme of administration, a scheme begun with such high promise, pursued with such tribulation, attended with such success, and concluded with such bitterness. Relieved of the burdens of office, he was free to retire to Brampton Castle to reflect upon the past four years. What lessons he drew from these years we do not know, but certain conclusions appear manifest to the historian. Among them five stand out as particularly significant. First, it is plain that Robert Harley, though he eschewed the name of undertaker, was only able to oust Godolphin and the Whigs from power because he could undertake to manage Parliament for the Queen. The day that Godolphin fell from office everyone knew that a new Parliament was inevitable. Secondly, Harley's deeply cherished plans to save the Queen from the tyranny of party by forming a mixed ministry went aground on the rocks of party passions, on the refusal of Whig to serve with Tory and of Tory to serve with Whig. Thirdly, he did successfully manage the Queen's affairs in Parliament for three years; he secured supplies, avoided censures, ratified the peace, and consolidated the debt, but he did so only by relying upon a Tory majority in the House of Commons and by having the Queen create a Tory majority in the House of Lords. Fourthly, the Tories demanded a price for their support: that more and more Tories be brought into office. The lord treasurer, though he clung to the control of patronage, as all court managers do, paid that price. Fifthly, his scheme of administration could succeed only as long as there was unity within the ministry and within the Tory party, but his own deviousness and Bolingbroke's recklessness finally broke that unity. In these last months, Dr. Stratford knew, Jonathan Swift knew, Ralph Bridges knew, what every parliamentary undertaker needed to know: a united party enjoying a majority in Parliament was the only sure support for a scheme of administration.

Conclusions

The Anatomy of a Parliamentary Undertaking

BY A PROCESS that was slow, halting, pragmatic, myopic, and experimental, English politicians during the reign of the Stuarts developed a mechanism for placing the executive power in the hands of those who led in Parliament. That mechanism was a parliamentary undertaking, though Englishmen after 1688 oftener called it a scheme of administration. Sir Henry Neville was the first to propose such an undertaking, in October 1611; Viscount Bolingbroke in July 1714 was the last Stuart politician to propose one—though by no means the last English politician to do so. Between those years there were a great variety of undertakings, which met with varying success. Furthermore, the mechanism itself changed through time, taking on more decisive, more refined, and more compelling features. Despite variety and change, however, these many undertakings and schemes had certain characteristics in common, enough to make it possible to draw the anatomy of a parliamentary undertaking.

At the heart of all such undertakings was an offer to manage Parliament successfully for the King if entrusted with high office. For particular promotions Neville undertook to carry the Parliament for His Majesty's profit and ends. In return for office, the Earl of Bedford and his friends engaged to procure the King a liberal revenue. Sir Richard Temple in 1663 undertook that the King's business should be effected and a large supply voted if he and his friends were given office. Four years later the Duke of Buckingham undertook that Parliament would vote money if the King dismissed the Clarendonians. Shaftesbury in 1679 and the Southamptons in 1680 un-

[234]

dertook to secure Charles II the money he needed to disband the army and set out a fleet if he agreed to the exclusion of the Duke of York and entrusted them with office. These offers to serve the King in return for office were largely the offspring of crises: of the failure of the Elizabethan polity in 1610, of the collapse of prerogative rule in 1640, of the disgrace at Chatham in 1667, and of the Exclusion Crisis in 1679 and 1680. After the Glorious Revolution, such offers became routine moves in the war of parties. The Whigs in 1693 offered to extricate William from all his difficulties if he would put his affairs into their hands. The Tories in 1700 undertook to carry the succession in the House of Hanover and secure the King a supply if given office. The Whigs in 1708 offered to carry the court through all its difficulties if the administration was put in their hands. And Robert Harley won the Queen's favor in 1710 by undertaking to rescue her from the tyranny of the Whigs.

It was an essential feature of such offers that the undertakers should come into office together. It was objected to Neville that he was not content to come in alone. Bedford's friends agreed that none would accept office until all were provided for. Temple wrote Buckingham in 1669 that he would have no foundation unless he brought in all his friends. The Earl of Essex in 1679 earned considerable obloquy by coming in before the rest. After the Glorious Revolution, the dictates of party ensured that undertakings would be a corporate enterprise.

It was likewise characteristic of an undertaking that those who proposed it were drawn from the opposition. John More was astonished that anyone should imagine that the King would name Neville secretary of state, for he was accounted a patriot and had opposed the courtiers. But gradually the sight of an opponent of the court negotiating for office became less startling. Indeed, what made a Neville or a Pym or a Shaftesbury or a Somers valuable to the King was the fact that he was a tribune of the people, well heard in Parliament and able to influence it. The parliamentary undertaker was preeminently a man who could speak for others, as Neville had spoken for the House of Commons in 1610 and Bedford for the noblemen and gentlemen of England in 1640. Their value to the King lay in their popularity in the two Houses.

Neville and Bedford had not opposed the King in order to win popularity and thereby preferment: they had opposed him because they were alarmed at the folly of his policies. The Earl of Newcastle, it is true, believed that men had opposed Charles I merely to be bought off with office, and at the Restoration he warned Charles II against this practice; but in fact the practice of opposing the King with a deliberate purpose to wrest office from him began in the 1660s, with Sir Richard Temple and his friends. In the 1666 session of Parliament, Temple led a formed opposition to the government, with the intent of driving out the Earl of Clarendon. By 1675 the Earl of Lindsey could complain to Danby of those who affected popularity merely to gain preferment. He was probably thinking of the Earl of Shaftesbury, but in truth Shaftesbury was less of a careerist than Temple or Howard or Seymour or even Danby himself in the 1660s. The passions aroused by the Popish Plot and the Exclusion Crisis gave a public face to Shaftesbury's private ambitions.

Few aspects of the politics of the reigns of William III and Queen Anne are more remarkable than the rapid rise of an explicit politics of opposition. In 1689 the Whigs seized upon miscarriages in Ireland and at sea to drive Carmarthen and Halifax from office; in 1692 they launched an attack upon Nottingham in order to drive him from office, an attack that succeeded in 1693 when the ministerial Whigs, angered at their neglect, joined with the extreme Whigs. It was Robert Harley who taught the Tories the art of opposition during the years from 1698 to 1700. The Tories proved apt pupils. By 1700 they were determined to puzzle the King's affairs, cross his politics, and confound his ministry until given office. Their business, they openly declared, was to break the ministry. The Whigs were not far behind in the politics of opposition. In 1706 they let Godolphin know that they would be against everything that might assist the Queen and the government unless their demands were met. In the session of 1707–08, they alternately came to the support of the government to prove their ability to do good and opposed it to prove their capacity for doing harm. Encouraged by the Earl of Nottingham, the High Flying Tories in 1711 and 1712 persisted in the politics of opposition, even though the leaders of the Tory party had won high office. They were determined, as they had been in 1701, to discredit the Whigs so thoroughly that they could never return to office. But, as Lord Somers told William III, the other side could play that game also. In 1714 the Whigs joined with the Hanoverian Tories to attack the government repeatedly. The Earl of Clarendon in the 1660s was deeply pained that any person should oppose the government simply because he was not of it, but the world of Clarendon did not survive the party passions of the reigns of William and Anne.

To propose an undertaking, one needed to negotiate with the King, and to negotiate with the King, one needed a broker at court. In every parliamentary undertaking in the seventeenth century, the undertakers possessed a friend or friends at court who promoted their cause. Neville had his Rochester, Bedford his Hamilton, Temple his Bristol, Shaftesbury his Monmouth, and the Southamptons their Sunderland. Sunderland, without a shadow of a doubt, was the supreme broker of the age. He negotiated for Shaftesbury in 1679, for the Southamptons in 1680, for the Whigs in 1693, for the Tories in 1700 (though the Earl of Jersey was the real power at court), and for the Whigs once again in 1701. For a brief moment in 1696, the Whigs thought they could do without a broker at court, but they soon found that they were mistaken. During the reign of Queen Anne, they used an initially reluctant Godolphin and an uneasy Marlborough as their intermediaries with the Queen. Robert Harley, in his turn, negotiated with the Queen through Shrewsbury, Somerset, and Mrs. Masham—that is, until he found his way up the back stairs at Kensington Palace in April 1710. By September of that year, he had become, in essence, the broker at court for a Tory party determined to wrest ever more offices from the Queen.

In the year 1701, toward the end of his career, the Earl of Sunderland wrote Lord Somers several letters setting forth the art of being a broker at court. In them he showed how delicate, how courteous, how subtle, how indirect, how informal one must be in negotiating with the King. The essence of the art was to persuade him to bring his critics into office while concealing from him the injury that this did to his prerogative. It is doubtful that such indirection deceived any monarch—James declared he would not have a secretary forced upon him by Parliament, and Queen Anne declared she would not be made a prisoner of the Whigs. Yet such indirection did wrap up necessity in a disguise acceptable to the political world. The prerogative, though invaded, was not *seen* to be invaded, which was more than could be said of the formal nomination of the King's ministers. In 1689 the Whigs debated whether the House of Commons should ask the King for permission to nominate faithful persons to him for the great offices. They decided that the House should not, for it would entrench upon his lawful prerogative. They resolved instead that these matters should be humbly offered to the King by private persons. The laws of England emphatically gave the King the right to choose his own ministers, but those laws did not forbid him to listen to the private remonstrances of great men at court before making his choice.

The results of a broker's negotiations were far oftener an understanding than an agreement. No monarch wanted to commit himself to naming the undertakers to office or to granting particular graces, yet he was willing to hold out the hope that such graces would be granted and suitable men brought into office. The anatomist of a parliamentary undertaking must examine with great care not only the officers whom the King named but the measures upon which he embarked, for the King might bestow office upon a man merely "to buy him off." There is a fine but exact line between a parliamentary undertaking, such as Neville proposed to James I, and a resort to the power of patronage, such as Bacon urged upon James. If the King embraced the policies of the opposition, conceded to them the graces they asked, then it was an undertaking; but if he clung to his own policies and refused those graces, then it was but a stratagem "to win men by office." It all depended upon whether Mohammed moved to the mountain or the mountain to Mohammed. When Charles

I detached Thomas Wentworth from the Country party and when Charles II gave office to Buckingham's lieutenant, Sir Thomas Osborne, it was no parliamentary undertaking, for these men agreed to serve the King on his terms. The Earl of Shaftesbury in 1675 clearly saw the distinction between entering the court upon one's own terms and entering it upon the King's, and thereafter refused to enter it upon any terms but his own. William III made the same distinction, but not the same choice. "He would have men come to his humour," he told Halifax, "not he to theirs."[1] Robert Harley fully concurred, writing in 1705, "The foundation is persons or parties are to come in to the Queen, and not the Queen to them."[2]

To persuade persons and parties to come into the court, the monarchs of England came increasingly to rely upon patronage and packing, upon the power of place and the power to influence elections. The Parliaments of the 1620s demonstrated that patronage and packing were frail reeds when divorced from any change in policy; in 1640 they failed totally. But after the Restoration, the dialect of recompense and rewards was heard again. In 1666 there were some 140 placemen in the House; by 1677 those corrupted by the court were said to number 215. Danby now began the systematic organization of the Excise pensioners and by allying the court pensioners and placemen with the Church party he came close to winning Charles a majority. But then came the Popish Plot and the Exclusion Crisis, which swept away the Danbean system; many placemen even voted for Danby's impeachment. Corruption only works, observed Sir William Temple, when the court falls into the true interest of the realm.[3]

After the Glorious Revolution, the court fell into the true interest of the realm and relied once again upon placemen. By 1692 there were about one hundred placemen in Parliament. But the Danbean formula no longer worked, for the spirit of party had arisen to wreck it. In 1692 thirty-four Whig placemen deserted the court and voted for the triennial bill. Nor could the power of patronage overcome defeat abroad. In the spring of 1693, the Earl of Sunderland hoped to win support for the government with a marquisate for Mulgrave, a regiment of horse for Brandon, and favors for the Earl of Bath's sons, but the destruction of the Smyrna fleet wiped out his plans. He now advised William to yield to the Whigs. During Queen Anne's reign, the managers had no illusion that they could manage the House of Commons solely through the placemen, there being only some eighty who could be depended upon. Four or five baskets full of preferments, observed Sir Miles Cooke, are not enough to feed five hundred people,[4] and there were usually more members who were angered at being overlooked than pleased by being remembered. The court at best hoped that the placemen might hold the balance between the two parties, as they did in the 1705 Parliament. But the managers discovered in 1708 that they could not prevent the electors of England from returning a sizeable Whig majority, nor did all of Harley's praise of moderation prevent the electors from returning large Tory majorities in 1710 and 1713. Notwithstanding Bacon's hopes, Danby's zeal, Henry Guy's bribes, and Harley's machinations, packing and patronage failed to win for the crown a significant party of its own.

The failure of packing and patronage drove the Stuart monarchs to listen to the promises of parliamentary undertakers, to Neville in 1612, to Bedford in 1641, to Buckingham in 1667, and to Shaftesbury in 1679. But having listened to them, they rejected their proferred undertakings. James scorned Neville's proposal; Charles I refused to give real power to Bedford and his confederates; Charles II toyed with the Anti-Clarendonians in 1667 and mocked the followers of Shaftesbury in 1679. In 1680 he spurned the Southamptons. These monarchs were able to reject and mock and spurn because they had a revenue that allowed them to govern without Parliament (or, as with Charles I in 1641, they were resolved to fall back upon the use of force). In the seventeenth century, the King's financial adversity was the undertaker's opportunity. The failure of projects in 1613, Charles's bankruptcy in 1640, Charles II's need for money to set out a fleet in 1667 and to disband the army in 1679 forced these monarchs to listen to undertakers. But there was another side to the coin: his solvency was their undoing. James I borrowed the money to do without parliaments until 1621; Charles II escaped from the Anti-Clarendonians in 1670 and 1671 by winning a sufficient revenue from the Church party, and he escaped from the Shaftesbury Whigs in 1681 by anticipating a growing revenue, especially an increasing customs. They deceived themselves, he remarked, if they "imagined that want of money would force me to extremities."[5]

After the Glorious Revolution, matters stood very differently. The King could no longer avoid "extremities" by proroguing Parliament. The two Houses deliberately voted him an inadequate revenue so that he must meet them. This decision, taken in 1690, was the most important single development in the history of parliamentary undertaking. Until then the King could reject a proposed undertaking; thereafter he could not. He could no longer "live of his own." The power of the purse fell irremediably into the hands of Parliament. William turned to the Whigs in 1693 and to the Tories in 1700 because only they could win him the supplies he needed from Parliament. Queen Anne yielded to the Whigs in 1708 and embraced the Tories in September 1710 because they alone could ensure that Parliament would vote the money she needed to govern her realm.

The King's financial dependence upon Parliament removed one great obstacle to parliamentary undertakings: the ability of the King to prorogue Parliament and govern without the undertakers. But there was a second great obstacle to parliamentary undertakings: the disrepute into which the undertakers fell when their undertaking became known. "This contracting sticketh in the House," declared a member of the Commons in 1614, and Neville only escaped censure by denying that he had undertaken to manage the House.[6] The Earl of Bedford and his friends fell into disrepute the moment they entered the council and sought to win the King two additional subsidies. In 1668 the Anti-Clarendonians were rendered suspect as undertakers before they had even entered into office. Shaftesbury and Essex quite lost their credit with the Country party upon taking office in April 1679. To prevent their leaders from being corrupted by the court, the Commons in June 1641 gave a first reading to a bill that would debar any member of the House from serving the King unless he first obtained the leave of the House. This was the first of many self-denying ordinances that were to be introduced into the House in the seventeenth century. They reflected how difficult it was for a man to don the livery of the court and still preserve his reputation in Parliament. The problem ran deep, for both Houses prized their independence, feared the influence of the court, hated pensioners, and resented any one man's undertaking to speak for them.

Though the problem ran deep, the politicians of Stuart England stumbled upon a solution: a political party that would remain loyal to an undertaker even though he donned the livery of the court. Neither Neville nor Bedford nor Temple could rely upon such a party, for it was not until the Exclusion Crisis that political parties emerged in English public life. Even then they were still in their infancy, with the result that Holles in 1679 lost all control of the House of Commons. In the autumn of 1680, Shaftesbury had so little control over the two Houses that he refused to enter office, or even to enter into negotiations for entering office, for fear of losing credit in Parliament. The years that followed the Glorious Revolution changed all this. Nothing is more astonishing than the swiftness with which political parties matured in the reigns of William and Anne, a story chronicled by a host of recent historians (Horwitz, Burton, Riley, Rowlands, Speck, Snyder, and Holmes). The success of Carmarthen and Nottingham in 1691 and 1692 arose in part from their having the Tory party behind them, and Somers and Montagu from 1693 onward depended upon the support of the Whigs. By 1696 the Whigs had formed a caucus, some fifty in number, known as "the Club", who concerted measures the night before Parliament met. During Queen Anne's reign, parties became even more vital in the management of Parliament. Not that they were the sole mechanism for managing the Queen's business there, for ministers still had to pursue the traditional arts of management—having bills ready, seeing to the attendance of the Queen's friends, moving supply at the right moment, avoiding divisive issues, preventing quarrels between the two Houses, winning victories abroad, and avoiding defeats at sea.

But increasingly it was party that supported the ministers who undertook to manage the Queen's business in Parliament. By 1708 Godolphin and Marlborough confessed that it had been a mistake to seek to divide the Whigs in the previous session. And Robert Harley discovered by 1711 that he must look to the Tory party for support. A ministry independent of party, Rochester told the Queen, was unworkable.[7]

Rochester might well have added that a government dependent upon party was unworkable unless the unity of the party was preserved. A parliamentary undertaker could not succeed in his undertaking unless he could hold his supporters together. Divisions between ministerial and Country Whigs fatally weakened the government between 1697 and 1700. Divisions between High Church and Moderate Tories brought down the government with which Queen Anne began her reign. Divisions between Treasury, Junto, and Whimsical Whigs weakened the government in 1707 and 1708, but the unity of the Whigs in 1708 and 1709 was the marvel of the political world. It did not last, however. Robert Harley came to power in the spring and summer of 1710 by skillfully exploiting divisions within the ranks of the Whigs. But he, in turn, fell from power in 1714 because of a want of unity within the Tory party, a want of unity that drove Dean Swift to despair. The undertaker who sought to support a scheme of administration on the basis of party must needs look to the unity of that party.

Political parties not only sustained the undertakers, they wrecked all the schemes of the managers to govern by mixed ministries. Charles II in 1679 embarked on the first such scheme, a Privy Council in which court and country politicians sat side by side, but he was merely toying with the opposition. William III believed far more earnestly in balanced counsels; he was an instinctive trimmer. He hoped that men of both parties or none, men of moderation, men who set loyalty to the crown above loyalty to party would serve him in council and high office. He therefore began his reign with a Cabinet Council composed of both Whigs and Tories and sought always to maintain such mixed ministries, but the insatiable demands of each party for office defeated all his purposes. By 1697 his Cabinet was wholly Whig; in 1700 it was largely Tory. Queen Anne was no less determined than William to escape from the tyranny of party by governing through a mixed ministry. Christian principles, she told Lord Somers, did not require that she put herself into the hands of any one party.[8] And she had skillful managers who sought to free her from party—Marlborough and Godolphin from 1702 to 1710 and Robert Harley from 1710 to 1714. Her reign was marked by a continual struggle between the managers, who would govern above party, and the politicians, who would govern through party. In that struggle the politicians ultimately prevailed. The extreme Tories broke the mixed ministry with which the Queen began her reign, and the Junto Whigs transformed the mixed ministry of 1705 into the one-party ministry of 1708. No politician regretted the failure of mixed ministries more than Robert Harley, who in 1705 had declared that parties should come into the Queen, not the Queen into parties.[9] Upon this principle he sought in the summer of 1710 to form a mixed ministry, but the Tories would not serve in the ministry unless he dissolved Parliament and the Whigs would not serve if he did. Harley finally advised the Queen to dissolve Parliament in September, upon which the Whigs resigned. In the ensuing elections, Harley pleaded for moderation, but the electors returned an overwhelming Tory majority. "A coalition-scheme is impracticable," wrote Nottingham in March 1711; and in June the House of Commons condemned those ministers who had "framed to themselves wild and unwarranted schemes of balancing parties."[10]

For wrecking mixed ministries, one of the most effective tools was resignation from office or a refusal to accept office. It was a weapon that worked silently, almost unobserved, and that could not be branded as an invasion of the prerogative. The Shaftesbury Whigs resorted to it in 1680 when they discovered that Charles had named them to the Privy Council only to ignore them. During William's reign Shrewsbury balked at serving William unless he removed certain men and embraced certain measures. Rochester in 1700 would not accept office until half a dozen conditions were met, and Godolphin in 1701 resigned because William turned to a mixed ministry. Resignation and the refusal to serve proved a particularly powerful weapon during the reign of Queen Anne. Rochester and Nottingham left the government in 1703 and 1704 because they were not content to serve with those who had the management of affairs. St. John, Mansell, and Harcourt resigned in 1708 because the Queen dismissed Harley. The Junto in the spring of 1709 threatened to resign unless Lord Orford was brought into the Admiralty. In 1710 even the moderate Lord Cowper declined office because his fellow Whigs were not employed. "To keep in," he said, "when all my friends were out would be infamous."[11] Lord Cowper's refusal was the decisive blow ending all Harley's dreams of a mixed ministry that would free the Queen from the dictates of party.

Harley may have lost the Whigs in September 1710, but he still retained the support of the Queen's servants. He might form a government based on a coalition of the Tories and the Court party, but he soon discovered that the Tories were not willing to allow him to exercise the power of patronage with no regard to their demands for place. Insensibly he had to exercise the power of patronage within limits set by party. One of the most significant developments of these years, one almost universally overlooked by historians, was the capture of patronage by party. In late 1641 John Pym told the Earl of Dover that if he looked for preferment he must comply with Parliament. But any patronage Pym had to bestow was independent of the King. It was not until 1693 that a set of undertakers won office because of their engagement to serve the King, and the Whigs then demonstrated that they sought more than the profits of office. Sir John Somers, named lord keeper, immediately demanded the right to nominate the attorney general. A fierce battle raged over the naming of the Customs and Excise commissioners, with Somers, Trenchard, and Shrewsbury insisting that men should be named who would not only administer those revenues efficiently but would support the King's affairs in Parliament. Except for Molesworth, whom the King could not abide, they won their demands. In 1700 when the Tories gained office, they were equally peremptory in their advice to the King on the bestowal of offices. Godolphin and Rochester advised William to name Trevor to the Common Pleas, Musgrave's son as clerk of the council, and Price as a Welsh judge.

The undertakers not only sought to nominate men to office but also to control the Court party in Parliament. Sir Richard Temple in 1663 made it a condition of his and Bristol's undertaking that the courtiers not obstruct their efforts in Parliament, and in 1670 he blamed Charles for not disciplining the Court party there. Once in office the Country party politician was less interested in destroying the Court party than in capturing it. In the spring of 1701, the Tories vehemently objected that the courtiers in the House of Commons had voted for the acquittal of Lord Somers, and they vowed to vote no supplies until William separated himself wholly from the Whigs. Harley himself chastized the King for not making the placemen stand more firmly behind his new ministers.

During Queen Anne's reign, the struggle for control of patronage raged on. Cowper declared in 1705 that he had accepted the office of lord keeper so that he might promote men to places who were in the true interest of England, and he sought to use the extensive patronage of his office to that end. Not even ecclesiastical appointments escaped the attention of the Whig Junto, as the prolonged quarrel over the appointment of Dawes and Blackall demonstrated. The Whigs finally acquiesced in the appointment of these two Tory clergymen, but only after the Queen had promised not to ignore their advice in the future. When Lord Orford entered the Admiralty in the 1709, he insisted on naming the other members of the commission, though the Queen prevented him from bringing in Jennings, just as William had kept out Molesworth. Harley would have liked to bestow office without regard to party, but he found his freedom of movement limited. In 1711 he was able to resist the demands of the October Club that Nottingham be named president of the council, but he found it politic to name Nottingham's nephew to the Jewell House, his cousin to the Board of Trade, and his son-in-law as paymaster of the marines. For the remainder of the Queen's reign, patronage was used rather to attach the Tory party to the government than to free the Queen from party. Oxford slowly redeemed his profligate promises to bring more Tories into the government. Though Somerset in August 1711 urged the Queen to name Lord Somers as lord privy seal, the Queen did not between September 1710 and her death name one Whig to office.

In April 1708 Robert Harley, still nursing the wounds occasioned by his fall from power in February, confided to a memorandum, "The power of the Crown ought to protect against the violence of men or party, now the power of the Crown is given to a party to destroy others."[12] By 1714 little had changed, except that the Tories were now exercising the power of the crown in an effort to destroy the Whigs. For the party out of power, for the party buffeted by these blows, there remained only one stratagem: seek a dissolution of Parliament and appeal to the electorate. It was the ultimate appeal of the discredited undertaker. The Duke of Buckingham in 1668 found that he and the Anti-Clarendonians had lost all credit in the House. He spent the next two years pressing the King for a dissolution. The Earl of Shaftesbury and his friends in 1675 saw that there was no purpose in their coming into court unless the Cavalier Parliament was dissolved. When Charles, as part of an undertaking reached with Lord Holles, finally dissolved that Parliament in 1679, they threw themselves furiously into the election of a new one. The Tories in 1700 likewise made the dissolution of Parliament a condition for undertaking to manage the King's affairs and likewise threw themselves furiously into the elections of a new one. The very next year, the Whigs, abetted by Daniel Defoe, resorted to the classic move of the politician who had lost control of the House: they engineered petitions for a dissolution. Similar petitions, now from Tory gentlemen, poured in upon the Queen in 1710, as the Whigs, paralyzed by fear of a dissolution, acquiesced in the dismissal of their colleagues from office. During that summer it was the universal judgment of men that Harley could only support his undertaking by advising the Queen to dissolve Parliament. For several months Harley resisted this judgment, but eventually yielded to the logic of the situation. He advised the Queen to dissolve

Parliament and sought to secure the election of a House of Commons that would support the Queen's new ministers.

James I, both in private conversation and public declaration, treated the undertakers with scorn, but a century later his successors could not. They could not because the parliamentary undertaker, bereft of power and credit in 1614, had become an irresistible force by 1714. The first explanation for this change was financial. The power of the purse had fallen into the hands of Parliament; no longer could the King postpone the problem of managing the two Houses by proroguing them. This did not mean, however, that he must hearken to the demands of the undertakers. He might seek to govern instead through a Court party or through a mixed ministry. The possibility of supporting a ministry of his choice through a Court party soon proved illusory: there were not enough places, those given places often proved disloyal, and those overlooked grew disgruntled.

Far more hopeful was government by mixed ministries, by men whose loyalty to the crown was greater than loyalty to party. The reigns of William and Anne were the scene of a continual struggle between the managers, who relied upon patronage and men's loyalty to the crown, and the undertakers, who relied upon party and their credit in Parliament. In the end, in 1697, in 1708, in 1711, the undertakers won out, for the spirit of party swept everything before it. It was the spirit of party that allowed the undertakers to retain their credit when they donned the livery of the court. It was the spirit of party that drove them to resort to the politics of opposition if denied office. It was the spirit of party that led them to threaten to resign if a monopoly of office were not given to their party. It was the spirit of party that gave them the majorities they needed in Parliament.

The power of the purse, gained at the Glorious Revolution, gave the undertakers the means to force their schemes of administration upon the monarch. The power of party, born of the Exclusion Crisis, gave them the means to make good their undertakings. Together the power of the purse and the power of party proved irresistible.

Epilogue

Though I have chosen to end this study with the accession of the House of Hanover, this does not mean that I believe that the year 1714 marks a sharp break in the history of schemes and undertakings. Quite the reverse, I believe that the circumstances that gave rise to such schemes and undertakings continued after 1714. In his book *The Growth of Political Parties, 1689–1742*, B. W. Hill has shown that party distinctions and jealousies contined until at least 1742, that schemes for a broadbottom ministry invariably failed because politicians refused to enter office except as a party, and that monarchs gave up favorites and employed those whom they detested in order to secure a fuller Civil List and the harmonious management of their affairs in Parliament. He has likewise shown that ministers, preeminently Robert Walpole, were able to secure a fuller Civil List and to manage Parliament harmoniously because they had the support of majorities there, particularly in the House of Commons, and that they secured these majorities by careful attention to the details of management, by the use of patronage, and by an appeal to party loyalty. Patronage, which quickly fell into the hands of the ministers, was never of itself enough to control the House of Commons; the ministers ultimately needed the support of a party there. As B. W. Hill concludes, "Walpole's control of Parliament arose out of his determination to keep his administration exclusively Whig. The price that both George I, in his last years, and George II paid for smooth-running affairs and an adequate Civil List was party control."[1]

After 1742 the spirit of party waned, but the role of the parlimentary undertaker did not. The Pelhamites, through a policy of reconciliation with their former opponents, built up a coalition in Parliament that allowed the politicians to force George II to dismiss his favorite, Carteret, in 1744, to take back the Pelhamites on their own terms in 1746, and to accept an unpalatable Pitt-Newcastle government in 1757. Because he could find no courtier who could manage Parlia-

Epilogue

ment for him, George II was forced to acquiesce in governments that were patently not those he would have chosen himself. The King, writes John Owen, retained "the right to appoint and dismiss ministers—though it rapidly became obvious that those ministers must be able to command the confidence of Parliament, and especially of the House of Commons, if the King's business was effectively to be carried on."[2]

The brief ministry of Lord Bute taught George III what the failure of Carteret had taught George II, that he must appoint ministers who could undertake to manage Parliament successfully for him.[3] As long as the King chose a parliamentary undertaker, he might name whom he wished as his chief minister. During the 1760s George III searched in vain for such a minister, but in 1770 he had the good fortune to find in Lord North a courtier who was also a politician, and in the policy of coercion in North America a cause that was popular in Parliament. Lord North's long tenure as the King's first minister rested on his ability to manage Parliament for the King, an ability that arose partly from the disarray of parties, partly from the use of patronage, and partly from the pursuit of policies popular in Parliament and the country. When these policies led to defeat in North America, Parliament overthrew Lord North.[4]

The King now turned to an equally astute parliamentary undertaker, William Pitt the younger, who in 1784 undertook to manage Parliament for the King. With the help of John Robinson's electoral management and a swing in public opinion in favor of the Tories, Pitt won a majority in Parliament, a majority that allowed him to make good his undertaking. In the ensuing twenty years, the King's failing health, the progress of "economical reform," and the reemergence of political parties greatly reduced the King's role in politics and enhanced that of the party leaders who could undertake to manage Parliament.[5]

During Queen Victoria's reign, a succession of politicians—Melbourne, Peel, Palmerston, Gladstone, Disraeli, and Salisbury—attained the highest office in the land because they could manage the Queen's affairs in Parliament successfully. They did not become prime minister because the British people elected them to that office or because the two Houses of Parliament elected them or even because the House of Commons elected them. The British people continued to reject all such schemes for the formal nomination of the monarch's first minister. The mechanism that finally brought responsible government to Britain was neither a popular nor a parliamentary election; it was a parliamentary undertaking. Margaret Thatcher is prime minister of Great Britain today because she, and only she, can undertake to manage the Queen's affairs in Parliament successfully. A parliamentary undertaking is an informal arrangement, a practical and very English arrangement, an arrangement whose roots lie far back in the political struggles of the seventeenth century. Sir Henry Neville, a pragmatical fellow, built better than he could ever have dreamed.

Notes

Abbreviations

Add. MSS	Additional Manuscripts
B.L.	British Library
B.R.O.	Berkshire Record Office
B.I.H.R.	Bulletin of the Institute of Historical Research
C.J.	Journal of the House of Commons
C.S.P., Dom.	Calendar of the State Papers, Domestic Series
C.S.P., Ven.	Calendar of State Papers and Manuscripts, Relating to English Affairs, Existing in the Archives and Collections of Venice
C.U.L.	Cambridge University Library
E.H.R.	English Historical Review
French Trans.	French Transcripts
H.L.Q.	Huntington Library Quarterly
H.M.C.	Historical Manuscript Commission
L.R.O.	Leicestershire Record Office
N.R.O.	Northamptonshire Record Office
P.R.O.	Public Record Office
S.P.D.	State Papers Domestic
S.R.O.	Scottish Record Office

Location of Manuscripts

Auchmar MSS	Scottish Record Office, Edinburgh
Ballard MSS	Bodleian Library, Oxford
Bishop Nicholson's Diary	Tullie House, Carlisle
Blenheim MSS	Blenheim Palace, Oxfordshire
Brydges Papers	Huntington Library, San Marino
Carte MSS	Bodleian Library, Oxford
Chatsworth MSS	Chatsworth House, Derbyshire
Clarendon State Papers	Bodleian Library, Oxford
Cottonian MSS	British Library, London
Coventry Papers	Longleat, Wiltshire
Dalhousie MSS	Scottish Record Office, Edinburgh
Egerton MSS	British Library, London
Finch MSS	Leicestershire Record Office
Finch-Halifax Papers	Chatsworth, Derbyshire
Finch-Hatton MSS	Northamptonshire Record Office
Forster MSS	Victoria and Albert Museum, London
Halifax Papers	Althorp, Northamptonshire
Hardwicke MSS	New York Public Library
Harleian MSS	British Library, London
Holles MSS	University of Nottingham Library, Nottingham
Isham MSS	Northampton Record Office
Lansdowne MSS	British Library, London
Levens MSS	Levens Hall, Westmorland

Notes

Lonsdale MSS	Cumberland and Westmorland Record Office
Newdigate News Letters	Folger Library, Washington, D.C.
Panshanger MSS	Hertforshire Record Office
Portland Papers	University of Nottingham Library, Nottingham
Roger Morrice's Entring Book	Dr. Williams Library, London
Sloane MSS	British Library, London
Spencer House Letter Book	Althorp, Northamptonshire
Stanhope MSS	Kent Record Office
Stowe MSS	British Library, London
Stowe MSS, H.L.	Huntington Library, San Marino
Trumbull MSS	Berkshire Record Office

PREFACE

1. Edmund Gosse, *The Life and Letters of John Donne*, 2:34.

2. James Spedding, *The Life and Letters of Francis Bacon*, 5:43.

3. B.L. Loan 29/237, fol. 193. This was the last known use in England; in Ireland it continued to be used into the mid-eighteenth century (see F. G. James, *Ireland in the Empire, 1688–1770*, pp. 132–33, 253–54, 268–71).

4. H.M.C., *Portland*, 3:451.

5. Jonathan Swift, *The Correspondence of Jonathan Swift*, ed. F. Erlington Ball, 2:190.

6. W. D. Christie, *The Life of Anthony Ashley Cooper, the First Earl of Shaftesbury*, 2:200–202.

CHAPTER ONE

1. More to Winwood, 29 October 1611, H.M.C., *Buccleuch MSS*, 1:101–2.

2. Elizabeth Read Foster, ed., *Proceedings in Parliament, 1610* (New Haven, Conn., 1966), 2:398.

3. Ibid., p. 344.

4. David Harris Willson, *The Privy Councillors in the House of Commons*, p. 126.

5. Ibid., pp. 128–29.

6. This sketch of Tudor methods of managing Parliaments is drawn from Sir John Neale's *Elizabeth I and Her Parliaments* (London, 1953, 1957).

7. H.M.C., *Buccleuch*, 1:102.

8. Willson, *Privy Councillors*, pp. 3–4, 13–16, 18–21. Of late it has become fashionable to deny that "parties" or "an opposition" existed in the 1610s and 1620s. It is undeniable that there existed no formally organized "party," no formally organized "opposition," but there did exist informally organized groupings and an informally organized opposition. Lord Ellesmere, shortly after 1610, described the secret conferences of the popular party and the great sway it exercised in the House of Commons. Sir Francis Bacon likewise declared that the opposition in 1610 arose partly "out of party" and complained that members "combined and made parties in Parliament." He also described the various elements "which made the popular party last Parliament." For Ellesmere's and Bacon's remarks, see ibid., pp. 120–21.

9. C.S.P., *Ven.*, 12:100.

10. Frederick Dietz, *English Public Finance, 1558–1614*, p. 121; S. R. Gardiner, *History of England from the Accession of James I to the Outbreak of the Civil War 1603–1642*, 2:13, 83; Robert Ashton, "Deficit Finance in the Reign of James I," p. 21; W. R. Scott, *The Constitution and Finance of English, Scottish, and Irish Joint-Stock Companies to 1720*, 3:517.

11. Thomas Birch, *Court and Times of James I*, 1:122.

12. S. R. Gardiner, ed., *Parliamentary Debates, 1610*, pp. 163–68.

Notes

13. Dietz, *English Public Finance*, pp. 142–43; Gardiner, *History*, 2:228; Chamberlain to Carleton, in Birch, *James I*, 1:291; Northampton to Rochester, B.L. Cottonian MSS, Titus F IV, fol. 332.

14. Spedding, *Life and Letters of Bacon*, 4:279–80, 365–68. There is no evidence that Bacon showed these memorials to James, but they clearly reveal the cast of mind that governed his advice to the King.

15. Ibid., pp. 370, 381. Bacon wrote in his essay "Of Negotiating," "If you would work any man, you must either know his nature and fashions, and so lead him; or his ends, and so persuade him; or his weakness and disadvantages, and so awe him; or those that have interest in him, and so govern him" (James Spedding, ed., *The Works of Francis Bacon*, 6:493–44).

16. Neale, *Elizabeth and Her Parliaments*, 2:243, 370–71; Willson, *Privy Councillors*, pp. 104–5, 117, 119–20; Le Fevre de Boderie, *Ambassades de Monsieur de la Boderie en Angleterre*, 2:199–200; David Willson, ed., *Parliamentary Diary of Robert Bowyer* (Minneapolis, 1939), pp. 366–67; *C.S.P., Ven.*, 12:110.

17. Spedding, *Life and Letters of Bacon*, 4:371; John Chamberlain, *The Letters of John Chamberlain*, ed. Norman McClure, 1:384.

18. Chamberlain, *Letters*, 1:338, 351–52, 355, 358–59; H.M.C., *Downshire*, 3:269, 308; H.M.C., *Portland*, 9:106, 157–58.

19. C.J., 1:485.

20. P.R.O., S.P.D., 14/74, No. 44. The advice is printed in S.R. Gardiner, *History of England*, 2:389–94. It is likely that the substance of Neville's advice was known in London in mid-June, for John Chamberlain wrote (*Letters*, 1:362): "A parliament is certainly expected after Michaelmas, and it is said the King will write to the shires and borough towns to choose the same men that were before as best acquainted with the business that is to be handled." It is incredible that James would want the same men chosen who served in 1610 unless he (or his favorites) were listening to Neville. Furthermore, Michaelmas was the date Neville proposed for the meeting of Parliament.

21. P.R.O., S.P.D., 14/74, nos. 451 and 46; other copies may be found in Harleian MSS. 4289, fols. 231v–233; Harleian MSS. 3787, fols. 185–86v; Lansdowne MSS. 486, fols. 17–20; Cottonian MSS. Titus F IV, fols. 13–14; Carte MSS. 125, fols. 131–33. The memorial is entitled "A Collection of such things as have been by several men desired to be obtained of his Majesty for the good of his people."

22. Neville proposed one other concession: a law stating more clearly what was treason and what was not. He had first offered a bill to this purpose in March 1604 (C.J., 1:153).

23. Foster, *Proceedings in Parliament*, 2:330–31.

24. Ibid., 1:119, 2:272, 279, 331 n; Gardiner, *Parliamentary Debates, 1610*, pp. 122–23.

25. Birch, *James I*, pp. 189, 191; H.M.C., *Buccleuch*, 1:111–14. David Willson (*Privy Councillors*, pp. 30, 32) dates the letter and memorial to Rochester "1614," but this could not be, for Rochester had become the Earl of Somerset by 1614 and the letter is addressed to Viscount Rochester. Internal evidence suggests the autumn of 1612 as the probable date. See Cottonian MSS, Titus F IV, for the letter to Rochester (fol. 349), the memorial on impositions (fol. 350), the administrative reforms (fol. 344), and the new concessions (fol. 346).

26. H.M.C., *Buccleuch*, 1:113.

Notes

27. Ibid., p. 112.

28. Ibid., p. 113. The three were probably Rochester, Overbury, and Neville.

29. Chamberlain, *Letters*, 1:387.

30. Berkeley to Phelips, 19 November 1612, Somerset Record Office, DD/PH 219/59.

31. Birch, *James I*, 1:122–23; J. E. Neale, "Commons Privilege of Free Speech in Parliament," in R. W. Seton-Watson, ed., *Tudor Studies Presented . . . to Albert Frederick Pollard*, pp. 384–85.

32. Sir Ralph Winwood, *Memorials of Affairs of State in the Reigns of Q. Elizabeth and K. James I*, 3:235–36; Foster, *Proceedings in Parliament*, 2:337–38; H.M.C., *Hastings*, 4:226–27.

33. Lake to Salisbury, 3 December 1610, B.L. Add. MSS. 4160, fol. 266v.

34. Owen Duncan, "Sir Henry Neville: Elizabethan Statesman and Jacobean Politician," pp. 1, 4, 6–8, 15–18, 50–51, 62–65, 68–69, 75–77. For the assessment see Lansdowne MSS.32, fol. 57.

35. Neville's dispatches to Robert Cecil, upon which this paragraph is based, are printed in Winwood, *Memorials of Affairs of State*, 3:16–185; see especially pp. 30–31, 61–63, 81, 94, 141, 179.

36. Ibid., p. 108; see also pp. 71, 154.

37. Duncan, "Sir Henry Neville," pp. 72–73.

38. P.R.O., S.P.D., 14/31/55.

39. Chamberlain, *Letters*, 1:445.

40. Arthur Slavin, *Politics and Profit: A Study of Sir Ralph Sadler, 1507–1547*, pp. 38–39.

41. Spedding, *Life and Letters of Bacon*, 2:342–52, 362.

42. Ibid., pp. 284, 348–50.

43. John Bruce, ed., *Diary of John Manningham, p. 135.*

44. C.S.P., *Ven.*, 1603–1607, p. 26.

45. Duncan, "Sir Henry Neville", p. 182.

46. Winwood, *Memorials of Affairs of State*, 2:217.

47. Ibid., p. 216.

48. Wilson, *Parliamentary Diary of Robert Bowyer*, p. 226.

49. Spedding, *Life and Letters of Bacon*, 4:74, 75n.

50. Winwood, *Memorials of Affairs of State*, 3:7; Cottonian MSS. Titus F IV, fol. 340v.

51. Sir Edward Peyton, in his "A Discourse of Court and Courtiers" (Harleian MSS. 3364, fol. 63v), calls Neville "our English Tacitus."

52. C.S.P., *Dom.*, 1611–18, p. 153; Chamberlain, *Letters*, 1:397; H.M.C., *Buccleuch*, 1:131; H.M.C., *Downshire*, 4:229.

53. Neville was executor of Sir John Norris's estate. Upon Norris's death his daughter, Lady Fenton, seized the estate and sought to carry it with a strong hand. Though Neville took the way of law and justice, Viscount Fenton complained of him to the King (Chamberlain, *Letters*, 1:403, 409). In May, Sir James Whitelocke drew up a legal brief showing the King's commission for inquiring into abuses in the Admiralty to be irregular. Northampton believed that Neville pro-

moted this opposition, but he could not prove it. Neville was not the author of Whitelocke's opposition, but he was an actor in it with greater men, so Whitelocke later wrote, though he concealed the fact from Northampton at the time (Sir James Whitelocke, *Liber Famelicus*, pp. 46, 113–18).

54. Neville to Winwood, H.M.C., *Buccleuch*, 1:131; P. R. V. Seddon, in his "Somerset," p. 58, dates this letter December 1612, not April 1613, as in *Buccleuch*.

55. H.M.C., *Mar and Kellie*, p. 151.

56. Chamberlain, *Letters*, 1:480; H.M.C., *Downshire*, 4:229.

57. John Nichols, *The Progresses, Processions, and Magnificent Festivities of King James I* (London, 1828), 2:757.

58. B.L. Add. MSS. 32, 023 B, fol. 215v.

59. Chamberlain, *Letters*, 1:515; Thomas Moir, *The Addled Parliament of 1614* (Oxford, 1958), pp. 31–51; Menna Prestwich, *Cranfield* (Oxford, 1966), pp. 149–50.

60. Cottonian MSS. Titus F IV, fols. 329v–330; P.R.O., S.P.D., 14/76 No. 23; Moir, *Addled Parliament*, pp. 200–201.

61. Gosse, *Life and Letters of Donne*, 2:34.

62. H.M.C., *Portland*, 11:30.

63. Cottonian MSS. Titus F. IV, fol. 351.

64. H.M.C., *Portland*, 11:30–31.

65. Cottonian MSS. Titus F IV, fol. 351.

66. M.H.C., *Downshire*, 4:340.

67. Cottonian MSS. Titus F IV, fol. 351. For Northampton's emphatic repudiation of the undertakers, see Linda Peck, *Northampton: Patronage and Policy at the Court of James I*, p. 207.

68. William Cobbett, ed., *The Parliamentary History of England from the Earliest Period to the Year 1803*, 1:1157.

69. C.J., 1:457, 464; Yale Center Transcript of MS. E237 (in the Kenneth Spencer Research Library), 9, 10, 11 May 1614; Moir, *Addled Parliament*, p. 45.

70. C.J., 1:462–63, 471; Chamberlain, *Letters*, 1:526.

71. C.J., 1:470–71; Yale Center transcript of MS. E237 (in the Kenneth Spencer Research Library), 2 May 1614. For arguments that Hoskyns was not a dupe of the Earl of Northampton, see Peck, *Northampton*, pp. 209–10.

72. Wallace Notestein, Frances Relf, and Hartley Simpson, eds., *Commons Debates 1621*, 7:634.

73. H.M.C., *Portland*, 9:27.

74. C.J., 1:485.

75. J. P. Cooper, ed., *Wentworth Papers, 1597–1628*, p. 76. There is no evidence that Wentworth actually delivered this speech.

76. Spedding, *Life and Letters of Bacon*, 5:43–44, 46.

77. Ibid., pp. 45–46.

78. C.J., 1:485; Notestein et al., *Commons Debates 1621*, 8:640; H.M.C., *Portland*, 9:132–33; Yale Center transcript of MS. E237 (in the Kenneth Spencer Research Library), 14 May 1614.

Notes

79. Birch, *James I*, 1:315.

80. Buisseaux to Puysieux, 21 May/1 June, 28 May/8 June, 12/22 June 1614, P.R.O., French trans.; Winwood to Carleton, *C.S.P., Dom.*, 1611–18, p. 237.

81. H.M.C., *10th Report*, pt. 6 (Bouverie), p. 84; Chamberlain, *Letters*, 1:607–8.

82. W. Gifford and F. Cunningham, eds., *The Works of Ben Jonson* (London, 1811), 3:250–51.

CHAPTER TWO

1. J. H. Wiffen, *Historical Memoirs of the House of Russell*, 2:125–26, 137, 141–51, 159, 192.

2. Spedding, *Life and Letters of Bacon*, 5:176–91.

3. [Edward Nicholas], *Proceedings and Debates in the House of Commons*, 1:11; Notestein et al., *Commons Debates 1621*, 2:12.

4. Sir John Eliot, *Negotium Posterorum*, 1:132–33.

5. P.R.O., S.P.D. 16/19/107, fol. 7.

6. Spedding, *Life and Letters of Bacon*, 7:115–16, 123–28, 145–49, 151–52.

7. John Hacket, *Scrinia Reserata: A Memorial Offered to the great deservings of John Williams, D.D.*, pt. 1, p. 50. Buckingham may have decided to swim with the tide even before receiving William's letter; indeed, he may never have received the letter. See Roger Lockyer, *Buckingham: The Life and Political Career of George Villiers, First Duke of Buckingham, 1592–1628*, p. 95.

8. Robert Ruigh, *The Parliament of 1624*, pp. 35–37; *C.S.P., Ven.*, 1623–1625, pp. 201, 216–17; Lockyer, *Buckingham*, p. 175. For a detailed account of Pembroke's electoral influence, see John K. Gruenfelder, *Influence in Early Stuart Elections, 1604–1640*, pp. 123–30.

9. Buckingham to James, Harleian MSS. 6987, fols. 200–202v. See also Christopher Thompson, "Origins of the Politics of the Parliamentary Middle-Group," *Transactions of the Royal Historical Society*, 5th ser., 22:73. Roger Lockyer (*Buckingham*, p. 184) concludes that Buckingham "now used the methods of the 'opposition' of 1621 for his own purposes."

10. Conrad Russell, *Parliaments and English Politics, 1621–1629*, pp. 149–51. The dialogue is in the Somerset Record Office, Phelips MSS.227/16.

11. Conrad Russell has, of course, asserted the opposite in his *Parliaments and English Politics*, but I do not find his arguments and evidence convincing. His cardinal error was to make the 1624 parliament a paradigm for all the parliaments of the 1620s. Consensus, not conflict, did mark the 1624 parliament, but the 1624 parliament was unique—and it was unique because only in 1624 was there an undertaking between the court and leading members of the popular party in the House of Commons. The other parliaments of the 1620s were, in my judgment, characterized by conflict, not consensus.

12. Chamberlain, *Letters*, 2:550; Hackett, *Scrinia Reserata*, 2:190; Russell, *Parliaments and English Politics*, pp. 154, 161–62, 173, 180, 189, 199–202.

13. Hacket, *Scrinia Reserata*, 2:14.

14. Ibid., pp. 17–18; S. R. Gardiner, ed., *Debates in the House of Commons in 1625*, xvii–xix, 90–91; *C.J.*, 1:811.

Notes

15. Joseph Meade to Martin Stuteville, Harleian MSS. 390, fols. 102, 108.

16. C.S.P., Ven., 19:416.

17. Willson, Privy Councillors, pp. 190–95.

18. Robert Ashton, "Deficit Finance in the Reign of James I," pp. 28–29; Robert Ashton, The Crown and the Money Market (Oxford, 1960), pp. 42–43, 174–75, 191. Conrad Russell, in The Origins of the English Civil War, p. 108, argues that Charles did successfully raise his revenue to about £1,000,000 a year, but Russell fails to observe that part of this revenue came from anticipations and the sale of royal lands.

19. The "Annals" of Bulstrode Whitelocke, B.L. Add. MSS. 37,343, fol. 206; Mary Frear Keeler, The Long Parliament, p. 21; R. N. Kershaw, "Elections for the Long Parliament," pp. 498–501; C.S.P., Ven., 1640–1642, p. 91. In his The Representative of the People: Voters and Voting under the Early Stuarts, Derek Hirst estimates that between 27% and 40% of the adult male population voted in these elections (pp. 104–5).

20. H.M.C., De L'Isle, 6:346. The fact that Lady Carlisle in Paris had already heard of Bedford's scheme dates its inception from early November.

21. Arthur Collins, Letters and Memorials of State (London, 1746), 2:666.

22. H.M.C., De L'Isle, 6:367–68. Other reports of the impending change were by W. Hawkins (ibid., p. 366), Montreuil (P.R.O. 31/3/72, 21/31 January 1641), and Salvetti Add. MSS.27,962 I, fol. 177v.

23. H.M.C., De L'Isle, 6:367, 369. The presumption must be great that Hamilton acted as the principal broker at court for Bedford and his confederates, for in the spring of 1641 there was talk that the Marquis of Hamilton would marry Bedford's daughter: as A[rchibald] Campbell wrote on 9 March to the Laird of Glenorchy (S.R.O., GD 112/40/2), "The Marquess of Hamilton I hear is to be married to the earl of Bedford his daughter."

24. Robert Baillie, The Letters and Journals of Robert Baillie, 1:292–93.

25. Edward Hyde, Earl of Clarendon, The History of the Great Rebellion and Civil Wars in England begun in the Year 1641, 1:280. Count Rossetti observed (P.R.O., 31/9, No. 19, fols. 391–92) that Jermyn counseled the Queen and Hamilton the King.

26. H.M.C., Cowper, 2:272. It is likely that this Mr. Stockdale was the same Stockdale, a messenger in the chamber, whom Windebanke harassed and whose petition against Windebanke delighted the Commons (Clarendon, History, 1:233n).

27. H.M.C., De L'Isle, 6:374.

28. Baillie, Letters and Journals, 1:305.

29. P.R.O., 31/3/72, dispatch for 18/28 February 1641.

30. C.S.P., Ven., 1640–1642, p. 126; the ambassador added "At present nothing is left to him [Charles] but the title and the naked show of king, and he does not know how to conceal the passions which naturally torture him" (p. 127).

31. P.R.O., 31/9, no. 20, fol. 7.

32. Peter Heylyn, Cyprianus Anglicus; or, the History of the Life and Death of the most Reverend and Renowned Prelate William by Providence Lord Bishop of Canterbury, p. 448; Clarendon, History, 1:258, 280–82; Bulstrode Whitelocke's Annals, B.L. Add. MSS. 37,343, fols. 219v–20; Edward Nicholas's Memorial for M. Sab-

Notes

ran, P.R.O., French Trans., 4/14 July 1644; Apology of George Lord Digby, P.R.O., S.P.D. 16/514/132.

33. *C.S.P., Dom.*, *1640–1641*, pp. 565–67.

34. Stowe MSS. 326, fols. 72v–73v, 92–95.

35. Russell, *Origins of the English Civil War*, pp. 111–14. Bedford himself (Bedford Office, London, Fourth Earl's Papers, nos. 6 and 7) calculated that the king could gain £420,000 from the sale of a third part of the rents of the lands of deans and chapters and £239,333 6s 8d from the sale of wardships. According to J. H. Wiffen (*Historical Memoirs of the House of Russell*, 2:186), Bedford left in one of his many books of miscellanies "an estimate of what might be yearly made unto his Majesty of the existing duties [probably customs], if they were settled by act of parliament." The result of his calculations, writes Wiffen, "was, that by the abolition of patents and monopolies alone, there would be an annual increase in revenue of £52,995; leaving an advantage of £36,400 above that which the late King enjoyed."

36. Clarendon writes that they undertook to secure the King tunnage and poundage for life (*History*, 1:281); but Sir John Harrison, who worked closely with Bedford, asked the Commons on 7 May to vote it for only three years (D'Ewes, Harleian MSS.163, fol. 145). Edward Montagu likewise wrote that the Commons intended to vote tunnage and poundage for three years (H.M.C., *Montagu of Beaulieu*, p. 130). For a full account of the House's inquiries into the King's revenues and expenses, see A. H. A. Hamilton, ed., *The Note Book of Sir John Northcote*, pp. 12, 59–60, 113–15.

37. Russell, *Origins of the English Civil War*, p. 96; Diane Willen, *John Russell, First Earl of Bedford*, pp. 101–10.

38. Gardiner, *History*, 7:139–40.

39. H. C. Darby, *The Draining of the Fens*, pp. 40–41, 57–60, 67. The Earl and Vermuyden had made the Bedford Level "summer land" but not yet "winter land"; hence both commissions could claim to be right (L. E. Harris, *Vermuyden and the Fens*, pp. 67–69).

40. Henry Wheatley, *London Past and Present*, 1:460–61; Gladys Thomson, *Life in a Noble Household*, pp. 38, 46.

41. Gardiner, *History*, 9:178–79, 198.

42. A. P. Newton, *The Colonizing Activities of the English Puritans*, pp. 68, 72, 76.

43. Clarendon, *History*, 1:247.

44. Edward Hyde, Earl of Clarendon, *State Papers Collected by Edward, Earl of Clarendon*, 2:110–12.

45. Thomson, *A Noble Household*, p. 36; Perez Zagorin, *The Court and the Country*, p. 76.

46. Clarendon, *History*, 1:241, 308–9.

47. Clarendon, *State Papers*, 2:112.

48. Daniel O'Neil to "Deer Will," S.R.O., D (W) 1778/I/i/14; Salvetti, B.L. Add. MSS.27,962 I, fols. 194–95; H.M.C., *De L'Isle*, 6:389; P.R.O., French Trans., 27 February/7 March 1641.

49. P.R.O., 31/9, no. 20, fols. 85, 136.

50. Sir John Harrison's discourse, Stowe MSS.326, fols. 73–73v.

Notes

51. H.M.C., *Cowper*, 2:279.

52. *C.S.P., Dom.*, *1640–1641*, p. 560; Mme Motteville, *Memoir on the Life of Henrietta Maria*, p. 21.

53. Baillie, *Letters and Journals*, 1:304.

54. "His Majesties Declaration . . . of 12 August 1642," in *The Works of King Charles the Martyr*, 2d ed. (London, 1687), p. 298; both Count Rossetti, the papal envoy (P.R.O., 31/9/20, fol. 31), and Montreuil, the French envoy (P.R.O., French Trans., 27 February/7 March 1641), reported that Charles named the councillors in order to save Strafford's life.

55. B.L. Add. MSS. 37,343, fol. 219v; Peter Heylyn, *Obersvations on the Historie of the Reign of King Charles: Published by H.L. Esq.* (London, 1656), p. 227; Clarendon, *History*, 1:334. Clarendon observed that there were few "who thought their preferments would do them much good if the Earl were suffered to live" (p. 282).

56. H.M.C., *Cowper*, 2:274.

57. O'Neil to "Deer Will," 23 February 1641, S.R.O., D (W) 1778/I/i/14.

58. David Dalrymple, ed., *Memorials and Letters Relating to the History of Britain in the Reign of Charles I*, p. 115.

59. Baillie, *Letters and Journals*, 1:310–11.

60. Clarendon, *History*, 1:282.

61. Heylyn, *Observations*, p. 227.

62. Baillie, *Letters and Journals*, 1:305.

63. Clarendon, *History*, 1:431.

64. The phrase is Clarendon's, ibid.

65. D'Ewes describes the scene on 29 May: "After the King had done speaking, during which time he looked twice or thrice upon his paper, he stayed a pretty while looking about, but there was not one man that gave any hum or the least colour of plaudit to his speech, which made him after some time of expectation to depart suddenly. Many were much grieved at this speech, because they saw no hope of dissolving the said Irish papist army" (Harleian MSS. 163, fol. 113).

66. The refusal to disband the army was only the breaking point in Pym's growing distrust of the King, not the sole cause of it. Charles's ecclesiastical policy during the previous sixteen years had also contributed to that distrust, as Anthony Fletcher (*The Outbreak of the English Civil War*, pp. xxix–xxx, 4–6, 27, 33, 59–62, 86, 102, 137–38) and Caroline Hibbard (*Charles I and the Popish Plot*, pp. 169–70, 188–203, 232–38) have shown.

67. Gardiner, *History of England*, 9:318, 343–45, 348–49, 357–58, 360–61, 364; H.M.C., *Cowper*, 2:281.

68. It was Bedford who asked Hyde to plead with Essex for Strafford's life and provoked the memorable answer, "Stone-dead hath no fellow" (Clarendon, *History*, 1:318–20).

69. D'Ewes, Harleian MSS. 163, fol. 105; H.M.C., *De Lisle*, 6:400, 402; *C.S.P., Dom.*, *1640–1641*, p. 569; P.R.O., French Trans., 27 February/8 March, 4/14 March, 8/18 April, 29 April/9 May, 6/16 May 1641.

70. P.R.O., French Trans., 23 April/3 May 1641.

71. Sir Philip Warwick, *Memoires of the Reigne of King Charles I*, pp. 163–64.

Notes

72. D'Ewes, Harleian MSS. 163, fols. 47–48.

73. Clarendon, *History*, 1:281.

74. P.R.O., French Trans., 25 March/4 April 1641; Clarendon, *History*, 1:346–48; H.M.C., *Cowper*, 2:286.

75. Baillie, *Letters and Journals*, 1:305.

76. O'Neil to "Deer Will," 23 February 1641, S.R.O. D (W) 1778/I/i/14.

77. Salvetti, 26 February 1641, B.L. Add. MSS. 27,962 I, fols. 194–95.

78. D'Ewes, Harleian MSS. 163, fols. 243v, 256.

79. Clarendon, *History*, 1:335.

80. Harrison's discourse, Stowe MSS. 326, fol. 73v.

81. Clarendon, *History*, 1:335. The term *undertaking* was used by contemporaries, but the only instance of the use of the term *undertakers* occurs in a pamphlet written by Edward Simmons, a devoted servant of Charles I, in 1645. Simmons calls those who led in Parliament in February 1641 "the undertakers." See Simmons, *A Vindication of King Charles*, p. 61. Though published in 1648, the pamphlet was written in 1645.

82. Clarendon, *History*, 1:334–35.

83. Gardiner, *History*, 9:374; Clarendon, *History*, 1:345.

84. Clarendon, *History*, p. 411.

85. Sloane MSS. 1467, fols. 87, 103v.

86. Clarendon, *History*, 1:345; the Elector Palatine to his mother, 7/17 August 1641, Forster MSS. 48.G.25, fol. 3.

87. H.M.C., *De L'Isle*, 6:405–6; C.S.P., *Dom.*, *1641–1643*, pp. 62, 63.

88. Hacket, *Scrinia Reserata*, 2:163.

89. H.M.C., *De Lisle*, 6:406, 409.

90. H.M.C., *Various Collections*, 8:54.

91. H.M.C., *De L'Isle*, 6:410; Salvetti, B.L. Add. MSS 27,961 I, fols. 280–281v.

92. For an excellent account of Pym's strategy in these months, see Fletcher, *The Outbreak of the English Civil War*, pp. 43–89.

93. H.M.C., *Montagu of Beaulieu*, p. 135.

94. H.M.C., *Buccleuch*, 1:288.

95. C.J., 2:349; John Nalson, *An Impartial Collection of Great Affairs of State*, 2:788.

96. Groen van Prinsterer, ed., *Archives ou Correspondance Inédits de la Maison D'Orange-Nassau* (Utrecht, 1859), 2d ser., 4:10–12.

97. Charles I, *Works*, pp. 296, 298.

98. B. H. G. Wormald, *Clarendon: Politics, History, and Religion 1640–1660* (Cambridge, 1951), pp. 124–25; Walter Yonge's Journal, B.L. Add. MSS. 18,777, fol. 156.

99. H. Wheatley, ed., *Diary of John Evelyn* (London, 1879), 4:152.

100. H.M.C., *Portland*, 1:593.

101. S. A. Strong, ed., *A Catalogue of Letters and Other Historical Documents Exhibited in the Library at Welbeck*, pp. 217–18; Sir Edward Walker, *Historical*

Notes

Discourses, p. 328; Sir Walter Scott, ed., *Secret History of the Court of James I*, 1:95–96; "A Confutation of Two Paradoxes, or Rather Two Vulgar Errors", in Harleian MSS. 6810, fols. 170–73.

102. Strong, *A Catalogue of Letters*, p. 217.

CHAPTER THREE

1. Edwin Gay has surveyed in magisterial fashion the fortunes and the debts of the Temple family: see "The Rise of an English Country Family: Peter and John Temple, to 1603"; "The Temples of Stowe and Their Debts: Sir Thomas Temple and Sir Peter Temple, 1603–1653"; and "Sir Richard Temple: The Debt Settlement and Estate Litigation, 1653–1675."

2. Stowe MSS, H.L., Morrice to Temple, 20 August 1660.

3. Godfrey Davies, "The Political Career of·Sir Richard Temple (1634–1697) and Buckingham Politics," pp. 48–50.

4. H.M.C., *Leybourne-Popham MSS*, p. 208.

5. Davies, "The Political Career of Sir Richard Temple," p. 83.

6. G. F. Trevallyn Jones, "The Composition and Leadership of the Presbyterian Party in the Convention," pp. 324, 332, 349, 353. Davies doubts that Temple sat in the Convention Parliament ("The Political Career of Sir Richard Temple," p. 85); but the Commons Journal shows him acting as messenger and teller for the House (see *C.J.*, 8:21, 22, 53, 110). Trevallyn Jones has published papers of Lord Wharton, now in the Bodleian Library, that show Temple to have been a member of the Presbyterian party and a lieutenant of Lord Wharton.

7. Clarendon, *State Papers*, 3:729–30.

8. *The Life of Edward Earl of Clarendon . . . Written by Himself*, 1:361; 2:42, 208, 344–45, 350–55; 3:707. For a vivid picture of this system in practice, see J. R. Jones, "Political Groups and Tactics in the Convention of 1660," pp. 169–71. For the preferment of Presbyterians, see Victor Sutch, *Gilbert Sheldon* (The Hague, 1973), pp. 64, 72.

9. Clarendon, *Life*, 2:343–44, 350–56, 434, 707–8; J. R. Jones, "Court Dependents in 1664," pp. 81–91. Servants of the King won many of the by-elections between 1660 and 1663 (W. C. Abbot, "The Long Parliament of Charles II," pp. 21–34).

10. *C.J.*, 8:502. An account of the King's message in Stowe MSS. 180, fol. 84, reads: "And after this his Majesty receiving by the petitioner's [Temple's] order and desire, and in his name, new professions of his duty and zeal to advance his Majesty's service, and that he was troubled to hear he was in his Majesty's displeasure as one who opposed his service; declaring he only opposed those who undertook to promote it and knew less of the sense of the House than he did, but that if his Majesty would trust him and his friends with the management of his affairs there, he would undertake to secure a liberal supply for his Majesty if the Courtiers did not obstruct it."

11. Here and below I have drawn upon four different accounts of Bristol's speech: Cobbett, *Parliamentary History*, 4:270–76; B.L. Loan 29/46/7; Carte MSS. 72, fols. 20–20v; Carte MSS. 36, fols. 80–81v.

12. Daniel O'Neil to the Duke of Ormond, 20 June 1663, in Dorothea Townshend, *George Digby, Second Earl of Bristol*, p. 224.

13. Recounted in his speech: see note 11 above.

14. Nathaniel Hodges to Dean Hodges, Clarendon State Papers 80, fols. 223–23v.

15. G. F. Trevallyn Jones, "The Bristol Affair, 1663," p. 21.

16. O'Neil to Ormond, in Townshend, *Bristol*, p. 224.

17. Clarendon State Papers 80, fol. 223.

18. Townshend, *Bristol*, p. 224. Some of the King's servants, wrote O'Neil (ibid.), "that found this fellow [Temple] was endeavouring to persuade the moderate as he had done the more passionate and zealous part of the House that those of the King's servants that were in the House had undertaken the very same things he did himself, persuaded the King to acquaint the House with Temple's undertaking."

19. See note 8, above.

20. *C.J.*, 8:499–502.

21. Samuel Pepys, *The Diary of Samuel Pepys*, ed. Robert Latham and William Matthews, 4:207.

22. For the full story of Bristol's attack on Clarendon, see Trevallyn Jones, "The Bristol Affair."

23. *C.J.*, 8:515.

24. P.R.O., S.P.D. 29/76, no. 8. In his message to the Commons, Charles declared that he had been informed "of several seditious discourses of Sir Richard Temple in dissuading persons to assist his Majesty, and using very scandalous expressions against the Government (for which his Majesty intends in a due time to have justice against the petitioner [Temple]" (Stowe MSS. 180, fol. 84).

25. H.M.C., *Third Report*, p. 93; *15th Report*, App. 7, p. 170.

26. Davies, "The Political Career of Sir Richard Temple," p. 55.

27. Bennet to Temple, 3 September 1663, Stowe MSS, H.L.

28. H.M.C., *Report VII*, p. 484; Caroline Robbins, "The Repeal of the Triennial Act in 1664." *H.L.Q.*

29. Carte MSS. 34, fols. 442, 448.

30. Egerton MSS. 2539, fol. 77.

31. Denis Witcombe, *Charles II and the Cavalier House of Commons*, pp. 59–60; H. C. Foxcroft, *The Life and Letters of Sir George Savile, Bart. First Marquis of Halifax*, 1:46–47.

32. Caroline Robbins, *The Diary of John Milward*, pp. 3, 33, 56.

33. Roger North, *Examen: or, An Enquiry into the Credit and Veracity of a Pretended Complete History*, p. 455.

34. Maxwell Schoenfeld, *The Restored House of Lords*, p. 201; P.R.O., S.P.D. 29/143, No. 157; Clarendon, *Life*, 3:711; Sir Alan Broderick in Carte MSS. 35, fol. 171.

35. Egerton, MSS. 2539, fols. 76–77; Witcombe, *Cavalier House of Commons*, pp. 53–55.

36 Witcombe, *Cavalier House of Commons*, pp. 55–58; Carte MSS. 35, fols. 30–30v, 238v, 259; Carte MSS. 47, fols. 138–38v.

37. Witcombe, *Cavalier House of Commons*, p. 64.

38. Carte MSS. 35, fol. 778v.

39. Egerton MSS. 2539, fol. 140.

40. Clayton Roberts, ed., "Sir Richard Temple's Discourse on the Parliament of 1667–1668," p. 142.

41. I have reconstructed this account of the undertaking from Buckingham's own account of it, as told to Sir John Doddington in 1669 (Doddington to Temple, 28 January 1669, Stowe MSS, H.L.) and from other bits and pieces. See especially Ruvigny's dispatches (P.R.O., French Trans., 9/19 September, 9/19 October, 19/29 December 1667), John Nicholas's letters (Egerton MSS. 2539, fols. 118v, 140), Pepys's Diary (8:449); the letters of Lord Conway and Lord Ossory (Carte MSS. 36, fols. 25 and 220, fol. 326v), and Thomas Carte's Life of James Duke of Ormond, 4:322–23.

42. P.R.O., French Trans., 7/17 November 1667.

43. Milward, Diary, pp. 99, 100, 112–15, 335; Anchitell Grey, Debates in the House of Commons, 1:23, 28.

44. Stowe MSS. 180, fol. 84.

45. Pepys, Diary, 8:596, 600; P.R.O., French Trans., 30 December 1667/9 January 1668, 2/12 January 1668; B.L. Add. MSS. 36,916, fol. 56.

46. Bulstrode Papers, in Alfred Morrison, The Collection of Autographed Letters and Historical Documents Formed by Alfred Morrison, 2d ser., 1:17, 23; H.M.C., Finch MSS, 1:493.

47. Pepys, Diary, 9:9.

48. Gilbert Burnet, History of My Own Time, 1:465.

49. P.R.O., French Trans., 10/20 February 1668; Milward, Diary, p. 179; B.L. Add. MSS. 36,916, fol. 66a.

50. P.R.O., French Trans., 13/23 February; Carte MSS. 36, fols. 155–55v.

51. Pepys, Diary, 9:71.

52. Egerton MSS. 2539, fol. 155v; Milward, Diary, pp. 189–90.

53. Carte MSS. 220, fol. 354.

54. Egerton MSS. 2539, fol. 170.

55. Temple's pursuit of Sir William Coventry is set forth in rich detail in the Coventry Papers at Longleat; see especially Coventry Papers CI, fols. 121, 133, 137, 145. Pepys confirms the story (Diary, 9:129).

56. Milward, Diary, pp. 191–92, 198; Grey, Debates, 1:85, 89–90, 93–94; Egerton MSS. 2539, fol. 160.

57. Grey, Debates, 1:99, 108; Milward, Diary, pp. 200, 212; Egerton MSS. 2539, fol. 166v.

58. Milward, Diary, pp. 285–86, 293; Grey, Debates, 1:148–49, 157; Pepys, Diary, 9:180.

59. E. Gay, "Sir Richard Temple, pp. 289–90; Clarendon, Life, 3:904.

60. Doddington to Temple, 28 January 1669, Stowe MSS, H.L.

61. Egerton MSS. 2539, fol. 193v.

62. P.R.O., French Trans., 14/24 February 1669; F. R. Harris, The Life of Edward Montagu, K.G., First Earl of Sandwich, 2:315.

Notes

63. Grey, *Debates*, 1:157–63, 169, 171–72, 176, 182–84, 204–6, 212–15; P.R.O., French Trans., 13/23 December 1669.

64. Roberts, "Sir Richard Temple's Discourse," pp. 138–44. When I edited the discourse for the *Huntington Library Quarterly* in 1957, I dated it June 1668; internal evidence now convinces me that Temple wrote it in January 1670 and was speaking about the 1669 session, not the one of 1668.

65. Violet Barbour, *Henry Bennet, Earl of Arlington*, pp. 162–64; Andrew Browning, *Thomas Osborne, Earl of Danby and Duke of Leeds*, 1:74–75.

66. Browning, *Danby*, pp. 73–74.

67. B.L. Add. MSS. 38,850, fols. 206v–7v. A summary of The Alarum is given in *C.S.P., Dom., 1668–69*, pp. 541–42.

68. P.R.O., French Trans., 27 December 1669/6 January 1670, 13/23 and 17/27 January 1670; Grey, *Debates*, 1:220–22, 227–28; Witcombe, *Cavalier House of Commons*, pp. 98–103; Alexander Grosart, ed., *The Complete Prose Works of Andrew Marvell*, 1:316.

69. Grey, *Debates*, 1:315–16, 321, 398. In March, Doddington wrote Temple: "I rejoice to find by my Lord Arlington that you are gracious with the King and that his Majesty is sensible you have served him this Session, I know the rest will follow and I see is coming" (Doddington to Temple, 6 March 1671, Stowe MSS, H.L.).

70. Gay, "Richard Temple" 6:273–77, 291.

71. Grey, *Debates*, 2:68.

72. Osmund Airy, ed., *Essex Papers*, 1:132.

73. *A Seasonable Argument to Persuade All the Grand Juries in England to Petition for a New Parliament* (Amsterdam, 1677), reprinted in Cobbett, *Parliamentary History*, vol. 4, app. 3; Merril Crissy and Godfrey Davies, "Corruption in Parliament, 1660–1677," pp. 107–14.

74. Witcombe, *Cavalier House of Commons*, pp. 98–103.

75. P.R.O., French Trans., 7/17 June 1669.

76. Burnet, *History of My Own Time*, 1:467.

77. [Thomas Baker,] *The Head of the Nile*, preface.

CHAPTER FOUR

1. W. D. Christie, *The Life of Anthony Ashley Cooper, the First Earl of Shaftesbury*, 2:200–202.

2. William Harbord to Essex, 9 January 1675, Stowe MSS. 207, fol. 22; Van Beuningen to the States General, 19/29 January 1675, B.L. Add. MSS. 17,766 QQQ, fol. 141v; Southwell to Ormond, 23 January 1675, Carte MSS. 72, fol. 257.

3. Southwell to Ormond, 16, 23, 26 January 1675, Carte MSS. 72, fols. 255, 257, 259.

4. Christie, *Shaftesbury*, 2:201.

5. I have drawn the argument of this paragraph largely from Denis Witcombe's perceptive analysis of Charles II's relations with the Cavalier House of

Commons (see Witcombe, *Charles II and the Cavalier House of Commons*, pp. 93, 98–104, 111–12, 119–20, 125–29, 136, 139–42, 166, 176–78).

6. K. D. H. Haley, *The First Earl of Shaftesbury*, pp. 315–16; Burnet, *History of My Own Time*, 1:536.

7. Ibid., 2:5–6, 8–10, 12; Sir Francis North's History of Faction, B.L. Add. MSS. 32,519, fol. 6v; Christie, *Shaftesbury*, vol. 2, Fragment of Stringer's Memoirs, App. 29; C.S.P., *Ven.*, *1673–1675*, p. 183.

8. Burnet, *History*, 2:16; Witcombe, *Cavalier House of Commons*, p. 130.

9. C.S.P., *Ven.*, *1673–1675*, pp. 27–28.

10. Burnet, *History of My Own Time*, 2:11.

11. C.S.P., *Dom.*, *1673*, p. 598; Stowe MSS. 203, fol. 149v.

12. Osmund Airy, ed., *Essex Papers*, 1:154.

13. C.S.P., *Ven.*, *1673–1675*, p. 176.

14. Stowe MSS. 204, fol. 73.

15. Haley, *Shaftesbury*, p. 360.

16. Airy, *Essex Papers*, 1:174.

17. C.S.P., *Ven.*, *1673–1675*, p. 177.

18. Stowe MSS. 204, fol. 237.

19. Stowe MSS. 207, fol. 112; Carte MSS. 72, fol. 257; Carte MSS. 38, fol. 275.

20. C. E. Pike, ed., *Essex Correspondence*, p. 18.

21. Bulstrode Papers, in Alfred Morrison, *The Collection of Autographed Letters and Historical Collections Formed by Alfred Morrison*, 2d ser., 1:287; H.M.C., Report VII, p. 492.

22. C.J., 9:327. For a full account of Finch's speech, see L.R.O. Finch MSS. pp. 37, fols. 21v–24v.

23. C.J., 9:323, 330.

24. Pike, *Essex Correspondence*, 2:4, 10; B.L. Add. MSS. 17,677 QQQ, fols. 238–39.

25. Orrery's Diary, Forster MSS. 47a, fols. 11–22. A newsletter of the time concurs with Orrery: "The highest Cavaliers and best Protestants are now convinced that persecution and English episcopacy are too narrow a foundation of our great monarchy to be built upon" (Bulstrode Papers, p. 301).

26. Orrery's Diary, Forster MSS 47a, fol. 26.

27. Haley, *Shaftesbury*, p. 388.

28. Browning, *Danby*, 1:167–74, 3:44–71.

29. Bulstrode Papers, in Morrison, *Collection*, 2d ser., 1:320; Stowe MSS. 208, fols. 61, 81; P.R.O., French Trans., 17/27 June 1675; B.L. Add. MSS. 17,677 QQQ, fols. 238, 243.

30. Forster MSS. 47a, fols. 26–28; P.R.O., French Trans., 11/21 November 1675; C.J., 9:373.74.

31. Bulstrode Papers, in Morrison, *Collection*, 2d ser., 1:320; C.S.P., *Dom.*, *1675–1676*, pp. 365–66; Van Beuningen, B.L. Add. MSS. 17,677 QQQ, fol. 332; C.J., 9:374, 382.

32. Haley, *Shaftesbury*, p. 398.

33. Andrew Browning, ed., *The Memoirs of Sir John Reresby* (Glasgow, 1936), pp. 114–15.

34. Browning, *Danby*, 2:67.

35. Osmund Airy, ed., *The Lauderdale Papers*, 3:131, 133; Burnet, *History of My Own Time*, 2:150; Henry Coventry to Laurence Hyde, Coventry Papers, XCII, fol. 25v.

36. P.R.O., French Trans., 6/16 June 1678. Barillon also wrote on 20/30 May: "I know that one negotiates with the heads of the Cabal to give money to pay off the troops and disband them."

37. Sir William Temple, *The Works of Sir William Temple, Bart.*, 2:429.

38. H.M.C., *Lindsey*, p. 377; North Papers, B.L. Add. MSS. 32,520, fol. 225. For similar opinions see W. D. Christie, ed., *Letters Addressed from London to Sir Joseph Williamson while Plenipotentiary at the Congress of Cologne in the Years 1673 and 1674*, 1:150; C.S.P., *Ven.*, *1673–1675*, pp. 162–63; *A Pacquet of Advice* (London, 1676), p. 4; *A Letter from Amsterdam* (London, 1678), p. 87.

39. Narcissus Luttrell, *A Brief Relation of State Affairs*, 1:3.

40. P.R.O., French Trans., 23 December 1678/2 January 1679.

41. Ibid.; Southwell to Ormond, Carte MSS. 38, fol. 1679.

42. P.R.O., French Trans., 30 December 1678/9 January 1679, 2/12 January 1679.

43. News Letter, Carte MSS. 72, fol. 429. "The Lord Treasurer and his cabal," wrote Barillon, "flatter themselves that by declaring against Catholics and France they will make the whole nation favourable, and money will be given to the present administration" (P.R.O., French Trans., 16/26 September 1678).

44. P.R.O., French Trans., 2/12, 13/23, 16/26 January 1679; Lyttleton to Hatton, B. L. Add. MSS. 29,577; fol. 181v.

45. See above, pp. 51, 54–55, 59.

46. Burnet, *History of My Own Time*, 2:187–88; P.R.O., French Trans., 20/30 January and 30 January/9 February 1679; Browning, *Memoirs of Reresby*, p. 168.

47. Haley, *Shaftesbury*, pp. 496–97.

48. L.R.O., Finch MSS. P.P. 57, News Letter, fol. 6.

49. Ibid.; H.M.C., *Ormond*, 4:311; Luttrell, *Brief Relation*, 1:6; Edward Maunde Thompson, ed., *Correspondence of the Family of Hatton*, 1:170–71; J. R. Jones, ed., "Shaftesbury's Worthy Men," p. 233.

50. Thompson, *Correspondence of the Family of Hatton*, 1:178; Henry Sidney, *Diary of the Time of Charles II*, 1:26.

51. Holles's undertaking may also have collapsed because his undertaking to borrow money from the chief Presbyterians in London for disbanding the army failed (P.R.O., French Trans., 30 January/9 February, 6/16 February 1679).

52. Browning, *Danby*, 3:6–7; Burnet, *History of My Own Time*, 1:187–88.

53. P.R.O., French Trans., 21 April/1 May 1679; Van Beuningen, B.L. Add. MSS. 17,677 SSS, fol. 247v.

54. Southwell to Ormond, 22 February, in Carte MSS. 39, fol. 21.

55. Danby to Rochester, 28 February 1685, in Morrison, *Collection*, 1st ser. 3:119. Danby wrote in his journal: "The King sent for me and [said] it would be both convenient for my selfe and for his service that I should quit my place of Lord Treasurer for that the Parliament would then forbear any further prosecution of me and would both give money and comply with him in what else he should desire of them . . . " (B.L. Add. MSS. 28,043, fol. 7).

56. P.R.O., French Trans., 7/17 April 1679.

57. Burnet, *History of My Own Time*, 2:208; P.R.O., French Trans., 17/27 March, 24 March/3 April 1679.

58. Charles Hatton to Lord Hatton, 15 April, B.L. Add. MSS. 29,572, fol. 112.

59. P.R.O., French Trans., 17/27 April 1679.

60. H.M.C., *Ormond*, 4:503–4.

61. Temple, *Works*, 1:413.

62. For an analysis of the composition of the new Privy Council, see Foxcroft, *Halifax*, 1:149n.

63. Laurence Hyde, Sir John Ernley, Sir Edward Dering, and Sidney Godolphin. The Commons showed their confidence in the new commission by assigning the money for disbanding the army to the Exchequer, not to the Chamber of London as originally planned (Van Beuningen, B.L. Add. MSS. 17,677 EE, fol. 105).

64. Sir Thomas Lee, Sir Thomas Meres, and Edward Vaughan. See Henry Horwitz, *Revolution Politicks: The Career of Daniel Finch Second Earl of Nottingham, 1647–1730*, p. 16, and Thompson, *Hatton Correspondence*, 1:179–81.

65. P.R.O., French Trans., 21 April/1 May 1679.

66. H.M.C., *Ormond*, 4:502, 5:3.

67. B.L. Add. MSS. 29,572, fol. 112. Barillon observed: "The House of Commons knows its force and sees well that the Court is in no condition to resist; thus in giving money one imposes on his Majesty conditions that serve to further the authority of Parliament, even in foreign affairs" (P.R.O., French Trans., 10/20 April 1679).

68. Lord Guildford's reflection, B.L. Add. MSS. 32,518, fol. 36v.

69. J. R. Jones, *The First Whigs: The Politics of the Exclusion Crisis, 1678–1683*, p. 75.

70. Shaftesbury expressed these fears with characteristic vehemence in a memorandum written on 6 March 1679 (P.R.O., Shaftesbury Papers, 30/24/6A, no. 334).

71. Edward Harley, 21 April 1679, B.L. Loan 29/183.

72. H.M.C., *Report XV*, pt. 5 (Foljambe), p. 129. For concurring judgments, see Browning, *Memoirs of Reresby*, p. 177; Henry Coventry, in H.M.C., *Ormond*, 5:67; and Sir Robert Southwell, H.M.C., *Ormond*, 4:502.

73. C.J., 9:609; P.R.O., French Trans., 5/15 May 1679. Burnet wrote, "There were also many in the House of Commons that finding themselves forgot, while others were preferred to them, resolved to make themselves considerable, and they infused in a great many a mistrust of all that was going" (*History of My Own Time*, 2:210). Or, as Ralph Montagu said, when many of his acquaintances were taken into the council and he was left out, "A pox on them: if he had thought

they would have gone without him, he would never have brought out my Lord of Danby's letter" (in Julia Cartwright, *Sacharissa*, p. 266).

74. P.R.O., French Trans., 8/18 May 1679; Browning, *Memoirs of Reresby*, p. 180; H.M.C., *Ormond*, 4:514; Grey, *Debates*, 7:265–78.

75. Campana de Cavelli, *Les Derniers Stuarts á Saint-Germain en Laye*, 1:265.

76. Burnet, *History of My Own Time*, 2:210.

77. Grey, *Debates*, 7:158–64, 236–60; *C.J.*, 9:620, 626.

78. P.R.O., French Trans., 27 March/6 April 1679.

79. P.R.O., French Trans., 3/13 April 1679; H.M.C., *Ormond*, 4:503–5, 5:58; Beuningen, B.L. Add. MSS. 17,677 EE, fol. 111v; Charles Hatton to Lord Hatton, B.L. Add. MSS. 29,572, fol. 118.

80. Carte, *Ormond*, 4:576.

81. Grey, *Debates*, 7:144–45.

82. H.M.C., *Ormond*, 4:520–21.

83. Sarotti to Venice, quoted in Leopold von Ranke, *A History of England Principally in the Seventeenth Century*, 4:84.

84. Haley, *Shaftesbury*, p. 552; Jones, *First Whigs*, pp. 94–106.

85. Sidney, *Diary*, 1:177–78, 182–85; H.M.C., *Report VI*, p. 741.

86. Christie, *Shaftesbury*, 2:356–58; Sidney, *Diary*, 1:270, 299; Hickman to Halifax, Halifax Papers, Box 5.

87. Haley, *Shaftesbury*, pp. 550–51.

88. Ibid., pp. 113, 413, 515; H.M.C., *Report VI*, app., p. 377; Jones, *First Whigs*, pp. 97, 182; J. R. Jones, "The First Whig Party in Norfolk," p. 18.

89. Sir Robert Reading to Ormond, Carte MSS. 243, fol. 473v.

90. P.R.O., French Trans., 24 May/3 June 1680.

91. Gilbert Burnet, "Some Unpublished Letters of Gilbert Burnet," ed. H. C. Foxcroft, pp. 8, 12.

92. Sir William Coventry to Halifax, Halifax Papers, Box 2.

93. Reading to Ormond, Carte MSS. 243, fol. 473.

94. P.R.O., French Trans., 5/15 April 1680.

95. Reading to Arran, Carte MSS. 39, fol. 65; Burnet, "Letters of Gilbert Burnet," p. 30.

96. P.R.O., French Trans., 17/27 June 1680.

97. Foxcroft, *Halifax*, 1:223–24.

98. P.R.O., French Trans., 27 September/7 October 1680.

99. Sidney, *Diary*, 2:106; Foxcroft, *Halifax*, 1:324–26.

100. Grey, *Debates*, 7:360–62; *C.J.*, 9:640.

101. Cartwright, *Sacharissa*, p. 266.

102. *C.S.P.*, *Dom.*, 1679–1680, p. 597; Sir Charles Lyttleton to Lord Hatton, B.L. Add. MSS. 29,577, fol. 277; H.M.C., *Ormond*, 5:378.

103. P.R.O., French Trans., 9/19 and 20/30 September 1680.

104. Prinsterer, *Archives*, 2d ser. 5:423.

Notes

105. P.R.O., French Trans., 7/17 and 11/21 October 1680. Van Citters reported on 5 October a rumor that Shaftesbury would be given the office of lord treasurer, an office he had long desired. On 8 October he wrote that Shaftesbury had met with some courtiers and had declared that he would promote His Majesty's authority, would act liberally, not destructively, in affairs, would appear one of His Majesty's most loyal servants, and would strive to ensure that the government should not become arbitrary or the Protestant religion be injured. On the twelfth Van Citters reported that the ministers here, in order to protect their own interests, take great care to give satisfaction to all the discontented and hold secret conferences with them (B.L. Add. MSS. 17,677 SSS, fols. 344–44v, 347v).

106. P.R.O., French Trans., 20/30 September 1680; in November, Shaftesbury complained that he no more understood the Commons than the Court (Sidney, Diary, 2:135).

107. P.R.O., French Trans., 25 October/4 November 1680.

108. C.J., 9:685–86.

109. Roger North, Examen, pp. 507–11, 515, 528, 533, 538–40, 552–53; Sidney, Diary, 2:107–8, 111, 113, 119; Sir John Dalrymple, Memoirs of Great Britain and Ireland, 1:355, 358; H.M.C., Ormond, 4:509, 515, 5:454; Temple, Works, 2:532; Prinsterer, Archives, 2d. ser., 5:423.

110. P.R.O., French Trans., 30 December 1680/9 January 1681.

111. H.M.C., Ormond, 5:541–42; P.R.O., French Trans., 30 December 1680/9 January 1681.

112. James Stanier Clarke, The Life of James the Second (London, 1816), 1:649; H.M.C., Finch, 2:99; P.R.O., French Trans., 3/13 January 1681.

113. Roger Morrice, Entring Book, 1:288–89.

114. Newdigate Newsletter L.C. 1025, 28 December 1680, in the Folger Shakespeare Library.

115. B.L. Loan 29/86/7; B.L. Add. MSS. 32,681, f. 129; Prinsterer, Archives, 2d ser., 5:466.

116. C.J., 9:695. Roger North wrote: "It is of the nature of that assembly [the House of Commons] to be averse to those who pretend to govern, for it hates to be imposed on; and whoever acts there in such a manner, as shews he thinks his sense ought to take place, is commonly ill heard; and slighted. And it was no sooner found that Sir William Jones had a spice of that temper, but his authority sunk, and little of his proposing would succeed" (Examen, p. 568). North's final remark reflects more of his animus against Jones than the actual record of events.

117. C.J., 9:695–96; Grey, Debates, 8:224–25. For Winnington's and Jones's continued leadership see Grey, Debates, 8:237, 244, 251, 253–54, 257–58, 268–71, 279, 283–88, 289–90.

118. H.M.C., Beaufort, p. 105.

119. P.R.O., French Trans., 3/13 January 1681.

120. Ibid.; C.J., 9:699, 702, 704.

121. Charles allowed this fact to guide his conduct. As Colonel Manser wrote in September 1680: "We understand that the King will stick close unto the Duke of York . . . it is said that he wants no money and that the Parliament shall know at meeting therefore they may sit and act provided that they meddle not with the Duke of York" (Carte MSS. 39, fol. 208). Charles's financial independence arose

far more from a retrenchment of expenditures, an increase in the customs, and anticipations on the revenues than from French subsidies: see C. D. Chandaman, *English Public Revenue, 1660–1688*, pp. 249–55; Glenn Nicholas, "English Government Borrowing, 1660–1688," pp. 81, 93–96.

CHAPTER FIVE

1. Grey, *Debates*, 10:11; Clayton Roberts, "The Constitutional Significance of the Financial Settlement of 1690."

2. Sunderland's Memoirs, Portland Papers, PwA 1219.

3. C.J., 10:300; Ranke, *History of England*, 6:162–63; Burnet, *History of My Own Time*, 4:287–89.

4. Morrice, Entring Book, 2:645. In 1692 it was moved in the House of Lords that an address be made to recommend my lord chief baron to His Majesty for the place of master of the rolls, but it was opposed as a thing without precedent for them to name anybody to the King for such an employment, upon which the debate ran to make an address to recommend him in general to His Majesty for some preferment, and this too was adjourned till tomorrow (B.L. Add. MSS. 34,096, fol. 164).

5. Foxcroft, *Halifax*, 2:230.

6. Ibid., p. 236.

7. John Lowther Lonsdale, "Memoirs of Lord Lonsdale," p. 94.

8. Luttrell, *Brief Relation*, 1:541, 599; Abel Boyer, *The History of King William III*, 2:86.

9. Gilbert Burnet, *A Supplement to Burnet's History of My Own Time*, ed. Helen Foxcroft, p. 313.

10. Dalrymple, *Memoirs of Great Britain and Ireland*, vol. 2, app. pp. 195–96; Lord Delamere voiced similar sentiments (*The Works of the Right Honourable Henry Late Lord Delamer, and Earl of Warrington* [London, 1694], pp. 82–86).

11. William Coxe, ed., *The Private and Original Correspondence of Charles Talbot, Duke of Shrewsbury*, p. 15. Six weeks before Shrewsbury wrote, on 9 November, Roger Morrice had observed that many wise men are of the opinion "there can be no Composition nor Temperament, but one of the Partyes must fall" (Entring Book, 2:645).

12. Morrice, Entring Book, p. 644; Dalrymple, *Memoirs of Great Britain and Ireland*, vol. 2, app., p. 182; Knatchbull's Diary, B.L. Add. MSS. 33,923, fol. 466; William Aiken, ed., *The Conduct of the Earl of Nottingham*, p. 53. The Tory spokesman in "A Dialogue Betwixt Whig and Tory", *Collection of State Tracts, Published on Occasion of the Late Revolution in 1688, and During the Reign of King William III*, 2:386, says: "But if the King will chuse any one Party, I think we of the Church are the most numerous and considerable, and are the fittest as such to be employed."

13. Gilbert Burnet, *History of His Own Time*, 4:66–71; Foxcroft, *Halifax*, 2:247. Sir John Guise observed in March, "I find this King and Queen extremely beholden to some people that would settle the Revenue for lives" (Grey, *Debates*, 10:20).

14. Dalrymple, *Memoirs of Great Britain and Ireland*, 2:186.

Notes

15. Morrice, Entring Book, 2:644–45; Dalrymple, *Memoirs of Great Britain and Ireland*, vol. 2, app. p. 199.

16. N. Japikse, *Correspondentie van Willem III en van Hans Willem Bentinck, eersten Graaf van Portland*, 1:64.

17. Foxcroft, *Halifax*, 2:243.

18. Japikse, *Correspondentie*, 1:70, 74, 81.

19. Foxcroft, *Halifax*, 2:247.

20. Constantijn Huygens, *Journal*, 1:248; on the changes in the two commissions, see Henry Horwitz, *Parliament, Policy, and Politics in the Reign of William III*, pp. 41, 52.

21. Horwitz, *Parliament, Policy, and Politics*, pp. 53, 63, 72–73, 111.

22. John Evelyn, *The Diary of John Evelyn*, ed. E. S. de Beer, 5:5; Morrice, Entring Book, 3:106.

23. Quoted in Horwitz, *Parliament, Policy, and Politics*, p. 51.

24. Morrice, Entring Book, 3:218; Ranke, *History of England*, 6:156; Horwitz, *Parliament, Policy, and Politics*, pp. 51–52, 56–57; H.M.C., *House of Lords MSS, 1690–91*, pp. iv–v. Constantijn Huygens commented on a Whig victory in a disputed election return in November 1690 (*Journal*, 1:360): "The Whigs in this Parliament begin to be most powerful."

25. Browning, *Danby*, 3:178–79; Dalrymple, *Memoirs of Great Britain and Ireland*, vol. 2, app., pp. 182–86; Burnet, *History of His Own Time*, 4:74.

26. For a list of placemen in William's reign, see Horwitz, *Parliament, Policy, and Politics*, pp. 359–66.

27. Ibid., pp. 54, 56–57, 108–9; Morrice, Entring Book, 3:138. Of the 1692 Abjuration Bill, Sunderland wrote Portland: "Then the oath was brought into the House of Commons, Seymour and many of the Court were violently against it, and so were the ministers in the House of Lords, when my Lord of Devonshire brought one of the like nature into that House" (Portland Papers, PwA 1219, [30] June 1693).

28. Foxcroft, *Halifax*, 2:129.

29. Grey, *Debates*, 10:32; Carte MSS. 130, fol. 327.

30. Anonymous, "State of the Parties," in Cobbett, *Parliamentary History*, vol. 5 app. 11.

31. Sidney and Coningsby to Portland, 27 September 1690, Portland Papers, PwA 299.

32. Browning, *Danby*, 1:491.

33. H.M.C., *Finch*, 4:231–33.

34. Horwitz, *Revolution Politicks*, p. 118.

35. R. Doebner, ed., *Memoirs of Mary Queen of England*, p. 39; Evelyn, *Diary*, 5:70.

36. Marion Grew, *William Bentinck and William III*, p. 210; H.M.C., *Portland*, 3:501.

37. "A Dialogue Betwixt Whig and Tory," in *A Collection of State Tracts . . . William III*, 2:390.

38. That the Whigs (and the Tories in their turn) acted for particular advantage and sought to engross all offices was a widespread complaint. See Sir Richard

Temple (Aiden, *Conduct of the Earl of Nottingham*, pp. 106–7), Rupert Browne (H.M.C., *Downshire*, 1:388), Blancard (H.M.C., *Report VII, Denbigh*, p. 211), Robert Harley (B.L. Loan 29/186, fol. 224), Paul Foley (B.L. Loan 29/135/7), and the anonymous authors of "A Dialogue Betwixt Whig and Tory" (*A Collection of State Tracts . . . William III*, 2:385, 387–88), "Some Short Considerations Upon the Present State of Affairs" (ibid., pp. 299, 301), and "The State of Parties" (ibid., pp. 208–12).

39. As the Earl of Portland put it, as early as February 1692, "the Whigs being many more in number, rather more than the other, and would expect (upon a removal) to have one they could confide in [as Secretary] and would take it ill if [they] had not such a one &c" (B.L. Add. MSS. 52,279, fol. 210).

40. Horwitz, *Parliament, Policy, and Politics*, p. 110.

41. Carte MSS. 79, fols. 345, 488.

42. Luttrell, *Brief Relation*, 3:18, 59–60; Burnet, *History of His Own Time*, 4:187–88.

43. Sunderland's Memoir, Portland Papers, PwA 1219.

44. Sunderland to Portland, 20 June 1693, Japikse, *Correspondentie*, 2:38–39.

45. Ibid., p. 38.

46. Sunderland to Portland, 2 May 1693, Portland Papers, PwA 1212.

47. H.M.C., *Portland*, 3:528.

48. Sunderland to Portland, 3 May 1693, Portland Papers, PwA 1212.

49. Sunderland to Portland, 19 July 1693, Portland Papers, PwA 1222.

50. H.M.C., *Finch*, 4:233.

51. Carte MSS. 233, fol. 194.

52. Carte MSS. 233, fols. 221–23. Sir Edward Harley may have referred to this meeting when he wrote Robert Harley, "'Tis said the great resort to the House with the new garden was of [illegible]. That gang is very busy and meet frequently" (B.L. Loan 29/142/2).

53. Japikse, *Correspondentie*, 2:42.

54. H.M.C., *Finch*, 4:233.

55. Robert Harley to Sir Edward, 5 August 1693, B.L. Loan 29/142/3.

56. Charles Hatton to Lord Hatton, 1 August 1693, B.L. Add. MSS. 29,574, fol. 206; H.M.C., *Johnstone*, p. 61; John Isham to Sir Justinian Isham, 8 August 1693, Northampton R.O., Isham Correspondence, 1484.

57. John Isham to Sir Justinian Isham, 8 August 1693, N.R.O., Isham MSS. 1484.

58. 2 August and 14 August 1693, Portland Papers, PwA 1227 and 1229/1.

59. Newdigate newsletter, L.C. 2213, 24 August 1693, in the Folger Shakespeare Library.

60. Foxcroft, *Halifax*, 2:172; L.C. to Halifax, 26 August 1693, Spencer House Letter Book, Althorp.

61. Shrewsbury to Wharton, 23 August 1693, Carte MSS. 233, fol. 256.

62. L. C. to Halifax, Spencer House Letter Book, 26 August 1693.

Notes

63. B.L. Add. MSS. 17,677 NN, fol. 220v.

64. John Isham to Sir Justinian Isham, 29 August 1693, N.R.O., Isham MSS. 1487.

65. On 19 September, L'Hermitage wrote that the Whigs heatedly demand Nottingham's dismissal (B.L. Add. MSS. 17,677 NN, fol. 257).

66. J. P. Kenyon asserts that Sunderland informed the Whig lords at Althorp that the King had agreed to name Russell admiral (*Robert Spencer, Earl of Sunderland*, p. 261); but Stephen Baxter rightly doubts that he did (*William III*, p. 437). Kenyon (p. 261) errs also in dating the meeting on 27 August and in declaring that Charles Montague was present. The meeting occurred a week earlier, and Lord Montague, not Charles, was present.

67. H.M.C., *Report VII, Denbigh*, p. 211.

68. N.R.O., Isham MSS. 1498 and 1499, H.M.C., *Portland*, 3:547; Luttrell, *Brief Relation*, 3:221; Thompson, *Correspondence of the Family of Hatton*, 2:197; Ranke, *History of England*, 6:217; B. L. Add. MSS. 17,677 NN, fol. 338.

69. Edward Maunde Thompson, ed., *Letters of Humphrey Prideaux*, p. 168.

70. Thompson, *Correspondence of the Family of Hatton*, 2:198. Bonnet believed that Shrewsbury refused office for the same reason he quit, "namely, some persons who are yet in the Ministry remain there" (Ranke, *History of England*, 6:218). Burnet believed that Shrewsbury refused office because he saw that William was turning to the Whigs from necessity, not choice (*History of His Own Time*, 4:215). Lord Capel was furious that Shrewsbury proved so scrupulous. "We have often been blamed," he wrote, "as men contented with nothing; and if the Church, the law, the fleet, the army (in regard to Talmash's great station), and the offering of both seals to be in the hands of our friends (the obstacle to common safety, my Lord Nottingham being removed) will not give content, what must, nay what will the world say of us?" (In Dalrymple, *Memoirs of Great Britain and Ireland*, 3:57.)

71. Pearl Finch, *History of Burley-on-the-Hill, Rutland*, p. 192; William wrote to Heinsius on 3 November that he saw that he would be forced to do things repugnant, without knowing whether they would succeed (B.L. Add. MSS. 34,504, fol. 130).

72. Doebner, *Memoirs of Queen Mary*, p. 61.

73. Aiken, *Conduct of the Earl of Nottingham*, p. 134.

74. Abel Boyer, *The History of King William the Third*, 2:375, 378; C.J., 11:12, 37.

75. C.J., 11:42, 66, 75, 117, 129–30, 132–33, 153, 158, 165, 168; L'Hermitage, B.L. Add. MSS. 17,677 OO, fols. 160v, 169, 194–95, 210–11, 213–14, 220, 243–45; Christopher Hatton, B.L. Add. MSS. 29,574, fol. 284v.

76. C.J., 11;71–72, 74–75; L'Hermitage, B.L. Add. MSS. 17,677 OO, fols. 173–75; Grey, *Debates*, 10:380–86.

77. Thompson, *Correspondence of the Family of Hatton*, 2:198.

78. I. F. Burton, P. W. J. Riley, and E. Rowlands, "Political Parties in the Reigns of William III and Anne: The Evidence of the Division Lists," pp. 30–31.

79. On two divisions concerning the condemnation of the Admiralty, the Whigs lost by 9 and 10 votes (C.J., 11:14, 21); on two early divisions on the treason bill and the triennial bill, they lost by 10 votes (C.J., 11:3, 13); yet they carried a duty on wine (later changed to a duty on tonnage) by 23 votes and a license fee on hackney coaches by 21 votes (C.J., 11:135, 169–70).

Notes

80 [Philip Yorke, Earl of Hardwicke, ed.,] *Miscellaneous State Papers*, 2:426–28; William Sachse, *Lord Somers A Political Portrait*, p. 93.

81. H.M.C., *Report VII, Denbigh*, p. 218.

82. Horwitz, *Parliament, Policy, and Politics*, pp. 128, 132.

83. Luttrell, *Brief Relation*, 3:299; Hatton, B.L. Add. MSS. 29,574, fol. 296.

84. The letters of Godolphin, Trenchard, Somers, and Shrewsbury are printed in *C.S.P., Dom., 1694–95*, pp. 179–86.

85. Luttrell, *Brief Relation*, 3:353.

86. Portland Papers, Sunderland to Portland, 5 August 1694, PwA 1240.

87. Commenting on the capture of Huy and Dixmunde, Christopher Hatton observed, "Certainly the Parliament the next sessions cannot do less than double their Votes and give ten millions considering how much is gained by the last 5 millions given" (B.L. Add. MSS. 29,574, fol. 331v).

88. *C.J.*, 11:175.

89. H.M.C., *Bath*, 1:51–52; Cobbett, *Parliamentary History*, 5:860–61.

90. Denis Rubini, *Court and Country*, pp. 111–12.

91. *C.S.P., Dom., 1694–1695*, pp. 365–66. Henry Horwitz has identified Coningsby as the author of this memorial (*Parliament, Policy, and Politics*, p. 218 n. 5).

92. Lawton, "Short State," in Cobbett, *Parliamentary History*, vol. 5, app. 104.

93. L'Hermitage, B.L. Add. MSS. 17,677 PP, 19 February/1 March 1695; *C.J.*, 11:236, 272; Boyer, *William III*, 3:23; B.L. Add. MSS. 29,574, fol. 396; *L.J.*, 15:546, 557, 577–78, 582; L'Hermitage, B.L. Add. MSS. 17,677 PP, 26 April/6 May 1695.

94. As L'Hermitage wrote, Foley was elected, "it being thought the Court was for Littleton." (B.L. Add. MSS. 17,677 PP, 15/25 March 1695).

95. Sunderland to Portland, 29 July 1695, Portland Papers, PwA 1248.

96. Guy to Portland, 31 May and 14 June 1695, Portland Papers, PwA 502 and 503.

97. Guy to Portland, 18/28 June and 12/22 July 1695, Portland Papers PwA 504 and 508; Musgrave to Harley, B.L. Loan 29/151/-.

98. Guy to Portland, 6 August, and Sunderland to Portland 18 August 1695, Portland Papers, PwA 511 and 1249.

99. H.M.C., *Portland*, 2:174; Coxe, *Correspondence of the Duke of Shrewsbury*, p. 399.

100. Burton, Riley, and Rowland, "Political Parties," p. 32. C. S. Emden writes: "The Whig victory in the election of 1695 was doubtless largely due to the substitution of Whig for Tory ministers, which had been proceeding in 1694" (*The People and the Constitution*, p. 141). He errs on two counts: first, the Whigs did not win a clear victory; secondly, there exists no evidence that court support contributed significantly to the number of seats they did win.

101. Burton, Riley, and Rowlands, "Political Parties," pp. 5–7; H.M.C., *Kenyon*, pp. 386–87.

102. Nottingham to his brother, 14 December 1695, Finch-Halifax MSS, Box 5.

Notes

103. Christopher Hatton, 10 January 1695, B.L. Add. MSS. 29,574, fols. 369–69v.

104. Boyer, *William III*, 3:113. Nottingham retired into the country once he saw that the opposition was divided and ineffectual.

105. H.M.C., *Hastings*, 2:252.

106. Horwitz, *Parliament, Policy, and Politics*, p. 156.

107. For Carmarthen's exploitation of the Preston Plot, see Browning, *Danby*, 1:495.

108. E. L. Ellis, "William III and the Politicians", in Geoffrey Holmes, ed., *Britain after the Glorious Revolution*, pp. 126–27. Robert Harley confessed that the discovery of the plot interrupted the scheme for a parliamentary council of trade (B.L. Loan 29/188, fol. 128).

109. *C.J.*, 11:519.

110. H.M.C., *Buccleuch*, 1:312.

111. Coxe, *Correspondence of the Duke of Shrewsbury*, p. 90; Guy to Portland, 31 May 1695, Portland Papers, PwA 502; Luttrell, *Brief Relation*, 3:467, 469; Horwitz, *Parliament, Policy, and Politics*, pp. 178–79, 230.

112. *C.S.P., Dom.*, 1696, pp. 318–19.

113. Somers to Portland, 18 August 1693, Portland Papers, PwA 1174.

114. Baxter, *William III*, pp. 339–41.

115. Coxe, *Correspondence of the Duke of Shrewsbury*, pp. 414, 417–20, 423, 424–27, 435; Carte MSS. 233, fols. 27–27v, 36, 38, 39. It was Somers who believed that Godolphin had been "tricked" and "cozened."

116. James Vernon, *Letters Illustrative of the Reign of William III from 1696 to 1708. Addressed to the Duke of Shrewsbury by James Vernon*, ed. G. P. R. James, 1:28, 30, 83.

CHAPTER SIX

1. James, *Letters to Shrewsbury from James Vernon*, 3:88–91.

2. John Trenchard, *Free Thoughts Concerning Officers in the House of Commons*, p. 2; a reprint of the preface to *The History of Standing Armies*, which was published in 1698.

3. W. D. Christie, ed., *Letters Addressed from London to Sir Joseph Williamson while Plenipotentiary at the Congress of Cologne in 1673–75*, 1:150.

4. Browning, *Memoirs of Reresby*, p. 112; P.R.O., French Trans., 7/17 June 1669.

5. "Short and Impartial Considerations upon the Present State of Affairs in England," in *Collection of State Tracts . . . William III*, 2:299.

6. B.L. Add. MSS. 17,677 OO, fol. 391. George Stepney wrote that Seymour and How were "grumbletonians" for being turned out (H. Manners Sutton, ed., *Lexington Papers*, p. 15).

7. This reflection occurs in a draft of a speech in the Finch-Halifax Papers, No. A 26. From internal evidence, I have dated it 1694, and I have hazarded the guess that it was drawn up by the Earl of Nottingham (though it may have been drawn up by Heneage Finch).

Notes

8. Anonymous, *The Militia Reformed*, 2:595. In the judgment of Denis Rubini ("Party and the Augustan Constitution, 1694–1716"), the distinction of Court and Country did extinguish that of Whig and Tory in the years from 1697 to 1701.

9. Carte MSS. 130, fol. 386.

10. Edward Harley's Memoirs, B.L. Add. MSS. 34,515, fols. 126–26v.

11. As the anonymous author of *The Militia Reformed* observed: "Interest or Conscience (real or mistaken) are the two principal Springs of all Division" (2:595). For the mounting opposition to a standing army, see Lois Schwoerer, *"No Standing Armies!" The Antiarmy Ideology in Seventeenth-Centruy England*, pp. 155–87.

12. C.S.P., Dom., 1698, pp. 102, 105.

13. Christian Cole, *Memoirs of Affairs of State*, p. 22.

14. H.M.C., *Report XIV*, pt. 9 (Onslow), p. 491.

15. C.J., 12:116, 125.

16. They maintained their unity by meeting regularly at the Whig Rose Club (James, *Letters to Shrewsbury from James Vernon*, 2:258).

17. R. Price to the Duke of Beaufort, Carte MSS. 130, fol. 391.

18. James, *Letters to Shrewsbury from James Vernon*, 1:478.

19. Coxe, *Correspondence of the Duke of Shrewsbury*, pp. 494, 505, 506, 523; C.S.P., Dom., 1697, p. 534.

20. Coxe, *Correspondence of the Duke of Shrewsbury*, pp. 532–33; James, *Letters to Shrewsbury from James Vernon*, 2:2.

21. C.S.P., Dom., 1698, p. 193; Paul Grimblot, ed., *Letters of William III and Louis XIV*, 1:436–38; Coxe, *Correspondence of the Duke of Shrewsbury*, p. 536.

22. James, *Letters to Shrewsbury from James Vernon*, 1:473–74.

23. Sunderland to Portland, 20 March 1699, Portland Papers.

24. Grimblot, *Letters of William III and Louis XIV*, 1:495–96.

25. Ibid., 2:71.

26. Coxe, *Correspondence of the Duke of Shrewsbury*, pp. 544–45.

27. Grimblot, *Letters of William III and Louis XIV*, 1:440.

28. Hardwicke, *State Papers*, 2:435.

29. Henry Horwitz, "Parties, Connections, and Parliamentary Politics, 1689–1714: Review and Revision," p. 56.

30. Hardwicke, *State Papers*, 2:435.

31. Coxe, *Correspondence of the Duke of Shrewsbury*, pp. 569–70.

32. James, *Letters to Shrewsbury from James Vernon*, 2:236–37; Coxe, *Correspondence of the Duke of Shrewsbury*, p. 572; Grimblot, *Letters of William III and Louis XIV*, 2:229.

33. C.S.P., Dom., 1698, p. 376.

34. James Lowther to Sir John Lowther, 6 January 1699, Lonsdale MSS. Tallard reported (P.R.O., French Trans., 19/29 December 1698) that in the debates on the standing army no one of the Court party was listened to.

35. Onno Klopp, *Der Fall des Hauses Stuart*, 8:274; James, *Letters to Shrewsbury from James Vernon*, 2:241, 268; Carte MSS. 288, fol. 261; Grimblot, *Letters of William III and Louis XIV*, 2:234.

Notes

36. Grimblot, *Letters of William III and Louis XIV*, 2:233, 324, 334.

37. James, *Letters to Shrewsbury from James Vernon*, 2:170–71, 279; Coxe, *Correspondence of the Duke of Shrewsbury*, p. 584.

38. James, *Letters to Shrewsbury from James Vernon*, 2:249.

39. Edward Harley to Sir Edward Harley, 28 January 1698 [1699], B.L. Loan 29/78/3.

40. *C.J.*, 12:199; James, *Letters to Shrewsbury from James Vernon*, 2:270–71; Luttrell, *Brief Relation*, 4:949; John Marriet to Mr. Pusey, B.L. Add. MSS. 34,730. fol. 250v.

41. Quoted in Horwitz, *Parliament, Policy, and Politics*, p. 253.

42. Granville to Halifax, 9 May 1699, Halifax Papers, Box 4.

43. Carte MSS. 228, fol. 310v; James Lowther to Sir John Lother, 13 and 16 May 1699, Lonsdale MSS; Coxe, *Correspondence of the Duke of Shrewsbury*, p. 579.

44. *C.S.P., Dom., 1699–1700*, pp. 175, 181, 189, 203, 210.

45. James, *Letters to Shrewsbury from James Vernon*, 2:371–76, 378–81.

46. Ibid., 2:397; P.R.O., French Trans., 24 December 1699/3 January 1700 and 31 December 1699/10 January 1700.

47. *Cursory Remarks upon Some Late Disloyal Proceedings*, 11:172, 179. Bishop Burnet (*History of His Own Time*, 4:422) concurred: "Those who opposed the King, resolved to force a change of the ministry upon him."

48. *C.J.*, 12:130.

49. B.L. Add. MSS. 30,000 D, fols. 47–48, 51–54.

50. Ibid.

51. Ibid., fols. 51–54; B.L. Add. MSS. 17,677 VV, fols. 158v–159; Edward Harley to his father, "Thurs. 11 clock," B.L. Loan 29/78/3.

52. James, *Letters to Shrewsbury from James Vernon*, 3:3, 6–8. Robert Harley, later reminiscing about events in 1700, declared that Sunderland had said that the King would have turned out Lord Somers to gain £200,000 from the Irish forfeitures: "This was offered and pressed very [much], but I would never enter into that negotiation, or give any encouragement to it" (H.M.C., *Portland*, 4:452).

53. James, *Letters to Shrewsbury from James Vernon*, 3:12–16; B.L. Add. MSS. 30,000 D, fols. 125–27; B.L. Add. MSS. 17,677 VV, fols. 207–298v.

54. James, *Letters to Shrewsbury from James Vernon*, 3:20–22; B.L. Add. MSS. 30,000 D, fols. 139–41; B.L. Add. MSS. 28,053, fols. 402–2v.

55. James Lowther to Sir John Lowther, 12 April 1700, Lonsdale MSS. 56.

56. James, *Letters to Shrewsbury from James Vernon*, 3:23–25.

57. Ibid., 2:393–94.

58. Ibid., 2:411–13.

59. James Lowther to Sir John Lowther, 21 January 1700, Lonsdale MSS; B.L. Loan 29/189, fol. 179; James, *Letters to Shrewsbury from James Vernon*, 3:20–21.

60. B.L. Add. MSS. 30,000 D, fols. 47–47v, 114v–15v, 118v–20; B.L. Loan 29/189, fol. 177. Two years later the Earl of Shaftesbury wrote to Benjamin Furley about Harley's role in this Parliament: "He is truly what is called in the world a great man, and it is by him alone that that party has raised itself to such a greatness as almost to destroy us. 'Tis he has taught 'em their popular game, and made them

able in a way they never understood, and were so averse to, as never to have complied with, had they not found it at last the only way to distress the government" (T. Forster, *Original Letters of Locke, Algernon Sidney, and Anthony Lord Shaftesbury*, p. 52).

61. Burnet, *History of His Own Time*, 4:429.

62. James, *Letters to Shrewsbury from James Vernon*, 3:35–36.

63. B.L. Loan 29/189, fol. 188. On 25 April, Tallard wrote to Louis XIV: "The Court applies itself entirely to finding the means to make the House of Commons more favorable the next session. One chief proposal has been to mix the Anglicans and Presbyterians in the administration, but neither the one party nor the other will consent. That has led to a proposal to win over the leaders of the strongest cabal in the Commons. But one finds this difficult, for those leaders are so flattered by the applause they receive from the whole nation and by the great role that they play that they do not wish to ally with the Court, forseeing that the opposing party will attack within a year and become as entirely superior as they are now" (P.R.O., French Trans., 27 April/7 May 1700).

64. Burnet, *History of His Own Time*, 4:431–33.

65. *Collection of State Tracts . . . William III*, 3:75.

66. P.R.O., French Trans., 27 April/7 May 1700; Le Neve, *The Lives and Characters of the Most Illustrious Persons British and Foreign Who Died in the Year 1712*, p. 208. The Duke of Bolton wrote Lord Somers in September 1700 that Shrewsbury "laboured mightily to convince me that my Lord Sunderland had no hand in the doing of it [Somers's dismissal]; and said, that my Lord Sunderland came to him, and was the most surprised in the world at its being done in this manner; and that my Lord Sunderland would have had the King send for your Lordship, and have told you, that, if you could have proposed a scheme to carry on his business, and preserve yourself, he would come into it; and upon this, it was supposed you would have quitted" (Hardwicke, *State Papers*, 2:438).

67. B.L. Add. MSS. 34,515, fol. 5; B.L. Loan 29/137/5, Roger Griffith to Harley; H.M.C., report 12, pt. 2, coke MSS, p. 398, B.L. Add. MSS. 17,677 VV, fol. 232; James, *Letters to Shrewsbury from James Vernon*, 3:55–56, 79, 85, 88–90; Southwell to Nottingham, L.R.O., Finch MSS, Box 4950, Bundle 30.

68. Southwell to Nottingham, L.R.O., Finch MSS, Box 4950, Bundle 20; H.M.C., *Portland*, 3:619; James, *Letters to Shrewsbury from James Vernon*, 3:49–50.

69. Coxe, *Correspondence of the Duke of Shrewsbury*, pp. 619–20; James, *Letters to Shrewsbury from James Vernon*, 3:38–42, 45–48, 50.

70. James, *Letters to Shrewsbury from James Vernon*, 3:53-54, 58–59, 62–63; P.R.O., French Trans., 27 April/7 May, 16/26 May 1700.

71. James, *Letters to Shrewsbury from James Vernon*, 3:94, 97, 105; B.L. Add. MSS. 17,677 VV, fol. 259v; B.L. Add. MSS. 30,000 D, fols. 212–12v.

72. B.L. Add. MSS. 30,000 D, fol. 211v.

73. B.L. Add. MSS. 17,677 VV, fol. 242v; B.L. Add. MSS. 30,000 D, fols. 207–8, 211v; Coxe, *Correspondence of the Duke of Shrewsbury*, p. 624; James, *Letters to Shrewsbury from James Vernon*, 3:51–52.

74. B.L. Add. MSS. 30,000 D, fol. 182v.

75. James, *Letters to Shrewsbury from James Vernon*, 3:94–95.

76. Bonnet, B.L. Add. MSS. 30,000 D, fol. 214; L'Hermitage, B.L. Add. MSS. 17,677 VV, fol. 259v.

Notes

77. James, *Letters to Shrewsbury from James Vernon*, 3:89, 97, 101.

78. Bonnet, B.L. Add. MSS. 30,000 D, fol. 211v.

79. James, *Letters to Shrewsbury from James Vernon*, 3:105, 116.

80. Rapin de Thoyras, *The History of England*, 3:281; L'Hermitage, B.L. Add. MSS. 17,677 VV, fols. 279, 353, 364, 366v.

81. H.M.C., *Bath*, 3:417; H.M.C., *Portland*, 3:628.

82. H.M.C., *Portland*, 3:630, 635; Luttrell, *Brief Relation*, 4:702.

83. L'Hermitage, B.L. Add. MSS. 17,677 VV, fols. 333, 334; Bonnet, B.L. Add. MSS. 30,000 D, fols. 313, 338; H.D. Montagu, Duke of Manchester, *Court and Society from Elizabeth to Anne, edited from the Papers at Kimbolton*, 2:82.

84. L'Hermitage, B.L. Add. MSS. 17,677 VV, fols. 333, 352; H.M.C., *Cowper*, 2:410.

85. G. V. Bennet, "Conflict in the Church," in Holmes, *Britain after the Glorious Revolution*, p. 166; Burnet, *History of His Own Time*, 4:506.

86. Burnet, *History of His Own Time*, 4:454, 458.

87. Klopp, *Der Fall des Hauses Stuart*, 9:154; Carte MSS. 228 fol. 368v; James Lowther to Sir John Lowther, 11 February 1700[1701], Lonsdale MSS.

88. Forster, *Original Letters*, p. 109.

89. As Speaker Onslow declares in a note to Burnet, *History of His Own Time*, 4:442.

90. H.M.C., *Portland*, 3:625; James, *Letters to Shrewsbury from James Vernon*, 3:129.

91. James, *Letters to Shrewsbury from James Vernon*, 3:107, 113–14, 125. Thomas Bateman wrote Sir William Trumbull, "My Lord Montague's is still the seat of politicks, and this night a consult is to be held there, which is to model a new Settlement to break country-party's and to do other wonders" (B.R.O., Trumbull MSS. Alph. L).

92. H.M.C., *Portland*, 3:625–26; B.L. Add. MSS. 34,515, fols. 6–8.

93. B.L. Add. MSS. 30,000 D, fols. 259–60.

94. John Oldmixon, *The History of England during the Reigns of King William and Queen Mary, Queen Anne, and King George I*, p. 208.

95. *Archaeologia*, 38:5.

96. F. J. L. Kramer, ed., *Archives ou Correspondance Inédite de la Maison D'Orange-Nassau*, 3d ser. (Leyde, 1907–9), 2:405.

97. For the emergence of a new Tory party in the 1690s, see Keith Feiling, *A History of the Tory Party, 1640–1714*, pp. 275–343.

98. L'Hermitage, B.L. Add. MSS. 17,677 VV, fols. 358, 362, WW, 109, 120; H.M.C., *Cowper*, 2:410; Walsh to Somers, Surrey Record Office, Somers MS.B/18. These changes in the commissions of the peace had little effect upon the election. See Lionel Glassey, *Politics and the Appointment of Justices of the Peace, 1675–1720*, p. 143.

99. Tallard, P.R.O., French Trans., 24 February/7 March and 7/18 March 1701; Klopp, *Der Fall des Hauses Stuart*, 9:191.

100. Klopp, *Der Fall des Hauses Stuart*, 9:118.

101. H.M.C., *Portland*, 3:629.

Notes

102. Tallard, P.R.O., French Trans., 5/15 February, 15/25 February, 24 February/7 March, 29 March/9 April 1701.

103. Klopp, *Der Fall des Hauses Stuart*, 9:208–9.

104. Harley Memoirs, B.L. Add. MSS. 34,515, fols. 10–11v.

105. H.M.C., *Portland*, 3:637–39; Oldmixon, *History of England in the Reigns of William and Mary, Anne, and George I*, p. 216.

106. James Lowther to Sir John Lowther, 23 January 1701, Lonsdale MSS.

107. Ballard MSS. 6, fol. 42.

108. L'Hermitage, B.L. Add. MSS. 17,677 VV, fol. 177; Bonnet, B.L. Add. MSS. 30,000 E, fols. 63–63v, 66v–70v; C.J., 13:447, 524; Andrew Browning, ed., *English Historical Documents, 1660–1714*, p. 134.

109. Tallard, P.R.O., French Trans., 9/20 February 1701.

110. Klopp, *Der Fall des Hauses Stuart*, 9:194.

111. Ibid., p. 200; P.R.O., French Trans., 21 March/1 April, 2/13 April, and 15/26 April 1701; B.L. Add. MSS. 30,000 E, fols. 96–96v, 105v, 110v–12v, 120, 144, 156; B.L. Add. MSS. 17,677 WW, fols. 196, 201v, 223, 230v–31; Matthew Prior, *History of His Own Time*, 1:223; Aiken, *Conduct of the Earl of Nottingham*, p. 137.

112. C.J., 13:489; Sachse, *Somers*, pp. 176–79.

113. Bonnet, B.L. Add. MSS. 30,000 E, fol. 152; Poussin, P.R.O., French Trans., 15/26 and 19/30 May, 13/24 June 1701; Evelyn, *Diary*, 5:461, 462.

114. Tallard and Poussin, P.R.O., French Trans., 22 March/2 April 19/30 May 1701; Bonnet, B.L. Add. MSS. 30,000 E, fol. 203.

115. Bonnet, B.L. Add. MSS. 30,000 E, fols. 73v–74v, 157v.

116. Ibid., fols. 234, 350, 259; H.M.C., *Downshire*, 1:804.

117. Bonnet, B.L. Add. MSS. 30,000 E, fols. 176v, 199, 235; Poussin, P.R.O., French Trans., 15/26, 19/30 May, 13/24 June 1701.

118. Klopp, *Der Fall des Hauses Stuart*, 9:274.

119. Ellis to Stepney, 6 May 1701, B.L. Add. MSS. 7074, fol. 15.

120. Luttrell, *Brief Relation*, 5:30; Bonnet, B.L. Add. MSS. 30,000 E. fols. 108–108v; Hardwicke, *State Papers*, 2:441.

121. Bonnet, B.L. Add. MSS. 30,000 E., fol. 259; Poussin, P.R.O., French Trans., 12/23 June 1701. Godolphin frankly confessed to Nottingham "that the people are generally unsatisfied with the proceedings of the Parliament," and then suggested those steps that led to the 12 June address (N.R.O., Finch-Hatton MSS. 4053).

122. James, *Letters to Shrewsbury from James Vernon*, 3:56.

123. H.M.C., *Cowper*, 2:432, 434; Normanby to Nottingham, 4 and 16 September 1701, L.R.O., Finch MSS, Box 4950, Bundle 22.

124. Burnet, *History of His Own Time*, 4:531; Klopp, *Der Fall des Hauses Stuart*, 9:498.

125. H.M.C., *Downshire*, 1:810. See also L'Hermitage, B.L. Add. MSS. 17,677 WW, fols. 378–79, for Tory threats against the Whig leaders.

126. Hardwicke, *State Papers*, 2:448–50, 451–52; Sachse, *Somers*, pp. 212–13.

127. Sachse, *Somers*, pp. 453–55; Harley Memoirs, B.L. Add. MSS. 34,515, fol. 13v. Somers did not speak lightly of the elections. Through William Walsh he had taken soundings of the electoral situation in Worcestershire. Walsh wrote to Somers on 26 October 1701, "If other Countreys seem as well settled, I think a Dissolution were very much to [be] wished for" (Surrey Record Office, Somers MSS. 371/14/B20a).

128. John Toland, *The Art of Governing by Parties*, pp. 110–11; *Limitations for the Next Foreign Successor*, 3:384; *The Dangers of Europe from the Growing Power of France*, 3:365); *The Claims of the People of England*, 3:5–7); and *Lex Vera* (London, 1702), p. 14.

129. Bonnet, B.L. Add. MSS. 30,000 E, fols. 395–95v; H.M.C., *Downshire*, 1:811; Klopp, *Der Fall des Hauses Stuart*, 9:498.

130. Hardwicke, *State Papers*, 2:457–60.

131. Ibid., p. 457.

132. James Lowther to Sir John Lowther, 30 December 1701, Lonsdale MSS, where Lowther insists that had the Northern members arrived in time the Whigs would have had a majority.

133. The foreign envoys in London saw clearly that William's power depended on a balance of parties, a balance such that each must seek to win the support of the court: see Bonnet, quoted in Ranke, *History*, 5:285; Robethon, quoted in Baxter, *William III*, p. 395; and L'Hermitage, B.L. Add MSS. 17,677 XX, fol. 210v.

134. Horwitz, *Revolution Politicks*, p. 164.

135. Klopp, *Der Fall des Hauses Staurt*, 9:503–4; Forster, *Original Letters*, pp. 174–75; L'Hermitage, B.L. Add. MSS. 17,677 XX, fols. 234–236v.

CHAPTER SEVEN

1. Geoffrey Holmes, *British Politics in the Age of Anne*, pp. 193–94; Keith Feiling, *History of England*, p. 598. Though I can agree with Edward Gregg that Queen Anne was more willful and had a clearer understanding than Holmes and Feiling suggest, I cannot agree that the Queen dominated the age and that she was not subject to the persuasion of favorites, as he suggests. See Edward Gregg, *Queen Anne*, pp. viii, 134–37.

2. W. A. Speck has shown that of 1,064 members of Parliament in Queen Anne's reign, 439 can be labeled as consistent Whigs, 495 consistent Tories, and only 130 waverers (of whom 59 were Tories who lapsed only once). Thus there were only 71 members who cannot "be identified as Tories or Whigs" (*Whig and Tory*, pp. 111–12).

3. Luttrell, *Brief Relation*, 5:152, 154, 164, 169, 170.

4. Burnet, *History of His Own Time*, 5:10.

5. Speck, *Whig and Tory*, p. 113.

6. Holmes, *Politics in the Age of Anne*, pp. 367–68.

7. H.M.C., *Portland*, 4:40, 42; B.L. Add. MSS. 29,588, fol. 83.

8. B.R.O., Trumbull Add. MSS. 133/5/1.

9. Cobbett, *Parliamentary History*, 6:25; Holmes, *Politics in the Age of Anne*, pp. 25, 461 n, 63; Speck, *Whig and Tory*, p. 28.

10. Lionel Gassey suggests that changes in the commissions of the peace did convince voters that the High Churchmen were all-powerful at court, and thereby helped them in the 1702 election (*Politics and the Appointment of Justices of the Peace*, pp. 148–49).

11. Luttrell, *Brief Relation*, 5:234, 241, 250, 272, 367, 372.

12. Ibid., 5:237–38, 265, 371, 403, 405–7.

13. There is a note in B.L. Loan 29/9/13, "Febr. 24: 1704/5," possibly by Robert Harley, that reads, "The Commons can by one sullen fit [at] the beginning of a session ruin any ministry. They can certainly draw the Lords after them, which the Lords cannot do the others. Lords the Court can make when they please, not the Commons."

14. William Coxe, *Memoirs of John Duke of Marlborough*, 1:207; H.M.C., *Portland*, 4:69.

15. Holmes, *Politics in the Age of Anne*, p. 415.

16. For Godolphin's and Harley's day-to-day management of Parliament, see B.L. Add. MSS. 28,055, fols. 3, 354; H.M.C., *Portland*, 4:47, 50–57, 65, 75; B.L. Loan 29/64/1, 2, 3, 4, 5, 8, 10, 11, 17; Henry Snyder, "Godolphin and Harley: A Study of Their Partnership in Politics."

17. Luttrell, *Brief Relation*, 5:237, 243, 261–62, 400, 401–2; Klopp, *Der Fall des Hauses Stuart*, 10:235–36; Cobbett, *Parliamentary History*, 6:49.

18. Thomas Jonson, a moderate Churchman, asserted that not religion but preferment to offices of profit was the concern of those who favored the bill (Thomas Heywood, ed., *The Norris Papers*, p. 108).

19. The best account of Rochester's and Nottingham's resignations is to be found in Horwitz, *Revolution Politicks*, pp. 187–88, 190–98. For the discontent of the High Church party, see Francis Atterbury, *The Epistolary Correspondence, Visitation Charges, Speeches, and Miscellanies of the Right Reverend Francis Atterbury, D.D., Lord Bishop of Rochester*, 3:158–59; 4:359–62, 366–69, 373–74, 381.

20. Lansdowne MSS. 773, fol. 29v.

21. Ibid., fol. 27v.

22. H.M.C., *Portland*, 4:147.

23. Patricia Ansell, "Harley's Parliamentary Management"; W. A. Speck, "The House of Commons, 1702–1714: A Study in Political Organization," p. 131; Henry Snyder, "Defeat of the Occasional Conformity Bill and the Tack."

24. H.M.C., *Portland*, 4:148; Trumbull Add. MSS. 133/29/3.

25. Burnet, *History of His Own Time*, 5:179; H.M.C., *Portland*, 4:148.

26. George Baillie, *Correspondence of George Baillie of Jerviswood*, p. 12.

27. Burnet, *History of His Own Time*, 5:179.

28. L'Hermitage, B.L. Add. MSS. 17,677 ZZ, fols. 521, 531v–532.

29. Bishop Nicolson's Diary, 10 December 1704.

30. George Baillie, *Correspondence*, p. 26.

31. Abel Boyer, *The History of the Life and Reign of Queen Anne*, p. 177. For Harley's negotiations with Newcastle, see H.M.C., *Portland*, 4:59, 185–87, 188, 189.

32. Klopp, *Der Fall des Hauses Staurt*, 11:355. For the seven tackers removed, see Snyder, "Defeat of the Occasional Conformity Bill," p. 186.

33. H.M.C., *Portland*, 4:176, 189; H.M.C., *Bath*, 1:69; Burnet, *History of His Own Time*, 5:218–19; L'Hermitage, B.L. Add. MSS. 17,677 AAA, fols. 248–48v, 299–99v, 304, 310–11, 322–23; Speck, *Whig and Tory*, pp. 106–8; Glassey, *Politics and the Appointment of Justices of the Peace*, pp. 166–68.

34. H.M.C., *Portland*, 4:223.

35. Ralph Bridges to Trumbull, Trumbull Add. MSS. 98, 27 June 1705.

36. Winston Churchill, *Marlborough*, 2:29.

37. H.M.C., *Bath*, 1:74–75.

38. George Baillie, *Correspondence*, p. 114.

39. Coxe, *Marlborough*, 1:484.

40. William Cowper, *The Private Diary of William First Earl Cowper*, p. 2. From Vienna, Sunderland wrote to congratulate Cowper: "I own I have expected this news with a great deal of impatience ever since I left England, and after this, I can't doubt but that everything will be done to the satisfaction of all honest men that wish well to their country" (Panshanger MSS. D/EP/F 56, fol. 96).

41. Japikse, *Correspondentie*, 2:564.

42. Dyer's News Letter, B.L. Loan 29/192, fol. 103; H.M.C., *Bath*, 1:74; B.L. Add. MSS. 28,055, fol. 316; Panshanger MSS. D/EP/F 55, fols. 115v, 118, and F 56, fols. 83–85.

43. For the careful management that led to this victory, see W. A. Speck's illuminating study, "The Choice of a Speaker in 1705."

44. L'Hermitage, B.L. Add. MSS. 17,677 AAA, fols. 513v, 532v, 538, 571–72v, 578–79, and BBB, fols. 28–29, 130; Abel Boyer, *The History of the Reign of Queen Anne, digested into Annals*, 4:191, 195–99, 203–10, 212–13.

45. B. Van Hoff, ed., *The Correspondence of John Churchill, First Duke of Marlborough, and Anthony Heinsius*, (The Hague, 1951), p. 230.

46. H.M.C., *Portland*, 4:291.

47. Luttrell, *Brief Relation*, 6:5, 8–9, 11–14, 16–18; L'Hermitage, B.L. Add. MSS. 17,677 BBB, fols. 49–50, 70v, 81–82, 86–88, 103v, 117, 122v–25; Godolphin to Harley, B.L. Loan 29/64/3.

48. Cropley to Shaftesbury, P.R.O. 30/24/20, 114 (3).

49. C.U.L., Add. MSS. 7093, fols. 74–75.

50. Cowper, *Diary*, p. 12.

51. Ibid., p. 19.

52. G. V. Bennett, "Robert Harley, the Godolphin Ministry and the Bishopric Crisis of 1707," pp. 730–32.

53. Ralph Bridges to Trumbull, 12 October 1705, Trumbull Add. MSS. 98.

54. Beatrice Brown, ed., *The Letters and Diplomatic Instructions of Queen Anne*, pp. 196–97, 199–200; Churchill, *Marlborough*, 2:203–5.

55. Thomas Somerville, *The History of Great Britain During the Reign of Queen Anne*, pp. 623–24; undated memorandum, B.L. Loan 29/10/4; Harley to Paulet, 21 September, B.L. Loan 29/143/7; Memorandums for 22 September and 25 September, B.L. Loan 29/9/38; H.M.C., *Bath*, 1:110; Coxe, *Marlborough*, 2:160–62.

56. H.M.C., *Portland*, 4:291.

57. B.L. Add. MSS. 56,105 L, 13 September 1706.

58. Coxe, *Marlborough*, 2:157.

59. Somerville, *Reign of Queen Anne*, p. 622.

60. Sarah Churchill, Duchess of Marlborough, *Private Correspondence of Sarah, Duchess of Marlborough* (London, 1838), 1:30–31.

61. Coxe, *Marlborough*, 2:139.

62. Churchill, *Marlborough*, 2:208.

63. Ibid., pp. 202, 207–10.

64. Herr Hoffmann, the imperial resident, declared that the Whigs remained silent because they were angry that Godolphin enjoyed their support but would not declare fully for them (Klopp, *Der Fall des Hauses Stuart*, 12:264–65).

65. William Carstares, *State Papers and Letters Addressed to William Carstares*, p. 759.

66. Somerset to unknown recipient, 12 February 1707, Stanhope MSS. 34/12.

67. Dr. Delane to Dr. Charlett, Ballard MSS. XXI, fol. 182; C.E. Doble, ed., *Remarks and Collections of Thomas Hearne*, 2:5; Luttrell, *Brief Relation*, 6:159.

68. Boyer, *Annals of Queen Anne*, 6:221–22.

69. Churchill, *Marlborough*, 2:280.

70. Wake MSS. 17, letter 174. Gilbert Burnet, who was at the Althorp meeting, wrote to Tenison: "I find our friends are so much out of humour, that I am afraid it may have ill effects." Lord Cowper agreed that the ordinary Whig was more extreme than his leaders. He wrote shortly before or on 8 September 1707: "As to 1st: Bishops—the Whig p[arty] would be ungovernable though their leaders should be satisfyed. They [the Whig leaders] could but loos[e] their Credit &c." (B.L. Add. MSS. 4292, fol. 46, quoted in Henry Snyder, "The Formulation of Foreign and Domestic Policy in the Reign of Queen Anne," p. 158).

71. H.M.C., *Portland*, 2:200–201.

72. James MacPherson, ed., *Original Papers Containing the Secret History of Great Britain from the Restoration to the Accession of the House of Hanover*, 2:378.

73. Boyer, *Annals of Queen Anne*, 6:252–57.

74. Joseph Addison, *The Letters of Joseph Addison*, ed. Walter Graham, pp. 79–80; Klopp, *Der Fall des Hauses Stuart*, 13:3.

75. H.M.C., *Portland*, 4:74–75.

76. Boyer, *Annals of Queen Anne*, 6:256–57; James, *Letters to Shrewsbury from James Vernon*, 3:292–93.

77. James, *Letters to Shrewsbury from James Vernon*, 3:300–301; H.M.C., *Egmont*, 2:219–21.

78. Speck, "The House of Commons," p. 161; Cropley to Shaftesbury, 11 December 1707, P.R.O., 30/24/20, 140.

79. So Sir John Cropley believed: see Cropley to Shaftesbury, 11 December 1707, P.R.O. 30/24/20, 140.

80. Godfrey Davies, "The Seamy Side of Marlborough's War," p. 39.

81. Burnet, *History of His Own Time*, 5:330–31; Cropley to Shaftesbury, 15 December 1707, P.R.O. 30/24/20, 136; Bennet, "Harley and the Bishopric Crisis," pp. 745–46.

82. H.M.C., *Lonsdale*, p. 118; James, *Letters to Shrewsbury from James Vernon*, 3:288–89, 291–92; Addison, *Letters*, p. 88; Cropley to Shaftesbury, 4 February 1708, P.R.O. 30/24/20 145 (1).

83. Manchester, *Court and Society*, 2:275–76; Nicholson's Diary, fols. 91–92; Luttrell, *Brief Relation*, 6:264–65.

84. Manchester, *Court and Society*, p. 273; James, *Letters to Shrewsbury from James Vernon*, 3:309–11.

85. James, *Letters to Shrewsbury from James Vernon*, 3:328–30; Burnet, *History of His Own Time*, 5:338; Luttrell, *Brief Relation*, 6:262.

86. Coxe, *Marlborough*, 2:364.

87. Brydges to Cadogan, 18 October 1708, Brydges Papers 57, Vol. 1, fol. 248; H.M.C., *Downshire*, 1:854.

88. Cropley to Shaftesbury, 15 December 1707, P.R.O. 30/24/20, 136.

89. Brydges to Cadogan, 24 December 1707, Brydges Papers 57, vol. 2, fol. 6. The Queen told Archbishop Sharp that she meant "to give no countenance to the Whig lords, but that all the Tories, if they would, should come in, and all the Whigs likewise that would show themselves to be in her interests, should have favour" (Thomas Sharp, *The Life of John Sharp, D.D., Lord Archbishop of York*, 1:323).

90. H.M.C., *Portland*, 4:448; Burnet, *History of His Own Time*, 5:330; Speck, "House of Commons," pp. 181–82, 185–87.

91. Cropley to Shaftesbury, 15 and 30 December 1707, P.R.O. 30/24/20, 136 and 141 (1).

92. Molesworth to Shaftesbury, 18 December 1707, P.R.O. 30/24/20, 137.

93. Jonathan Swift, *The Correspondence of Jonathan Swift*, ed. F. E. Ball, 1:73.

94. Henry Snyder, ed., *The Marlborough-Godolphin Correspondence*, 2:916–17, 931–32.

95. B.L. Loan 29/237, fol. 193. H.M.C., *Portland*, 2:200 (which prints part of the letter and misdates it; for the correct dating, see Henry Snyder, "Godolphin and Harley," p. 265).

96. Swift, *Correspondence*, 1:76.

97. There was remarkable agreement among observers, whether Whig, Tory, or neutral, on the offices to be bestowed: see Addison, *Letters*, pp. 91–92, 94–95; L'Hermitage, B.L. Add. MSS. 17,677 CCC, fols. 321v–22; Coningsby, "History of Parties," p. 8; and B.L. Add. MSS. 22,217, fol. 6, where Lord Strafford confirms that Poulett was to be secretary of state. Though he named no names, James Lowther observed: "You will hear by this post of great alterations at Court. Harley and his friends had laid a deep design to rout all the Whigs and turn them all out, not excepting the great Ministers for supporting them" (Lonsdale MSS, Lowther to Gilpin, 12 February 1707[8]). In June, James Craggs referred to "the late Ministers of the new Scheme" (Craggs to Stanhope, 1 June 1708, Stanhope MSS 34/5).

98. Sir John Cropley wrote on 4 February 1708, "Harley has at last secured a good reception with the Torys" (P.R.O. 30/24/21, 145, 1).

99. For the story of Harley's fall, see W. A. Speck and Geoffrey Holmes, "The Fall of Harley in 1708 Reconsidered," an exhaustive and incisive study, which is, however, usefully corrected on several points by Henry Snyder, "Godolphin and Harley."

Notes

100. Somers to Portland, Portland Papers, PwA 1188; Japikse, *Correspondentie*, 2:567; Cropley to Shaftesbury, 19 February 1708, P.R.O. 30/24/21, 148 (2).

101. Cropley to Shaftesbury, 19 February 1708, P.R.O. 30/24/21, 148 (2); James, *Letters to Shrewsbury from James Vernon*, 3:357–58, 360; Luttrell, *Brief Relation*, 6:273.

102. Japikse, *Correspondentie*, 2:567; Addison, *Letters*, pp. 91–92.

103. Addison, *Letters*, p. 94; L'Hermitage, B.L. Add. MSS. 17,677 CCC, fols. 322–23v; James, *Letters to Shrewsbury from James Vernon*, 3:355–56. All but two of the Country Whigs deserted Peter King on this occasion and followed the Junto (Addison, *Letters*, p. 94).

104. Addison, *Letters*, pp. 94–95.

105. Speck, "House of Commons, 1702–1714", pp. 220–23.

106. Cropley to Shaftesbury, 19 February 1708, P.R.O. 30/24/21, 148 (2); Addison, *Letters*, pp. 100, 110.

107. Brown, *Letters of Queen Anne*, p. 246.

108. Snyder, *Marlborough-Godolphin Correspondence*, 2:969.

109. Ibid.; Sarah Churchill, *Private Correspondence*, 1:121. Erasmus Lewis wrote Robert Harley, "The notion of extinguishing the names of Whig and Tory and assuming the distinction of Court and Country party, which the great men were once themselves fond of, seems now to be taken up by their adversaries" (22 May 1708, H.M.C., *Portland*, 4:490).

110. Craggs to Stanhope, 1 June 1708, Stanhope MSS. 34/5.

111. Speck, *Whig and Tory*, p. 113.

112. Cropley to Shaftesbury, P.R.O. 30/24/21, fol. 52.

113. Speck, "House of Commons", p. 22. Halifax wrote Montrose on 28 October 1708, "From the time we broke with the Ministers, about the Council in North Britain, it was very visible they would carry things with a high hand, and by encouraging their own creatures, and discountenancing others, try to obtain the majority of the ensuing elections by that influence, though they had lost the authority of the Council" (Auchmar MSS. GD 220/5).

114. Coxe, *Marlborough*, 2:424. For an example of Whig propaganda, see [Arthur Maynwaring,] *Advice to the Electors of Great Britain, Occasioned by the Intended Invasion from France*, pp. 1–4. Henry Snyder has identified Arthur Maynwaring as the author of this anonymous pamphlet ("Daniel Defoe, the Duchess of Marlborough, and the *Advice to the Electors of Great Britain*," *H.L.Q.*, 29 [1965–66]:53–62.

115. For these various efforts, see Sarah Churchill, *Private Correspondence*, 1:142–43; Coxe, *Marlborough*, 2:518; Speck "House of Commons", p. 237; Somerset to Stanhope, 24 June 1708, Stanhope MSS. 34/12; Maynwaring to Duchess of Marlborough, Blenheim MSS. e 25; George Baillie, *Correspondence*, p. 194; Earls of Marchmont, *A Selection from the Papers of the Earls of Marchmont*, 3:335.

116. Earls of Marchmont, *A Selection from the Papers of the Earls of Marchmont*, p. 331; George Baillie, *Correspondence*, pp. 193–95; H.M.C., *Eighth Report*, p. 42.

117. Nathaniel Hooke to Torcy, P.R.O. 31/3/195, 23 July 1708.

118. Quoted in Holmes, *Politics in the Age of Anne*, p. 238.

119. Halifax to Marlborough, 6/17 July 1708, Blenheim MSS. B. 1–7.

120. Churchill, *Marlborough*, 2:474.

121. Hooke to Torcy, 23 July 1708, P.R.O. 31/3/195.

122. Hardwicke MSS. 33, fols. 125–26; Rare Books and Manuscripts Division, The New York Public Library, Astor, Lenox and Tilden Foundations.

123. Sunderland to Newcastle, 19 October 1708, in G. M. Trevelyan, *England under Queen Anne*, 2:414–15.

124. Sunderland to Montrose, 26 October 1708, Auchmar MSS. G D 220/5.

125. Lansdowne MSS. 1236, fol. 249.

126. Sunderland to Newcastle, 4 November 1708, in Trevelyan, *England under Queen Anne*, 2:416.

127. Craggs to Erle, 5 November 1708, Erle MSS. 2/12, fol. 23v.

128. Burnet, *History of His Own Time*, 5:383–85; Sarah Churchill, *Private Correspondence*, 1:158; Boyer, *Annals of Queen Anne*, 8:271, 276; H.M.C., *Downshire*, 1:869.

129. L'Hermitage, B.L. Add. MSS. 17,677 DDD, fols. 91–92; James Cartwright, ed., *The Wentworth Papers*, pp. 77–78; Klopp, *Der Fall des Hauses Stuart*, 13:207.

130. L'Hermitage, B.L. Add. MSS. 17,677 CCC, fol. 685; J. H. Plumb depicts this as a major defeat for the government (*Sir Robert Walpole: The Making of a Statesman*, 1:143); but it did not seem so to Henry Newton, who wrote to Joseph Addison, "The house was in debate upon the recruits when the cannon were firing for the capitulation of Ghent, and therefore went very cheerfully into the measure for raising recruits proposed by the Court and modified by Sir Peter King and some others" (Addison, *Letters*, p. 124).

131. Quoted in Horwitz, *Revolution Politicks*, p. 217.

132. Bishop Nicolson's Diary, 10 December 1704.

133. So reported James Craggs to Marlborough, as quoted in Henry Snyder, "Queen Anne versus the Junto" p. 330.

134. Ibid., pp. 331–39.

CHAPTER EIGHT

1. B.L. Loan 29/237, fol. 193.

2. Stratford to Harley, 8 August and 8 October 1708, B.L. Loan 29/158/7; Harley to Stratford, 20 August and 10 October 1708, B.L. Loan 29/171/2; Bromley to Harley, 12 October 1708, B.L. Loan 29/127.

3. L'Hermitage, B.L. Add. MSS. 17,677 DDD, fols. 30v–31v.

4. Bromley to Harley, 20 August 1709, B.L. Loan 29/128/3.

5. H.M.C., *Bath*, 1:191–92.

6. H.M.C., *Portland*, 4:504–5.

7. Notes by Harley, 3 May 1708, 3 April 1708, 10 April 1710, and 21 May 1710, in B.L. Loan 29/10/20, 29/10/21, 29/10/22.

8. H.M.C., *Bath*, 1:191, 195, 196; Rivers to Harley, 15 July 1708, B.L. Loan 29/156/3. Godolphin in July 1709 reported that Harley was busy strengthening his party, spreading insinuations against himself and Marlborough, and negotiating with Shrewsbury, who had recently been with the Queen (Snyder, *Marlborough-Godolphin Correspondence*, 3:1327–28).

Notes

9. H.M.C., *Portland*, 2:205; Coxe, *Marlborough*, 3:133–34.

10. Sarah Churchill, *Private Correspondence*, 1:208–10; H.M.C., *Portland*, 4:7, 538. An illuminating account of Harley's activities in winning over the Whig lords may be found in Angus McInnes, *Robert Harley: Puritan Politician*, pp. 117–19.

11. B.L. Add. MSS. 35,853, fol. 25v; Holmes, *Politics in the Age of Anne*, p. 207.

12. H.M.C., *Portland*, 4:486, 495, 499, 510, 524–26, 532, 536.

13. Klopp, *Der Fall des Hauses Stuart*, 13:421; Coxe, *Marlborough*, 3:134; Brydges Papers 57, vol. 3, fol. 204.

14. Jonathan Swift asserts that soon after Dr. Sacheverell's trial (which ended 20 March), Harley, by Mrs. Masham's intervention and the Queen's command, was brought up the back stairs (Jonathan Swift, "Some Considerations Upon the Consequences Hoped and Feared from the Death of the Queen," in *Prose Works*, 8:102).

15. H.M.C., *Portland*, 4:486, 496, 511, 524, 526, 636.

16. George Lockhart, *The Lockhart Papers*, 1:317.

17. John Cropley observed, "If this is all the ministry and Whigs can do against the Tories, I fear we shall be soon overpowered" (Cropley to Stanhope, 21 March 1710, Stanhope MSS. 34/16); see also Klopp, *Der Fall des Hauses Stuart*, 13:421.

18. Swift believed it was done pursuant to Harley's advice ("Memoirs of 1710," *Prose Works*, 8:117).

19. Coxe, *Marlborough*, 3:142–53; Holmes, *British Politics*, pp. 210–13.

20. H.M.C., *Portland*, 4:535, 536.

21. Ibid., p. 537.

22. Cropley to Stanhope, 23 April 1710, Stanhope MSS. 34/16.

23. Sarah Churchill, *Private Correspondence*, 1:301.

24. Cropley to Stanhope, 23 April 1710, Stanhope MSS. 34/16.

25. Plumb, *Walpole*, 1:158; Cartwright, *Wentworth Papers*, p. 112.

26. Cropley to Stanhope, 23 April 1710, Stanhope MSS. 34/16.

27. Philip Roberts, ed., *The Diary of Sir David Hamilton 1709–1714*, p. 8.

28. H.M.C., *Portland*, 4:542–43.

29. Brydges to Drummond, Brydges Papers 57, vol. 3, fol. 270.

30. H.M.C., *Portland*, 4:542–43.

31. "May 30: 1710 Memdm," B.L. Loan 29/10/19.

32. Burnet, *History of His Own Time*, 6:7n.

33. Godfrey Davies and Clara Buck, "Letters on Godolphin's Dismissal in 1710," p. 240.

34. Burnet, *History of His Own Time*, 6:7n; Snyder, *Marlborough-Godolphin Correspondence*, 3:1508–13; H.M.C., *Portland*, 2:210. Coningsby confirms Dartmouth's observation that the scheme went no further than the removal of the Marlborough family, but he reports that Shrewsbury wished to ally with Godolphin and the moderates of both parties, and not with the Junto lords ("History of

Parties," p. 16). It is quite likely that Shrewsbury sought to work with Godolphin but that Harley, as Brydges reported, preferred not to.

35. L'Hermitage, B.L. Add. MSS. 17,677 DDD, fol. 524; Coxe, *Marlborough*, 3:232.

36. Coxe, *Marlborough*, 3:232, 238; Sarah Churchill, *Private Correspondence*, 1:320; Brydges Papers 57, vol. 3, fols. 274–75.

37. Coxe, *Marlborough*, 3:220; Snyder, *Marlborough-Godolphin Correspondence*, 3:1417.

38. Sarah Churchill, *Private Correspondence*, 1:318.

39. Churchill, *Marlborough*, 2:718.

40. Bromley to Grahme, 13 May 1710, Levens MSS; Sarah Churchill, *Private Correspondence*, 1:314.

41. Klopp, *Der Fall des Hauses Stuart*, 13:432.

42. B.L. Add. MSS. 31,143, fol. 486v.

43. Snyder, *Marlborough-Godolphin Correspondence*, 3:1553.

44. [Arthur Maynwaring,] *Four Letters to a Friend*, p. 22; for the attribution of this pamphlet to Maynwaring, see Henry Snyder, "The Last Days of Queen Anne: The Account of Sir John Evelyn Examined."

45. H.M.C., *Bath*, 3:437.

46. Cropley to Stanhope, 17 June 1710, Stanhope MSS. 34/16.

47. Davies and Buck, "Godolphin's Dismissal," pp. 230–31.

48. Boyer, *Annals of Queen Anne*, 9:235.

49. Coxe, *Marlborough*, 3:248–50.

50. H.M.C., *Portland*, 4:545.

51. Davies and Buck, "Godolphin's Dismissal," pp. 231n, 232; Coxe, *Marlborough*, 3:257–59.

52. Lowther to Gilpin, 8 June 1710, Lonsdale MSS.

53. Klopp, *Der Fall des Hauses Stuart*, 13:437–38.

54. Halifax to Harley, B.L. Loan 29/151/9; Halifax to Newcastle, B.L. Loan 29/238, fol. 328; H.M.C., *Portland*, 2:211–12; Peter to Thomas Wentworth, B.L. Add. MSS. 31,143, fol. 508.

55. W. Jessop to Newcastle, 18 July 1710, Holles MSS.Pw 2/139.

56. H.M.C., *Portland*, 7:3, 5; L'Hermitage, B.L. Add. MSS. 17,677 DDD, fol. 548; Cartwright, *Wentworth Papers*, pp. 123, 128.

57. Cartwright, *Wentworth Papers*, p. 123. Halifax wrote Newcastle that the Whigs had promised to lay aside all heats and resentments, and that he was engaged to see that it was performed; but "the friends of our ministers grew jealous of these transactions" and "pushed to make a strike that might make a reconciliation impracticable" (H.M.C., *Portland*, 2:216). It is unlikely that Harley trusted these Whig promises.

58. Duchess of Marlborough to the Bishop of Sarum, Bodleian Add. MSS. A. 191, fol. 3v; Coxe, *Marlborough*, 3:272–74, 281; Churchill, *Marlborough*, 2:741; Grey to Neville, 1 August 1710, B.L. Loan 29/152/1.

59. H.M.C., *Portland*, 2:211.

60. H.M.C., *Bath*, 1:198.

Notes

61. Klopp, *Der Fall des Hauses Stuart*, 13:460; Davies and Buck, "Godolphin's Dismissal," p. 228.

62. For Godolphin's and Marlborough's awareness of Harley's malice, see Coxe, *Marlborough*, 3:206, 274; for Harley's belief that the Queen might rightly lay aside a favorite whose power had grown dangerously, see his memorandum of 10 July 1710, B.L. Loan 29/10/20.

63. Daniel Defoe, *The Secret History of the October Club, Part I*, p. 45.

64. Roberts, *Diary of Sir David Hamilton*, p. 15.

65. H.M.C., *Portland*, 2:217–18; Harley's Memoirs, B.L. Add. MSS. 34,515, fols. 139v–40; Godfrey Davies and Marion Tinling, "Correspondence of James Brydges and Robert Harley," p. 461; Dyer's News Letter, 26 August 1710, B.L. Loan 29/321.

66. H. T. Dickinson, ed., "The Letters of Henry St. John to the Earl of Orrery 1709–1711, p. 148; H.M.C., *Fourteenth Report*, App. 3, p. 210; Marlborough believed that such an offer to the elector was part of "the very foundation of Mr. Harley's scheme" (Snyder, *Marlborough-Godolphin Correspondence*, 3:1601). Henry Snyder believes that Lord Rivers did have oral instructions to make the offer, but that the elector rejected the feelers so decisively that Rivers did not press it ("Godolphin and Harley," p. 270).

67. Lowther to Gilpin, 8 August 1710, Lonsdale MSS.

68. Lady Roxburgh to Nottingham, Leicestershire R.O., Finch MSS, Box 4950, Bundle 23. Richard Onslow (Burnet, *History of His Own Time*, 6:11), Abel Boyer (*The Political State of Great Britain*, 1:2), and Daniel Defoe (*The Secret History of the October Club, Part I*, pp. 44–45) also declared that Harley in early August designed a mixed ministry or coalition.

69. Lowther to Gilpin, 10 August 1710, Lonsdale MSS; James to William Brydges, 2 September 1710, Brydges Papers 57, vol. 4, fol. 135; Harley to [Boyle?], 11 August 1710, Chatsworth MSS, 1st ser., 102.2; Cropley to Shaftesbury, [ca. 1 September 1710,] P.R.O. 30/24/21.

70. B.L. Loan 29/160/8.

71. H.M.C., *Portland*, 2:214.

72. Ibid., pp. 215–16.

73. Ibid., pp. 216–17.

74. Ibid., p. 219. L'Hermitage agreed with Harley, writing on 11 August 1710: "One is confirmed in the belief that Parliament will be dissolved by the fact that affairs would not be permitted to go on well in the present one" (B.L. Add. MSS. 17,677 DDD, fol. 572v). Defoe declared that "the endeavours to preserve the Parliament was with a design to overthrow and destroy the new Ministry (*Secret History of the White Staff*, 1:10).

75. L'Hermitage, B.L. Add. MSS. 17,677 DDD, fols. 551–52. James Brydges wrote that some believed that the animosity between the two parties had grown to such a height that the new Ministry would be given entirely to the Tories. "Of this sort is the Duke of Somerset who though entirely averse to the thoughts of keeping my late Lord Treasurer or the Duke of Marlborough is yet for the Ministry's declaring themselves upon a Whiggish bottom and measures, which not being judged by what I can understand practicable has so disgusted his Grace, that he is gone into the country" (Davies and Buck, "Letters on Godolphin's Dismissal," p. 235).

Notes

76. H.M.C., *Portland*, 4:551; Hutton to Charlett, Ballard MSS. 35, fol. 132; Cartwright, *Wentworth Papers*, p. 135.

77. H.M.C., *Portland*, 4:563, 7:6; Snyder, *Marlborough-Godolphin Correspondence*, 3:1597.

78. Harley's Memoirs, B.L. Add. MSS. 34,515, fols. 139–39v.

79. Monckton to Cowper, 28 August 1710, Panshanger MSS. D/EP F55, fol. 113.

80. Cartwright, *Wentworth Papers*, p. 135; Bromley to Grahme, 1 September 1710, Levens MSS; James to William Brydges, 2 September 1710, Brydges Papers 57, vol. 4, fol. 135.

81. Harley's Memorandum, "12 Sept. 1710," B.L. Loan 29/10/19; Bromley to Grahme, 1 and 11 September 1710, Levens MSS; Francis Atterbury, *The Epistolary Correspondence, Visitation Charges, Speeches, and Miscellanies of Atterbury*, 1:26; Burnet, *History of His Own Time*, 6:12.

82. Harley's Memorandum, "12 Sept. 1710," B.L. Loan 29/10/19; Defoe, *Secret History of the October Club, Part I*, p. 45.

83. Lowther to Gilpin, 10 August 1710, Lonsdale MSS; Cartwright, *Wentworth Papers*, p. 131.

84. *The Private Diary of William First Earl Cowper, Lord Chancellor of England*, pp. 43–44.

85. Lord North and Grey wrote Nottingham, "This change is gone farther than they that laid the plan of it ever intended." (L.R.O., Finch MSS, Box 4950, Bundle 23, 9 October 1710).

86. H.M.C., *Portland*, 2:219.

87. Ibid., p. 219.

88. B.L. Loan 29/10/19.

89. Clement, *Faults on Both Sides*, in *Somers Tracts*, 12:695–700. Simon Clement probably wrote it at Harley's direction (Burnet, *History of His Own Time*, 6:12).

90. Swift, *Correspondence*, 1:207–8; Abel Boyer declared that the court sought only "such a majority of the High Church in the House of Commons, as might countenance the New Scheme" (*Annals of Queen Anne*, 9:248).

91. Speck, *Whig and Tory*, pp. 85–87, 96–97, 113, 123.

92. The words are John Kaye's; see Kaye's Diary, 29 January 1711, Staffordshire R.O., D (W) 1778/V/200, pp. 1–2.

93. In a disputed election return, see William Bishop to Dr. Charlett, 22 January 1711, Ballard MSS. 31, fol. 89.

94. The Commons brought all these complaints together in an address that they presented to the Queen on 4 June (Cobbett, *Parliamentary History*, 6:1026–31).

95. L.R.O., Finch MSS, Political Papers 150; Burnet, *History of His Own Time*, 6:37.

96. B.L. Loan 29/11/9.

97. Lord Balmerino to Henry Maule, 26 January 1711, S.R.O., Dalhousie MSS. GD 45/14/352.

Notes

98. Klopp, *Der Fall des Hauses Stuart*, 13:486; Horwitz, *Revolution Politicks*, pp. 226–27.

99. *C.J.*, 16:684.

100. Cartwright, *Wentworth Papers*, p. 180; Holmes, *Politics in the Age of Anne*, p. 343; Swift, "Memoirs of 1710," *Works*, 8:125–26. Sir Arthur Kaye's words are quoted in Horwitz, *Revolution Politicks*, 224.

101. Horwitz, *Revolution Politicks*, pp. 225–26.

102. Cartwright, *Wentworth Papers*, pp. 189–90; Kaye's Diary, 26 March 1711, Staffordshire R.O., D (W) 1778/V/200, fol. 3; Luttrell, *Brief Relation*, 6:707.

103. H.M.C., *Portland*, 4:683–84.

104. Brydges Papers 57, vol. 5, fol. 134.

105. Boyer, *Annals*, 10:225–27; Swift, *Correspondence*, 1:278. The Duke of Shrewsbury remained as lord chamberlain, but he was hardly a Whig any longer and he was not, because of his timidity, informed of hazardous enterprises.

106. Brydges Papers 57, vol. 5, fol. 134.

107. Holmes, *Politics in the Age of Anne*, pp. 310–11.

108. George Baillie to Montrose, 4 December 1711, Auchmar MSS. G D 220/5; H.M.C., *Portland*, 5:116; George Lockhart, *The Lockhart Papers*, 1:366; Cartwright, *Wentworth Papers*, pp. 216–17.

109. Holmes, *Politics in the Age of Anne*, pp. 400–401.

110. H.M.C., *Portland*, 5:120, 125.

111. Swift, "Enquiry into the Behaviour of the Queen's Last Ministry," *Works*, 8:147.

112. Roberts, *Diary of Hamilton*, p. 29.

113. Kinnoul to Oxford, 16 November 1711, Dupplin to Oxford, 23 November 1711. Annandale to Oxford, 27 November 1711, Kinnoul to unknown recipient, 3 December 1711, B.L. Loan 29/198; McInnes, *Harley*, pp. 140–43; Ralph Bridges to Trumbull, 5 and 14 December 1711, Trumbull Add. MSS. 136/1 and 136/3.

114. Cartwright, *Wentworth Papers*, p. 224; Holmes, *Politics in the Age of Anne*, p. 387. Abel Boyer describes the failure of the court to win over lords by preferment and closeting (*Annals of Queen Anne*, 10:281).

115. Burnet, *History*, 6:87; Boyer, *The Political State of Great Britain*, 3:417–18; *Annals of Queen Anne*, 11:121.

116. Boyer, *Annals of Queen Anne*, 10:315; *The Works of the Right Hon. Henry St. John Lord Viscount Bolingbroke*, 1:332; H.M.C., *Portland*, 3:417–18; Boyer, *Annals of Queen Anne*, 11:121.

117. H.M.C., *Portland*, 5:167.

118. Strafford, to whom St. John had written on 12 December the good news of a promised change at court, made these remarks in February 1712 (James Macpherson, *Original Papers; Containing the Secret History of Great Britain from the Restoration to the Accession of the House of Hanover*, 2:350).

119. H.M.C., *Portland*, 5:209; Anonymous, 28 October 1712, B.L. Loan 29/11/1; *Lockhart Papers*, 1:411–13.

120. *Examiner*, vol. 3, no. 15, for 12 January 1713.

121. Defoe, *The Secret History of the White Staff, Part I*, pp. 22–25.

Notes

122. Ibid., pp. 25–27; *Lockhart Papers*, 1:412–13; H.M.C., *Portland*, 5:271; Cartwright, *Wentworth Papers*, p. 324; Bishop Nicholson's Diary, 16 March 1713.

123. Ralph Bridges to Trumbull, 9 June 1713, Trumbull Add. MSS. 136/1.

124. *Lockhart Papers*, 1:413–14.

125. Harley's Memoirs, B.L. Add. MSS. 34,515, fol. 162.

126. Ballard MSS. 31, fol. 104v.

127. Justinian Isham to Sir Justinian Isham, 23 June 1713, N.R.O., Isham Correspondence 2325; Speck, "House of Commons," p. 79. William Bishop reported that half the Scottish members voted against the bill out of anger at the malt bill, which would mean more than twenty members; he believed that Hanmer may have carried forty members (Ballard MSS. 31, fols. 104, 105v). Speck declares that thirty-five of the nearly eighty Tories who voted against the bill were "Whimsicals," that is, regular opponents of the government ("House of Commons," p. 79).

128. Jonathan Swift, *The Letters of Jonathan Swift to Charles Ford*, ed. David Nichol Smith, p. 13. The Tory journalist William Pittis declared that they deserted "by reason of the great body of Traders that appeared against the Bill" (*The History of the Third Session of the Last Parliament*, p. 128).

129. Swift, *Correspondence*, 2:47–48; Bateman to Trumbull, 19 June 1713, Trumbull MSS. Alph. LI. Bolingbroke declared, "The Court were willing to have dropped the Bill, rather than to have made a breach among our friends; but the body of Tories absolutely refused to part with it" (*Works*, 2:425).

130. Ballard MSS. 31, fol. 104.

131. Swift, *Correspondence*, 2:47.

132. Macpherson, *Original Papers*, 2:419–20. Defoe asserted that the vote on the Treaty of Commerce was less a dispute about trade than "an arrow shot at the present administration" (Daniel Defoe, *The Letters of Daniel Defoe*, ed. George Harris Healey, pp. 418–19).

133. Boyer, *Political State of Great Britain*, 6:163–64; Brydges to Marlborough, 18 August 1713, Brydges Papers 57, vol. 9, fols. 168–69.

134. George Lockhart wrote, "Everybody now expected that my Lord Oxford, even for his own sake, would perform what he had so frequently and solemnly undertaken; but his Lordship jogged on in the old way, nothing being done to encourage and strengthen those by whom the Ministry had been hitherto supported, and without whom they were not in a condition to stand their ground" (*Lockhart Papers*, 1:438). For Bolingbroke's scheming in late July and early August, see Holmes, "Harley and St. John," *Britain after the Glorious Revolution*, pp. 225–56.

135. Boyer, *History of the Life and Reign of Queen Anne*, p. 515.

136. Speck, *Whig and Tory*, p. 113. The Earl of Oxford in March 1714 estimated that there were 240 Tories and 151 Whigs in the House, and that there were fifty-odd persons dependent upon the court (B.L. Loan 29/10, "19 March").

137. *Examiner*, vol. 5, no. 11 (4 January 1714); St. John, *Works*, 2:611–12, 624; H.M.C., *Portland*, 5:373, 7:188; "May 14, 1714," B.L. Loan 29/10/8; "May 23, 1714," B.L. Loan 29/10/19.

138. Among such pleas, see the letters of Warrington to Oxford, B.L. Loan 29/127/1; Sussex to Oxford, B.L. Loan 29/155/6; Lansdowne to Oxford, B.L. Loan

Notes

29/311/3; Paget to Oxford, B.L. Loan 29/153/1; and Herbert to Oxford, B.L. Loan 29/146/6.

139. Harcourt to Oxford, 16 March 1714, B.L. Loan 29/138/5.

140. St. John, *Works*, 2:625–66.

141. Macpherson, *Original Papers*, 2:585. Plunkett, a Jacobite agent, wrote to Sir William Ellis on 7 October 1713, "[Mr. Netterville] tells me, the House of Commons will let no prime minister govern for the future, but manage the main point, and make the Crown dependent on them" (ibid., p. 440).

142. Memorandum, 26 March 1713/14, B.L. Loan 29/138/5.

143. 29 March 1713/14, B.L. Loan 29/138/5.

144. Swift, "Enquiry into the Behaviour of the Queen's Last Ministry", *Works*, 8:154–55.

145. H.M.C., *Portland*, 5:405.

146. Ibid., p. 404.

147. She dismissed John Aislabie from the Admiralty and Mr. Egerton, Mr. Sidney, and Mr. Holms from the Guards (Bromley to Strafford, 2 April 1714, B.L. Add. MSS. 31,139, fols. 78–78v). Bromley added that more changes were talked of among the military and civil employments. George Vernon wrote, "They are assured in the House of Commons that there will suddenly be many removes made of persons now in employment" (H.M.C., *Dartmouth*, 1:320).

148. A. N. Newman, ed., "Proceedings in the House of Commons, March–June 1714", p. 213.

149. Macpherson, *Original Papers*, 2:587–89.

150. Boyer, *Political State of Great Britain*, 7:313–15, 346–48.

151. Ralph Bridges to Trumbull, 23 April 1714, Trumbull MSS. Alph. LV.

152. *Lockhart Papers*, 1:462; "May 23, 1714," B.L. Loan 29/10/19.

153. John M. Kemble, ed., *State Papers Illustrative of the Social and Political State of Europe*, p. 495.

154. Klopp, *Der Fall des Hauses Stuart*, 14:605–6.

155. H.M.C., *Portland*, 8:189.

156. Cartwright, *Wentworth Papers*, p. 391. Later Peter Wentworth wrote, "It has been said that the Lord Treasurer has given out that if it had not been for him the Pretender had been here long ago and 'tis supposed of late he has been taken into grace and favour of the Whigs, and that he has promised them if they impeach Lord B——— he will not oppose them, and that underhand he has given them some matters to go upon" (ibid., p. 394).

157. [David Jones, ed.,] *The Works and Life of the Right Honourable Charles Late Earl of Halifax*, pp. 255–57; Klopp, *Der Fall des Hauses Stuart*, pp. 618–19.

158. Klopp, *Der Fall des Hauses Stuart*, pp. 616–18.

159. Ralph Bridges, 5 July 1714, Trumbull MSS. Alph. LV.

160. Swift, *Correspondence*, 2:190.

161. Macpherson, *Original Papers*, 2:635. Oxford himself held Bolingbroke's scheme in contempt, writing, "Nobody would join in their scheme. . . . They haven't any credit but what your [the Queen's] conduct gives them" ("June 8, 1714," B.L. Loan 29/10/8). Henry Snyder doubts that the Queen would have given the white staff to Bolingbroke ("The Last Days of Queen Anne,").

Notes

CONCLUSIONS

1. See above, p. 113.
2. See above, p. 174.
3. See above, p. 86.
4. See above, p. 143.
5. See above, p. 96.
6. See above, p. 28.
7. See above, p. 219.
8. See above, p. 192.
9. See above, p. 174.
10. See above, p. 219.
11. See above, p. 216.
12. See above, p. 200.

EPILOGUE

1. B. W. Hill, *The Growth of Political Parties 1689–1742*, p. 189. Linda Colley in her recent history of the Tory party, *In Defiance of Oligarchy: The Tory Party 1714–60*, likewise argues that the dichotomy of Whig and Tory remained important after 1714: "General election after general election [demonstrated] that throughout this period, one-party whig government had been superimposed on a two-party, predominantly tory, state" (p. 290).

2. John Owen, *The Eighteenth Century, 1714–1815*, p. 95.

3. John Brooke, *King George III*, pp. 179, 199, 211, 222, 224, 235, 253–54.

4. Richard Pares, *King George III and the Politicians*, pp. 93–142, and especially p. 109, where he concludes, "Ministries of politicians could not be formed without some negotiations."

5. For William Pitt's implication in the intrigues that led to the dismissal of the Fox-North coalition and his undertaking to serve the king, see John Cannon, *The Fox-North Coalition*, pp. 127–33, 145–47).

Selected Bibliography

MANUSCRIPTS

Althorp House, Northamptonshire (Earl Spencer)
    Halifax MSS   Letters to George Savile, first
                                     Marquis of Halifax
    Spencer House Letter Book   Transcriptions of letters to the
                                     Marquis of Halifax

Bedford Estate Office, London (Duke of Bedford)
    Bedford MSS VIII, XI, XXVIII   Papers of Francis Russell, fourth
                                     Earl of Bedford

Berkshire Record Office, Reading
    Trumbull MSS   Papers of Sir William Trumbull

Blenheim Palace, Woodstock (Duke of Marlborough)
    Blenheim MSS E 25   Marlborough Papers
    Blenheim MSS B 1–7   Godolphin Papers

Bodleian Library, Oxford
    Add. MSS. 191   Letters to Gilbert Burnet
    Ballard MSS
        10   Letters to Dr. Charlett from Eng-
                              lish noblemen, 1690–1720
        11   Letters to the Duke of Bucking-
                              ham, Dr. Charlett, and others
        12   Letters from Dr. George Hickes to
                              Dr. Charlett, 1684–1715
      20–24   Letters and papers on literary and
                              antiquarian subjects addressed
                              to Dr. Charlett, 1680–1721
      31–32   Letters from William Bishop to
                              Dr. Charlett
      33–36, 38   Letters and papers chiefly on lit-
                              erary subjects address to Dr.
                              Charlett, 1676–1722
      39   Letters addressed to Dr. Charlett,
                              1678–1711
    Carte MSS
      34–39   Correspondence and papers of the
                              first Duke of Ormonde
      47   Letters chiefly to the Duke of Or-
                              monde, 1652–83
      72   Newsletters, addressed to the first
                              Duke of Ormonde, 1660–85
     125   Correspondence and papers of the
                              Wharton family, 1603–1716

130 — Correspondence and papers of the Duke of Beaufort, including letters from Robert Price, 1688–99

220 — Correspondence and papers of the first Duke of Ormonde, including some of the Earl of Ossory's papers, 1664–1687

222 — Newsletters, 1662–84

228 — Miscellaneous papers relating to English history from 1625 to 1701, from the Wharton and Huntington collections

243 — Correspondence and papers of the first Duke of Ormonde, 1670–1681

Clarendon State Papers 80 — Papers of Edward Hyde, first Earl of Clarendon, July–December 1663

British Library, London
Additional Manuscripts
1467 (Sloane)
4160, f. 266v — Sir Thomas Lake to Salisbury
4292 — Letters collected by Thomas Birch
17,677 EE through SSS — Dispatches of the Dutch Ambassadors
18,777 — Journal of Walter Yonge, 1642–45
22,217 — Strafford Papers
27,962 I — Dispatches of Amerigo Salvetti, the Florentine agent
28,043 — Leeds-Godolphin Correspondence
28,053 — Leeds-Godolphin Correspondence
28,055 — Leeds-Godolphin Correspondence
29,572 — Hatton Correspondence
29,573 — Hatton Correspondence
29,577 — Hatton Correspondence
30,000 D and E — Dispatches of Friedrich Bonnet, the Prussian agent
31,139 — Wentworth Papers
31,143 — Wentworth Papers
32,023 B — Dispatches of the Piedmontese agent

32,518	Reflections of Francis North, Lord Keeper Guildford
32,519	Francis North's History of Faction and other observations
32,520	Papers of Francis North
33,923	Diary of Sir John Knatchbull
34,096	Sir William Colt Newsletters
34,504 fol. 130	William III to Heinsius
34,515	Edward Harley's Memoirs
34,730	Correspondence of the Mariett family of Alscot, in Gloucestershire
35,853	Hardwicke Papers, vol. DV, letters and papers relating to the Churchill family
36,916	John Starkey Newsletters
37,343	Bulstrode Whitelocke's Annals of His Own Time, 1643–1645
38,850	"The Alarum"
52,279	Sir William Trumbull's Diary
56,105 L	Queen Anne's letter to Lord Godolphin of 30 August 1706, with a draft of Godolphin's reply
Cottonian Manuscripts Titus F IV	Parliamentary Papers, *temp*. James I
Egerton Manuscripts 2539	Letters of John Nicholas
Harleian Manuscripts 163	The Parliamentary Diary of Sir Simonds D'Ewes
390	Newsletters from Joseph Meade to Sir Martin Stuteville
3364	Sir Edward Peyton's "A Discourse of Court and Courtiers"
3787 and 4289	Sir Henry Neville's Memorials
6810	"A Confutation of Two Paradoxes"
Lansdowne Manuscripts 32	Miscellaneous papers, among them a subsidy book of taxation of the Commons, 1581
486	Transcriptions from Titus F IV in the Cotton library
773	Letters from Charles D'Avenant to his son Henry, 1703–7

Bibliography

Manuscripts on Loan from the Duke of Portland

29/7	Draft of Speeches by Robert Harley
29/8	Newsletters
29/9	Privy Council Minutes, 1704–8
29/10 and 11	Memoranda by Robert Harley
29/46	News Sheets, Broadsides, Parliamentary Affairs
29/64, 65, 70	Letters to Auditor Harley
29/74 and 75	Letters to Sir Edward Harley
29/125 through 189	Letters to Robert Harley
29/192	Dyer's News Letter
29/198	Letters to Robert Harley, Earl of Oxford, from Scottish peers
29/237	Cavendish Papers, 1696–1707
29/238	Cavendish Papers, 1708–1716
29/309	Bolingbroke to Robert Harley
29/312	Musgrave and Harcourt to Harley
29/320 and 321	Dyer's News Letters for 1709 and 1710

Stowe Manuscripts

180	Collection of Miscellaneous Papers concerning state affairs in the seventeenth century, including papers relating to Sir Richard Temple
203	Papers relating to Arthur Capell, Earl of Essex, Vol. IV (Letters from Sir Joseph Williamson and Sir William Temple)
204	Essex Papers, Vol. V (Letters from Sir Joseph Williamson)
207	Essex Papers, Vol. VIII (Letters from Sir Charles Harbord and Sir William Temple)
208	Essex Papers, Vol. IX (Letters from Francis, Lord Aungier, Sir William Temple, and Sir Arthur Forbes)
326	Papers concerning the customs, by Sir John Harrison

Chatsworth House, Derbyshire (Duke of Devonshire)

Finch-Halifax Papers, A 26	Draft of a speech, probably by the second Earl of Nottingham
Chatsworth MSS, 1st series, 102.2	Robert Harley to [Henry Boyle], 11 August 1710

[302]

Bibliography

Christ Church, Oxford University
  Wake MSS

Papers of Archbishop William Wake

Churchill College, Cambridge University
  Erle MSS

Letters to Thomas Erle, *temp.* Queen Anne

Cumberland and Westmorland Record Office, Carlisle
  Lonsdale MSS

Letters of James Lowther to William Gilpin and to Sir John Lowther of Whitehaven

Dr. Williams Library, London
  Roger Morrice's Entring Book

Diary of a leading Nonconformist minister in the reigns of Charles II, James II, and William III

Folger Shakespeare Library, Washington, D.C.
  Newdigate Newsletters

Newsletters addressed to members of the Newdigate family of Arbury, Warwickshire, 1674–1715

Hertfordshire Record Office
  Panshanger MSS

Papers of the first Earl and Countess Cowper

Huntington Library, San Marino, California
  Stowe MSS
  Brydges Papers 57, vols. 2–9

Papers of Sir Richard Temple
Papers of James Brydges, first Duke of Chandos

Kent Record Office, Maidstone
  Stanhope of Chevening MSS

Correspondence of James, first Earl of Stanhope

Leicestershire Record Office, Leicester
  Finch MSS

Papers of Daniel Finch, second Earl of Nottingham

Levens Hall, near Kendal, Westmorland, (Mr. and Mrs. O. R. Bagot)
  Levens MSS

Letters of William Bromley to James Grahme

Longleat House, Warminster, Wiltshire (Marquis of Bath)
  Coventry Papers

Papers of Henry and William Coventry

  Thynne Papers

The Official and Private Correspondence of the Thynne family, 1542–1780

New York Public Library, New York
  Hardwicke MSS. XXXIII

Papers of John Lord Somers

Bibliography

Northamptonshire Record Office, Northampton
  Isham MSS   Letters of John Isham to Sir Justinian Isham
  Finch-Hatton MSS   Letterbooks and Papers, 1702–1716, of the Finch and Hatton Families

Nottingham, University of Nottingham Library
  Portland MSS   Correspondence of Hans Willem Bentinck, first Earl of Portland
  Holles MSS   Correspondence of John Holles, first Duke of Newcastle

Public Record Office, London
  State Papers Domestic
    14/74/44   [Neville's] Advice to the King to hold a Parliament
    14/74/45   Copy of the above, with a Collection of such things as have been desired to be obtained of His Majesty for the good of his people
    14/74/46 and 47   Copies of the above Collection
    16/514/132   The Apology of George Lord Digby
    PRO 29/76/8   Petition of Sir Richard Temple to the King
    29/143/157   Memoranda for the management of the King's 100 servants or officers
    30/24/20   Papers of the Earls of Shaftesbury
    31/3/74–195   Transcripts of the dispatches of the French ambassadors, made by Armand Baschett
    31/9/18–23   Transcripts of Carlo Rossetti's dispatches

Scottish Record Office, Edinburgh
  Dalhousie MSS   Letters of Henry Maule of Kelly
  Auchmar MSS   Letters to James Graham, Marquess of Montrose

Somerset Record Office, Taunton
  Phelips MSS   Papers of Sir Robert Phelips
Staffordshire Record Office, Stafford
  Dartmouth MSS   Papers of William Legge, first Earl of Dartmouth

Surrey Record Office, Kingston
  Somers MSS   Papers of John Lord Somers

Bibliography

Tullie House, Carlisle
  Diaries of Bishop William Nicolson
Victoria and Albert Museum, London
  Forster MSS
Diary of Roger Boyle, first Earl of
Orrery

PRINTED PRIMARY SOURCES

Parliamentary Proceedings

Cobbett, William, ed. *The Parliamentary History of England from the Earliest Period to the Year 1803*. London, 1806–20.

Foster, Elizabeth Read, ed. *Proceedings in Parliament 1610*. New Haven, Conn., 1966.

Gardiner, Samuel Rawson, ed. *Debates in the House of Commons in 1625*. Camden Society, n.s., vol. 6. London, 1873.

————, ed. *Parliamentary Debates, 1610*. Camden Society, vol. 81. London, 1862.

Grey, Anchitell. *Debates in the House of Commons, from the Year 1667 to the Year 1694*. London, 1763.

Journals of the House of Commons, 1547–1714. London, 1742–.

Journals of the House of Lords, 1578–1714. London, 1767–.

Newman, A. N., ed. "Proceedings in the House of Commons, March–June 1714." *Bulletin of the Institute of Historical Research 34 (1961)*: 211–17.

[Nicholas, Edward.] *Proceedings and Debates in the House of Commons*. Oxford, 1766.

Notestein, Wallace, Francis Relf, and Hartley Simpson, eds. *Commons Debates, 1621*. New Haven, Conn., 1935.

Willson, David, ed. *Parliamentary Diary of Robert Bowyer*. Minneapolis, 1939.

Official Documents

Calendar of State Papers, Domestic. Edited by M. A. E. Green et al. London, 1857–1924.

Calendar of State Papers, Venetian. Edited by Horatio F. Brown and Allen B. Hinds, London, 1900–1940.

Kramer, F. J. L., ed. *Archives ou Correspondance Inédite de la Maison D'Orange-Nassau*. Troisième Série, Leyde, 1907–9.

Prinsterer, Groen van, ed. *Archives ou Correspondance Inédite de la Maison D'Orange-Nassau*. Deuxième Série, Utrecht, 1857–61.

Historical Manuscript Commission Reports

H.M.C. *Third Report*, Appendix.

Bibliography

H.M.C. *Sixth Report*, Appendix, p. 377.
H.M.C. *Seventh Report*, Denbigh (Blancard Correspondence).
H.M.C. *Eighth Report*, Appendix.
H.M.C. *Tenth Report*, Appendix IV, Bouverie.
H.M.C. *Twelfth Report*, Appendix II, Coke.
H.M.C. *Fourteenth Report*, Appendix IX, Onslow.
H.M.C. *Fifteenth Report*, Appendix V, Foljambe; Appendix VI, Somerset and Ailsbury.
H.M.C. *Bath MSS*, vols. 1 and 3.
H.M.C. *Beaufort MSS*.
H.M.C. *Buccleuch MSS*, vols. 1 and 2.
H.M.C. *Cowper MSS*, vol. 2.
H.M.C. *Dartmouth MSS*, vol. 1.
H.M.C. *De Lisle MSS*, vol. 6.
H.M.C. *Downshire MSS*, vols. 1, 3, and 4.
H.M.C. *Egmont MSS*, vol. 2.
H.M.C. *Finch MSS*, vols. 1, 2, and 4.
H.M.C. *Hastings MSS*, vols. 2 and 4.
H.M.C. *House of Lords MSS, 1690–91*.
H.M.C. *Johnstone MSS*.
H.M.C. *Kenyon MSS*.
H.M.C. *Leybourne-Popham MSS*.
H.M.C. *Lindsey MSS*.
H.M.C. *Lonsdale MSS*.
H.M.C. *Mar and Kellie MSS*.
H.M.C. *Montagu of Beaulieu MSS*.
H.M.C. *Ormond MSS*, vols. 4 and 5.
H.M.C. *Portland MSS*, vols. 1 through 11.
H.M.C. *Various Collections*, vol. 8.

Pamphlets and Newspapers

Anonymous. *A Dialogue Betwixt Whig and Tory*. London, 1692. Reprinted in *A Collection of State Tracts, Published on Occasion of the Late Revolution in 1688, and During the Reign of King William III*. London, 1705–7.
———. *A Letter from Amsterdam*. London, 1678.
———. *A Seasonable Argument to Persuade All the Grand Juries in England to Petition for a New Parliament*. Amsterdam, 1677. Reprinted in Cobbett, *Parliamentary History*, vol. 4.
———. *Cursory Remarks upon Some Late Disloyal Proceedings*. London, 1699. Reprinted in Walter Scott, ed., *Somers Tracts*, 2d ed., vol. 6. London, 1811.

Bibliography

―――. *Limitations for the Next Foreign Successor*. London, 1701. Reprinted in *A Collection of State Tracts, Published on Occasion of the Late Revolution in 1688, and During the Reign of King William III*. London, 1705–7.

―――. *Short and Impartial Considerations Upon the Present State of Affairs in England*. London, 1692. Reprinted in *A Collection of State Tracts, Published on Occasion of the Late Revolution in 1688, and During the Reign of King William III*. London, 1705–7.

―――. *State of the Parties, and of the Publick, as Influenced by those Parties in this Conjuncture*. London, 1692. Reprinted in *A Collection of State Tracts, Published on Occasion of the Late Revolution in 1688, and During the Reign of King William III*. London, 1705–7.

―――. *The Claims of the People of England*. London, 1710. Reprinted in *A Collection of State Tracts, Published on Occasion of the Late Revolution in 1688, and During the Reign of King William III*. London, 1705–7.

―――. *The Dangers of Europe from the Growing Power of France*. London, 1701. Reprinted in *A Collection of State Tracts, Published on Occasion of the Late Revolution in 1688, and During the Reign of King William III*. London, 1705–7.

―――. *The Militia Reformed*. London, 1698. Reprinted in *A Collection of State Tracts, Published on Occasion of the Late Revolution in 1688, and During the Reign of King William III*. London, 1705–7.

―――. *The Present Disposition of England Considered*. London, 1701. Reprinted in *A Collection of State Tracts, Published on Occasion of the Late Revolution in 1688, and During the Reign of King William III*. London, 1705–7.

[Baker, Thomas.] *The Head of the Nile*. London, 1681.

[Clement, Simon.] *Faults on Both Sides*. London, 1710. Reprinted in Walter Scott, ed., *Somers Tracts*, vol. 12. London, 1811.

Defoe, Daniel. *The Secret History of the White Staff: Part I*. London, 1714.

―――. *The Secret History of the October Club: Part I*. London, 1711.

Hampden, John. *Some Short Considerations concerning the State of the Nation*. London, 1692. Reprinted in *A Collection of State Tracts, Published on Occasion of the Late Revolution in 1688, and During the Reign of King William III*. London, 1705–7.

Lawton, C. *A Short State of our Condition, with Relation to the present Parliament*. London, 1693. Reprinted in vol. 5 of Cobbett, *Parliamentary History*.

[Maynwaring, Arthur.] *Advice to the Electors of Great Britain Occasioned by the Intended Invasion from France*. London, 1708.

―――. *Four Letters to a Friend*. London, 1710.

Oldisworth, William. *Examiner*, vol. 3 no. 15 (12 January 1713) and vol. 5, no. 11 (4 January 1714). London, 1713–14.

Pittis, William. *The History of the Third Session of the Last Parliament*. London, n. d. (ca. 1713).

Bibliography

Toland, John. *The Art of Governing by Parties*. London, 1701.

Trenchard, John. *Free Thoughts Concerning Officers in the House of Commons*. London, 1701.

Letters, Diaries, Memoirs, Contemporary Histories

Addison, Joseph. *The Letters of Joseph Addison*. Edited by Walter Graham. Oxford, 1941.

Aiken, William, ed. *The Conduct of the Earl of Nottingham*. New Haven, Conn., 1941.

Airy, Osmund, ed. *Essex Papers*. Vol. 1. Camden Society, London, 1890.

Airy, Osmund, ed. *The Lauderdale Papers*. Camden Society, London, 1884–85.

Atterbury, Francis. *The Epistolary Correspondence, Visitation Charges, Speeches, and Miscellanies of the Right Reverend Francis Atterbury, D.D., Lord Bishop of Rochester*. London, 1783–90.

Baillie, George. *Correspondence of George Baillie of Jerviswood*. Edinburgh, 1842.

Baillie, Robert. *The Letters and Journals of Robert Baillie*. Edinburgh, 1841.

Boderie, Le Fevre de. *Ambassades de Monsieur de la Boderie en Angleterre*. N.p., 1750.

Booth, Henry, Lord Delamere and Earl of Warrington. *The Works of the Right Honourable Henry Late Lord Delamer, and Earl of Warrington*. London, 1694.

Boyer, Abel. *The History of King William the Third*. London, 1702–3.

———. *The History of the Life and Reign of Queen Anne*. London, 1722.

———. *The History of the Reign of Queen Anne, digested into Annals*. London, 1703–15.

———. *The Political State of Great Britain*. London, 1711–14.

Brown, Beatrice, ed. *The Letters and Diplomatic Instructions of Queen Anne*. London, 1935.

Browning, Andrew, ed. *English Historical Documents, 1660–1714*. London, 1953.

———, ed. *Thomas Osborne Earl of Danby and Duke of Leeds*. Vols. 2 (Letters) and 3 (Papers). Glasgow, 1951.

Bruce, John, ed. *The Diary of John Manningham*. London, 1868.

Burnet, Gilbert. *History of His Own Time*. Oxford, 1823.

———. *History of My Own Time*. Edited by Osmund Airy. Oxford, 1897–1900.

———. "Some Unpublished Letters of Gilbert Burnet." Edited by Helen Foxcroft. *Camden Miscellany, vol. 11*. London, 1907.

———. *A Supplement to Burnet's History of My Own Time*. Edited by Helen Foxcroft. Oxford, 1902.

[308]

Bibliography

Carstares, William. *State Papers and Letters Addressed to William Carstares.* Edinburgh, 1774.

Cartwright, James, ed. *The Wentworth Papers.* London, 1883.

Charles I. *The Works of King Charles the Martyr.* 2d ed. London, 1687.

Christie, W. D., ed. *Letters Addressed from London to Sir Joseph Williamson while Plenipotentiary at the Congress of Cologne in 1673–75.* Camden Society, London, 1874.

Cole, Christian. *Memoirs of Affairs of State.* London, 1733.

Coningsby, Thomas, "History of Parties," *Archaeologia*, vol. 38. London, 1860.

Cooper, J. P., ed. *Wentworth Papers, 1597–1628.* Camden Society, 4th ser., vol. 12. London, 1973.

Cowper, William first Earl. *The Private Diary of William First Earl Cowper, Lord Chancellor of England.* Eton, 1833.

Coxe, William, ed. *Memoirs of John Duke of Marlborough.* London, 1818.

Coxe, William, ed. *The Private and Original Correspondence of Charles Talbot, Duke of Shrewsbury.* London, 1821.

Dalrymple, David, ed. *Memorials and Letters Relating to the History of Britain in the Reign of Charles I.* Glasgow, 1766.

Dalrymple, Sir John, ed. *Memoirs of Great Britain and Ireland.* London, 1790.

Davies, Godfrey, and Clara Buck, eds. "Letters on Godolphin's Dismissal in 1710." *Huntington Library Quarterly* 3 (1939–40): 225–42.

————, and Marion Tinling, eds. "Correspondence of James Brydges and Robert Harley." *Huntington Library Quarterly*, vol. 1, no. 4 (1938), pp. 457–72.

Defoe, Daniel. *The Letters of Daniel Defoe.* Edited by George Harris Healey. Oxford, 1955.

Dickinson, H. T., ed. "The Letters of Henry St. John to the Earl of Orrery 1709–1711". *Camden Miscellany Vol. XXVI.* Camden Society, 4th ser., vol. 14. London, 1975.

Doebner, R. ed. *Memoirs of Mary Queen of England.* Leipzig, 1886.

Doble, C. E., ed. *Remarks and Collections of Thomas Hearne.* Oxford, 1886.

Eliot, Sir John. *Negotium Posterorum.* London, 1881.

Evelyn, John. *Diary of John Evelyn, Esq. F.R.S. To which are added a selection from his Familiar Letters and the Private Correspondence between King Charles I and Sir Edward Nicholas and Between Sir Edward Hyde (afterwards Earl of Clarendon) and Sir Richard Browne.* Edited by William Bray. London, 1879.

————. *The Diary of John Evelyn.* Edited by E.S. de Beer. Oxford, 1955.

Forster, T, ed. *Original Letters of Locke, Algernon Sidney, and Anthony Lord Shaftesbury.* London, 1830.

Bibliography

Gifford, W., and F. Cunningham, eds. *The Works of Ben Jonson*. London, 1811.

Grimblot, Paul, ed. *Letters of William III and Louis XIV*. London, 1848.

Grosart, Alexander, ed. *The Complete Prose Works of Andrew Marvell*. Blackburn, Lancashire, 1873–75.

Hacket, John. *Scrinia Reserata: A Memorial Offered to the great deservings of John Williams, D.D.* London, 1693.

Hamilton, A. H. A., ed. *The Note Book of Sir John Northcote*. London, 1877.

Heylyn, Peter. *Cyprianus Anglicus: Or, the History of the Life and Death of the most Reverend and Renowned Prelate William by Providence Lord Archbishop of Canterbury*. London, 1668.

Heywood, Thomas, ed. *The Norris Papers*. Chetham Society, 1846.

Hoff, B. van, ed. *The Correspondence of John Churchill, first Duke of Marlborough, and Anthony Heinsius*. The Hague, 1951.

Huygens, Constantijn. *Journal*. Werken van het Historish Genootschap, N.S., No. 23. Utrecht, 1876.

Hyde, Edward, Earl of Clarendon. *The History of the Great Rebellion and Civil Wars in England begun in the Year 1641*. Oxford, 1888.

———. *The Life of Edward Earl of Clarendon . . . Written by Himself*. Oxford, 1761.

———. *State Papers Collected by Edward, Earl of Clarendon*. Oxford, 1767–86.

Japikse, N., ed. *Correspondentie van Willem III en van Hans Willem Bentinck, eersten Graaf van Portland*. The Hague, 1927–35.

[Jones, David, ed.] *The Works and Life of the Right Honourable Charles Late Earl of Halifax*. London, 1715.

Jones, J. R., ed. "Shaftesbury's Worthy Men." *Bulletin of the Institute of Historical Research* 30 (1957): 232–41.

Kemble, John M., ed. *State Papers Illustrative of the Social and Political State of Europe*. London, 1857.

LeNeve, John. *The Lives and Characters of the Most Illustrious Persons British and Foreign Who Died in the Year 1712*. London, 1714.

Lockhart, George. *The Lockhart Papers*. London, 1817.

Lonsdale, Sir John Lowther, first viscount. "Memoirs of Lord Lonsdale." *English Historical Review* 30 (1915): 90–97.

Luttrell, Narcissus. *A Brief Relation of State Affairs*. Oxford, 1857.

MacPherson, James, ed. *Original Papers: Containing the Secret History of Great Britain from the Restoration to the Accession of the House of Hanover*. London, 1775.

McClure, Norman, ed. *The Letters of John Chamberlain*. Philadelphia, 1929.

Marchmont, Earls of. *A Selection from the Papers of the Earls of Marchmont*. London, 1831.

Bibliography

Montagu, H. D., Duke of Manchester, ed. *Court and Society from Elizabeth to Anne, edited from the Papers at Kimbolton*. London, 1864.

Morrison, Alfred. *The Collection of Autographed Letters and Historical Collections Formed by Alfred Morrison*. First Series, London, 1883–91. Second Series, London, 1882–93.

Motteville, Mme de. *Memoir on the Life of Henrietta Maria*. Camden Society, n.s., vol. 31. London, 1883.

Nalson, John. *An Impartial Collection of Great Affairs of State*. London, 1682–83.

North, Roger. *Examen: Or, An Enquiry into the Credit and Veracity of a Pretended Complete History*. London, 1740.

Oldmixon, John. *The History of England during the Reigns of King William and Queen Anne, and King George I*. London, 1735.

Pepys, Samuel. *The Diary of Samuel Pepys*. Edited by Robert Latham and William Matthews. Berkeley, Calif., 1970–76.

Pike, C. E., ed. *Essex Correspondence*. Camden Society, 3d ser., vol. 24. London, 1913.

Prior, Matthew. *History Of His Own Time*. London, 1740.

Ranke, Leopold von. *A History of England Principally in the Seventeenth Century*. Vol. 6 (Bonnet's dispatches). Oxford, 1875.

Robbins, Caroline, ed. *The Diary of John Milward*. Cambridge, England, 1938.

Roberts, Clayton, ed. "Sir Richard Temple's Discourse on the Parliament of 1667–1668." Huntington Library Quarterly, Vol. 20, No. 2.

Roberts, Philip, ed. *The Diary of Sir David Hamilton 1709–1714*. Oxford, 1975.

St. John, Henry Viscount Bolingbroke. *The Works of the Right Hon. Henry St. John Lord Viscount Bolingbroke*. London, 1798.

Scott, Walter, ed. *Secret History of the Court of James I*. Edinburgh, 1811.

Sidney, Henry. *Diary of the Time of Charles II*. London, 1843.

Simmons, Edward. *A Vindication of King Charles*. N.p., 1648.

Spedding, James, ed. *The Life and Letters of Francis Bacon*. London, 1857–74.

———. *The Works of Francis Bacon*. London, 1858.

Snyder, Henry, ed. *The Marlborough-Godolphin Correspondence*. Oxford, 1975.

Strong, S. A., ed. *A Catalogue of Letters and Other Historical Documents Exhibited in the Library at Welbeck*. N.p., 1903.

Sutton, H. Manners, ed. *Lexington Papers*. London, 1851.

Swift, Jonathan. *The Correspondence of Jonathan Swift*. Edited by F. Erlington Ball. London, 1910.

———. *The Letters of Jonathan Swift to Charles Ford*. Edited by David Nichol Smith. Oxford, 1935.

————. *The Prose Works of Jonathan Swift.* Edited by Herbert Davis and Irvin Ehrenpreis. Oxford, 1953.

Temple, Sir William. *The Works of Sir William Temple, Bart.* Edinburgh, 1754.

Thompson, Edward Maunde, ed. *Correspondence of the Family of Hatton.* Camden Society, n. s., vol. 22. London, 1878.

————. *The Letters of Humphrey Prideaux.* Camden Society, n. s., vol. 15. London, 1875.

Vernon, James, *Letters Illustrative of the Reign of William III from 1696 to 1708 Addressed to the Duke of Shrewsbury by James Vernon.* Edited by G. P. R. James. London, 1841.

Walker, Sir Edward. *Historical Discourses.* London, 1705.

Warwick, Sir Philip. *Memoires of the Reigne of King Charles I.* London, 1701.

Whitelocke, Sir James. *Liber Famelicus.* Edited by John Bruce. Camden Society. London, 1858.

Winwood, Sir Ralph. *Memorials of Affairs of State in the Reigns of Q. Elizabeth and K. James I.* London, 1725.

[Yorke, Philip, earl of Hardwicke, ed.] *Miscellaneous State Papers.* London, 1778.

Secondary Sources

Abbot, W.C. "The Long Parliament of Charles II." *English Historical Review* 21 (1906):21–34.

Ansell, Patricia. "Harley's Parliamentary Management." *Bulletin of the Institute of Historical Research* 34 (1961):95–97.

Ashton, Robert. "Deficit Finance in the Reign of James I." *Economic History Review*, 2d ser., 10 (1957–58):15–29.

Barbour, Violet. *Henry Bennet, Earl of Arlington.* Washington, D.C., 1914.

Baxter, Stephen. *William III.* London, 1966.

Bennet, G.V. "Robert Harley, the Godolphin Ministry, and the Bishopric Crisis of 1707." *English Historical Review* 82 (1967):726–46.

Birch, Thomas. *Court and Times of James I.* London, 1848.

Brook, John. *King George III.* St. Albans, 1974.

Browning, Andrew. *Thomas Osborne, Earl of Danby and Duke of Leeds.* Volume I, Life. Glasgow, 1951.

Burton, I. F., R. W. J. Riley, and E. Rowlands. "Political Parties in the Reigns of William III and Anne: The Evidence of the Division Lists." *Bulletin of the Institute of Historical Research*, Special Supplement no. 7 (November 1968).

Cannon, John. *The Fox-North Coalition.* Cambridge, England, 1969.

Carte, Thomas. *Life of James Duke of Ormond.* Oxford, 1851.

Bibliography

Cartwright, Julia. *Sacharissa: Some Account of Dorothy Sidney, Countess of Sunderland, Her Family and Friends, 1617–1684*. London, 1893.

Cavelli, Campana de. *Les Derniers Stuarts à Saint-Germain en Laye*. Paris, 1871.

Chandaman, C. D. *English Public Revenue, 1660–1688*. Oxford, 1975.

Christie, W. D. *The Life of Anthony Ashley Cooper, the First Earl of Shaftesbury*. London, 1871.

Churchill, Winston. *Marlborough*. London, 1947.

Colley, Linda. *In Defiance of Oligarchy: The Tory Party, 1714–60*. Cambridge, England, 1982.

Crissy, Merril, and Godfrey Davies. "Corruption in Parliament, 1660–1677." *Huntington Library Quarterly* 6 (1942–43):106–14.

Darby, H. C. *The Draining of the Fens*. Cambridge, England, 1956.

Davies, Godfrey. "The Political Career of Sir Richard Temple (1634–1697) and Buckingham Politics." *Huntington Library Quarterly* 4 (1940):47–83.

———. "The Seamy Side of Marlborough's War". *Huntington Library Quarterly* 15 (1951–52):21–44.

Dietz, Frederick. *English Public Finance, 1558–1614*. London, 1964.

Emden, C. S. *The People and the Constitution*. Oxford, 1933.

Feiling, Keith. *A History of the Tory Party, 1640–1714*. Oxford, 1924.

———. *History of England*. New York, 1948.

Finch, Pearl. *History of Burley-on-the-Hill, Rutland*. London, 1901.

Fletcher, Anthony. *The Outbreak of the English Civil War*. London, 1981.

Foxcroft, H. C. *The Life and Letters of Sir George Savile, Bart. First Marquis of Halifax*. London, 1898.

Gardiner, Samuel Rawson. *History of England from the Accession of James I to the Outbreak of the Civil War, 1603–1642*. London, 1883.

———. *History of the Great Civil War, 1642–1649*. London, 1891–94.

Gay, Edwin F. "The Rise of an English Country Family: Peter and John Temple, to 1603". *Huntington Library Quarterly* 1 (1937–38):367–90.

———. "The Temples of Stowe and Their Debts: Sir Thomas Temple and Sir Peter Temple, 1603–1653." *Huntington Library Quarterly* 2 (1938–39):399–438.

———. "Sir Richard Temple. The Debt Settlement and Estate Litigation, 1653–1675." *Huntington Library Quarterly* 6 (1942–43):255–91.

Glassey, Lionel. *Politics and the Appointment of Justices of the Peace, 1675–1720*. Oxford, 1979.

Gosse, Edmund. *The Life and Letters of John Donne*. London, 1899.

Gregg, Edward. *Queen Anne*. London, 1980.

Grew, Marion. *William Bentinck and William III*. London, 1924.

Gruenfelder, John K. *Influence in Early Stuart Elections, 1604–1640*. Columbus, Ohio, 1981.

Bibliography

Haley, K. H. D. *The First Earl of Shaftesbury*. London, 1968.

Harris, F. R. *The Life of Edward Montagu, K.G., First Earl of Sandwich*. London, 1912.

Harris, L. E. *Vermuyden and the Fens*. London, 1953.

Hibbard, Caroline. *Charles I and the Popish Plot*. Chapel Hill, N.C., 1983.

Hill, B. W. *The Growth of Political Parties, 1689–1742*. London, 1976.

Hirst, Derek. *The Representative of the People? Voters and Voting under the Early Stuarts*. Cambridge, England, 1975.

Holmes, Geoffrey, ed. *Britain after the Glorious Revolution*. London, 1969.

———. *British Politics in the Age of Anne*. London, 1967.

Horwitz, Henry. *Parliament, Policy, and Politics in the Reign of William III*. Manchester, England, 1977.

———. "Parties, Connections, and Parliamentary Politics, 1689–1714: Review and Revision." *Journal of British Studies* 6 (November 1966):45–69.

———. *Revolution Politicks: The Career of Daniel Finch Second Earl of Nottingham, 1647–1730*. Cambridge, England, 1968.

James, F. G. *Ireland in the Empire, 1688–1770*. Cambridge, England, 1973.

Jones, J. R. "Court Dependents in 1664". *Bulletin of the Institute of Historical Research* 34 (1961):81–91.

———. "Political Groups and Tactics in the Convention of 1660". *Historical Journal*, vol. 6, no. 2 (1963):159–77.

———. "The First Whig Party in Norfolk." *Durham University Journal*, n.s., 15 (1953–54):13–21.

———. *The First Whigs: The Politics of the Exclusion Crisis 1678–1683*. Oxford, 1961.

Keeler, Mary Frear. *The Long Parliament*. Philadelphia, 1954.

Kenyon, J. P. *Robert Spencer, Earl of Sunderland*. London, 1958.

Kershaw, R. N. "Elections for the Long Parliament". *English Historical Review* 38 (1923):496–508.

Klopp, Onno. *Der Fall des Hauses Stuart*. Vienna, 1875–88.

Lockyer, Roger. *Buckingham: The Life and Political Career of George Villiers, First Duke of Buckingham, 1592–1628*. London, 1981.

Macpherson, James. *The History of Great Britain from the Restoration to the Accession of the House of Hanover*. London, 1775.

McInnes, Angus. *Robert Harley: Puritan Politician*. London, 1970.

Neale, Sir John. "Commons Privilege of Free Speech in Parliament." In *Tudor Studies Presented . . . to Albert Frederick Pollard*. Edited by R.W. Seton-Watson. London, 1924.

Newton, A. P. *The Colonizing Activities of the English Puritans*. New Haven, Conn., 1914.

Nicholas, Glenn. "English Government Borrowing, 1660–1688." *Journal of British Studies* 10 (May 1971):83–104.

Bibliography

Owen, John. *The Eighteenth Century, 1714–1815*. New York, 1974.

Pares, Richard. *King George III and the Politicians*. Oxford, 1953.

Peck, Linda. *Northampton: Patronage and Policy at the Court of James I*. London, 1982.

Plumb, J. H. *Sir Robert Walpole: The Making of a Statesman*. London, 1956.

Prestwich, Mena. *Cranfield: Politics and Profits under the Early Stuarts*. Oxford, 1966.

Ranke, Leopold von. *A History of England Principally in the Seventeenth Century*. Oxford, 1875.

Robbins, Caroline. "The Repeal of the Triennial Act in 1664". *Huntington Library Quarterly* 12 (1948–49):121–40.

Roberts, Clayton. "The Constitutional Significance of the Financial Settlement of 1690." *Historical Journal* 20 (1977):59–76.

Rubini, Denis. *Court and Country*. London, 1967.

———. "Party and the Augustan Constitution, 1694–1716." *Albion* 10 (1978):195–202.

Ruigh, Robert. *The Parliament of 1624*. Cambridge, Mass., 1971.

Russell, Conrad. *The Origins of the English Civil War*. London, 1973.

———. *Parliaments and English Politics, 1624–1629*. Oxford, 1979.

Sachse, William. *Lord Somers: A Political Portrait*. Manchester, England, 1975.

Schoenfeld, Maxwell. *The Restored House of Lords*. The Hague, 1967.

Schwoerer, Lois. *"No Standing Armies!" The Antiarmy Ideology in Seventeenth-Century England*. Baltimore, 1974.

Scott, W. R. *The Constitution and Finance of English, Scottish, and Irish Joint-Stock Companies to 1720*. Cambridge, England, 1910–12.

Seddon, P. R. V. "Somerset." *Renaissance and Modern Studies* 14 (1970):48–68.

Sharp, Thomas. *The Life of John Sharp, D.D., Lord Archbishop of York*. London, 1825.

Slavin, Arthur. *Politics and Profit: A Study of Sir Ralph Sadler, 1507–1547*. Cambridge, England, 1966.

Snyder, Henry. "Defeat of the Occasional Conformity Bill and the Tack." *Bulletin of the Institute of Historical Research* 41 (1968): 172–92.

———. "The Formulation of Foreign and Domestic Policy in the Reign of Queen Anne." *Historical Journal* 11 (1968): 144–60.

———. "Godolphin and Harley: A Study of Their Partnership in Politics." *Huntington Library Quarterly* 30 (1966–67): 241–71.

———. "The Last Days of Queen Anne: The Account of Sir John Evelyn Examined." *Huntington Library Quarterly* 34 (1970–71): 261–76.

———. "Queen Anne versus the Junto: The Effort to Place Orford at the Head of the Admiralty." *Huntington Library Quarterly* (1972): 323–42.

Bibliography

Somerville, Thomas. *The History of Great Britain during the Reign of Queen Anne*. London, 1798.

Speck, W. A. "The Choice of a Speaker in 1705." *Bulletin of the Institute of Historical Research* 37 (1964): 20–46.

———. *Whig and Tory*. London, 1970.

———, and Geoffrey Holmes. "The Fall of Harley in 1708 Reconsidered." *English Historical Review* 80 (1965): 673–98.

Sutch, Victor. *Gilbert Sheldon*. The Hague, 1973.

Thomson, Gladys. *Life in a Noble Household*. New York, 1937.

Thoyras, Rapin de. *The History of England*. London, 1789.

Townshend, Dorothea. *George Digby, Second Earl of Bristol*. London, 1924.

Trevallyn Jones, G.F. "The Bristol Affair." *Journal of Religious History* 5 (June 1968): 16–30.

———. "The Composition and Leadership of the Presbyterian Party in the Convention." *English Historical Review* 79 (April 1964).

Trevelyan, George Macaulay. *England under Queen Anne*. London, 1930–34.

Wheatley, Henry. *London Past and Present*. London, 1891.

Wiffen, J. H. *Historical Memoirs of the House of Russell*. London, 1833.

Willen, Diane. *John Russell, First Earl of Bedford*. London, 1981.

Willson, David Harris. *The Privy Councillors in the House of Commons*. Minneapolis, 1940.

Witcombe, Denis. *Charles II and the Cavalier House of Commons*. Manchester, 1966.

Zagorin, Perez. *The Court and Country*. London, 1969.

Dissertations

Duncan, Owen. "Sir Henry Neville: Elizabethan Statesman and Jacobean Politician." Ph.D. dissertation, Ohio State University, Columbus, Ohio.

Speck, W.A. "The House of Commons 1702–1714: A Study in Political Organization." Thesis submitted for the degree of Doctor of Philosophy at the University of Oxford, September 1965.

Index

Abjuration, bills of, 117–18, 274 n. 27
Addison, Joseph, 190, 290 n. 130
Admiralty, complaints against, 182–84, 189
"Advice Touching the Holding of Parliament, An," 10–11
"Alarum, The," 75
Alienations, restraint of, 12 23
Almanza, Battle of, 185, 188, 190
Althorp, Northamptonshire: meetings at, 99, 123, 124, 125, 130, 181; Sunderland retires to, 140, 141
Anglesey, Arthur Annesley, first Earl of, 66, 67, 71
Anglesey, John Annesley, fourth Earl of, 205, 206, 210
Anglican party. See Church party
Anne, Queen: 109, 165, 240, 241, 242, 244, 245, 247, 288 n. 89; as Princess, 115, 154; character of, 166, 284 n. 1; employs Tories, 167, 168; dismisses Tories, 170, 172; appoints Cowper lord keeper, 174; appoints Sunderland secretary of state, 178, 180; appoints Montagu and Somers, 190–96; appoints Orford to the Admiralty, 197; clings to prerogative, 191, 196, 238; and bishopric crisis, 181, 184, 186; supports Harley in 1708, 187, 188; supports Harley in 1710, 203, 204, 205, 207, 211, 215; turns to Tories, 217, 221, 222, 223, 232–33; and 1714 crisis, 229, 231, 232, 297 n. 147, 297 n. 146
Anti-Clarendonians, 116, 136, 240, 241, 247; seek preferment, 66, 67, 68; lose reputation, 68, 69; oppose supply, 70, 71; seek dissolution in 1669, 72, 73, 74; secure office, 76

Argyle, John Campbell, second Duke of, 200, 201, 202, 204, 229, 230
Arlington, Henry Bennet, first Earl of, 68, 95, 267 n. 69; urges reliance on patronage, 59, 60; relations of, with Temple, 63, 65; builds a court party, 74, 75, 76; divides court party, 81, 83 84
Army plot of 1641, 48–49
Atterbury, Sir Francis, Bishop of Rochester, 215, 227, 231

Bacon, Sir Francis, 36, 50, 56, 59, 80, 109, 110, 120, 238, 240; advice of, to James I, 7–8, 9, 15, 32, 33, 256 n. 14; defends Parry, 26; scorns undertaking, 14, 28, 30; on "Negotiating," 256 n. 14; on "party," 255 n. 8
Baillie, Dr. Robert, 39, 46, 47
Balanced counsels. See Mixed ministries
Bank of England, 126, 133, 181, 209, 211
Barillon, Paul, 91, 92, 95, 100, 101, 103, 105, 269 nn. 36 and 43, 270 n. 67
Bath, Sir John Granville, first Earl of, 120, 240
Baxter, Stephen, 133, 276 n. 66
Bedford, Francis Russell, fourth Earl of, 72, 86, 90, 92, 93, 116, 127, 166, 234, 235, 236, 237; compared to Neville, 31; early career of, 42–43, 260 n. 23, 261 n. 39; purposes of, in 1640, 44–45, origin of his undertaking, 31–32, 38, 39, 40–41, 260 n. 20; inquiries of, into revenue, 41–42, 261 n. 35; failure of undertaking of, 46–51; and Strafford, 49, 262 n. 68; death of, 46, 47, 50, 51

[317]

Index

Bedford, William Russell, fifth Earl of, 43, 78, 128

Bedford level, 42, 43

Berkeley, Sir Maurice, 8, 14, 16, 26

Billingbeare, Berkshire, 10, 17, 22, 30

Blackall, Dr. Offspring, 181, 182, 184, 186, 246

Blenheim, Battle of, 171

Bodley, Sir Thomas, 22, 30

Bolingbroke, Henry St.John, first Viscount, 171, 234, 245, 296 n. 129; opposes trimming, 162, 168; place of, in 1708 scheme, 188; resigns, 189; and 1710 scheme, 200, 202, 203, 206, 207, 215; opposes Somerset, 221; supports Harley, 223, 225, 227, 228, 229; breaks with Harley, 230, 231, 232; scheme of, in 1714, 231, 232, 297 n. 146

Bonnet, Friedrich (Prussian resident), 125, 146, 147, 152, 158, 161, 276 n. 70

Bourbon, House of, 183, 222

Boyer, Abel, 208, 293 n. 68, 294 n. 90, 295 n. 114

Boyle, Henry, 185, 187, 189, 190, 192, 212, 215

Boyne, Battle of, 118

Brandon, Charles Gerard, Viscount, 120, 240

Bridges, Ralph, 231, 233

Bristol, John Digby, first Earl of, 39, 47, 52

Bristol, John Digby, second Earl of: as Lord Digby, 40, 41, 46, 52; as Earl of Bristol, 60, 61, 62, 80, 102, 237, 246

Bromley, William, 199, 221, 223, 229, 297 n. 147

Brooke, Robert Greville, second Lord, 43, 47

Brydges, James, 211, 212, 227, 291 n. 34, 293 n. 75

"Broker," role of, in undertakings, 14, 38–39, 55, 102, 120, 123, 130, 133, 237–38

Bromley, William, 170, 173, 192, 200, 202, 207, 227

Brydges, James, 184, 205–6, 207

Buckingham, George Villiers, first Duke of, 34, 35, 36, 37, 209, 259 nn. 7 and 9

Buckingham, George Villiers, second Duke of, 72, 80, 86, 92, 160, 234, 235, 240; undertaking of, in 1667, 65, 66, 67, 68; conduct of, in 1669, 71, 72, 74–75; loss of power of, 75, 76; seeks dissolution, 72, 247

Buckingham and Normanby, John Sheffield, third Earl Mulgrave, first Marquis of Normanby, and fifth Duke of, 120, 129–30, 172, 188, 215, 220, 239

Burleigh, William Cecil, Lord, 59, 84, 108

Burnet, Gilbert, 77, 81, 151, 270 n. 73, 276 n. 70, 280 n. 47, 287 n. 70

Cadiz, defeat at, 168

Canary patent, 64, 65

Capel, Sir Henry, later Lord, 92, 95, 97, 99, 100, 132, 276 n. 70

Carleton, Sir Dudley, 20, 22

Carlisle, Charles Howard, first Earl of, 78, 105, 164

Carteret, John, 249, 250

Carteret, Sir George, 71, 73

Cavalier party, 58, 59, 70, 74

Cavendish, William. See Devonshire, first Duke of

Catherine of Braganza, Queen, 97, 98

Cecil, Robert. See Salisbury, first Earl of

Chamberlain, John, 7, 9, 14, 22, 26, 35, 256 n. 20

Charles I, 92, 136, 236, 238–39, 240; as Prince, 18, 34, 35; personal rule of, 37; prosecutes Bedford, 31, 43; listens to undertaking, 38, 39, 40, 41, 43, 45, 46; seeks to save Strafford, 46, 47, 48, 262 n. 54; spurns Say's undertaking, 51, 52, 260 n. 30; takes up sword, 49, 52, 53, 54, 262 n. 66; remarks of, to Lady Bedford, 50; at Isle of Wight, 55

Charles II, 129, 137, 235, 236, 239, 240, 241, 243, 244, 246, 247; at

Restoration, 57–58, 59, 60; and Temple's undertaking, 60, 61, 62, 63, 264 n. 10, 265 n. 24; defends prerogative, 64; and Buckingham's undertaking, 66, 67, 68, 70, 71; turns to Church party, 72, 73, 74, 77; rewards Temple, 75, 267 n. 69; as parliamentary manager, 79, 81, 82, 105, 108; follows Danby's advice, 85, 86, 87, 88; dissolves Parliament, 89; and the Privy Council scheme, 92–97, 109; dismisses Danby, 270 n. 55; seeks Dutch alliance, 99; resists Exclusion, 94, 102, 272 n. 121; spurns South-amptons, 104, 105; dissolves Parliament, 105–6

Chatham, disaster at, 67, 86, 109, 235

Chester, bishopric of, 181, 186

Cholmondeley, Hugh Cholmondeley, first Earl of, 223, 227

Church party (also Anglican), 206, 231, 239, 241; opposes Comprehension, 68; conduct of, in 1669, 74; strength of, 77, 84, 273 n. 12; William turns to 114, 115, 116, 117, 118, 154, 155; Anne declares for, 168; as threat to court, 171; in 1710 elections, 217

Churchill, John. See Marlborough first Duke of,

Cinque ports, 8, 116

Civil list, 132, 134, 139, 160, 225, 249

Clarendon, Edward Hyde, first Earl of, 77, 109, 152, 166, 236, 237; intercedes for Strafford, 262 n. 68; comments on Bedford's undertaking, 40, 43, 45, 46, 47, 48, 50, 51, 261 n. 36, 262 n. 55; as parliamentary manager, 59, 60; impeached, 61, 66, 67; flees to France, 67, 71

Clifford, Sir Thomas, later first Lord: as court manager, 59, 60, 74, 76, 109, 110; attacked in "Alarum," 75; as treasurer, 80; intrigues by, against Shaftesbury, 81

Commissions of peace, changes in 127, 156, 161, 168, 173, 282 n. 98

Commons, House of: in 1610, 3–4, 12, 15; attacks undertakers, 25, 26, 27,

28, 29; in 1641, 49, 50, 52, 53; purged, 55; in 1663, 62, 63; in 1668, 68, 70, 71; anger of, at chancellor, 80; rejects Self-Denying bill, 83; in 1675, 84; condemns ministers, 86; impeaches Danby, 88, 90; in 1679, 93, 94, 95, 96, 270 nn. 63 and 67; in 1680, 102, 103, 104; censures ministers, 105; votes no impeachments, 116; passes Place Bill, 117; defeats abjuration, 117–18; votes address, 126; exonerates Montagu, 139; in 1698, 142; condemns Admiralty, 144; and Kidd affair, 145; in 1700, 147, 148; condemns Partition, 158; in 1703, 169, 170; defeats Tack, 171; exonerates Godolphin, 172, 175; Harley on power of, 285 n. 13; and Regency bill, 176; and Almanza, 185; attacks Admiralty, 183; and supply bill, 189, 195–96; in 1711, 217, 218, 219; and peace, 221, 222; rejects Treaty of Commerce, 225; and Protestant Succession, 230; in 1714, 230, 231, 296 n. 136; condemns balancing schemes, 244

Composite ministries. See mixed ministries

Comprehension, bill for, 66, 68, 69

Compton, Spencer, 175, 187, 192

Coke, Sir Edward, 8, 21, 34

Coningsby, Thomas, first Lord and later Earl of, 118, 129, 140, 155, 210, 277 n. 91, 291 n. 34

Conventicles, bills against, 69, 73, 75, 79, 83

Conway, Edward, third Viscount, 65, 82

Cooke, Sir Miles, 143, 240

Cottington, Francis Cottington, first Lord, 38, 41, 45, 46, 51

Council of Trade, 131, 132, 278 n. 108

Country party: in 1666–67, 64–65; apostates from, 76; in 1678, 86, 87; in ascendancy, 89, 91, 92, 96; in 1693 and 1694, 127, 128; opposes standing armies, 138; attacks Montagu, 139; and election of Speaker, 142; pamphleteers of, 143; opposes court, 143, 146

Index

Court-Country polarity, 137–38

Court managers: lack of power of, 128; fall of, 130, 132; Sunderland as, 140; and 1701 elections, 156; in 1702, 164, 165; ally with Tories, 168, 169, 170; ally with Whigs, 173, 177; creed of, 174; cling to power by, 189, 191–92, 196, 198; and 1708 elections, 192; in 1710, 210, 211; struggle of, with party, 224; cling to patronage by, 233

Court party, 4, 246; in 1610, 8; in 1666, 64; failure to discipline by, 73; in 1669, 74; allied with Church party, 75; fear of, 76; divisions within, 80; Danby's reliance on, 83, 84, 85, 86, 88; collapse of, 87, 89; as means of management, 109; in 1694, 129; in 1695, 130, 131; in 1696, 134; weakness of, in William's reign, 135, 143; in 1698, 279 n. 34; in Charles II's reign, 105; Tories seek support of, 157; holds balance, 191; weakness of, 217, 230, 248; undertakers seek to control, 246

Covent Garden, 31, 42, 43

Coventry, Sir William, 66, 69, 70, 71, 82, 83

Cowper, William, first Lord and later Earl of, 208, 222, 245, 246, 287 n. 70; appointed lord keeper, 174, 191, 196; grasps at patronage, 177, 182; returns to Junto, 192; named lord lieutenant, 212, 215; resigns, 215–16

Craggs, James, 207, 288 n. 97

Croft, Sir Herbert, 15, 16, 26, 27

Cropley, Sir John: courted by Godolphin, 187; deplores cowardice of Whigs, 204; employed by Harley, 212; reports by, 176, 186, 190, 191, 204, 208, 288 n. 98, 291 n. 17

Customs, votes of, 42, 49, 53, 261 n. 36

Danby, Sir Thomas Osborne, first Earl of, later first Marquis of Carmarthen and first Duke of Leeds, 66, 68, 71, 74, 76, 98, 102, 110, 129, 130, 132, 135, 145, 236, 239, 240, 242; seeks

greater revenue, 82; creates Court-Anglican party, 83, 84, 85, 86, 269 n. 43; impeached, 87, 88, 89, 90; dismissed, 91, 270 n. 55; feared by Shaftesbury, 93; letter of, to King, 94; named lord president, 113; and Church party, 114; manages Parliament, 116, 117, 118, 119; opposed by Whigs, 137

Dartmouth, William Legge, first Earl of, 172, 206–7, 207, 216, 227

Dawes, Sir William, Bishop of Chester, 181, 182, 184, 186, 230, 246

Declaration by Charles I, 12 August 1641, 54

Declaration of Indulgence, 60, 61, 79, 81

Defoe, Daniel, reports by, 170, 171, 211, 224–25, 247, 293 nn. 68 and 74, 296 n. 132

Devonshire, William Cavendish, first Earl and first Duke of, 118, 128, 192, 274 n. 27; opposes exclusion, 95; resigns, 97; left in office, 167, 170; as ally of Junto, 187, 190, 192, 194

Digby, George. See Bristol, John Digby, first Earl of; Bristol, John Digby, second Earl of

Digges, Sir Dudley, 8, 26, 27, 33

Dissenters, 115, 170, 173, 213, 230. See also Nonconformists

Dorchester, Evelyn Pierrepont, first Marquis of, 194, 210

Dover, Henry Carey, first Earl of, 54, 245

Duncombe, Sir Charles, 139–40, 211

Dutch, the, 65, 79, 82, 91, 99, 124, 163, 209

Ecclesiastical Commission, 154, 161

Elections, parliamentary: in 1603–10, 264 n. 9; from 1610 to 1640, 260 n. 19; in 1679, 96–97; in 1690, 116; in 1695, 130–31, 277 n. 100; in 1698, 141, 142; in 1701, 156, 164, 282 n. 98; in 1702, 167–68, 285 n. 10; in 1705, 173; in 1708, 187, 191–92, 289 n. 113; in 1710, 214, 217, 294 n. 90; in 1713, 227–28; in 1784, 250; failure of court influence in, 240

Index

Harcourt, Sir Simon, later first Earl of, 228, 229, 245; as solicitor, 150, 151, 173; and Harley's 1708 scheme, 188; resigns, 189; named attorney general, 215; and 1714 scheme, 231

Harbord, William, 82, 83, 102, 103, 104

Harley, Sir Edward, 93, 104, 144, 147, 275 n. 52; memoirs of, 155; and Dr. Williams, 213; folly of, depending on party, 225, 226

Harley, Robert, later first Earl of Oxford, 169, 228, 235, 236, 237, 239, 240, 243, 244, 245, 246, 247, 285 n. 13; reports by, 121, 123, 125, 149, 278 n. 108; leads Country party, 127, 129, 131, 136; negotiates with Sunderland, 133, 136; in opposition, 138, 142, 149, 280 n. 52; and 1700 scheme, 150, 151, 152; as Speaker, 154, 156, 164; in 1701, 158, 159, 162; for resolution about impeachments, 165; as secretary of state, 170–90 passim, 288 nn. 97–98; allies with Bromley, 199, 200; distrust of, 201, 202, 291 n. 14; 1710 scheme of, 203, 205, 206, 207, 209, 293 n. 66; seeks mixed ministry, 210, 211, 212–13; turns to Tories, 214, 215, 216; resists Tory demands, 217, 219; created Earl of Oxford, 220; and management of Parliament, 220–27 passim, 296 n. 134; in 1614, 228–33 passim, 296 n. 136, 297 n. 156; *Faults on Both Sides*, 216

Hatton, Charles, 93, 125

Hedges, Sir Charles, 153, 164, 167, 178

Henrietta Maria, Queen, 39, 45, 46, 48, 52

Henry IV of France, 17, 19, 30

Henry VIII, 16, 18, 42

Hertford, William Seymour, third Earl and later first Marquis of, 34, 38, 39, 44, 51

Heylyn, Peter, 40, 46, 47

High Tories. *See* Tories: High

Hoffmann, Johann, 156, 172, 207, 209, 211, 287 n. 64

Hollies, Denzil, later first Lord, 100, 247; prosecuted in 1629, 51; rumored to become secretary of state, 40, 51, 54, 55, 59; to be removed from Council, 67; meets with York, 78; dismissed, 87; 1679 undertaking of, 89, 90, 91, 242, 269 n. 51

Holles, Sir John, 8, 24, 27

Horwitz, Henry, 119, 242, 277 n. 91

Hoskyns, John, 4, 27, 258 n. 71

How, Jack, 140, 146, 278 n. 6

Howard faction, 6, 9, 22, 23, 25

Howard, Sir Robert, 122, 236; opposes court, 63; as Anti-Clarendonian, 67, 69, 70, 71, 72; leader of Country gentlemen, 75; gains office, 76; for supply, 81

Hyde, Edward. *See* Clarendon, Edward Hyde, first Earl of

Hyde, Lawrence. *See* Rochester, Lawrence Hyde, first Earl of

Impeachments: of Middlesex, 35; of Strafford, 45, 46–47, 49; of Clarendon, 62, 66, 67; of Penn, 69; of Orrery, 73; of ministers in 1674, 82; of Danby, 83, 87, 88, 90, 94, 114; of Whig lords, 148, 158, 159, 161, 165; of Sacheverell, 217

Impeachment, threat of: against Percy and Jermyn, 52; against Ormond, 73; against Arlington, 74; against Sunderland, 140; against Harley, 189; against Bolingbroke, 232, 297 n. 156

Impositions, 4, 12, 14, 15, 29, 35

Indemnity, bill of, 114, 115

Ireland, 48, 111, 113, 115, 119, 146, 194

Irish cattle, importation of, 63, 64, 65, 76

Irish forfeiture bill. *See* Resumption of forfeited Irish lands, bill for

Isham, John, 123, 124, 125

Jacobites, 127, 162, 168, 192, 194, 230

James I, 38, 61, 92, 109, 238, 240, 348; spurns Great Contract, 4; as

Index

[325]

Index

Purveyance, 3, 4, 6, 7, 12

Pym, John, 235, 245; opponent of court, 21; on Neville's death, 30; to be chancellor of the Exchequer, 38, 40, 51, 52; plan of, to increase revenue, 41; meets with Bedford, 43; drafts petition, 44; meets with King, 46; distrusts King, 48, 262 n. 66; loses control of House, 49, 50; favors parliamentary nomination of ministers, 52, 53; and patronage, 54

Queensberry, James Douglas, first Duke of, 192, 200, 201

Raby, Lord. *See* Strafford, Thomas Wentworth, Earl of

Recoinage, 131, 134

Recruitment bill, 187–88, 190, 196, 198, 290 n. 130

Regency, bill for, 175, 176

Resignation from office: by Whig councillors in 1680, 97; by Shrewsbury in 1690, 116; by Rochester in 1703 and Nottingham in 1704, 170; by St. John, Mansell, and Harcourt in 1708, 189; by the Whigs in 1710, 215–16; threats of, by Marlborough, 189, 203; threats of, by the Whigs, 197, 207; practice of, 244–45

Restraining Orders, 221, 223

Resumption of forfeited Irish lands, bill for, 137, 146, 146–47, 149, 159, 220, 223

Revenues: under James I, 6; in 1641, 37–38, 41, 260 n. 18, 261 n. 35; in 1677, 82–83; in 1678, 88; in 1680, 96, 99, 106, 272 n. 121; anticipated in 1630s, 37; plans to limit, 42; inadequate vote of, in 1690, 107, 116, 117; determines fate of undertakings, 240, 241

Revolution Settlement, 106

Richmond, James Stuart, third Duke of, 53, 55

Rivers, Richard Savage, second Earl of, 200, 201, 203, 205, 212, 213, 293 n. 66

Robartes, John, first Baron, later first Earl of Radnor, 91, 92

Rochester, Robert Carr, first Viscount, later first Earl of Somerset, 39, 42, 102, 209, 256 n. 25, 257 n. 28; works for Neville, 3, 9, 10, 13, 22; receives signet, 13; turns from Neville, 23, 30; offers graces, 24

Rochester, Lawrence Hyde, first Earl of, 174, 194, 243, 244, 245, 246; named to Treasury, 270 n. 63; favors setting out a fleet, 99; enters Council, 118; scheme of, in 1700, 150, 151, 152, 153, 154, 155; relies on Harley, 156; seeks control of patronage, 157; attacked by Whigs, 159; presses on King, 161; opposes Whigs, 166; allies with managers, 167, 168; resigns, 170; attacks government; 170, Queen spurns, 186, 212; as president of the Council, 215, 218–19; opposes mixed ministries, 219; death of, 220

Rochester, bishops of. *See* Atterbury, Francis; Ward, Seth

Russell, Conrad, 34, 35, 259 n. 11, 260 n. 18

Russell, Edward, later first Earl of Orford, 151, 208, 245, 246; named Admiral, 118, 276 n. 66; dismissed, 120; at Althorp, 124; named Admiral, 125, 127, 133; accused by Fenwick, 133, 134; named treasurer of the Navy, 134; relations of, with Sunderland, 140, 150; attacks upon, 143, 144, 145, 146; impeached, 158, 159; censured, 168, 169; as member of the Junto, 182, 184, 194, 196, 197, 198; resigns, 216

Russell, William, Lord, 90, 94, 95, 97, 101, 102, 103, 104

Ryswick, Peace of, 137

Sacheverell, William, 202, 204, 213, 217, 225, 291 n. 14

St. John, Oliver, 38, 39, 41, 42, 43, 44, 48, 40, 58

Salisbury, Robert Cecil, first Earl of, 3, 4, 9, 16; as lord treasurer, 6; electoral management of, 8; justifies impositions, 14–15; and Neville, 17, 18–19, 19, 20; his graces, 24; death of, 7, 9, 13

[327]

Index

Sandys, Sir Edwin, 8, 16, 26, 34

Savile, Sir Henry, 16, 22, 30

Savile, Thomas, Lord, 39, 47, 52

Say, William Fiennes, first Viscount, 89; dines with Buckingham, 34; named to Council, 39; to be master of the wards, 38, 40, 46; meets with Bedford, 43; opposes Strafford, 47; named to office, 50, 51; his undertaking, 51–52; at Isle of Wight, 55

Schemes of administration: Bedford's, 260 n. 20; Temple's, 92, 95; Sunderland's in 1693, 121, 123; Whigs' in 1693, 122, 126; Tory scheme in 1700, 149, 150, 151, 152, 153, 154, 155, 156, 281 n. 66; Whigs in 1701, 163; Sunderland's in 1701, 164; nonparty in 1704, 170; Whigs' in 1705, 172; Whigs' in 1706, 179; Harley's in 1706, 179–80; four schemes of 1707–8 (Whigs', 186; Queen's, 186; Godolphin's, 187; Harley's, 188, 189, 288 n. 97); success of Whigs', 195–98; Harley's in 1710, 199, 200, 203, 204, 206, 211, 215, 293 n. 66, 294 n. 90; dependent on party, 230, 232, 233; coalition, 219; Bolingbroke's, 231–32, 297 n. 156

Scotland: proposed union with, in 1607, 21; war against, 37, 43, 44, 49; Charles I seeks army from, 52; Jacobite plot in, 168; succession in, 171; Privy Council of, 184–85, 187, 289 n. 113; justices of the peace in, 185; elections in, 192; mismanagements in, 195; invasion of, 196

Scottish Lords, 218, 222, 225, 228

Scottish MPs, 296 n. 127

Security, Act of, 171, 172, 175

Self-denying resolutions: in 1641, 50; in 1675, 83; in 1679, 94; in 1680, 104; summary of, 241–42

Settlement, Act of, 176

Seymour, Sir Edward, 155, 236; opposes court, 63, 64, 67; well-heard in House, 69; attacks Ormond, 69; opposes supply, 70, 71; as Anti-Clarendonian, 73; treasurer of the Navy, 76; a grumbletonian, 278 n. 6;

enters Council, 118; named to Treasury, 118; in opposition, 134, 138, 147, 148; dines with King, 149; as comptroller of Household, 167; dismissed, 169, 170

Shaftesbury, Anthony Ashley Cooper, first Earl of, 90, 122, 138, 234, 235, 237, 240, 241, 247, 270 n. 70; as Lord Ashley, 67; letter of, to Carlisle, 78, 79, 105; as lord chancellor, 80; opposes Clifford, 81; urges King's divorce, 82; rumor of an undertaking by, 85; ordered to leave town, 87; delighted at dissolution, 89; undertaking of, in 1679, 91, 92, 93; and control of Commons, 95, 98, 242; anger of, at King, 96, 97, 100; undertaking of, in 1680, 99, 101, 272 n. 105; rages against Southamptons, 103, 104; not a careerist, 236, 239

Shaftesbury, Anthony Ashley Cooper, third Earl of, 154, 161, 187, 212, 280 n. 60

Sheffield, Edmund, Lord, later Earl of Mulgrave, 9, 10

Shrewsbury, Charles Talbot, twelfth Earl of and (after 1694) first Duke of, 215, 245; named secretary of state, 113; supports a mixed ministry, 114; resigns, 116, 118; and 1693 undertaking, 121, 122, 123–24; refuses office, 125, 276 n. 70; named secretary of state, 127–28; and patronage, 128; favors Triennial bill, 129; reconciles Sunderland and Whigs, 130; accused by Fenwick, 133, 134; relations of, with Whigs, 140, 141, 142, 145, 151, 155, 281 n. 66; negotiates with Harley, 290 n. 8, 200, 201, 237; favors Sacheverell, 202; named lord chamberlain, 204; role of, in 1710 crisis, 207, 208, 210, 211, 291 n. 34, 295 n. 105

Sidney, Henry, later Earl of Romney, 101, 104, 118

Smith, Jack, 210; as a leading Whig, 140, 143, 145, 146, 147, 149; resigns from Treasury, 153, 161, 164; elected Speaker, 173, 175; wooed by Godolphin, 187; as chancellor of the

Index

Supply, vote of: in 1610, 3–4; in 1641, 49; in 1665–66, 64; in 1668, 70–71; in 1670, 75; in 1673, 81; in 1675 and 1677, 85; in 1678, 86; in 1679, 96; in 1689, 115; in 1690, 116, 118; in 1691–92, 116; in 1692–93, 116; in 1693–94, 126; in 1694–95, 128–29; in 1695–96, 131; in 1696–97, 134; in 1697–98, 139; in 1699–1700, 149; in 1700, 147, 155, 160; in 1701, 168; in 1706, 180; in 1708, 195; in 1710–11, 217; in 1711, 220; in 1714, 231; ability of Whigs to carry, 198; Temple's promise of, 264 n. 10

Supply, withholding of: urged by Owen, 4; in 1640, 42; in 1641, 49, 53; in 1668, 70–71; in 1669, 72-73; in 1674, 82; in 1679, 93, 94, 96; in 1690, 107; in 1697, 138; threat to, in 1663, 61–62; in 1701, 157, 159, 160; opposed indirectly, 166

Tacking, practice of, 171, 172, 173, 186, 223, 225

Tallard, Count, 141, 142, 146, 158, 279 n. 34, 281 n. 63

Tankerville, Forde Grey, first Earl of, 145, 151, 152, 153

Temple, Sir John, 38, 39, 52

Temple, Sir Richard, 80, 93, 102, 127, 134, 136, 234, 235, 236, 237, 242, 246; debts of, 57; in convention, 265 n. 24; undertaking of, in 1663: 60, 61, 62, 264 nn. 10 and 67, 265, n. 18; in opposition, 63, 64, 65; and Buckingham's undertaking, 65, 66; named commissioner for trade, 68; in 1668 Parliament, 70; in France, 71; as Anti-Clarendonian, 72; his discourse, 73, 237 n. 64; goes over to court, 75, 76, 267 n. 69

Temple, Sir William, 76, 86, 92, 95, 100, 239

Ten Propositions, 52

Test Act, 81

Tories: Hanoverian, 230, 237; High, 212, 213, 216, 218, 219, 237, 243, 244

Tory party, 241, 242, 243; in 1689, 109, 111, 114; in office 1690–93, 113, 115, 116, 118, 275 n. 38; driv-

en from office, 119, 121, 134; attacks Trenchard, 129; and land bank, 133; goes into opposition, 131, 137, 138, 236; divided, 142, 145; attacks Somers, 147, 148; scheme of, in 1700, 149, 151, 235; wins elections, 155–56; in 1701 Parliament, 157, 158–59, 160, 161; in Anne's first Parliament, 164, 164–65, 167, 168, 284 n. 2, 170–71; divides over Tack, 171; in 1705–8 Parliament, 173, 175, 177, 179, 180, 182, 183–84, 184–85; opposes recruiting bill, 185; suspicious of Harley, 188; opposes government, 185, 189, 190, 196; loses 1708 elections, 192; supports Harley's scheme, 199, 200, 202, 203, 215, 232; determined on Peace, 205; demands dissolution, 207, 209, 214, 244, 247; wins 1710 elections, 217; seeks to drive Whigs from government, 217–18, 219, 225, 226, 247; supports Harley, 221, 223; wins 1713 elections, 227–28; seeks to control patronage, 233, 245, 246; division of, in 1714, 228

Townshend, Charles, second Viscount, 194, 221

Townshend, Horatio, Lord, 98, 100

Treason, law of, 131, 132, 276 n. 79, 256 n. 22

Trenchard, John, 120, 121, 122, 127, 128, 136, 245; A History of Standing Armies, 136

Treaty of Commerce: with France, 225, 226, 230, 296 nn. 127–29, 132; with Spain, 230, 231

Trevor, Sir John, 130, 135, 157, 246; named secretary of state, 67, 76; as envoy to France, 68; as Speaker, 117, 121, 129; as court manager, 116, 123; as protégé of Sunderland, 140; refuses seals, 150

Triennial Act: of 1641, 40, 42, repeal of, in 1663, 63, 69; of 1693, 118, 125, 276 n. 79, 127, 129, 173, 191

Trimming, practice of: by William III, 113, 114, 118, 120, 135, 145, 165; by Queen Anne, 168, 226, 243

Triple Alliance, 70, 79

Index

be made lord lieutenant of Ireland, 190, 192, 193, 194, 195, 196; resigns, 216; jest about foreman by, 223; papers of, 264 n. 6

Whig party, 229, 242; led by Southamptons, 99; leaders given office, 109, 113; distinction between Tories and, denounced, 111; seeks to drive Tories from office, 114, 137, 236; rejects formal nomination of ministers, 112, 238; seeks office in 1690, 115, 116, 275 n. 38; strength of in 1690, 115, 116, 274 n. 24; William turns to, 118; clamor of, for office, 119, 120, 275 n. 39, 121, 122 (in 1693, 124, 125, 126, 235, 241; in 1694, 127, 128, 129, 245, 276 n. 79); wins 1695 elections, 277 n. 100; manages Parliament successfully, 130, 131, 132, 133; gains monopoly of office, 134, 139, 140, 141, 142; failure of management by, 145, 146, 148; aversion of, to Sunderland, 150, 151; in disarray, 153, 154–55; in 1701 Parliament, 156, 158, 159, 284 n. 127; seeks dissolution, 160, 247; William returns to, 161, 162, 163; in 1702 Parliament, 164, 165; removed by Anne, 167; in Anne's first Parliament, 168, 171, 171–72, 172, 284 n. 2; presses for office after 1705, 173, 174, 175, 244; allies with court, 177; demands control of church appointments, 178, 246; strength of, in Commons, 179; practices politics of opposition, 180, 181, 182–83, 184, 185, 186, 189, 190, 236, 287 n. 70; wins 1708 elections, 191, 192; exploits power of the purse, 193; prevents censure of Godolphin, 196; demands Orford's appontment, 197; forms ministry, 198; impeaches Sacheverell, 202; division of, in 1710, 204, 243; fear of dissolution of, 204, 205, 207, 208, 209, 210; negotiations of, with Harley in 1710, 206, 210, 292 n. 57, 215; loses elections, 214; in 1711 Parliament, 220, 225; none preferred, 227; attacks government, 237; Harley negotiates with in 1714, 297 n. 156

Whigs: Country, 187, 190, 191, 196, 222, 243, 289 n. 103; Junto, 184, 185, 189, 243, 246; Lord Treasurer's, 187, 189, 191, 243; Ministerial, 236, 243; Shaftesbury, 244. See also Whig party

Whimsicals, 176, 187, 230, 296 n. 127, 243

Whitelocke, Bulstrode, 40, 46

Whitelocke, Sir James, 22, 257 n. 53

William III, 101, 165, 235, 237, 240, 241, 242, 243, 244, 245, 246; given crown but insufficient revenue, 107; seeks to balance parties, 109, 113; defends prerogative, 110, 111, 112, 126; turns to Tories, 115, 116; opposes abjuration bill, 117; still a trimmer, 118, 120; relies on Dutchmen, 122; turns to Whigs, 125, 276 nn. 70–71; refuses Wharton preferment, 125; vetoes place bill, 126; yields on patronage, 127, 128; accepts Triennial bill, 129; turns further to Whigs, 130, 132, 133, 134; relations of, with Whigs in 1698 and 1699, 138, 140, 141, 142, 144, 145; defends Irish grants, 146, 147; prorogues Parliament in 1700, 148; dismisses Somers, 148, 149; turns to Tories, 151, 152, 153, 154, 156; asks Tories not to attack Whigs, 159, 161–62; prorogues Parliament in 1701, 160; negotiates with Somers, 162; dissolves Parliament, 163; returns to trimming, 164, power of in 1701, 284 n. 133; would have men come to his humor, 239

Williams, John, Bishop of Lincoln, 34, 35, 36, 52, 259 n. 7

Williamson, Sir Joseph, 74, 107

Windsor: Neville's interviews at, 10, 13, 30; conference at, 145; garden house at, 201

Winnington, Sir Francis, 88, 102, 103, 104, 105, 140, 144

Winwood, Sir Ralph, 3, 13, 14, 21

Woburn Abbey, 42, 140

Worcestershire, elections in, 284 n. 127

Index

Wotton, Sir Henry, 9, 10, 13

Wyndham, Sir William, 223–24, 227, 230, 231

York, James Duke of. *See* James II